Motivation and Dynamic Structure

by

RAYMOND B. CATTELL

and

DENNIS CHILD

Holt, Rinehart and Winston
London · New York · Sydney · Toronto

Contents

PREFACE   vii

ACKNOWLEDGEMENTS   x

1. *The Foundations of Motivation Measurement*   1

2. *Dynamic Structure: Ergs and Sentiments*   22

3. *Dynamic Traits related to Structured Learning Theory and
   Situational Modification*   59

4. *Integrative Behavior and the Dynamic Calculus*   88

5. *Contributions from Animal Motivation*   113

6. *Motivation related to Physiology and Neurology*   136

7. *The Dynamic Calculus and Clinical Psychology*   158

8. *Motivation in Education: the Dynamics of Structured Learning
   Theory*   184

9. *The Dynamics of Daily Work and Occupation Adjustment*   204

10. *The Dynamic Calculus of Group Life*   232

Appendix 1. Factor Analysis   256

Appendix 2. Elementary Matrix Algebra   259

vi   *Contents*

BIBLIOGRAPHY   262

SUBJECT INDEX   279

AUTHOR INDEX   283

Preface

In the comparatively uncharted and vitally important realms of motivation, every systematic attempt to understand the fundamental issues involved deserves to be studied and evaluated. There are very few psychological or sociological areas which cannot benefit in some way from a sound knowledge of motivation, both in theoretical researches and in the day to day setting of education, industry, clinics, counseling and the like. Thus, over a period of some thirty years, the senior author has tried to assemble a consistent model, one which is explicit in its terms of reference, careful in its elaboration within the limits of a young science and mindful of the speculations and findings of others in the field. As with any scientific theory, there will be hard facts, tentative conclusions, errors of judgement and numerous questions unanswered—for the test of a good theory is not only in the answers it provides, but in the hypotheses and experiments it generates. It is anticipated that the model presented here will fulfil this expectation.

The book is for any student of the behavioral sciences, but especially in psychology. Basically, it is aimed at the undergraduate, or the graduate wanting a springboard for more advanced work. But we do not pretend that the book is for those who are looking for a soft option. In psychology it is still not unusual—especially in so-called humanistic psychology—to write a book making few demands and appealing to the lowest intellectual calibre rather than to the mind prepared to grapple with the true majesty of the subject. In medicine, chemistry, or engineering, the hoax is scarcely possible because the student is satisfied only if he can meet difficulties and perform effectively in his profession and in facing the real demands of nature. The book written with the purpose of smoothly avoiding difficult problems is as popular with a certain type of teacher as with the student—for, in fact, it needs no teacher. This book needs a teacher—and a good one—for it deals with new ideas on the frontiers of research in human dynamics. The principles and formulae are going to demand thorough study by both student and lecturer, and will need the classroom discussion and illustrative expression that only a good teacher can give. This does not mean that our treatment is specialized and recondite—and aimed only at the graduate student. On the contrary, it simply addresses itself to the common, central, everyday basic issues in the psychology of motivation. It *does* ask, however, that they be treated, not as a kind of gossip about people, but as a serious, integrated, and potent scientific analysis. Perhaps only the undergraduate psychology major will need to get to grips in this fashion (and *he* will be a deprived and underprivileged psychologist if he is denied this more mature and disciplined treatment). But any undergraduate worthy of his entrance examination should find absolutely no insuperable obstacles in terms of unusual demands beyond an ordinary science and mathematical background. One does not wish to protest against imaginary obstacles, but the above introductory comments spring from actual experience that reactionary circles exist in which any truly systematic, quantitative approach to motivation is rejected in favor of an easy ramble, eclectically savoring a series of theoretical and poorly constructed viewpoints, from which the student returns with indigestion and disillusionment about the readiness of psychology to take its place with developed sciences.

The emphasis here is on a well-knit presentation in which the student can reason from experiment to theoretical model and back to new inferences for experiment. It begins with the evidence on human dynamic structure *as it stands*, and for this the student has to grasp the logic of correlation and factor analyses, but need not get entangled in any technicalities of calculation. From this, it proceeds, naturally, to ask how such structures arose. Since a surprising proportion of workers in the field of motivation have failed to address themselves to this problem, the explanations here rest on relatively few fundamental researches, and much has to be left at the hypothetical level.

However, there is enough circumstantial evidence about the genetic and learning origins of several of the patterns to permit a consistent picture. The problem of conflict and interaction of dynamic structures is then taken up in Chapters 3 and 4. At this level, one leaves the simple empirical realities of structure and enters into theoretical superstructures which various psychologists are likely to question at specific points. However, the model, as a whole, is surely not one that can be considered peculiar, for it is the simplest possible, namely, a linear additive model. Despite the novelty of their names, as far as new readers are concerned, such models as the dynamic lattice and the dynamic calculus are mathematically simple, and conceptually virtually inevitable in any attempt to develop the subject. It is pointed out to the reader that some psychologists may prefer more elaborate theory at certain points, and such is possible, but modifications of our simpler approach are scarcely justified at this stage in our experimental findings.

Having presented a well-knit model capable of handling most of the data of quantitative experiment and broad clinical and ethological observation as it exists today, the authors proceed to visit two more specialized fields which are considered to be crucial adjuncts to the totality of the topic of motivation. These concern the augmentation of human motivation principles through sharing the evidence with that of animal experimentation, and a consideration of physiological processes which research has shown bear some relationship to the outward manifestations of human activity.

Finally, the design of the book calls for turning the principles clarified in dynamics as a basic science upon various applied areas, primarily educational, clinical, industrial, and social psychology. Here space compels restriction (from an immense volume of publications) to experimental and statistical work which is so fundamentally designed as to integrate with the basic model. After all, these developments need to be pursued in detail only by the graduate student with his specialty in one of them, and to these we have indicated sufficient reading.

As regards advice on the art of using the book in course work, the authors abide by their opening implication that active anticipation of "difficulties", according to the particular omissions in the students' background, is essential. It is sad to have to admit, in this day and age, that one of the main omissions in the psychology student's background is still elementary algebra and statistics, such as would enable him to take the logic of the factor model in his stride. However, as background reading to a number of the more technical issues raised in this book, students are advised to read *The Scientific Analysis of Personality*, by R. B. Cattell, Penguin, 1965. As a means of fitting the contents into a backcloth of other theoretical formulations, the student might like to consult the following general texts: C. N. Cofer and M. H. Appley, *Motivation: Theory and Research*, Wiley, New York, 1964; P. T. Young, *Motivation and Emotion*, Wiley, New York, 1961; R. N. Haber, *Current Research in Motivation*, Holt, Rinehart and Winston, 1966 (light on physiological aspects which can be supplemented with J. E. Hokanson, *The Physiological Basis of Motivation*, Wiley, New York, 1969).

Raymond B. Cattell
Institute for Research on Morality and Self Realization
Boulder
Colorado
U.S.A.

Dennis Child
University of Bradford
England.

Acknowledgements

The authors would like to acknowledge and thank the following sources for permission to reprint information indicated in the body of the text. The acknowledgements are presented in the order in which they appear in this book. John L. Horn, "Motivation Concepts from Multivariate Experiment" in Raymond B. Cattell (Ed.), *Handbook of Multivariate Experimental Psychology*, © 1966 by Rand McNally and Company, pp. 617–618, 628 (table 1.1, pp. 8–10, table 1.3, p. 16 and table 10.5 p. 251). Diagrams 21 and 38 in Raymond B. Cattell: *The Scientific Analysis of Personality* (Pelican Original, 1965) © Raymond B. Cattell, 1965 (figure 2.2, p. 24 and figure 3.1, p. 60). Table 4 from the *Motivation Analysis Test Handbook* (1964), reproduced by permission of the Institute for Personality and Ability Testing, Champaign, Illinois, U.S.A. (table 2.13, p. 51). K. Rickels, R. B. Cattell, C. Weise, B. Gray, R. Yee, A. Mallin, and H. G. Aaronson, Controlled Pharmacological research in private psychiatric practice. *Psychopharmacologia*, 9, 288–306 (1966), reproduced by permission of Springer-Verlag (figure 3.2, p. 62). P. T. Young, and J. T. Greene, Quantity of food injested as a measure of relative acceptability, *J. Comp. Physiol. Psychol.*, 46, 288–294, Copyright (1953) by the American Psychological Association (figure 5.3, p. 120). Edward J. Murray, *Motivation and Emotion*, © 1964 by permission of Prentice-Hall, Inc., Englewood Cliffs, New Jersey (figure 6.1, p. 137). N. Calder, *The Mind of Man*, © 1970 with the permission of B.B.C. Publications, London (figure 6.2, p. 138). H. Jasper in W. Penfield and T. C. Erickson (Eds.)., *Epilepsy and Cerebral Localization* published by C. C. Thomas, Springfield, Illinois (figure 6.3, p. 144). Donald B. Lindsey, "Psychophysiology and Motivation", in *Nebraska Symposium on Motivation*, 1957, ed. by Marshall R. Jones, reprinted from Fig. 4, p. 66 and Fig. 6, p. 69 by permission of University of Nebraska Press (figure 6.4 (b) and (c), p.145). Donald B. Lindsey, "Emotion" in the *Handbook of Experimental Psychology* by S. S. Stephens (Ed.) by permission of John Wiley and Sons, Inc, © 1951 (figure 6.4 (a), p. 145). K. M. B. Bridges,

Emotional Development in early infancy, *Child Development*, 1932, **3**, 324–341, figure 1, p. 340, by permission of the Society for Research in Child Development, Inc., (figure 6.5, p. 154). Pages 25, 26, 29 and 27, respectively from the *Preliminary Descriptive Manual for Individual Assessment with the Motivation Analysis Test*, reproduced by permission of the Institute for Personality and Ability Testing, Champaign, Illinois, U.S.A. (figures 7.1, 7.2, 7.3, and 7.4 on pp. 160, 161, 163 and 165 respectively). R. B. Cattell and H. J. Butcher, *The Prediction of Achievement and Creativity*, Table XL, page 215, by permission of Bobbs-Merrill Co., Inc., (table 8.1, p. 187). R. B. Cattell, K. Barton, and T. E. Dielman, The prediction of school achievement from motivation, personality, and ability measures, *Psychological Reports*, 1972, **30**, 35–43 (tables, 8.2 and 8.3, pp. 187 and 190). Cross-cultural personality profiles from *Handbook of the 16 PF*, reproduced by permission of the Institute for Personality and Ability Testing, Champaign, Illinois, U.S.A.

1 The foundations of motivation measurement

1 Scientific methods in investigating human dynamics Many philosophers, writers and psychologists have speculated about the basic forces or urges which impel man to respond to his environment. Some, notably McDougall, Freud, Murray, Maslow, Hull and more recently the ethologists Lorenz and Tinbergen, have argued for innate mechanisms such as "drives", "needs", "tensions" and "instincts" which are said to have enabled both animals and man to survive the hostilities of their surroundings. Others, like Watson and Skinner, have supposed that all patterns of motivation are acquired.

The variety and complexity of these numerous propositions is illustrated in the works of McDougall, Freud, Murray, Maslow, Young, Berlyne, and others. McDougall (1908) listed no less than fourteen instincts or propensities—"complex inherited tendencies, common to all members of a species" (Burt, 1941) such as gregariousness, acquisitiveness, and self-assertion. Freud proposed moving forces of life and death in the form of libidal, ego and thanatos instincts. Maslow (1943) posited a hierarchy of human needs starting with a broad base of prepotent organic physiological needs and passing through safety, love, esteem, and self-actualization, to the need for man to acquire knowledge and understanding. Murray listed 20 "needs" which have been taken seriously in test construction by Jackson (1965) and Edwards (1954). Whilst most of the foregoing proposals have some face validity, that is, a certain common-sense feel about them, there has been an alarming absence of appropriate experimental and analytical methods to substantiate the claims made. As they stand they scarcely belong to a mature science.

Experimental psychologists looking for firmer foundations have fastened their attention to animal motivation research. This has the advantage that powerful manipulation can be used, and physiological alterations arranged, including vivisection. But although certain general laws may transfer, much of the transmission to human affairs is by analogy only. And the vast investment of human motivation in cultural domains scarcely has any counterpart.

Our plan of study here is to bring human and animal dynamics as far as possible into an illuminative whole. But one of the novelties of the contribution we have to make here is that we propose to turn the hitherto one-way traffic, from animal to human, into a two-way traffic, since we believe that the multivariate experimental methods that have clarified human motivation can contribute new certainties to animal and physiological motivation study.

The field of motivation, interest, drive, acquired dynamic patterns, conflict, defense mechanisms, emotion, and the physiology of needs is an extremely complex one. At the clinical level of observation and reasoning which has hitherto carried personality and motivation study along, certain rough concepts have emerged about unitary drives, the ego, defense mechanisms, conflict and anxiety, etc. But science rests on measurement and measurement rests on defining what has to be measured. So long as McDougall says there are fourteen instincts, Freud three, and animal experimenters cannot agree whether curiosity, assertion, and gregariousness are primary or secondary learned behaviors, deriving from primary physiological needs, comparable measurements are difficult.

One of our contentions here will be that this area can be considerably advanced by the use of multivariate experiment. What does that mean? It means in the first place the use of what we call factor analysis to discover what the unitary entities are. For example, we shall bring evidence before long to show that by correlating various interests (readinesses to respond) in men or animals and finding by factor analysis *what coheres*, the definite number and the definite nature of drives in man or other animal species can be discovered. There is no need to stay with the clinical hunches of say, McDougall, Freud, and Murray, or the subjective elaborations of Maslow.

Secondly, multivariate experiment offers us a chance to get at important relations without manipulation, which cannot be done with animals. Nature does its own powerful experiments with human emotional learning. From there, without adding to the manipulation, we can tease out by superior statistical analysis the connections we cannot establish directly. For example, if we want to know what domination by a larger sibling does to emotional development we can put young rats in cages with aggressive siblings and see what happens; but with humans we must take a lot of families as they exist and work out by correlations and variance analyses the relation conceived.

However, both bivariate (classical) experiment and multivariate (newer, analytical) experiment begin with measurement and mathematical models, and in this respect differ markedly from the clinical or social observation, or even the animal ethology methods (see chapter 3). This does not mean that we are going to reject hunches for good experiments coming from clinical or social observation, or animal ethology, or education. But it *does* mean that we shall not believe theories from such sources until they have been placed on a firm basis of quantitative experiment.

Fortunately, the clinical–qualitative approaches, which generated most motivational theory during the first half of this century (and which still dominate the amateur psychological analyses of popular journalism), have given way in professional psychological research for the last twenty years to an increasing output of experimental investigation. The time is ripe to put this into perspective and that is what this book can perhaps achieve.

2 The outline of larger structures rests on the stimulus–response element The basis of behavioristic psychology lies in stimulus–response connections. Parenthetically we should not make the mistake of confusing Behaviorism with reflexology, which rests everything on the reflex model, as in Pavlov's work. This is a subdivision within Behaviorism, which simply says that psychology as a science must be based on behavior, observed by many, not introspection, observed unreliably by one. (Watson took liberties when he called reflexology behaviorism.) What elements of behavior one chooses to begin with is another matter.

In most animal and much human behavior the stimulus–response element has a single "bit" of behavior subjected to measurement. But there are some advantages in human behavior in starting with units slightly more complex, such as a stimulus which is a whole situation, e.g. sitting at supper, entering school, and responses which are whole courses of action or processes rather than atomistic "reflexes", e.g. giving a bad boy a "lecture", riding away on a bicycle, doing an evening's study. The larger elements can be broken down later into description in smaller ones if we wish; but to get along quicker we are entitled to use our common sense and use any one of the above courses of action or a "response", and to measure, say, the length of time the parent "lectures" the bad boy.

In later analyses here we shall use, both with animals and humans, sometimes a single act as our element, and sometimes a whole course of action. In humans it will be seen later that the term "attitude" comes as close as any other to defining an element in which a given situation creates a given course of action. The situation may be that the boss refuses to raise my salary; my attitude may be the response (perhaps expressed, perhaps inhibited) that I will get up and move to a job elsewhere. An attitude so defined is a reasonable "size" in the totality of behavior, and as we shall see, practicably measurable as to its strength.

Before we turn to tidy and extend this concept of measuring an attitude, let us, however, ask why we want to measure it. What in fact are the big questions of dynamic structure and motivation that we are interested in? First we want to know what the number and nature of human drives may be. Then we can ask the same about some higher mammals. Next we shall ask "How do we acquire new interests and motives?" and "Do these patterns of interest show any order in a given culture?" For example, are sentiments to parents, school, sport, job, religion, etc., describable, enduring structures, and can the amount of interest locked up in them be measured? What happens when a course of action dictated impulsively by an innate drive comes into conflict with one of these sentiments? Is there such a thing as a person's "total interest"? If drives exist, what is the relation of these tension levels to experiences of stimulation and deprivation?

An examination of the nouns and verbs in the above will show that language has forced upon us such concepts as drives, "patterns of interest", "conflicts between dynamic structures", and so on. Clearly we must begin by finding out if unitary structures of this kind exist, and, if so, what they are in our species and culture. This is called the *taxonomic stage* of science, and although psychology has been a bit immature—especially in the motivation field—about this taxonomic task, compared, say, to the systematic job done by botany, chemistry, or zoology, it cannot afford to neglect it. The first three chapters of this book will therefore lay a firm foundation of structure. We shall ask what structures exist and define these clearly before proceeding to the relations and processes among them.

3 The promise of unitary dynamic traits from the foundation in attitude measurement

When we say anywhere in science that there is a "unity" we do so through observation that the parts appear together, grow together, disappear together. Statistically this means that they correlate. For example, half a dozen physiological signs derive from low oxygen supply in the blood. The proof that they rest on a single influence—if we could not manipulate oxygen level experimentally—would be that they form a cluster of positively intercorrelating variables. More precisely, to discover and demonstrate this we should correlate these and other variables (across say 100 people with degrees of oxygen deficiency) and show by factor analysis that it is more than a cluster and in fact a single factor (see end of book in appendix I for a note and references on factor analysis).

Similarly, if we want to check whether there is such a thing as a single sex drive we should take perhaps fifty attitude-interests, some involving sex and some not, and measure them on, say, 200 people and by correlating the variables and factoring see if any such single factor appears. The finer points of such correlations will be taken up later, for, to begin at the beginning, it is necessary to *ask first how we shall measure the strength of interest in a single attitude-interest*. The present chapter will be devoted to this problem, after which we shall be in a position to evaluate and understand the correlational evidence for structure.

The validation of measures of the strength of motive or interest will therefore first be pursued in relation to *attitude elements* as briefly introduced above. The term "strength of an attitude" is used here in a highly specific defined sense as a measure of *the strength of a course of action, or tendency to a course of action, in response to a stimulus*. It is not to be confused with the popular or loose "ballot box" psychological meanings which have become associated with the concept. Thus for some sociologists and even educators an attitude represents a static opinion or inclination for or against an object, idea, or institution without a corresponding course of action (e.g. when one holds an attitude or opinion about a political party, or music, without necessarily responding in a way which belies the attitude). On the contrary, attitudes as defined in the present context *always* proceed to a course of action even if that action is a simple verbal response without a physical correlate. Logically, if there was no action or reaction to a stimulus in thought, word, or deed, there would be no evidence to suggest that the attitude even existed. There must be some mode of response for us to detect an attitude.

One or two cautionary remarks are therefore needed to avoid the confusion which may arise if the reader has already got accustomed to sociological uses of "attitude". One problem in this use is that the investigators have generally been prepared to accept the individual's purely verbal behavior as evidence of his attitude (giving yes/no answers to a set of statements). This naïve, verbal, conscious method of response represents only one of many ways by which we can tap the domain of human attitudes. There can be a world of difference between what a person thinks he might do or say in a given situation and what that person actually does. If a child is asked how many ice cream cones he would enjoy, he might say a dozen. In practice, he might enjoy the first six, but once he becomes satisfied he may begin to experience aversion to eating more. As we shall see later, there are several devices available, drawn from such diverse psychological fields as memory, perception, selective attention, retroactive inhibition, animal research, neurophysiology, and psychodynamics, from which we can gain a more detailed and realistic knowledge of both the magnitude and direction of attitudinal responses. The point to be emphasized is that action or a tendency to action is not only (or necessarily) verbal, but physiological, emotional, and intellectual.

Further, negative or inhibited attitudes must be regarded as attitudes in the sense we have defined above. We might hold strong views about the inadequacies of a boss, head teacher, or professor, but decline to do anything about it. But the fact that overt action is stifled or inhibited does not mean that a tendency to action is not present. An attitude shall exist even though the action involved occurs in varying degrees of introspection.

Clearly, there is a hierarchy of stimulus–response relationships which vary within each situation. The problem is to break into this hierarchy at a point where we can make a meaningful measure and we have taken the attitude to be the point of entry. Obviously, an attitude is dependent upon many stimulus–response activities because the tendency to respond to a situation involves a number of motor responses connected with "subsituations". Where the reactions to subsituations compound to give a consistent response pattern, we have an attitude. To encompass response patterns, several *devices* or test-situations have been used, such as spontaneous attention towards competing interests or muscle tension accompanying the pursuit of an interest; so that whilst changing the incentives we note the performance in motivational situations. These will be met with later.

In turn, attitudes interact to give higher order patterns of action as in habits, generalized attitudes, and sentiments. Habits, like attitudes, are acquired tendencies to respond consistently to given stimuli but they are larger and more inclusive units of behavior. Moreover, habits also involve cognitive as well as conative and affective (in a word—orectic) behavior. We develop habits of thinking which are acquired strategies of mental action for the solution of problems. Generalized attitudes are frequently used by clinical psychologists to describe such human reactions as hostility or insecurity, but later it will be shown that both generalized attitudes and sentiments are more complex and dependent on several attitudinal elements.

What do we need to know about an attitude in order to measure it? Cattell (1957) has suggested a paradigm in the following form:

In these circumstances	I	want so much	to do this	with that
(*stimulus situation*)	(*organism*)	(*interest-need of a certain intensity*)	(*specific goal, course of action, response*)	(*object concerned in action*)

An example of an attitude statement might be, "I want to become proficient in my chosen career", "I want to know more science", or "I want to see organized religion maintain or increase its influence".

Thus, for a person in a particular situation, the parts are (a) the nature of the course of action, (b) the intensity of the interest in the course of action, and (c) the object involved in the action. Some have suggested that we need to add the phrase "until something happens" and, whilst it does not influence the analyses to be described, it seems sensible to indicate that an attitudinal motive persists (the word "until") in the absence of satisfaction or frustration ("something happens"). The paradigm contains rather more than the traditional stimulus–organism–response model (S–O–R) of many learning theorists, because there are two qualifying terms "want so much" and "to do this" which require a consideration of both the *magnitude* and *direction*, respectively, of the attitude. The direction we will return to in the next chapter, but we shall have to consider first the important place given to interests-need in the measurement of attitudes.

4 What do psychologists consider are manifestations of strength of interest? Typically we speak of the "strength of interest" in a course of action, i.e. in an attitude (granted the given prevailing situation). But how do psychologists consider that the strength of an interest or motive is manifested and best judged? Fortunately, the psychological literature is rich in measures of interest from physiological, clinical, and learn-

ing theory research going beyond the paper and pencil, yes/no, attitude scales and intended to sample the manifold ways by which manifestations of motivation strength and interest are displayed. For example, a boy who is interested in a girl would tend to recall and reminisce about her, and, the more interested he is, the more he is likely to remember; clinical research indicates that unapproved motives, highly likely in boy–girl friendships, tend to be repressed, so that projection or "misperception" can be used to explore these hidden motives; physiological functions are likely to change with the memory or sight of the girl—psychogalvanomic reflexes, heartbeat and blood pressure are most likely to respond; the boy is more likely to perceive things about her more rapidly when he is interested than when he is not, even to the point of misrepresenting or exaggerating his perceptions.

The number of legitimate signs of motivation strength mentioned by psychologists in various fields—clinical psychology, learning, education, physiological psychology—is by now considerable. Some sixty-eight psychological principles of motivation measurement—see table 1.1—have been proposed (Horn, 1966) for the construction of test devices—a "principle" being a tenet in motivation theory by which we can assemble test material. For example, given two courses of action, a person is more likely to choose the course in which he is most interested; a person is more likely to experience physiological changes (heartbeat, muscle tension) with something which interests him than with something else which does not. Going back to the "boy meets girl" example above and referring to the list of principles in table 1.1, it will readily be seen that in a test of preferences (1) where two stimuli are presented, a person is going to choose the stimulus which most interests him (the girl associations rather than the President of the United States or a geography textbook). His fantasy ruminations (12) will dwell on the subject of girls when the opportunity is given. His attention to matters of greatest interest (34) will be more persistent than for less interesting matters. His heart will beat faster when he thinks of the girl (27). Thus by building on these human reactions to situations, we can gain some idea of his strength of interest.

However, it is not sufficient to pull out from the psychological literature a

Table 1.1 Some principles of motivation measurement applied to constructing test devices

---

With increase in interest in a course of action expect increase in:

1. **Preferences.** Readiness to admit preference for course of action.
2. **Autism:** misperception. Distorted perception of objects, noises, etc., in accordance with interest (e.g. Bruner coin perception study).
3. **Autism:** misbelief. Distorted belief that facts favor course of action.
4. **Reasoning distortion:** means–ends. Readiness to argue that doubtfully effective means to goal are really effective.
5. **Reasoning distortion:** ends–means. Readiness to argue that ends will be easily reached by inapt means.
6. **Reasoning distortion:** inductive.
7. **Reasoning distortion:** deductive.
8. **Reasoning distortion:** eduction of relations in perception (e.g. analogies).
9. **Utilities choice.** Readiness to use land, labor, and capital for interest.
10. **Machiavellism.** Willingness to use reprehensible means to achieve ends favoring interest.
11. **Fantasy choice.** Readiness to choose interest-related topic to read about, write about, or explain.
12. **Fantasy ruminations.** Time spent ruminating on interest-related material.
13. **Fantasy identification.** Prefer to be like individuals who favor course of action.
14. **Defensive reticence.** Low fluency in listing bad consequences of course of action.
15. **Defensive fluency.** Fluency in listing good consequences of course of action.
16. **Defensive fluency.** Fluency listing justifications for actions.
17. **Rationalization.** Readiness to interpret information in a way to make interest appear more respectable, etc., than it is.
18. **Naïve projection.** Misperception of others as having one's own interests.
19. **True projection.** Misperception of others as exhibiting one's own reprehensible behavior in connection with pursuit of interest.
20. **Id projection.** Misperception of others as having one's own primitive desire relating to interest.
21. **Superego projection.** Misperception of others as having one's own righteous beliefs relating to interest.
22. **Guilt sensitivity.** Expression of guilt feelings for nonparticipation in interest-related activities.
23. **Conflict involvement.** Time spent making decision under approach–approach conflict (both alternatives favor interest).
24. **Conflict involvement.** Time spent making decision under avoidance–avoidance conflict (both alternatives oppose interest).
25. **Threat reactivity:** psychogalvanic resistance drop when interest threatened.
26. **Threat reactivity:** increase cardiovascular output when interest threatened.
27. **Physiological involvement:** increase cardiovascular output when interest aroused (threatened or not).
28. **Physiological involvement:** finger temperature rise when interest aroused.
29. **Physiological involvement:** increase muscle tension when interest aroused.
30. **Perceptual integration.** Organize unstructured material in accordance with interest.
31. **Perceptual closure.** Ability to see incomplete drawings as complete when material is related to interest.

Table 1.1 *cont.*

---

32. **Selective perception.** Ease of finding interest-related material imbedded in complex field.
33. **Sensory acuity.** Tendency to sense lights as brighter, sounds as louder, etc., when interest is aroused.
34. **Attentivity.** Resistance to distractive (lights, sounds, etc.) when attending to interest-related material.
35. **Spontaneous attention.** Involuntary movements with respect to interest-related stimuli (e.g. eye movements).
36. **Involvement.** Apparent speed with which time passes when occupied with interest.
37. **Persistence.** Continuation in work for interest in face of difficulty.
38. **Perseveration.** Maladaptive continuation with behavior related to interest.
39. **Distractibility.** Inability to maintain attention when interest-related stimuli interfere.
40. **Retroactive inhibition** when interest-related task intervenes.
41. **Proactive inhibition** by interest-related task.
42. **Eagerness: effort.** Anticipation of expending much effort for course of action.
43. **Activity: time.** Time spent on course of action.
44. **Eagerness: money.** Anticipation of spending much money for course of action.
45. **Activity: money.** Money spent on course of action.
46. **Eagerness: exploration.** Readiness to undertake exploration to achieve interest-related ends.
47. **Impulsiveness: decisions.** Speed of decisions in favor of interest (low conflict).
48. **Impulsiveness: agreements.** Speed of agreeing with opinions favorable to interest.
49. **Decision strength.** Extremeness of certainty for position favoring course action.
50. **Warm-up speed: learning.** Speed warming-up to learning task related to interest.
51. **Learning.** Speed learning interest-related material.
52. **Motor skills.** Apt performance to affect interest.
53. **Information.** Knowledge affecting and related to course of action.
54. **Resistance to extinction** of responses related to interest.
55. **Control.** Ability to co-ordinate activities in pursuit of interest.
56. **Availability: fluency.** Fluency in writing on cues related to course of action.
57. **Availability: free association.** Readiness to associate to interest-related material when not oriented by cue.
58. **Availability: speed of free association.** Number of associations when interest aroused.
59. **Availability: oriented association.** Readiness to associate interest-related material with given cue.
60. **Availability: memory.** Free recall of interest-related material.
61. **Memory for rewards.** Immediate recall of reward associated with interest.
62. **Reminiscence.** Ward–Hovland effect. Increased recall over short interval of interest-related material.
63. **Reminiscence.** Ballard–Williams effect. Increased recall over long intervals of interest-related material.
64. **Zeigarnik recall.** Tendency to recall incompleted tasks associated with interest.
65. **Zeigarnik perseveration.** Readiness to return to incompleted task associated with interest.
66. **Defensive forgetfulness.** Inability to recall interest-related material if goal not achievable.

Table 1.1 *cont.*

---

67. **Reflex facilitation.** Ease with which certain reflexes are evoked when interest aroused.
68. **Reflex inhibition.** Difficulty in evoking certain reflexes when interest aroused.

Source: Cattell (1957), Cattell and Horn (1963), Cattell, Radcliffe, and Sweney (1963); from Horn (1966).

collection of measures without also showing their validity. These devices only have the status of *hypotheses*. There are broadly two ways—common in psychometrics—whereby we can go about examining the validity of the individual devices. (1) We can set up real life *criteria* which are held, *a priori*, to define strength of interest. In this case we took the amount of time and the percentage of his income that the individual is ready to spend on the given interest. (2) We can pool the scores on *all* the devices that psychologists believe to be interest strength measures and find the correlation of each device with the pool of all. This democratic analogy in science at least assumes that what we are measuring corresponds to what most people are talking about, i.e. that it is *semantically* correctly placed. But as will be shown in the next section one must take some better criterion in the end than a mere average of an arbitrary pool; we must find the factors in the pool. However, in the earliest experiments (Cattell, 1957), it seemed desirable to include the "external criteria"—time and money spent on an interest. With these as concrete criteria (see Cattell and Warburton, 1967 on criteria) the devices mentioned above representing psychologists' conceptions and practices in motivation measurement were intercorrelated to reveal those most consistently related to each other and to the external criteria of the earlier work.

To recapitulate, the first aim is to be able to measure that brick in the house of motivation structure we call the attitude. That is to say, we want to measure the strength of a person's interest in pursuing a course of action in a given situation.

5   The riddle of motivational components   Before such multivariate methods as factor analysis were available the naïve psychologist would have taken the pool of manifestations as his empirical definition of motivation strength. Thus traditional attitude psychology would lead us to believe that there is probably only one source of variance which is sufficiently evaluated by using two-way choice items. The pool is better than this.

The logical possibility exists, however, that even this heap is not really all of one kind of "substance." Upon making this necessary check (in the 1950s) Cattell and his coworkers (see Cattell and Baggaley, 1956, 1958) found no fewer than seven primary factors were needed to explain the source of variance in these motivation manifestations. That is to say there are actually seven (or even eight) distinct kinds of manifestations that can vary independently. The same person, in regard, say, to his interest in sports, can be high on one and low on another.

What is the nature of these distinct components? The reply is that it is still something of a riddle, which we shall return to from time to time. One theory, which we shall sketch here, is that they are what psychoanalysis has called the ego, the id, and the superego components in motivation, plus some others that psychoanalysis has not previously seen. Another is that they represent the contributions respectively to the amount of stimulation going on, the amount of physiological need, and the amount of deprivation of expression that exists. Yet another is that they represent components in the interest laid down at different stages of maturation. Yet another is that they represent *states* in motivation, such as degree of arousal, anxiety, tension, etc.

At any rate, let us consider what the actual motivation measurement devices are that come together in these *primary motivational components* as we shall call them. Table 1.2 contains the devices used to measure the attitudes and the seven columns headed with the letters of the Greek alphabet contain the average loadings or, in other words, the extent to which each device correlates with the component. The largest, and therefore the most significant, loadings have been blocked off to show the regularity of the patterns which have emerged from many experiments.

The Greek letters at the head of each column are a recognition that one should not be too quick to leap to theoretical titles. The letters hold and identify the patterns as such while research is finding out more about them. It should be remembered that the factors extracted are common to all individuals in the analysis, although the extent, as we have said, will vary from one person to the next.

The alpha component.   We all have strong desires to do or say things and occasionally carry them through without counting the cost. In children this tendency is somewhat untamed and one frequently hears one saying "I want to . . ." or "I am going to . . ." no matter how antisocial or destructive it may be. The devices having the highest correlation with the alpha component seem to reflect this quality. Distorted reasoning, where there is a tendency to argue that the ends or goals which a person is seeking will be easy to reach (even when they are clearly not so to everyone else), and autism, where one believes in those things which fit one's desires, are two prominent aspects of this component. There is also decisiveness in choosing on a preference test containing "I want to do this" items. We find rationalization (inventing reasons to justify one's beliefs) and quick decision time in deciding what one wants. Therefore, it appears as a component which signifies determination, sometimes irrational, in the quest to satisfy personal desires at a conscious level. It has been called the *conscious id* component because of its likeness to the Freudian concept of the id—that cauldron of untutored desires expressed in such terms as "I wish "or "I want" without due regard for censorship.

Table 1.2   Summary of primary motivational components (average loadings)

Devices	Average loadings							Number of studies
	Alpha	Beta	Gamma	Delta	Epsilon	Zeta	Eta	
Distortion of reasoning	41							8
Autism*	43		30					9
Preferences	48		49					11
Fantasy: topics to explain	44		30					3
Fantasy: books to read	48							2
Decision time	33							4
Perceptual closure	37							2
Naïve projection	36							2
True projection	−45							1
Id projection	38							1
Defensive fluency on good consequences	27							2
Information*		29						11
Learning a language		40						5
Perception integration		37						1
Availability: free association speed		50						2
Auditory distraction		41						2
Warm up speed		31						1
Fantasy: time spent ruminating		39						2
Availability: free association*			38					5
Perseveration: low perceptual integration			32					2
Superego projection			28					1
Availability: oriented association			54					2
Selective perception			38					2
Expectancy: effort to be expended			23					2

Table 1.2 *cont.*

Devices	Average loadings							Number of studies
	Alpha	Beta	Gamma	Delta	Epsilon	Zeta	Eta	
Physiological involvement:								
Systolic blood pressure change				−48				4
Diastolic blood pressure change				−44				3
Psychogalvanic response deflection				39				3
Decision speed				42				2
Retroactive inhibition				31				1
Physiological threat activity:								
Deflection of PGR to threat					34			2
Memory for cues					−40			3
Interference: reminiscence by recall					−54			5
Utilities (time and money spent)*					36			2
Impulsiveness: decision speed						54		2
Impulsiveness: agreement speed						49		2
Decision strength						42		2
Fluency on cues							33	2
Persistence: perceptual task							−44	2

* Devices used in the construction of MAT and SMAT.

The beta component. Maturity brings with it more reasoned judgments and a regard for information and knowledge about how the individual relates to other people, i.e. the scheme of things. The second column in table 1.2 contains a number of devices which indicate a mature interest and contact with reality. High correlations show up on information and perceptual skills and a capacity to learn in those areas of greatest interest to an individual. He can quote fluently those rewards which follow from a given course of action. Even in the face of perceptual competition, he is able to pursue and pick out those things which interest him most. This is illustrated by the phenomenon known as the "cocktail party effect" in which one's name or a matter of particular interest can be picked out from a conversation in which one is not immediately involved. The actual experiment involved an auditory stimulus of interest to the listener overlaid with other auditory stimuli (noise and conversation) of no special interest. The interested listener was able to pick out the relevant stimulus (competitive inhibition).

The beta component bears a strong resemblance to the Freudian "ego". Interests and attitudes grow through contact with reality by accumulating knowledge and skills, by concentrating and attending to the relevant cues, and by being ready to take effective action on behalf of an interest. This latter point is shown quite well by the large galvanic skin reflex response correlating with the factor.

The gamma component. The devices which characterize this component have the "I ought to be interested, but . . ." quality about them which favors the Freudian concept of the superego, that is displaying restraint and inhibition as a product of societal pressures. The devices of expectancy and perseveration in which the individual shows interest by the number of times he is prepared to repeat a process in order to be rewarded, represent a will to achieve what is required. The presence of some devices which figure in the alpha component (preferences and autism) would strengthen the argument that this component contains the vestiges of restrained willfulness.

The delta component is almost completely physiological in content. Here we find measures such as rise in blood pressure, psychogalvanic deflection and speed of decision-making which strongly suggest autonomic and peripheral reactions of the body to increased interest in an object. There has been much support from physiological research (see chapter 5) that our body mechanisms are part and parcel of our reaction to interesting stimuli, in both the tasteful and distasteful sense. Poets and authors have written about it and musical composers depend on it for the effects which their work might have on the autonomic system. Some people experience "butterflies" in their stomachs at the sight or sound of certain stimuli; others experience goose pimples at the sound of a piece of music. The delta component may, therefore, be revealing some of the physical concomitants of a state of interest.

The epsilon component ranks amongst the most intriguing. Here we find three manifestations of conflict: psychogalvanic reflex response, poorness of memory for given material and poorness of reminiscence. It will be remembered that reminiscence occurs when there is an improvement in recall, after a period of rest from a learning task, beyond that recalled immediately after the learning task. Clinical psychologists have shown for a long time that if a word is given to a mental patient which touches on one of his complexes, he reacts sharply on the psychogalvanometer. Half an hour later, the patient will have a very poor memory for the word and little, if any, spontaneous reminiscence. Normally, large galvanic responses are associated with stronger memory for words, yet here we find a curious inversion effect. This has led to regarding the component as tied to unconscious memories which arise from the repression of conflicting experience and this bears a resemblance to the Freudian definition of "complexes". Therefore, this component, along with all the others, makes a contribution to the total interest strength, but differs from them in deriving from unconscious motives laid down in earlier conflict experiences.

6   The concepts of integrated and unintegrated motivation   To the sociologist, and some social psychologists, accustomed to representing the strength of an attitude by a single number, and to performing extensive calculations therefrom, the evidence that seven or so distinct scores are needed will come as a shock. Quite possibly these components will behave differently over time or in predictions of voting, work, donations, and other behaviors in the line of the given attitude.

Fortunately, we can, to a certain degree, simplify this problem by taking out what are called *second-order* or *second-strata* factors. A second-order factor is simply a common, broad factor found from factoring the correlations among primary factors. (For the above seven or eight primaries are to some extent mutually correlated.) It is thus a broad influence at the back of several primaries. Second-strata factors are familiar incidentally in other fields. Thus Thurstone's primary mental abilities will condense to fluid and crystallized intelligence (Cattell, 1963); the sixteen personality factors of Cattell (16 PF, 1970) will give about eight broad personality dimensions, to three of which the Eysenckian typologies of extraversion, psychoticism, and neuroticism are initial approximations, and so on.

The factoring of primaries was awaited with much interest and the verdict when it came was clear that there are two major second-order factors, and possibly a small third factor. Thus, it is possible to group the primary factors to yield more general, all-inclusive structures which, for reasons that will soon be apparent, are referred to as the integrated or I component and the unintegrated or U component.

The integrated second-order, as table 1.3 shows, contains the beta (ego) and gamma (ideal self) primary components. The unintegrated contains the

Table 1.3   Loading patterns of U and I factors (second-order)

Primary component	Adults		Children		Average of several studies (using Fisher's z)	
	I_I*	II_U†	I_I	II_U	I_I	II_U
Alpha	19	*42*	−07	*53*	08	*44*
Beta	*75*	18	*24*	−07	*58*	06
Gamma	*35*	−18	*51*	06	*36*	−07
Delta	04	22	−08	−01	−01	*11*
Epsilon	−06	12	09	*47*	02	*28*

* I_I = rotated second-order simple structure giving integrated component.
† II_U = rotated second-order simple structure giving unintegrated component.
Decimal places are omitted, so that the first value for alpha is really +0.19.
Significant loadings are italicized.
Source: from Horn in Cattell (1966c).

alpha (id), delta (physiological) and epsilon (repressed complexes), whilst the uncertain and provisional zeta and eta factors became part of minor factorial debris. It helps to visualize this if we set out the resolution of the seven primaries and their relationship to the two major second-order components from table 1.3 in graphical form as in figure 1.1.

Here it is easy to see that α, δ and ϵ fall in one group and β and γ on another axis. The "rotation of axes", as it is called in factor analysis, is a bit chancy with so few points, but the evidence shows that these two—U and I—are somewhat negatively correlated (otherwise they would be drawn orthogonally) and strikingly consistent in their arrangement from one analysis to the next.

In interpreting these components, the possibility has been considered that they are not straightforward motivation factors, but some combination (additive or product) of motivation and ability. For example, the device we have called "information" (table 1.1 and the examples in MAT and SMAT in the final section of this chapter), which loads on (correlates with) the I component, might be dependent not only on the *selective* memory of an individual thus reflecting his interest, but also on his memory as an aspect of his general ability. The question arises, to what extent and in what ways does a measure of heightened interest depend on the intellectual skills which an individual brings with him to any situation? This we know, that when strongly motivated most abilities will, over a certain range, at least, increase in power, so that these "shapes" we have found in U and I might be, say, in U a temperamental tendency to strong autonomic expression, and in I a general intelligence and educational level, similarly augmented in expression when motivation is strong. This "product model" as it is called will be duly examined later in competition with the additive model, which says the components are sheer motivation and have nothing to do with abilities. Certainly they do not

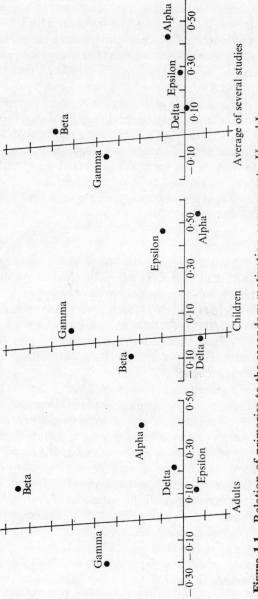

Figure 1.1 Relation of primaries to the secondary motivation components, U and I

look much like abilities. Indeed various checks that have been applied—such as correlation with ability measures—show that they are indeed the general stuff of motivation, (Cattell, Radcliffe, and Sweney, 1963).

The work of Sweney, DeYoung, and others discussed later in fact suggests that the U component is a relatively unintegrated, unrestrained, and spontaneous component in interest which is susceptible to momentary stimulation and is in part unconscious or preconscious. The integrated component on the other hand is a relatively firm, reality-oriented, cognitively invested, experienced and aconsciously integrated and controlled interest component. To get a single score for a person's attitude interest strength we could simply add I and U measures, but there is little advantage in doing this if they behave differently with time and circumstances. Thus adding what a person owns in life insurance to what he owns in real estate might give us a single score of "what he is worth" in worldly wealth; but the two have different reaction to inflation and one is not available to him till he dies! So it is not a very functional addition, and similarly U and I components are most meaningfully kept as separate scores on separate kinds of tests.

7   The nature of practical tests of motivation strength   Within any one science the basic researcher may be a bit inclined to look down on technological applications as mere by-products. But as between sciences it has wisely been said that the best test of whether the theories of a science are bogus, dressed-up scholarship or genuine is shown by the extent of the technology resulting. The theory of relativity and the nuclear power plant are closely connected.

Psychology has not unjustly been accused through the first half of this century of filling libraries with theories more academic than scientific. What does motivation theory contribute to the measurement and prediction of interest strength in school achievement, clinical therapy and other fields?

The fuller utility will appear in due course (chapters 8 and 7), but here we should pause at least to ask to what *concept-valid* measures the above basic research leads. Out of nearly one hundred devices that have now been tried for validity against the components—factor estimates of α, β, γ, δ, ϵ, ζ, η, U and I, etc.—some eight to ten have repeatedly stood out as combining the highest loadings with experimental practicability. Some are individual tests, such as require appreciable apparatus, and these, alas, have received little further use. But others are either pencil and paper or can be adapted to group administration. The latter are illustrated here in excerpts from two standardized instruments known as the Motivation Analysis Test (MAT, 1964; Sweney, 1969) and the School Motivation Analysis Test (SMAT, 1970). Revisions of Form A and a parallel Form B are in preparation. A children's form (CMAT) is in preparation by Burdsal. These have become the most frequently used devices for research in motivation, and consequently the central source of information in both the elaboration of the dynamic structure (described in the following chapter) and applied research into such fields as conflict, school achievement, learning, professional behavior of physicians, and the motivational profiles of various occupational groups (see subsequent chapters).

In order to compile a good test of motivation, the devices had to be reliable, appear consistently and significantly in the factor analyses, be conveniently administered to groups, easily scored, indirect and therefore resistant to faking, and to represent, as far as possible, the two secondary factors I and U. With these criteria in mind, Cattell and his coworkers (MAT, 1964) chose one device from each of the alpha, beta, gamma, and epsilon components. Delta was excluded because the physiological tests require individual administration, although forms of the delta factor test do exist for those able to spend the time administering them. Thus, test devices from beta and gamma were chosen to represent I and from alpha and epsilon to represent U.

The tests chosen are shown by an asterisk in table 1.2. Below will be found some examples of items from MAT.

Examples from MAT (Motivation Analysis Test)

Autism (alpha and U component)

1. What percentage of people feel that a person's status is properly shown by his appearance and that "clothes make the man or woman?"

80%   50%   20%   0

2. The money spent by cities to protect their citizens from atomic attack has gone up in ten years by:

20%   50%   100%   200%

Utilities (epsilon and U component)

1. More research money should be spent on:
   (a) Dressing the nation in smarter styles and new fabrics
   (b) Finding cures for radiation sickness
2. More newspaper articles should stress:
   (a) self-control in facing sexual distractions
   (b) gaining happiness by being socially useful

Information (beta and I component)

1. A stoic is:
   (a) a person who seeks pleasures of a physical nature
   (b) a basic coin in Ethiopia
   (c) a person not affected by passions
   (d) a small hay stack in a field

2. Which of the following has the highest reputation as a man of honesty and principle?
   (a) Talleyrand
   (b) Charlie Chaplin
   (c) Theodore Roosevelt
   (d) Woodrow Wilson

Paired Words (gamma and I component)

Red $\Big\langle$ cross / lips   Country $\Big\langle$ club / cottage

Examples from SMAT (School Motivation Analysis Test)

Autism

1. What percentage of children want to be captain of a team?

   15%   30%   45%   60%

Utilities

1. If your friends wouldn't let your brother (or sister) join your club, you should:
   (a) leave unless they agree to let him in
   (b) keep your own position in the club anyway
2. Our angry feelings are given to us to:
   (a) be controlled and checked on most occasions
   (b) help us enjoy a quarrel

Information

A protractor is used for measuring:
(a) straight lines
(b) circles
(c) areas
(d) angles

Word Association (paired words)

Choose the word more natural you. Give to your *first* reaction

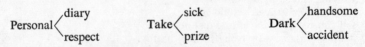

Personal $\Big\langle$ diary / respect   Take $\Big\langle$ sick / prize   Dark $\Big\langle$ handsome / accident

To this point, we have defined a basic unit of motivation in the form of an attitude and shown, by the use of factor analytical techniques, some major components of motivated behavior. The tool for measuring the intensity of motivation was interest and from interest devices standardized tests were compiled (MAT and SMAT). In the next chapter, we shall use these basic measures to establish a dynamic structure theory of motivation.

8 Summary 1. From the era of subjective or qualitative theories about drives and other dynamic structures we have moved into the use of multivariate experimental methods, more powerful than bivariate experiment in defining and measuring the *patterns* with which dynamic concepts are concerned.

2. To discover the outlines of dynamic structure it is necessary to correlate and find what behaviors "go together". To do this one must take what may be called "bits" or elements of behavior from primary observation, and for this we take the stimulus–response element. In humans this is most conveniently taken at a slightly higher level than that of a single act. The unit actually taken is the attitude, defined as a specific course of action in response to a particular situation.

3. The next problem is that of measuring the strength of interest in such a course of action objectively, i.e. other than by a verbal self-estimate. Psychology in its various fields—clinical, physiological, learning, perception—has accepted an array of indicators as manifestations of strength of motivation. These stake out an area but do not tell us whether one or several factors exist in "motivation strength".

4. Factor analytic experiments show that sixty or more manifestations do not present a single dimension but that there are seven or eight primary *motivation components*. The nature of these components has not been settled, but theories have been put forward, e.g. that the component indexed as α is the psychoanalytic id, β the ego, and γ the superego component.

5. In any case these (which incidentally correlate well with concrete criteria such as time and money spent on an interest) are the criteria by which the concept validity of any device one wants to try is examined.

6. Although it would seem at first as if seven or eight distinct measures must be used to fix the total strength of interest in an attitude, a second-order factoring shows that the primaries fall into two main secondaries called the Integrated (I) and Unintegrated (U) components. These are practically uncorrelated and suggest that this minimum of two is indispensable.

7. A fuller understanding of the nature of the seven to eight primaries and two to three secondaries must await extensive work on their predictive powers, their changes with stimulation and deprivation, etc., now that they can be reliably identified and measured. However, promising theories, and a model in a formula, already exist.

8. The nature of the tests most effective for group administration is set out. In the MAT and SMAT batteries, four devices give two scores, U and I, for each attitude. Parenthetically, the verbal inventory type of device (as in the Strong or Kuder) accounts for only 10 to 20 percent of the total interest variance as measured by objective devices. On this broader foundation of measurement of strength of interest the exploration of human dynamic structure can more reliably proceed.

2 Dynamic structure: ergs and sentiments

1 Tracing dynamic connections: subsidiation and the lattice

The purpose of developing tests of interest strength of an objective kind and of known validity is primarily to reach a basis for finding the goals of motivated behavior and the paths which lead to these goals. This system we call *dynamic structure*. The practical psychologist will, of course, find many uses for objective measurement of interest strength *per se*, but to anyone interested in the basic and constantly debated issues of how motives are pursued and attained in man and animals, the chief opportunity is that of exploring the dynamic structure of motivation. Past conceptions of what dynamic structure is have been extremely varied, from the biogenic views of the biologist and animal psychologist stressing innate instincts or drives, to the sociogenic beliefs of the sociologist who sees all the patterns of motives as derived from cultural institutions and personal experience. As the nature of the dynamic structure unfolds, it will become clear that both these points of view possess something of value.

When we do something such as taking a degree, going to a dance, or even washing the dishes, our motives are rarely simple; they frequently consist of an intricate network of subsidiary motives. The essence of this chapter is to demonstrate one way of finding and interpreting this network or *dynamic lattice*. To get some preliminary facts about structure, one would start with an adequate battery of test devices as shown in the last chapter, either by measuring U and I components separately, or putting them together, and using these to measure each of a wide array of human attitude interests. Thus, we could take in attitudes concerning one's career, one's friends, one's entertainment interests, religion, politics, and so on. If, say, three or four hundred typical adults in our culture were measured on, say, fifty or sixty attitudes of that kind, and the attitudes were then correlated, it would be possible to see how interests are typically arranged. As a first step, we could look at the matrix containing all the correlations and see what clusters exist, i.e. which sets of attitudes tend to go together in strength, or we could proceed further to factor analysis, and ask what underlying influences are responsible for the patterns seen. Almost certainly one set of patterns we would look for is that concerning the mammalian drives, since it would be reasonable to expect that people would vary on the strength of their drives, such as sex or fear, and that, in consequence, all attitudes which serve the interest of sex or the interest of security would similarly tend to vary together (if there is indeed a single underlying drive).

This is, in fact, what systematic research next set out to do; but we need not go into it entirely blindly, since clinical and other evidence has given us some ideas about the way in which attitudes are typically organized, and by taking some account of what we know, we might be able to choose the attitudes more strategically before seeking the verdict of the above empirical correlations.

If we accept the position of most clinicians, ethologists, and the psychoanalysts, as well as the systematically worked out position of McDougall and other psychologists, we would suppose that all motivation is aimed at ultimate biological goals, such as satisfying hunger, satisfying thirst, being self-assertive, escaping to security, mating, and so on. In the complexities of civilization, we do not go directly to these goals, but reach certain sub-goals, and so proceed by steps.

The basic unit in this structure is called a *subsidiation chain* as represented in figure 2.1. If we ask a person why he is studying a foreign language, for instance, he may reply that he is studying it in order to qualify as an interpreter.

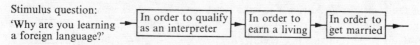

Stimulus question: 'Why are you learning a foreign language?' → In order to qualify as an interpreter → In order to earn a living → In order to get married →

Figure 2.1   A simplified subsidiation chain

If you then ask him why he is qualifying as an interpreter, he will say because that is a good way of earning a living. If you ask him why he wants to earn a living, he will say, perhaps, to get married or to eat. In this way, one can proceed along a number of sub-goals which eventually finish at an instinctual goal that the person is unable to explain or justify further. For example, if you ask him why he wants to eat, he may say in order to live, but this is a sophisticated reply, since eating is an ultimate satisfaction in itself. Even if we set aside for a moment the fact that people do not always know what the links in a subsidiation chain are, i.e. that they go underground or unconscious at certain places, and also the fact that most people will not honestly tell us all their motives, we can, nevertheless, recognize that these subsidiation chains are typical of our motivation structure. They also exist in animal experiments in that a rat will push open a door (e.g. a Skinner box)–in order to enter a room where there is a lever–in order to press the lever–in order to get a pellet of food. And this habit chain will get well established.

Both everyday observation and clinical depth analyses point to a second feature in this structure, namely, that the subsidiation chains criss-cross in the dynamic life patterns of a typical individual. This is due to the fact that certain sub-goals operate simultaneously as a means to quite different ultimate drive goals. For example, the sub-goal of having a bank account on which one can safely draw is contributed to perhaps by such attitudes as, "I want a higher salary", "I do not want to pay so much income tax", "I want to resist advertisements and save my money". When this sub-goal is attained, it is a stepping stone for several different subsidiation chains. For example, one may go on to the satisfaction of hunger made possible when funds exist. Another may go on to the satisfaction of the need for security, e.g. by paying insurance against illness. Another may go on toward a sexual goal, and so on. The result of this is what has been called a dynamic lattice, as shown in figure 2.2, in which a series of attitudes, as shown on the left, go through certain intermediate goals which are labelled *sentiment level goals*, and so on to *ergic goals* at the right-hand side.

The reader may be interested to try out some of these particular attitudes, and see if his own views of how they subsidiate in the particular person coincide with those which are set out, purely hypothetically as yet, in figure 2.2. It will be remembered from the last chapter that an attitude is a course of action in

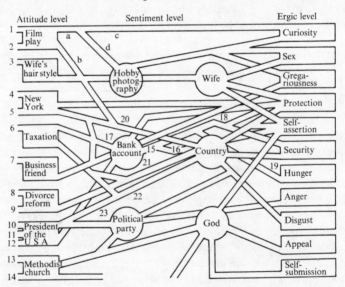

Figure 2.2   Fragment of a dynamic lattice showing attitude subsidiation, sentiment structure, and ergic goals
Source: Cattell (1965).

relation to a stimulus situation and involving an object. The typical paradigm was presented as:

In these circumstances	I	want so much	to do this	with that
(*Stimulus situation*)	(*organism*)	(*interest intensity*)	(*response*)	(*object*)

In terms of the dynamic lattice, each sub-goal is a new situation, making a new course of action possible. The object is often a "sentiment object" that is "used" by several other attitudes, and the course of action is a link in any one of the chains moving the person on from one condition or sub-goal to another.

One can, of course, set out either a *common* dynamic lattice to suggest what is the most common structure for people in our culture, or one *specific to each individual*, which would have its own idiosyncrasies relative to a standard pattern. The dynamic lattice, if the above were furnished with figures showing the strengths of interest in the particular courses of action, and showing various feedbacks, which for simplicity are not included in the initial diagram above, would be the most complete statement we could make about a person's interests and dynamic structure. It is this on which we should start our analysis and attempt our derivation of dynamic laws, as, indeed, Freud and others have attempted. But the question is how do we penetrate the mass of observed behavior and reach a dependable statement of the dynamic lattice? In everyday life we have many ways of deciding what people's dynamic goals are, and forming our own shrewd ideas of "what makes them tick". In fact, the average human being has become very good at this, in an intuitive sense, because his survival has often depended upon being sophisticated about the motives of other people. Nevertheless, as with most arts, the best practitioners might have great difficulty in setting out explicitly just what signs and what inferences they judge to be motives. Psychology in the past has used the psychoanalytic couch, employing such methods as free association (i.e. talking aimlessly and without inhibitions), hypnotism, and projection. By these means, the psychoanalyst has had some success in finding the roots of those neurotic attitudes which we call symptoms. However, this still remains an art regarding which people may disagree and which does not yield quantitative results.

A better way exists. In response to the question "Why are you learning a foreign language?" we set out in figure 2.1 a simple, linear chain of responses. If we schematize a slightly more complex dynamic lattice as shown in figure 2.3, it will be seen that a whole set of attitudes ultimately subsidiate to an ergic goal A and another set of attitudes ultimately subsidiate to ergic goal B. These subsidiations overlap, as in attitudes 1, 2, 5, and 6, but distinct courses can be plotted nevertheless.

But, before we proceed, let us state the meaning of the term *ergic* as used above. One of the diseases of psychology is that its discussions often originate over nothing but semantic confusions, and this has been particularly true about

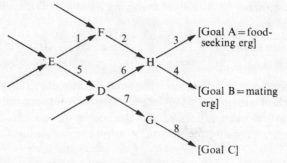

A, B, and C are final ergic goals;
D, E, F, G, and H are sub-goal stimuli;
1 to 8 are attitudes forming the subsidiation chain.
Thus, attitude 1 could be "I want to qualify as an interpreter"
    attitude 2 could be "I want to earn a living"
    attitude 3 could be "I want to eat"
    attitude 4 could be "I want to get married"

Figure 2.3   A dynamic lattice

the words instinct and drive. For example, the word instinct carries all sorts of connotations from literary writing and from animal studies that are not intended in the human case. Accordingly, when the first multivariate experimental analyses of human motivation patterns revealed what we shall describe in a few paragraphs as *human ergs* or drive patterns, Cattell suggested that the word *erg* be used to rescue an operationally defined concept from the trailing clouds of confusion that come with terms like instinct. Roughly, however, an instinct is an erg, which will shortly be defined in an operational way. The word comes from the Greek root *ergon*, the same as is used for an erg in physics, and means a source of power or work. This is desirable because the drives are the motive powers behind most of our energies. The adjective ergic (pronounced with a soft g as in urge) will then define anything that has to do with ergs. Now the assumption expressed in figure 2.3 is that all the attitudes which normally subsidiate to ergic goal B, the goal of mating, tend to be simultaneously stronger in a person whose need for mating is greater than in another, who is colder. Also, we can suppose that through alternations of gratifications and deprivation, ergs will alter their tension levels in the same individual from hour to hour and if this is the case, then the whole set of attitudes shown in figure 2.3 should rise and fall to some extent together. The correlation will not be complete, because, as shown in attitudes 1, 2, 5, and 6, two different ergs are involved in them, so that their variance is only partially accounted for by one erg.

It is precisely in disentangling a number of distinct influences operating over a set of variables that factor analysis, if properly used, can do for us what no other method can. We might measure sixty attitudes sprinkled over the whole area of what might be called a person's total life interest, measure them for a sizeable sample of people by the objective devices above, and inter-correlate them, and perform a factor analysis to see what attitudes vary together (R-technique). We would then want to check on this by doing the same on one person at a time, measuring the fifty to sixty attitudes every day for, perhaps, a hundred and fifty days, to see how they change together (P-technique). The outcome of such experiments is the topic of the next section.

2 The appearance of the ergic drive structures

From the standpoint of a century of speculation about human and mammalian drives, beginning with Darwin, the outcome of these new methods is extremely interesting. The work begun by Cattell and his coworkers twenty years ago shows, both through R-technique (individual differences) and P-technique (fluctuation within single individuals), that we do indeed have drive patterns that are highly similar to those found in the higher mammals by the ethologists such as Lorenz (1967 and Tinbergen (1951), and speculated on by McDougall (1908). Since the higher mammals, and particularly the apes, resemble us in their general physiology as Darwin first clearly brought out, it would indeed be strange if we did not also share with them certain constitutional impulses, emotions, and tendencies to inborn, spontaneous attention to certain objects. Of course, these behaviors are enormously modified by cultural experience in man, to the point where their very existence could be doubted, but these more refined methods of analysis do show that there must be some underlying organization producing a functional unity of these interests.

The ergic structures in the following tables emerging from factor analysis are shown by setting out the actual attitudes that have been measured, along with a loading (see Appendix I) which is the approximate average from the factor loading in several different studies. Thus, table 2.1 shows the fear or security-seeking erg, and it will be noticed that all the attitudes have in common the seeking of safety. Thus, the person who has a high score on this factor is simultaneously interested in avoiding obliteration in nuclear war, reducing danger of death by accident and disease, avoiding economic catastrophies, wishing personally never to be an insane patient in a mental hospital, taking out insurance against illness, and so on.

In evaluating the consistency of these factor patterns, the reader must remember that the short list of attitudes with definite loadings, as shown in table 2.1, is selected by the factor analysts from among thirty or forty attitudes that are quite different in their content and field. What examination of research data will clearly show, however, is that (a) all attitudes that have to do in any way with fear are brought together by the uniquely rotated factor, and (b) that attitudes that do not have anything to do with fear are *not* brought into the factor pattern. The last statement needs a little qualification since occasionally a number of attitudes appear with lower loading which, at first sight, one would not, perhaps, think of as belonging to the given erg. For example, in table 2.2 which follows, we have a set of attitudes which predominantly and obviously are expressions of the sex drive, but we also have there a liking for smoking, for fine foods, for listening to music, and for wanting to travel and explore. Fortunately, through the explorations of psychoanalysis, the appearance of

Table 2.1   Security-seeking (fear, escape)

	Loadings
I want my country to get more protection against the terror of the atom bomb	.5
I want to see any formidable militaristic power that actively threatens us attacked and destroyed	.5
I want to see the danger of death by accident and disease reduced	.4
I want to see those responsible for inflation punished	.4
I want never to be an insane patient in a mental hospital	.4
I want to see a reduction of income tax for those in my bracket	.3
I want to take out more insurance against illness	.3
I want to become proficient in my career	.3
I want my country to have power and influence in the world	.3
I like to take part in political arguments	.3

Table 2.2   Attitudes defining the sex erg

	Loadings
I want to fall in love with a beautiful woman	.5
I want to satisfy my sexual needs	.5
I like sexual attractiveness in a woman	.5
I like to see a good movie now and then	.4
I like a novel with love interest and a ravishing heroine	.4
I like to enjoy smoking and drinking	.4
I want to see more good restaurants serving attractive food	.3
I want to listen to music	.3
I want to travel and explore the world	.3

Table 2.3 Ergs of gregariousness, parental protectiveness, explorational curiosity, and self-assertion

Erg	Major attitudes	Loadings
Gregariousness erg	I like to take an active part in sports and athletics	.5
	I would rather spend free time with people than myself	.4
	I like to watch and talk about athletic events	.4
	I enjoy the spirit of comradeship in my professional associates	.4
	I like indoor sociable games	.3
	I dislike solitary, constructive hobbies	.3
	I have no wish to disagree with authorities	.3
	I do not enjoy hunting and fishing	.3
	I want to belong to a good club with plenty of social life	.2
	I want to see more movies and plays	.2
Parental protectiveness	I want to help the distressed, wherever they are	.5
	I want to insure the best possible education for my children	.5
	I want my parents never to be lacking the necessities of comfortable living	.4
	I want to save my wife unnecessary drudgery	.4
	I want to see, for everyone, the danger of death by accidents and disease reduced	.4
	I want to see the congenial way of life of my native country preserved	.4
	I do *not* want (need) the help and advice of my parents	.4
	I do *not* want to drive myself beyond reason (or to fight)	.3
Exploration (curiosity)	I like to read books, newspapers, and magazines	.5
	I want to listen to music	.5
	I want to know more about science	.4
	I like to satisfy my curiosity about everything going on in my neighborhood	.3
	I want to see more paintings and sculpture	.3
	I want to learn more about mechanical and electrical gadgets	.3
	I like to see a good movie or play	.3
	I am not interested in being smartly dressed	.3
Self-assertion	I want to be smartly dressed, with a personal appearance that commands admiration	.4
	I want to increase my salary	.4
	I want to be first-rate at my job, excelling colleagues	.4

Table 2.3 *cont.*

Erg	Major attitudes	Loadings
Self-assertion (*cont.*)	I want to belong to a good club or follow a team	.4
	I want to keep a good reputation, with those who can help my career	.4
	I enjoy trying to make a profit in business deals	.3
	I like to take part in political arguments	.3
	I want to avoid damaging my sense of self-respect	.3
	I like to own a home and have things I can call my own	.3
	I would rather spend free time by myself than with others	.2

these items does not puzzle us as much as it would if we had taken a purely biological approach, looking only at the higher mammals. For, in the concept of oral eroticism, the Freudian sees smoking as, in part, a sexual expression, and he also sees a certain fraction of the interest in food deriving from sublimated sex. (Even before Freud, there was a folk-saying that "A full stomach is a good corrective for an empty heart".) The psychoanalytic observation that the arts are a cultural sublimation of sex will also give us understanding for the appearance of the attitude on music. As to the desire to travel and explore, we can, perhaps, turn to the studies of the animal psychologists, who show, especially in the male, that restless exploratory behavior is partly motivated by sex, and indeed, the "Weltreise" institution for the wanderlust of adolescence points in the same direction.

However our initial purpose is not so much to explain the more odd expressions as to make clear that the primary expressions, which are the most highly loaded, do indeed pick out particular drives. A number of other important instances are shown in table 2.3, which brings together the loading patterns for gregariousness, parental protectiveness, explorational curiosity and self-assertion.

The above examples are all from R-technique, with substantial numbers of people. To complete the range of evidence, the factor analyses of individuals studied by P-technique, i.e. repeated measurements on the attitudes of a single individual over many occasions, factored by correlations over those occasions, are presented in table 2.4. It will be seen that essentially the same patterns emerge—only the salient loadings appear in the table of Cross's work (1951). Yet a third type of analysis, the dR technique, has been used (Cattell, De Young, and Horn, 1974) and successfully confirms the basic structure of dynamic factors.

Table 2.4 P-technique in dynamic structure studies

	Mating erg	Parental-protective erg	Self-sentiment	Narcism	Appeal-dependence erg	Escape-fear erg	Self-assertive erg	Fatigue	Passive sympathy (or gregarious erg)	Play
Make love to beautiful women	51									
Go to good movie or play each week	42									
Session number		24								
Know more about science		25								
Never damage self-respect			41	35	−36					
Control mental process			41							
Rather spend free time with people				−43					−22	
More time to enjoy my own company				41						
Parents never lacking necessities	23				46					
Feel I'm in touch with God					38					
Take active part in athletics and exercise						−41	−37			29
America get more protection from bomb						49				
Danger of death by accidents and disease reduced						30	−36			
Increase salary							41			
Have command of people							18			
Listen to music								30		
Spend more on smoking and drinking				20			21	−51		
Help distressed		34						34		
Some place to turn for help			−36	−29					28	−31
More time to enjoy sleep and rest			−34					35		−32
Insure best education for children	−29									33

Source: Cattell and Cross (1952).
Only salient loadings visible.

3 The appearance of sentiment structures

It will be noticed that in figure 2.2, no model has been set up as to how the intermediate goals between the attitudes, on the one hand, and the ergs, on the other, should express themselves in the correlational relationships among attitudes.

The reason for this is the sufficient one that it is not yet easy on *a priori* grounds to argue just what these sub-goals would produce in the way of attitude relationships. However, it quickly became apparent in the empirical results that new patterns exist beyond those due to ergs.

These patterns certainly do not resemble anything which our biological relatives, the primates and the higher mammals, possess. In fact, even at a first glance, one can see that they center upon certain social institutions, such as the family, one's job, one's church, one's chief recreational hobby interest, one's country, and so on. These *new dynamic structures, visible as common reaction patterns to persons, objects or social institutions, and upon which all people seem to have some degree of endowment,* though differing considerably, have been called *sentiments.* The common use of the word sentiment has always had this connotation, and it has been further specialized to mean just this in the writings of McDougall and in the experiments of the senior author. A simple example of the religious sentiment pattern is shown in table 2.5.

Another well-defined pattern of this kind is found in the sentiment to one's career. Naturally, this differs somewhat according to the particular profession or job, and the example given below in table 2.6 is one that has been found

Table 2.5 Religious sentiment

	Loadings
I want to feel that I am in touch with God, or some principle in the universe that gives meaning and help in my struggles	.6
I want to see the standards of organized religion maintained or increased throughout our lives	.6
I want to have my parents' advice and to heed their wishes in planning my affairs	.4
I want my parents never to be lacking the necessities of comfortable living	.3
I do not want to see birth control available at all	—.2
I want more protection against the atom bomb	.2
I want my country to be the most powerful and influential	.2
I want to help the distressed, wherever they are	.2
I do not want to spend more time playing cards	—.2

Table 2.6 Sentiment to profession (Air Force)*

	Loadings
I want to make my career in the Air Force	.70
I like the excitement and adventure of combat flying	.63
I want to get technical education such as the Air Force provides	.58
I enjoy commanding men and taking the responsibilities of a military leader	.44
I do not want to take more time to enjoy rest and to sleep later in the mornings	−.41
I like being up in an airplane	.41
I want to satisfy my sense of duty to my country by enlisting in its most important defense arm in threatening times	.39
I want to become first-rate at my Air Force job	.36
I do not want to spend more time at home puttering around	−.36

* Here, as in other tables setting out factors, the signs of the loadings are given as they occur for all the positively directed ("I want") attitudes in the original list of variables. For the reader's convenience in reading the list of salients the qualifying "not" is inserted whenever the loading has gone negative. The attitudes thus read consistently as they stand and need no change.

among Air Force men who are aspiring to officer status as a pilot within the military structure. That they are characterized by all sorts of interests that would naturally go together in the profession is at once obvious. As the above and further examples below are scanned, it will become evident that a generalization is possible at the operational level which completely distinguishes the sentiments from the ergs. In the ergs, we see a set of attitudes which, although embedded in diverse cultural areas (consider the fear attitudes in table 2.4 in their distribution over health insurance, war, personal integrity, etc.), are, nevertheless, all bound by the quality of seeking a particular *biological* goal. On the other hand, in sentiments, we have just the opposite principle of unification, in that although the biological emotional qualities of the component attitudes are all different, they are bound by a common *social* institution. For example, in the sentiment to career above, there are such diverse emotional satisfactions as the excitement of combat flying, the satisfaction of a sense of duty, the self-asserted satisfaction of commanding men, and whatever that plexis of almost organic satisfactions is that makes one enjoy being up in an airplane.

This entire difference in character invites one to look for an entire difference in origin. The bringing together of these attitudes with different ergic roots is almost certainly due to their being trained and rewarded in common by some cultural institution. That is to say, the manner of the individual's life is such that he, in contrast to some other individual low on the sentiment, encounters more frequently what the conditioning theorist would call a "reinforcement schedule" that is simultaneously applied across all those attitudes. The possibility of aggregates of attitudes being built up by social learning situations into single structures has long been recognized though there has previously been no experimental demonstration of their existence and particular natures. (Cattell in 1946 used the expression, "environmental mold source trait" showing that a factor would be expected to be generated by a particular mold in the environment to which all individuals are exposed in a learning situation, which operates more on some individuals than others.)

Another easily found pattern is that of the sentiment to sports and games, as shown in table 2.7.

Table 2.7   Sports and games

	Loadings
I like to watch and talk about athletic events	.75
I like to take an active part in sports and athletics	.63
I enjoy hunting and fishing trips	.27
I do not like to make things with my hands in wood, metal, or clay, to paint, etc.	−.20
I like to get into a fight, particularly if my rights are involved	.20
I like to spend (some of) my spare time playing cards with the fellows	.16

One would expect on general developmental grounds that the sentiment structure would be less developed and less stable in children than in adults, and the researches of Sweney (Cattell, Sweney, and Radcliffe, 1960; Sweney and Cattell, 1961; Delhees, Cattell, and Sweney, 1971) seem to support this. The patterns in children are more numerous and more fragmentary as illustrated in table 2.8.

We should also expect sentiments to be more local to their particular cultures. As yet, there has been no systematic investigation across cultures, with the exception of the work with the Motivational Analysis Test by Cattell and Radcliffe (1961) in Australia, which, as might be expected, shows much the same pattern as in America and Britain. However, experiment with objective measures will doubtless extend in due course to other cultures and this point can be checked. Meanwhile, we can speak of subcultures and notably the male and female subcultures in our own society. For example, the sentiment of mechanical interests, as shown in table 2.9, shows itself clearly among men but not nearly so clearly among women, and one must suppose that the training influences which characteristically bring on this pattern in boys and men are weaker in the environment of women.

Finally, a sentiment about which we shall have much to say later in regard to its central organizing role in personality is what has been called the self-sentiment. This is the set of attitudes and interests which grow up around the self-concept as studied so intensively throughout the fifties of this century. Most of the researches dealt with cognitive aspects of the self-concept, but to a dynamic psychologist the more important aspect is the forces which gather around this self-concept. As table 2.10 shows, a well-defined sentiment can be located which has to do particularly with the individual's interests in maintaining self-respect, maintaining good social reputation, obtaining a high level of self-control, being good at his job, and so on.

Table 2.8 Comparison of sentiment structure in adults and children

Sentiment	Major attitudes	Average loadings	
		Adult	Children
Self-sentiment	To control impulses and mental processes	40	32
	Never to damage self-respect	35	27
	To excel in my line of work	38	
	To maintain good reputation	37	34
	Never to become insane	39	
	To be responsible, in charge of things	31	
	To know about science, art, literature	31	
	To know more about myself	33	
	To grow up normally		28
Superego sentiment	To satisfy sense of duty to church, parents, etc.	41	
	Never to be selfish in my acts	41	
	To avoid sinful expression of sex needs	33	
	To avoid drinking, gambling—i.e. "vice"	21	
	To maintain good self-control	28	31
	To admire and respect father		28
Religious sentiment	To worship God		34
	To go to church		33
Career sentiment	To learn skills required for job	34	
	To continue with present career plans	33	
	To increase salary and status	27	
Sweetheart sentiment	To bring gifts to sweetheart	51	
	To spend time with sweetheart	41	

Table 2.9   Mechanical, material interest (or construction erg)

	Loadings
I enjoy a good car or motorcycle for its own sake	.51
I like to handle mechanical things—gadgets, engines, etc.	.46
I enjoy buying and selling things and trying to make a profit in business deals	.40
I do not want to have my parents' advice and heed their wishes in planning my affairs	−.31
I like to own a home and have things I can call my own	.30
I like being way up in an airplane	.29
I am not interested in my parents' never lacking the necessities of comfortable living	−.25
I want to know more about physical science— electricity, chemistry, engineering	.20
I like to make things with my hands in wood, metal, or clay, to paint, etc.	.15

On the whole, it has been surprisingly easy to sort the obtained dynamic structure factors into ergs and sentiments, respectively, but of course, there are a few patterns that are rather puzzling, and actually they exist in this area of the self-sentiment. There are, in fact, three patterns which show appreciable concern with attitudes that have to do with the self. One is the self-sentiment pattern shown above, another is the self-assertive drive, which is shown in table 2.3 above, and a third is the superego pattern which is shown in table 2.10.

The distinction between the self-assertive erg and the self-sentiment can usually be made by observing that the sentiment has a number of attitudes in which self-respect, self-control, and various attitudes of obligation are involved. On the other hand, in the self-assertive drive, the attitudes are those of achievement, competitiveness, pride, and independence. They necessarily overlap to some extent because, as we shall argue later, the self-sentiment draws rather strongly upon the power of the self-assertive drives; however, with a proper choice of attitudes in a crucial experiment, it is always possible to separate them. Parenthetically, the literature of psychology for the last thirty years, by the free and undefined use of the word aggression, has tended to muddy the waters here. Aggression could mean either striving for eminence and power, as in the self-assertive erg, or pugnacity. As can be shown by these analyses, the real goal of pugnacity is destructiveness, and although it may be slightly more associated with self-assertive behavior (because of the situation that self-assertive behavior tends to be obstructed), it really has no special organic connection with self-assertion. This matter is discussed further below.

In regard to the third pattern, the superego, the problem of separation is that between it and the self-sentiment. The superego is to some degree concerned with social reputation and obligations, but the emphasis on conscience and fundamental moral values as distinct from social values, etc., is usually clear enough to enable it to be identified when the superego and self-sentiment patterns turn up in the same research. Incidentally, the intensive studies of the superego structure by Gorsuch (1965) and by Horn (1961) have left no doubt about the particular forms of the superego and its distinction from the self-sentiment. The differences and the cooperative functions of the self-sentiment and the superego pattern are discussed later in this chapter under personality integration. Moreover, it will be noted that the "need for achievement" which McClelland, Atkinson, and others have intensively studied is almost certainly a dual entity formed by the combination of the self-sentiment and the self-assertive. Indeed, the extent to which a society can be designated "an achievement society" is probably best expressed by the degree to which the self-sentiment and, for that matter, also the superego of members of the society, enable them to accept self-assertion as a legitimate and desirable motive. The question of possible confusion of the superego with the inverse of the narcistic ego (the word narcistic rather than the more cumbersome narcissistic will be used throughout) will be discussed in the next section.

4   The nature of ergs and ergic tension

With the division of dynamic structures into ergs and sentiments, illustrated by actual examples, in the sections above, it is now time to turn to a more thorough examination of the concept of the erg. Obviously, this concept should be reached inductively, by consideration of the actual patterns that have emerged, but that induction should spread over a wider field of evidence than the purely psychometric evidence we have so far studied. As to the actual number and naming of ergs in human beings, another decade of systematic research extending that in section 2 above might reasonably be expected to give us a complete picture. At present, if we add to the well-replicated patterns from different researches a number of patterns which have appeared in fragmentary forms in single researches, we would reach a list of ergs much as is set out in table 2.11.

In general, the nature of this list far better fits the list compiled by Mc-Dougall, of some sixteen human and primate drives, than it does that of Murray, which really is a dictionary-based list, and that of Freud, which attempts apparently too great a reduction, beginning initially with an attempt at a monistic theory of sexual drive alone, and belatedly introducing aggression and perhaps fear.

In the early stages of the above work of the fifties, the absence of an erg of pugnacity (or aggressiveness) seemed to support the contemporary view of many psychologists that aggressiveness is not instinctive or a drive. Both McDougall and Freud, and more recently the ethologists in relation to animal

Table 2.10   Evidence for the dynamic factor structure

Attitudes	Factors (pattern)										
I want:	Fear	Mating	Assertiveness	Narcism	Pugnacity	Self-sentiment	Superego	Career	Sweetheart	Home–parental	Residual
1. Protection from A-bomb	55	−18	−32	−06	45	00	−17	10	−13	16	−26
2. To avoid disease, injury	84	−01	−21	16	−20	−16	12	20	04	−12	−15
3. To fall in love	04	68	11	09	10	09	11	−28	−18	07	06
4. To satisfy sexual needs	−16	60	12	08	−14	−06	−10	08	03	−38	−01
5. To dress smartly	−18	01	67	25	−21	−23	03	−29	−21	29	−06
6. To increase salary, status	24	17	47	16	−28	16	02	32	−16	−30	−06
7. To enjoy delicacies	62	−20	16	58	10	14	−00	03	11	−05	19
8. To rest, have easy time	−13	−01	47	24	31	43	−07	−20	17	−35	38
9. To destroy our enemies	−07	−20	17	05	80	−06	14	04	07	−07	−00
10. To see violent movies	02	25	−23	55	38	−22	−05	−00	02	−21	−09
11. To control impulses	32	−07	−05	−12	14	42	31	−29	09	−06	−59
12. Never to damage self-respect	−10	−11	−08	17	−13	90	−06	16	11	06	04
13. To maintain reputation	−22	−34	03	42	−29	58	26	−04	−29	01	−12
14. Never to be insane	05	23	06	09	14	84	30	06	−04	15	−15
15. A normal sexual adjustment	17	55	02	−07	22	47	−04	28	25	19	10
16. To know myself better	44	13	01	−04	−09	43	10	−18	06	09	18

17. To look after family	23	−19	−08	−02	−00	16	01	−08	−04	36	71
18. To be proficient in career	37	10	69	11	22	45	−12	19	−04	17	−07
19. To satisfy sense of duty	06	−21	19	−15	−15	−08	61	25	23	−10	−41
20. To end all vice	−07	17	−68	−18	−00	34	55	17	−09	−03	19
21. To be unselfish	−04	06	19	−01	10	02	73	−03	10	10	12
22. To avoid impropriety	05	19	−27	09	−17	−04	82	−10	−11	23	−18
23. To learn my job well	04	02	25	17	00	08	04	79	05	−03	07
24. To stick with my job	13	05	−15	−61	−11	−11	35	58	−03	−16	07
25. To spend time with sweetheart	−05	−11	−11	11	00	−01	−02	−07	83	13	06
26. To bring gifts to sweetheart	03	12	10	−06	01	−00	01	01	83	13	−09
27. My parents to be proud	−11	09	28	−01	−03	26	01	04	08	80	−06
28. To depend on my parents	10	−00	09	−20	−23	−00	−05	−05	−00	87	09

Source: adapted from Cattell, Horn, and Butcher (1962) for the Motivation Analysis Test Handbook (1964).

Table 2.11   Hypothesized list of human ergs

Goal title	Emotion	Status of evidence
Food-seeking	Hunger	Replicated factor; measurement battery exists
Mating	Sex	Replicated factor; measurement battery exists
Gregariousness	Loneliness	Replicated factor; measurement battery exists
Parental	Pity	Replicated factor; measurement battery exists
Exploration	Curiosity	Replicated factor; measurement battery exists
Escape to security	Fear	Replicated factor; measurement battery exists
Self-assertion	Pride	Replicated factor; measurement battery exists
Narcistic sex	Sensuousness	Replicated factor; measurement battery exists
Pugnacity	Anger	Replicated factor; measurement battery exists
Acquisitiveness	Greed	Replicated factor; measurement battery exists
Appeal	Despair	Factor, but of uncertain independence
Rest-seeking	Sleepiness	Factor, but of uncertain independence
Constructiveness	Creativity	Factor, but of uncertain independence
Self-abasement	Humility	Factor, but of uncertain independence
Disgust	Disgust	Factor absent for lack of markers
Laughter	Amusement	Factor absent for lack of markers

behavior, have included an instinct of aggression. The tendency to anger and to a destructive type of behavior in animals is very clear, and one may say that common observation does not suggest that it is lacking in humans. At first, our explanation of this lack was that we are measuring in the ergs the primary sources of energy, as defined below. Now a very good argument can be made that the pugnacious erg does not have a constant energy of its own, but that it consists of a transformation of the energy operative at the time in any drive that is thwarted. The so-called "frustration–aggression" theory of Dollard *et al.* (1939) would seem to require that aggression is motivated by frustration, and it is a little surprising that experiments have not been done to connect the intensity of destructive behavior with the intensity of the drive that was operative (using a comprehensive array of drives) before the thwarting occurred.

However, a simpler explanation, it seemed to us, was that we had not used devices involving pugnacity in sufficient number to give proper representation to such a drive. Accordingly, Cattell and Baggaley (1958) widened the scope of pugnacity. There was a distinct tendency in the factor analysis results for the pugnacious behavior to fall on the same factor as the erg of fear, i.e. the need for security, and also some suggestion of loading on the self-assertive erg. This would make good psychological sense in that in the present generation, with much of that inhibition lifted from sex, which characterized the period in which Freud's theories developed, the principal frustrations remaining would seem to be to self-assertion and to the need for security, due to the very considerable threat of wars. The issue awaits further experiments, but certain rotations, notably in the work of Baggaley, do seem to give also a distinct pugnacity–sadism factor, and this seems to be confirmed by the work of Horn (1966). On this basis, two attitudes "I want to see our enemies destroyed" and "I like to see movies with real violence in them" were added to the MAT, and loaded .8 and .4 respectively on a pugnacity erg. The same erg also had some loading on a fear attitude, namely, "I want to get protection from nuclear bombs", suggesting that the individual is ready to express his own pugnacity in insuring this safety. Nevertheless, the probable conclusion is that pugnacity is an erg of relatively small, inherent appetitive power and that it is "parasitic" upon the other drives for its immediate energies.

A second discrepancy between these objective test findings and the general biological and ethological approach was the absence in our data of a "territorial imperative" instinct pretty well demonstrated in animals, and the presence in our data of a second version of the sex drive which had not been mentioned by ethologists. It is quite possible that the former will appear as more suitable variables are factored, and it might even turn out to be identical with the self-assertive erg. The interesting point regarding the sex drive is that our findings here agree well with Freud, suggesting that there is a more auto-erotic, self-directed, pure sensuous narcistic drive as part of the general sex interest. Psychoanalysis has, of course, made much of the forms and varieties of the sex drive, setting aside the normal, heterosexual-directed mating drive as a form from which there are many deviations, such as a fixation at the homosexual stage, etc. However, we may be justifiably suspicious that many of these forms are pathological deviations in a relatively small segment of the population, due to special circumstances, genetic or environmental, and not needed in the explanation of the major sexual behavior of the majority of people. Nevertheless, it does seem clear that in the majority of people there is this narcistic erg with a generalized erotic–sensuous satisfaction goal, which is somewhat correlated with, but essentially a distinct drive from, the heterosexual mating and courtship behavior drive. This cannot be left as a firm conclusion, however, without leaving the door ajar to what may eventually be inferred from the fact that there is a very high negative correlation between this pattern and that of the superego. In some studies this negative correlation is such that some factor analysts would leave this as a bipolar factor with narcisism at one pole and superego demands at the other. Our present judgment is that this latter is not the true picture, and that the superego is negatively correlated with several drives, possibly as a product of this culture and at this time, particularly with the narcistic drive.

As Vance Packard in the *Status Seekers* and Robert Ardrey in *African Genesis* have recognized, the drive of the self-assertive erg is much involved in status hierarchies in man and animals ("who pecks whom" among hens and who leads the group among baboons). Incidentally, this erg is not necessarily socially disrupting as one might at first imagine, for the hierarchy is usually quickly established and gives rules for individual behavior, reduces fighting and provides leadership systems.

Another erg which sociologists have frequently seen fit to hypothesize (from Karl Marx to Thorstein Veblen) is an "instinct of workmanship", or the "desire for effectiveness", or the "need for creativity" as others have called this urge to manipulate the world. The evidence from multivariate experiment on attitudes and interest measures for an underlying *constructive erg* is tolerably complete, but the erg is weaker (smaller on loadings on any array of variables) than sex, hunger, security (fear avoidance) and other older biological ergs. And the frustration of the constructive erg (except when blended with self-assertion), though commented on by sociologists, has not been recognized by clinicians as noticeably productive of neurosis.

The ergs obtained operationally as uniquely determined factors in objective motivation strength measures thus align themselves, as a glance at table 2.11 will show, very well with the most convergent conclusions from clinical psychology, ethology, and sociology, but the next step in our putting a theory together does involve the assumption that, because of this parallelism, we are speaking about the same things. For Freud, McDougall, and the ethologists above, "an instinct" as they see it has always had three parts: (1) an innate tendency to perceive certain objects as more significant than others; (2) a tendency to experience a certain emotion in relation to what is perceived; (3) a purely conative impulse to perform certain acts in relation to the perceived object more readily than others in the interests of self-preservation. Up to this point, a connection has not been experimentally established between the patterns of the ergs and these three steps in a process, nor have we demonstrated directly, as yet, e.g. by twin studies, that the strength of these ergs is innately given.

In the animal world, the particular and peculiar sequence of events in the instinctual process is relatively clear. Such performances as recognizing a member of the opposite sex in the same species, being emotionally moved thereby, entering into courtship rituals, and so on to mating is easily visible in many species. So also is the hunting behavior of sudden attention to an object which is innately recognized as a suitable prey, the stalking behavior, and again the consummatory response of hunting down and killing the prey. Such procedures are accompanied by characteristic inward emotional and excitation sequences, in so far as we can perceive in the higher mammals and the primates emotional expression similar to our own. If anyone is skeptical about the characteristic nature of these instinctual processes, and their innateness, mathematical methods now exist for describing a process and showing that it is similar from one member of a species to another (Cattell, 1966, 1972), while the innateness of these responses has been repeatedly shown by experiments such as those of Lorenz and Tinbergen in which young animals have been removed from their parents before they have had a chance to learn by imitation (see chapter 5). Of course, the necessary environmental stimuli have to be present, but that is another matter. Also, it can be shown that, at first, many animals seem to inherit only parts of the process, and that a certain amount of experience, perhaps over and above maturation, is necessary to get the different parts coordinated into a whole.

In man, it is obvious that the inherent plasticity in instinctual behavior—a plasticity which increases from the insect through the lower animals and so to the mammals (see chapter 5)—permits substantial changes in the pattern, and indeed, makes the fabric of the ergic pattern largely environmental. It is probably still true to say that we have no positive evidence that if the young man and woman were brought up quite apart from society, they would accomplish mating—but it is a little hard to doubt it! If we look at the dynamic lattice in figure 2.2, it is evident that the ergic goals on the right, such as eating food, responding more readily with fear to thunder and the dark, and copulating, are largely inborn, relatively unlearned responses—or at least responses that are learned far more readily than any random behavior would be. But in the history of the culture, these direct satisfactions have usually been blocked or hedged in by rituals in various ways, and one must realize that the spread of the dynamic lattice distally from the ergic goals is a result of the numerous intermediate steps that now become necessary, if we are to live together in civilized life, to achieve a goal that was originally more directly reached. The dynamic lattice grows from right to left, in the way that we have arranged the diagram above. And by the time we get to the extreme left, we are dealing with whole series of attitudes and courses of action that are learned as means to ends to the goals on the right. Incidentally, the significance of this, as Freud points out in *Civilization and its Discontents*, is often misunderstood to mean that ergic satisfactions are harder to attain and less frequently attained in civilized than in barbaric or primitive life. This is not so. When societies move from hunting to agriculture, their food supply was actually much more assured, and a greater satisfaction of a greater number occurred, but it occurred through conditions which required more foresight and planning, more respect for a neighbor's property, and so on. Thus, the complication of the instinctual life is a stress but not a frustration. In more intensive studies of this phenomenon, the term *deflection strain* is used to indicate the psychological strain which occurs from approaching instinctual goals in more circuitous and complex ways, and doubtless there are psychological limits to the amount of deflection strain that an organism of a given level of development can take. But that is another story, to be discussed under conflict in a later chapter.

As the systematic investigation of ergs proceeds, it is likely that researchers will map out the whole subsidiation system—which we may call a *tract*—for each erg, as it typically occurs in our culture, and as is indicated in quite approximate ways in figure 2.3. The pattern that we have picked up by factor analysis across a section of attitudes, as shown in figure 2.2, is our evidence for the existence of the erg. Actually, this cross-section may turn out not to be all at the same distance from the goal, but it suffices to show which set of attitudes are all part of the tract going to a particular ergic goal.

What we are defining by this pattern, therefore, is admittedly not innate in the widest sense, because it could be shown that the pattern will be peculiar to a particular culture in its more distal approaches, though all these cultural patterns will get more alike as we approach the consummatory goal. Exactly the same problem exists about innateness, however, in regard to intelligence, in that, although we know that about 80 percent of the individual variance in intelligence is inherited, the form in which intelligence is expressed depends very much upon the culture. What we are saying is that, within one culture, where everyone learns the same things, innate differences of intelligence will lead to some people learning all of those things more quickly and deeply than others will. Similarly, in regard to ergs, we are saying that there is a source of energy or reactivity of a particular kind, all connected with a particular goal, and that if there are certain patterns in reaching that goal in a given culture, then some people show a greater interest in and reactivity to those ways of behaving than others do. The kind of energy is innate, but the mode of its expression is, at least in its more distal behaviors, more dependent upon the culture.

In any case, the proof of innate differences in drive strength levels is going to be more difficult than the corresponding proof for intelligence, because ergic tension levels alter all the time with degree of stimulation and degree of deprivation. Actually, this supplies us with one more proof of the unitary character of the drive energy, because in what is called dR (or differential R) factor analysis or P-technique (see above), we measure people from day to day and find that the factor analysis of change scores shows the same functional unities in change as it does in individual differences. Statistically, we do not know how much of the individual difference on a given day, therefore, is real individual difference and how much is the fluctuation of the pattern. Consequently, one would have to measure each person, say on ten to twenty occasions on the manifestations believed, by loading pattern, to be those of, say, sex, fear, etc., if we want to pursue the usual methods in behavior genetics to examine, for example, by twin comparisons, the innateness of dispositions to particular ergic reactivities.[1]

---

[1] Here we make our first step operationally and conceptually towards the idea of a specific quality of energy, i.e. of reactivity in each erg. The problem of demonstrating and defining this has held up some of the most penetrating thinkers in the field. Thus, Sir Cyril Burt (1955) in "Permanent contributions of McDougall" comments on Ashby's and McDougall's attempts to use homeostasis. He notes that as in our description of the process above, striving ceases when a particular kind of goal is achieved, which may be considered a particular kind of homeostasis. McDougall, he points out, always gave conation, "a second characteristic—self-correction". Psychic energy, or "Horme" as he preferred to call it, is "directed energy"—a concept that he never succeeded in making quite clear. The possibility of making it clear seems to begin with the factor analytic separation of ergs.

5 The nature of engrams: sentiments and complexes

The distinction we have drawn above between the innate source of energy connected with particular survival goals (ergs such as parental protectiveness, mating, food seeking) and the many ways in which these might be expressed as a result of cultural vagaries, calls for a concept which describes the latter dynamic pattern at the same order of complexity as the erg. The term used is an *engram* and represents whatever structures arise from experience and persist in one form or another. Thus, not only sentiments but habits and attitudes (and complexes to be dealt with later) are species of the engram. But before we can understand the operation of engrams we need first to say more about the relationship between ergs and sentiments and the possible origins of sentiments.

It is evident from the factor analytic work that the relation of ergs to sentiments is a relatively randomized one, as illustrated schematically in the factor loading matrix in table 2.10. That is to say, the attitude variables which demarcate one sentiment, for example "Career", are likely to have other loadings which are associated with several different ergs, as shown in the variables 3, 5, 6, 11, 15, and 19 in the matrix above, all of which are highly loaded on the Career sentiment, but which have their other loadings on distinct ergs. Conversely, the attitude courses of action that are loaded on one erg, e.g. on the Assertiveness erg in table 2.10, are quite likely to distribute their other appreciable loadings on several different sentiments [variables 18 (Self-sentiment), 20, 22 (Superego), 23 (Career), and 27 (Parental)]. Only occasionally will one get some systematic and substantial relation between a drive and a sentiment, as to some extent between the self-sentiment and the self-assertive erg, or between the sentiment to a sweetheart and the sex erg. In general, the necessary complications of culture require that several sentiments be subsidiated to one erg, and one sentiment to several ergs. For example, the need for security will be partly contributed to by medical insurance, partly by religion, partly by national defense, i.e. a patriotic sentiment, and so on to other sentiments.

The most complete list of sentiments to date is shown in table 2.12 gathered from several experimental sources.

Now in the history of psychology over the last fifty years, it will be recognized that when instincts or drives were driven from the field (except among animal psychologists) by the attacks of sociologists and Watsonian behaviorists in the twenties and thirties, the sentiments were the only structures left in command of the field. They were not always called by that name, but variously called aggregates of attitudes, sociological response patterns, habit formations, habit hierarchies, secondary drives, and so on. But "instincts" had to come back to fill a theoretical void. As Burt remarked in 1955, "During the last few years the pendulum has started to swing forward again. Under such innocent aliases as 'drives', 'needs', 'urges', or the like, the outlawed concept has begun to show its face in several unexpected quarters"; and, to quote the historian

Gardner Murphy (1949), "With the passing of the intense wave of anti-McDougall feeling, instinctive mechanisms have now come slowly back into place". The new slogan—"purpose of behaviorism" —would be an excellent title for what McDougall called a "hormic psychology". Actually, the scientific weakness of McDougall's position, as the senior author argued with McDougall in 1938, was that he had no methodology, such as we have developed in multivariate experimental methods, to demonstrate the existence and nature of the more complex patterns, which have been discussed in this chapter.

Thus, sentiments are now firmly established as factor patterns, and their relation to ergs is clear. But the manner in which they grow up has not been

Table 2.12*   Hypothesized list of human sentiments

S_1 *Profession* (1)	S_{15} *Theoretical–logical.* Thinking, precision (2) (8) (10)
S_2 *Parental family, home* (1)	S_{16} *Philosophical-historical.* Language, civics, social–cultural, esthetic rather than economic (2) (3) (6) (7)
S_3 *Wife, sweetheart* (1)	
S_4 *The self-sentiment* (1). Physical and psychological self	
S_5 *Superego* (1)	S_{17} Patriotic–political (1) (7)
S_6 *Religion.* This has emphasis on doctrine and practice, on high social and low esthetic values (1) (4) (7) (8)	S_{18} *Sedentary–social games.* Diversion, play club and pub sociability; cards (2) (10)
	S_{19} *Travel-geography.* Possibly Guilford's autism here
S_7 *Sports and fitness.* Games, physical activity, hunting, military activity (1) (2) (3)	S_{20} *Education–school attachment*
	S_{21} *Physical–home-decoration– furnishing*
S_8 *Mechanical interests* (1) (2) (5)	S_{22} *Household–cooking*
S_9 *Scientific interests.* High theoretical, low political; math. (2) (3) (4) (5) (6) (7) (9)	S_{23} *News–communication.* Newspaper, radio, TV
S_{10} *Business–economic.* Money administrative (2) (3) (4) (5)	S_{24} Clothes, self-adornment
S_{11} *Clerical interests* (2) (4)	S_{25} Animal pets
S_{12} *Esthetic expressions* (2) (10)	S_{26} Alcohol
S_{13} *Esthetic–literary appreciation.* Drama	S_{27} Hobbies not already specified
S_{14} *Outdoor–manual.* Rural, nature-loving, gardening, averse to business and "cerebration" (2) (5) (6)	

* References:

(1) Cattell *et al.* (4 studies)	(9) Strong (1949)
(2) Guildford *et al.* (1954)	(10) Thorndike (1935)
(3) Thurstone (1931)	*See also*
(4) Gundlach and Gerum (1931)	(11) Cottle (1950)
(5) Torr (1953)	(12) Hammond (1945)
(6) Carter, Pyles, Bretnall (1935)	(13) Crissy and Daniel (1939)
(7) Ferguson, Humphreys, Strong (1941)	(14) Vernon (1949)
(8) Lurie (1937)	(15) Miller (1968)

properly experimentally demonstrated yet. Our theory, as stated in the opening section, is that a sentiment pattern comes into existence through certain individuals being systematically more experienced and rewarded in certain courses of action than are others. This is due to their having greater involvement by the necessities of their life in certain institutions. For example, a married man develops a whole lot of attitudes about his home which are not developed by an unmarried man. And if we believe, as some near cynics do, that some people are more married than others, then there could be a continuum of experience, reward, and punishment, simultaneously scheduled on each of perhaps fifty attitudes which have to do with the adjustment to married life. This is what we would then recognize as a simple structure factor in objective motivational measurements.

There are, however, some complex and thorny problems yet to be straightened out in the concept of sentiment, especially relating to the mode of its representation in the dynamic lattice.

In a standard stimulus–response paradigm for an attitude, as used above, each attitude involves an object (though not simply for or against an object, as in the "Polling" definition). Is a sentiment identified by, and centred upon, an object of this kind, or does it constitute a large sub-goal or plexis in the middle ranges of the dynamic lattice, as suggested earlier? Or, indeed, are these two concepts really different?

If a sentiment is simply a sub-goal, it is a little difficult to account for positive correlations among the attitudes which subsidiate to it. Consider the maintenance of a bank account as a sub-goal, as it undoubtedly is, with various attitudes subsidiating to keeping it in the black, and various attitudes running from it toward this, that, and the other mode of interesting expenditure. Actually, one could argue that if one way of filling the bank account is strong, the others need not be so strong. For example, if the man's course of action in his profession is very rewarding salary-wise, then he may not have so strong an attitude about Aunt Jane's will. Probably, the only way in which some positive correlation among the subsidiating attitudes can be accounted for is by supposing that any such sub-goal is fully conscious and much considered. If Person A thinks a good deal about his bank account, and Person B does not, the Person A is likely to allot more psychological reward to every one of the attitudes which promises to help the bank account.

If, on the other hand, we approach the sentiment as an object, then we reach a position which is somewhat different, but not entirely so. Consider a young man who has a new car. Several distinct attitudes with several distinct goals develop which share the cost as an object, though scarcely as a sub-goal. For example, he may say, "I want my car in order to take out my girl" (in which we might detect a sexual objective), and again, "I want my car to be in good condition in order that I can get to business on time" (in which we might detect a self-assertive, ambitious goal, and perhaps the sentiment to a career), and again "I want my car so that I can 'show off' to my peers" (where we would see both gregarious and self-assertive satisfactions). It then becomes evident that the very *existence* of the car becomes necessary for each of these courses of action and these different goals and sub-goals, though otherwise they may not be psychologically related. Consequently, if we were to investigate correlations in a group of young men, half of whom possess cars and half of whom did not, we might expect to find some positive correlation among these attitudes since the existence of the car as a means to the given end rewards all of them. Or, again, between husband or wife, there are many attitudes and different kinds of satisfaction involved, but all of them depend upon the existence of the person; further, we might say that the total sentiment strength or investment would be expected to be equal to the sum of the strengths of all these attitudes.

The placing of an object that is not a sub-goal in the dynamic lattice really requires an extra dimension, or some line linking the objects involved in a set of attitudes going to various sub-goals by a line indicating that they all utilize a common object. Inasmuch as people become conscious of the objects that they "use", it might, however, be said that they become sub-goals in the sense that the individual subsidiates a lot of attitudes to insuring the continued existence of that object—his car, his wife, and, as we shall see in a moment, himself. Certainly, wherever a sentiment factor is found, it seems that we can find an object, or range of objects, upon which the thought of that sentiment is concentrated and upon which the attitudes converge. Furthermore, it now

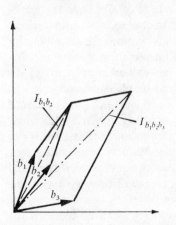

Method 1

$I_{b_1 b_2 b_3}$ is the final resultant found by first obtaining the resultant $I_{b_1 b_2}$ for b_1 and b_2 and then locating the resultant between $I_{b_1 b_2}$ and the remaining vector b_2 to give $I_{b_1 b_2 b_3}$.

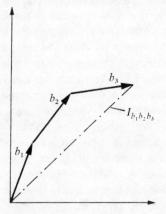

Method 2

Join the vectors head to tail as shown. The line which joins the tail of b_1 to the head of b_3 is the same resultant $I_{b_1 b_2 b_3}$ as in Method 1.

Figure 2.4 Summation of attitude vectors for one sentiment to give total strength of interest $I_{b_1 b_2 b_3}$

becomes possible to make a quantitative statement about the individual's amount and quality of interest or investment in that sentiment object. To do this, we have only to take the attitude vectors and add them algebraically. For the moment, we can demonstrate the process using geometry. If we collect all the attitudes that are involved in a particular sentiment, we could obtain for them a single vector which could be represented in familiar geometrical "summation of forces" terms, as shown in figure 2.4 by two methods, showing the total strength of interest in the continued existence of the object. The length of the vector represents the intensity of responses and the direction defines the relationship between the vectors.

This resultant vector essentially states the total satisfaction, and the kind of satisfaction, that anyone gets in a particular sentiment. Such a calculus has all kinds of interesting possibilities, both in clinical and in social psychology. For example, when we come to issues of conflict, effective prediction may well depend upon knowing the total strength of a given sentiment. And in social psychology, these measures of the strength of sentiments could help the economist, for example, understand the expenditures and investments connected with sentiments.[1] One of the experimental checks that could be made on the correctness and utility of this summation of the total interest in the sentiment represented by a vector, would be to measure the amount of pugnacity generated by anything which threatens the existence of the sentiment object. If we accept the theory we have adopted above that the total strength of pugnacious behavior is a simple function of the strengths of the ergic tendencies that are blocked, then it should follow that any threat to the existence of the object would evoke pugnacious behavior proportional in strength to the summated ergic tensions.

One consequence of the attitudes highly loaded on sentiments having strong contributions from this learned habit strength, and having ergic tension contributions which spring from different ergs, is that the motivation springing from a sentiment is likely to be more constant and dependable than that springing from an erg. The tension of ergs will vary from day to day with degrees of stimulation and satisfaction, but the strength of sentiments should stay relatively constant over time, both because they are an average of a variety of different ergic tensions and also because these habit strength terms expressing the amount of learning that has gone on necessarily remain constant at the level reached by past experience.

In the account above, we have said nothing about a second species of object

---

[1] Incidentally, a side-issue that would arise here concerns the meaning also of the loading of the attitudes in a sentiment upon other sentiments. Does that mean that they also add to the strength of sentiment? Our tentative answer is no because we shall soon be making a distinction between the idea of energy which is represented by the ergic tensions involved, and the idea of habit strength due to repetition, which constitutes the sentiments' contributions and which is quite a different thing.

attachment, namely, the *complex* of psychoanalytic theory. Sentiments and complexes collectively will be referred to as *engrams* or M factors. Engrams may be defined as structures which arise from experience with objects, institutions or individuals giving rise to persistent sentiments and complexes. The reason for omitting complexes is obvious: no investigation seems to have been made in multivariate experimental terms. As far as one can see, a complex should show itself in much the same way as a sentiment does by certain attitudes being very strong, certain aversions and prejudices being simultaneously strong, and so on in a manner that should lead to the appearance of a single factor. The chief difference would be, presumably, that when the interests are tapped by conscious methods, e.g. the usual opinionnaire or questionnaire, the individual would not necessarily, consciously, show the awareness of the strengths of the attitudes. Thus, a discrepancy between the conscious, consulting room self-report on attitudes, on the one hand, and the measurements by other, indirect devices on the other, might distinguish these patterns. Actually, this distinction comes very close to that between the integrated/unintegrated components discussed in the last chapter, and, in fact, Sweney (1969; see also Williams, 1959; Delhees, 1968; Horn and Sweney, 1970) has argued cogently that when a large discrepancy between the integrated and the unintegrated measurement for the same attitude or sentiment structure is found, we are dealing with a complex, or, at the very least, a strong conflict about a sentiment. However, this issue belongs to the chapter on conflict below. The difference between sentiments and complexes may also need P-technique to bring it out, i.e. factor analysis of the single individual, if it should prove that there are virtually no "common complexes" but only those peculiar to the individual's experience.

6 The relation of dynamic structures to the total personality

The question all psychologists will pose at this point is, "What is the relation of these dynamic structures to what we think of as the total personality structure?" The possibility that individuals will differ in the natural strength of their ergs has long been embodied in the concept of "dispositions". Thus, we speak of a person as being of a fearful, or an amorous, or an assertive disposition. The correlations in table 2.13 show that, indeed, over a two, three, or four month interval, the scores of individuals on the Motivational Analysis Test, which measures ergic tension levels and sentiment strengths, do remain appreciably constant. That is to say, while we recognize that ergic tensions may change with provocation and deprivation levels, yet there is certainly an overall individual stability about them. Indeed, if the correlations in table 2.13 were corrected for attenuation due to the unreliability of the measures, there would be quite appreciable stability. Thus, there is a

Table 2.13 Stability coefficients for dynamic factors

Dynamic factor		Stability coefficients		
		Over five weeks*	Over six months†	
		Adults	Children	
			I	U
Fear	E	.48	.29	.14
Mating	E	.51	.58	.20
Assertiveness	E	.53	.34	.23
Narcism	E	.53	.43	.17
Pugnacity	E	.41	.45	.20
Career	S	.39	—	—
Sweetheart	S	.47	—	—
Home–parental	S	.65	.23	.25
Superego	S	.46	.38	.07*
Self-sentiment	S	.69	.46	.05*
School sentiment	S	—	.39	.10*

* *Motivation Analysis Test Handbook* (1964).
† Bartsch (1973, personal communication). Note the insignificant values (asterisks) in the U component of some sentiment factors amongst children.
E is an erg, S a sentiment.

legitimate basis for speaking of differences of disposition as part of the description of individual personality. It must be pointed out in looking at table 2.13, however, that most of the people concerned are staying in much the same life situation, and that we do not know for certain what would happen if they could all be placed in very different life situations, satisfactions, and deprivations. Further experiment is necessary, but, if we can assume that the stable situations are of much the same kind for various people in the experimental group, then we can assume that the description in terms of dispositions is an important part of the description of a stable personality. Although table 2.13 does not bring it out too clearly, there is additional evidence elsewhere (for example, in Kline and Grindley's work (1974) where the standard deviations for the sentiments are lower than for the ergs—see figure 3.5) that the sentiments show a higher degree of stability than the ergic tensions, as would be expected from the arguments above.

In the writings of most psychologists, it is evident that there is a conception of personality which is something different from the individual's particular interests. Thus, to describe a person's sentiments by saying that he is a person who is very much attached to his home, that he is keen on athletics, and that he has little interest in mechanical hobbies, seems to leave a lot of his personality undescribed. It is also generally accepted, at least from common-sense observation, that persons of very different personalities may, to some extent, have the same interests, and that persons of very different interests may, to some extent, have the same personality. Thus, for example, among persons who are very interested in psychology, there is almost as wide an array of personality types as in the population at large. And, among people who could all be described as of a warm, sociable disposition (i.e. affectic, high on the A factor, in the personality test called the 16 PF), there are some whose interests may be strongly in religious work, some who are salesmen, and others who would be political in their interests, and so on.

The qualifications of general personality factors, many of which are temperament factors, started somewhat earlier than did the multivariate experimental exploration of the dynamic field, although they have since been developing in parallel. In the medium of measuring personality by questionnaires, for example, we recognize now some twenty or more primary personality factors, such as surgency, dominance, affectia, ego strength, parmia, etc. As more general contributors or organizers of these, we recognize some eight second-order personality factors, such as exvia–invia (the precise core in the popular notion of extraversion vs. introversion), anxiety, cortertia, independence, and so forth. In objective personality tests, there are also some twenty personality factors measured by actual "behavior in miniature situations", and these also have what is generally thought of as a temperamental character (for more detail, see Cattell and Warburton, 1967).

The distinction between temperament traits, ability traits, and dynamic trait modalities is one which the average psychologist makes intuitively. If asked to state exactly how he distinguishes the modalities, he would generally have considerable difficulty in coming to an operational statement. Nevertheless, an operational statement is possible, though we shall not pursue it here since it is somewhat complex. Briefly, it may be defined by saying that dynamic traits are goal directed, and are connected with behavior which typically ceases when some consummatory goal is reached. The temperament and ability traits are teased out by measures made in the course of behavior which constitutes the dynamic trait. For example, if we have a rat running a maze for food, the speed with which he will run (i.e. reflecting his interest) is likely to be largely a measure of the strength of his motivation. The relations and discriminations that he will make at certain points in the maze (assuming he has had earlier experience) will be measures of his abilities, e.g. memory and spatial ability. The changes in tempo as interest waxes and wanes, measured, possibly, using the ratio of the performance in the first half to that in the second half of the maze, is the best indication of a temperament trait, as in a fast starter versus a slow starter, and so on. Similarly, in human traits, ratio scores are frequently what we would interpret as temperament; note also that measures of how well people do when their motivation is about equal are generally considered measures of abilities. Any actual performance is almost invariably a combination of such traits, and we may write an equation to represent this.

If we think of these traits as vectors in the multidimensional life space of people, characteristically explored by factor analytical methods, we may quantify and summarize the behavioral performance P_j using an additive behavioral equation thus:

$$P_j = b_{ja}A + \cdots + b_{jt}T + \cdots + b_{ja}D + \cdots$$

where the b terms are behavioral indices determining the contribution of each trait to the total behavior in question, the A's represent ability factors, such as intelligence, verbal ability, spatial ability, etc., the T's represent temperament traits, such as surgency, affectia, parmia, premsia (general sensitivity), etc., and the D's represent dynamic traits, covering both the ergs (E's) and the engrams (M's) discussed above.

Another way of stating this is to say that in interests, i.e. dynamic traits, we are always scoring responsiveness to interest in a *particular* kind of behavior, which may be very narrow as, say, when we talk about interest in raising geraniums, or fairly broad, as when we speak of sex interest. That is to say, we are unlikely to find anything more than a specific factor for interest in geraniums, but we are likely to find a broad factor, as shown in table 2.2 above, for the interests that arise from the sex drive. Now, when we come to temperament traits (or, for that matter, abilities too), we are really taking a still broader set of measures. If we say that an individual is surgent (F factor in the 16PF), we mean that he is quick, impulsive, and lively in whatever he does. Thus, if we took thirty interests and measured certain ratios in regard to the speed with which the person warms up, the impulsiveness of his behavior, the lack of fall off in performance with fatigue, etc., then we should be measuring a general personality trait of surgency. Thus, a personality trait may be considered an abstraction from a whole lot of dynamic traits, and, in consequence, we should not expect it to have much correlation with any one of them. Consequently, the difference between general personality traits and dynamic traits is, therefore, partly in the type of measurement made (the ratio type, etc., in the former) and partly in the generality, in that the personality-trait type of measure needs to be taken across a large number of particular interests.

Actual correlational study with abilities, general personality (temperament) traits, and the dynamic traits already known bears out very definitely this independence. The correlations of ability traits with personality traits is only small and sporadic, and the correlation of temperament traits with dynamic traits is relatively minor. Although this is the general rule, there are, of course, some interesting exceptions, and a fair amount has been written about the small and special associations of some abilities with some temperament traits. Actually, in the dynamic area, there are one or two instances of rather powerful bridgings which we must now discuss. In effect, if a dynamic trait is very broad, i.e. not something like an interest specifically in athletics or in raising geraniums, it may produce styles of behavior running so broadly across a personality that it becomes, in effect, a general personality factor classifiable with the temperamental factors.

The two major instances of this are the dynamic factors we have already called the self-sentiment and that which has been recognized in the superego, the loading patterns for which have been set out in table 2.10. As indicated before, the self-sentiment is a set of attitudes which take the self-concept as their object, and have to do with the physical, emotional, and social characteristics of the self. For reasons that are discussed more fully in chapter 4, this becomes a sentiment with a very large investment, due to the maintenance of the physical self, the emotional integrity, and the social reputation being necessary prerequisites for a very large number of other satisfactions.

A sentiment already mentioned previously, the origin of which is less clear (unless we accept the psychoanalytic explanations exactly as they stand), is the superego. Here experiment clearly supports the Freudian concept of a set of attitudes, all of which have to do with maintaining moral standards, and which cause the individual to feel guilty and unhappy if he offends against these standards. Although superego may seem only another word for conscience, it has some additional meaning which is worth retaining, from clinical work, and also from the experimental findings we are now dealing with. The pattern of this structure, from factoring objective motivation measures, is shown in table 2.10.

This also influences a very broad array of a person's behavior, coming into all kinds of special interests too, and in consequence, showing up in those general personality behaviors which are picked up by ratings, questionnaires, and objective tests devised to find general personality dimensions. In fact, what is now clear, is that the two factors which have been named self-sentiment and superego here, are essentially the same as those that have been picked up in the general personality tests by the 16 PF, the High School Personality Questionnaire (HSPQ), the Children's Personality Questionnaire (CPQ), etc., as factors Q_3 and G. These have, in their own right, both through the questionnaire content and through the things to which they related themselves, such as school achievement, freedom from delinquency, freedom from automobile accidents, etc., been identified as the self-sentiment and the superego (Gorsuch, 1965, obtained a correlation of .46 between superego sentiment and the G factor). Now it becomes possible to check this by actual correlations of the measures, and the results show very clearly that the motivation test approach and the personality test by questionnaire are zeroing in on the same two concepts here.

Nevertheless, as table 2.14 shows, the factors in the 16 PF and the dynamic structure factors in the MAT and other measures are largely independent. There *are* some significant correlations among them, but they are mainly small. This table is partly that published in the original, first investigation of the relation of dynamic structure to personality factors (Cattell, 1957), but is, in part,

Table 2.14 Relation of dynamic modality factors to general personality factors

Dynamic Traits	A Affectia	B Intelligence	C Ego weakness	E Dominance	F Surgency	G Superego strength	H Parmia	I Premsia	L Protension	M Autia	N Shrewdness	O Guilt-proneness	Q₁ Radicalism	Q₂ Self-sufficiency	Q₃ Self-sentiment	Q₄ Ergic tension
Sex	.02	.15	.02	—.02	.11	—.30*	—.11	—.06	.20*	.31*	.11	.27*	.27*	.19*	.19*	.31*
Gregariousness	.33*	.05	.15	—.01	.22*	—.18*	.17	—.06	—.08	.01	.01	.01	—.11	—.33*	—.31*	.03
Parental protectiveness	.06	—.15	.09	—.25*	—.09	.12	—.08	.04	—.07	.01	—.15	.06	—.09	—.16	—.12	.05
Exploration (curiosity)	—.14	.09	.01	.02	—.10	.07	—.06	.21*	.01	.13	—.09	.04	.29*	.13	.09	—.00
Fear; escape	—.07	—.12	—.09	—.01	—.16	.19*	.15	.01	—.06	—.17	—.02	—.20*	.09	—.13	.27*	—.23*
Self-assertion	.24*	.11	.06	.15	—.00	—.01	.32*	—.06	—.20*	.03	.03	—.06	.21*	—.12	.07	—.10
Narcistic vs. superego	.02	.08	.05	.07	.13	—.37*	—.12	—.15	.21*	.35*	.12	.22*	.27*	.22*	—.39*	.26*
Air Force	.01	.01	.11	.23*	.13	.14	.38*	—.09	—.24*	—.13	.13	—.38*	—.05	—.07	.21*	—.41*
Sports	—.00	—.11	.02	—.02	—.08	—.06	—.02	—.16	—.12	—.03	—.01	—.09	—.20*	—.04	—.08	—.00
Religious sentiment	.01	—.18*	.03	—.19*	—.05	.26*	.01	.20*	—.14	—.22*	—.16	—.12	—.34*	—.33*	.25*	—.10
Mechanical, materialistic interest	—.03	.10	.01	.10	.01	.11	.10	—.13	—.05	—.01	.04	—.12	.16	.15	.06	—.18*
Self-sentiment	.11	.10	.04	.20*	—.05	.13	.34*	.05	—.31*	—.15	—.02	—.22*	.06	—.18*	.34*	—.25*
Rest-seeking	—.10	.03	—.03	—.09	—.20*	.10	—.04	—.04	—.02	.04	.06	.14	.10	.05	.06	.09

* Significant at 1 % level.

strengthened by correlations found in more recent forms of both tests which have, therefore, reduced the attenuation due to unreliability of scales. Comparison with the intercorrelation table in the MAT Handbook reveals a certain randomness in the correlations except for superego and self-sentiment. It will be seen that though 74 percent of the correlations are nonsignificant, there are some which invite hypotheses and further research. For example, the gregariousness erg does relate positively to effectia, as one would expect, but one is disinclined to call this an identity and to suppose rather that people of affectic (warmhearted, sociable) temperament are stronger in their gregarious disposition, though affectia and gregariousness are not identical. This is suggested for example by the fact that gregariousness is also significantly correlated with surgency, which is quite different from affectia. One also sees an appreciable correlation of the strength of the religious sentiment with the strength of the superego, but again, one would argue that religious attachment may help to strengthen superego, though the superego is, itself, a different structure. However, the two correlations which are such that they could indicate measurement of one and the same thing, after due allowance for instrument factors, are those between the superego and self-sentiment in the questionnaire and the superego and self-sentiment in the dynamic structures.

Our conclusion must, therefore, be that we are in the main in three different domains in ability, temperament, and dynamic structure factors, but that there are some interesting connections, suggesting intriguing hypotheses about mutual effect for further research. Meanwhile, all three need to be measured in any attempt at a full description of the individual person.

7   Summary   1. The next step in systematic research, after discovering how to measure sheer interest strength objectively, is to intercorrelate measures made by such devices upon a very comprehensive array of dynamic measurements, i.e. measurements on attitudes taken as "courses of action".

2. Although in an exploratory approach we need to keep open-minded, and to insure this by taking what is called a representative design of experiment by using great diversity of interest variables, yet, we do not enter entirely blindly, and without prior views on dynamic structure. Thus, we have the concept that attitudes subsidiate one to another eventually finishing up at consummatory goals in drives or ergs. Further, it is obvious from clinical work that these subsidiation chains form a lattice structure in which the subsidiated attitudes go through sub-goals to these final ergic goals. This hypothesis can be tested by insuring that we have at least two or three attitudes representing each supposed drive.

3. Among the most clear-cut factor structures which emerge from such research are patterns which immediately suggest the principal mammalian,

primate drives as located in the study of the higher animals by ethologists and others. These are called ergs rather than instincts, because of the confusions associated with the instinct concept, and they turn out to be in number and nature much nearer to the list suggested by McDougall than that by Murray or Freud, though they do contain a narcistic sex component hypothesized by Freud. In any case, an entirely new and positive basis is now provided for theory and experiment regarding the presumably innate ergic patterns in man.

4. Along with these patterns that strike the eye at once as representing functional unities due to innate ergs are other patterns which represent aggregates of attitudes brought together by learning within each of several distinct social institutions. These have been called sentiments. The basic operational distinction of ergs and sentiments is that ergs contain a set of attitudes utilizing different cultural features, but sharing a common emotion and ergic goal, whereas the sentiments, reciprocally, have quite diverse emotional, ergic components but center upon a single cultural purpose. Sentiments seem to be better formed in adults than children, but so far, only a limited number of them have been explored, and a substantial field of investigation remains.

5. Although ergs are picked up here operationally as unique simple structure factors, the theoretical conception includes much more, particularly, the notion of a unitary process over time. This process is easily recognized in all kinds of animals, but the plasticity of man hides it in a lot of cultural specificities. Methods exist for locating characteristically repetitious processes from initial provocation to consummatory goal, but have, so far, not been applied in man. There is a sense in which the factor analytic extraction of ergic patterns rests on a sequential track in the dynamic lattice, even if not on a time sequence observation. Since the same patterns are found in longitudinal P-technique study in individuals as in R-technique, we must suppose that ergic tension varies appreciably from occasion to occasion, but other evidence shows that there is also a tendency in every individual to a fairly characteristic level, indicating his disposition. The specific ergic tensions may be considered "energies with direction".

6. The growth of common sentiment structures seems to be due to differential exposure to schedules of experience and reward set up as particular patterns by various social institutions, such as church, family, hobby group, career, etc. When sentiments and ergs are examined side-by-side in the same matrix, it is usual to find the loading patterns randomized with respect to one another. Thus, each sentiment may call upon a variety of ergs. Further analysis and experiment is needed concerning the question of whether a sentiment needs to be represented in the lattice as a sub-goal or as an object shared by attitudes subsidiating in different directions. In either case, we can write a vector, summing the different attitudes which have to do with the sentiment, which describes the nature and strength of the individual's total investment in a given sentiment. It is suggested that the equation for this total strength could be

checked by measuring the amount of pugnacity evoked when the existence of the sentiment object is threatened. It is possible that, apart from the ergic tensions which enter a sentiment, there is a contribution different in kind and close to what is considered habit strength, representing the number of repetitions of the learning experience, etc. This would mean that sentiments contribute a different kind of "interest strength" to a particular attitude to that contributed by ergs.

7. Little is known from multivariate experiment about what are clinically recognized as complexes. It is possible, though not probable, that no complexes will be found as common traits, i.e. by R-technique, but that they are always individual in form, and therefore discoverable only by P-technique. The chief differentiation of the complex from the sentiment may turn out to be discrepancy in the amount of self-conscious integrated component in the former compared with the amount of the unintegrated, U component.

8. Personality study recognizes three modalities of traits: abilities, general personality or temperament traits, and dynamic or interest trait structures. Although usually distinguished only intuitively, they can be distinguished operationally, by procedures including the fact that temperament traits are more frequently ratio difference scores, that dynamic traits are goal-directed from stimuli to consummatory responses, and that general personality traits are averages or abstractions across the behavior in a lot of dynamic traits. On this basis, one would expect that abilities, temperament traits, and dynamic traits would occupy factor analytically different domains, and that any specific piece of behavior would, in general, be a sum of the effects of all three of them. Experiment demonstrates that this is essentially the case, though certain of the more general dynamic structure traits also enter into what are generally and properly thought of as general personality traits. For example, the levels of the broad ergic tension factors have long been called personality "dispositions". More specifically, the two very broad sentiments which are called the self-sentiment and the superego structure appear also as factors in questionnaires and objective tests of general personality, due to the fact that they affect broadly the whole style of behavior. This is verified by the substantial correlations obtained between the measures of self-sentiment and of the superego in the two modalities when the effect of instrument factors is allowed for. There exists some other slighter, but meaningful, connections across media, e.g. that of the gregariousness erg with affectia, which deserves to be investigated in terms of a more complex connecting mechanism.

3 Dynamic traits related to structured learning theory and situational modification

1 Personality learning examined by adjustment process analysis

Having grasped what research has to tell us about the form of dynamic structure, one naturally asks next "how did such structure arise?" In other words, how did we acquire the web of attitudes, habits and sentiments woven into such a complex interactive pattern as the dynamic lattice? In the cognitive field of psychology the theme is referred to as "learning theory"; on the emotional side, as in clinical work, it is known as "getting adapted" (successfully or unsuccessfully). In the context of dynamic structure, what is not the result of genetic maturation (as in the genotypic ergs) is *personality learning* in the wider sense, and *dynamic learning or adaptation* when specifically related to dynamic traits. The assumption throughout the chapter will be that personality learning is multidimensional change in response to multidimensional situations (and there can be few situations, except in psychological laboratories, which are not). This chapter will concentrate on the understanding of the rise of sentiments and the modulation of ergs by situations.

Approaching the matter in the broadest context, familiar to the clinician and the educator, one can perceive a model which puts the story of dynamic adaptation in a nutshell. This model is shown in the *Adjustment Process Analysis* chart in figure 3.1 which speculates on the possible paths and outcomes taken by an individual in the process of gratifying an erg. When stimulation first occurs there is a *chiasm* A, or *first dynamic crossroads*, with three possible outcomes depending on the internal conditions or choices of the organism and the nature of the external situation. If the individual finds immediate satisfaction (A_1), then no learning occurs and the drive subsides temporarily. Where there is no immediate gratification, we find either obstruction (A_2) as when a traveller in the desert can see water in a mirage but cannot reach it, or continued deprivation (A_3), when the traveller cannot even see water. Continued attempts to circumvent the barrier now lead to chiasm B.

Extreme annoyance may succeed in breaking the barrier (B_1) if it happens to be of that kind. However, he may not succeed (B_2) and thus remain in a state of rage, or he may stay deprived and in a state of phantasy (B_3). The subjects in the Minnesota Starvation Studies (Keys, 1952) who were put on a semi-starvation diet for six months began to experience phantasies of food — banquets, and dining halls of delicious delicacies paraded in their minds.

Having learnt that rage or phantasy do not satisfy an erg, other possibilities such as despair-appeal (C_1) [the thirsty man in the desert prays for water, the Minnesota subjects begged the researchers for more food], renunciation of the idea of ever satisfying the erg (C_2) or becoming hopelessly ensnared in an aggressive or pugnacious cycle (C_3) are tried. Beyond chiasm C at the D, E, and F chiasms which are more appropriate to human than animal behavior, we see still more complex emotional adjustment problems. After failure and anxiety, the most discussed branch in this tree of attempted adaptation, is a move to "forget" the ill-fated dynamic need by repression (E_3). From this there may be one more step (chiasm F) to the cul-de-sac of neurosis.

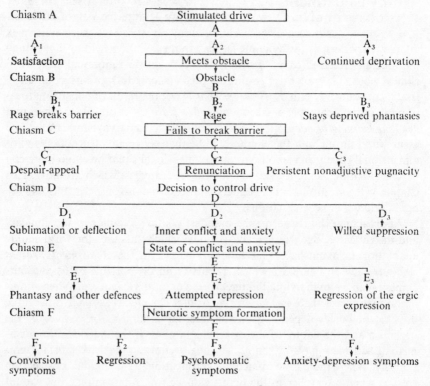

Figure 3.1 The Adjustment Process Analysis chart
Source: Cattell (1965).

At each choice point—a choice not entirely in the hands of the individual but greatly affected by the circumstances of the environment—just a few paths constitute the possible sequels. Some lead back to normal adjustment or *homeostasis*[1] (ready for the next "aboriginal" situation). But many lead into chiasms requiring more subtle kinds of emotional learning and adjustment which have an abiding effect on future problem-solving.

Now any and all of the attempts at "self-expression" which constitute the stuff of our lives can have their history and outcome traced in a shorthand form from the APA chart. For example, A_2, B_2, C_2, D_2, E_1, records that the individual was stimulated, met a barrier, failed to break it, persisted between ineffective rage and despair, and settled for an adjustment of substitute satisfaction by phantasy. In a precise analysis quantities would be assigned to the degrees of each kind of response and sequel.

The APA chart as given above is of course an abstraction and as such incomplete. It does not state the particular erg or life object involved, and, therefore, one must recognize that being thwarted in wanting to join a sports club is in general much less of a frustration than being deprived of nourishment. The actual working out of what a particular life situation will do to the personality requires that the real life objects be filled in with appropriate weights. An excellent and penetrating analysis expanding in qualitative terms what the various chiasms and paths may mean to personality has recently been contributed by the Cartwrights (*Psychological Adjustment, Ego and Id*, 1971). From such studies one would hypothesize, for example, that repeated failure to solve the problem at chiasms C and D will lead to reduction of ego strength— factor C in the 16PF, HSPQ, and other general personality factor scales.

It is known that factors C, E, and F (a) become significantly lower in neurotics (persons forced to chiasm F), (Cattell and Scheier, 1961), and (b) improve under psychotherapy (Hunt, 1944). Also there are indications that if a person is prevented, by a combination of therapy and tranquillizers, from experiencing emotional upsets (low factor C behavior) over a period of as little as six weeks his ego strength increases (figure 3.2).

Turning from these specific instances towards a general model of personality learning which incorporates them, we find one that is suitable for the present crude stage of researches in this area in what has been called the *multidimensional learning matrix calculation*. It supposes that any path of experience— now considered as filled in from figure 3.1 with specific life object definitions, e.g. pass or failure in a high school examination—is likely on an average to

---

[1] Homeostasis, as we shall see in chapter 5, is a concept introduced by Cannon (1932) to describe the process whereby the body attempts to control the physio-chemical conditions inside the body within the narrow limits sufficient for survival. In its original form it was related to physiological body needs which are self-regulatory such as food, water, oxygen, and temperature of the body. But the concept has widened in recent years to include other kinds of motives such as curiosity and general body activity.

produce slight changes in each of several personality factors as a result of *changes in trait scores*. As such it can be written as a learning vector, with illustrative trait change values, thus:

$$\begin{array}{c} \text{Personality factor} \\ \begin{array}{ccccc} A & B & C & D & \ldots & Q_4 \end{array} \end{array}$$

Path X, one experience $\quad +.2 \quad 0 \quad -.1 \quad +.3 \quad\quad -.4$

Now if we know how frequently the person repeats this experience (and assume each experience summatively contributes the same effect), the whole calculation of learning change can be conducted by what is called matrix algebra, as shown in table 3.1. The learning vector could have been any row from the **L** matrix shown in table 3.1.

If the psychologist reading this is not yet familiar with matrix calculations (which constitute today the bulk of psychological calculations on the computer) he need not feel that he has to understand it in detail (see brief notes in appendix II). The important thing is that—since we can actually measure the personality change profile and know the frequency of experience matrix—it is possible to calculate the learning matrix, **L**, which yields such values as we set out above. That is, reading along the rows in the learning law matrix, it states the power

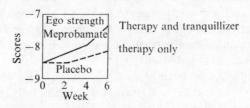

	Change in drug therapy group (1)	*t* value (2)	Change in placebo-therapy group (3)	*t* value (4)	Difference (1) and (3)	*t* value
Ego strength	1.24	2.88 $p>.005$	.48	.83 (n.s.)	.76	1.11 (n.s.)
Guilt-proneness	.52	1.21 (n.s.)	1.05	2.69 $p>.01$	−.53	.97 (n.s.)

Source: Rickels *et al.* (1966).

Statistical evaluation of effect of therapy and tranquillizer upon ego strength (C) and guilt-proneness (O)

Figure 3.2 Effect of experience of therapy, reducing emotional upsets, upon ego strength (C)

Table 3.1 Learning calculation by learning summary matrix model

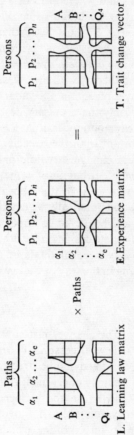

Personality

| Paths | | | | Persons | | | | Persons | | |
| α_1 $\alpha_2 \ldots \alpha_e$ | | | $\times$ Paths | p_1 $p_2 \ldots p_n$ | | | $=$ | p_1 $p_2 \ldots p_n$ | | |

A
B
· · ·
Q₄

α_1
α_2
· · · α_e

A
B
· · ·
Q₄

Personality

L. Learning law matrix   E. Experience matrix   T. Trait change vector

$\alpha_1, \alpha_2, \ldots, \alpha_e$ represent paths through the Adjustment Process Analysis chart
A, B, ..., Q₄ represent personality factors

of a given experience (path) to produce changes on each of several personality factors. Or, if we take a column instead of a row, it states for a given personality factor (A, B, C, etc.) what the nature of the changes are as produced by each of a variety of experiences.

This is only a first and relatively crude approach to learning laws. That is why it has been called the Learning Summary Matrix Model, since it presents the final change from a given experience without analyzing the factors of reward, etc., which contribute in detail. If we wish to get down to the details of mechanism and the why's and wherefore's of a particular piece of learning taking place—as one might in a Hullian equation—then the empirical, descriptive laws yielded by matrix **L**, must be further broken down, as will be discussed later. But this is the necessary experimental beginning, if we are to concern ourselves with the rise of *whole dynamic structures* and not, as in so much reflexological learning theory, with an isolated bit of behavior, such as the frequency of pecking by a pigeon in a Skinner box. However, the present chapter will aim to master only the necessary descriptive phase of structured learning, leaving dynamic explanation until later.

Perhaps still more important than the capacity of the structured learning theory description to handle change in whole patterns is the fact that this approach can handle the real life behavior of humans *in situ*, i.e. as it naturally occurs, without having to remove it to the laboratory. The latter has severe limitations, in that ethically and practically we cannot introduce manipulations in the laboratory strong enough to change important aspects of personality. The nonmanipulative multivariate design on the other hand, can, by the method above, tease out by more advanced methods of analysis what learning experiences in life are producing in the way of changes in well-known personality structures.

2 Learning as change in the bearing of traits upon behavior

The changes just considered are in traits, and in general personality and ability traits as much as in the dynamic structures with which this book is chiefly concerned. For economy of statement we shall use the proper term of a *vector* of trait changes (any column in matrix **T** in table 3.1 above). A vector of course is only a set of numerical values in an agreed order, which can in geometry be represented as an arrow of particular length and particular direction (see figure 3.3, page 66).

In this section we are going to meet the more subtle idea that a learning experience will do more than change an individual's endowments on a vector of trait scores. *It will normally also change the way in which he combines his capacities in bringing them to bear on a given performance.*

This has been shown clearly and conclusively in the realm of cognitive and physical skills by the different experimental approaches of Fleishman and Hempel (1954, 1956), Tsujioka (1970), and Tucker (1966). Yet actually the principal is more important and more urgently in need of study in the motivational field. Here we are fully aware that exactly the same action may be carried out by different people for different reasons.[1] Also, as emotional learning proceeds, one and the same person may initiate a course of action with one motive and transfer to a different motive as time goes by. A young man might take up the career of a sailor because he wants to escape from the restrictions of home, but pursue it later because it satisfies career ambitions. There must be many wealthy men who started out with the intention of making money, but who have since become hooked on the subtleties of business dealings for their own sake, almost in an esthetic sense.

In theory this change could occur without any change in the actual, absolute strength of the attitude itself, though in most cases both trait change and trait rearrangements would occur, very probably producing some change in the strength of the particular course of action. But let us first examine the composition of an attitude by means of a geometrical representation of the factor equation (3.1), where for practical purposes let us say all the loadings that matter fall on just two ergs, E_1 and E_2 (two engrams M_1 and M_2 or any combination of E's and M's would be just as permissible), thus:

$$a_{ij} = b_{j1} E_{1i} + b_{j2} E_{2i} \qquad (3.1)$$

Here the attitude course of action a_j or response has its strength best estimated for individual i by the strength of his two ergic tensions E_1 and E_2, and the weight in the *behavioral indices*, b_{j1} and b_{j2} which are the loadings found by factor analysis. These b's may vary from 0 to ± 1.0. Now either of these b's is actually a (partial) regression coefficient, a tangent showing how rapidly the strength of a_j increases from person to person according to a person's endowment in E. This is shown in figure 3.3. The essentials of this figure hold regardless of whether the factor analysis is what we have been calling R-technique (factoring across people) or P-technique (across occasions for a particular person). In the latter case the b values will represent how the interest in the attitude *for that particular person*, changes with the levels of his ergic tensions.[2]

---

[1] There is, for example, the authentic story of the visiting clergyman who was touched by the kindness of a "tough" prisoner in feeding some of his own limited food to a nest of young rats. The prisoner proudly pointed out, however, that rats in that wing had been known to attack the warders.

[2] It is possible, as elementary algebra will suggest, to have constants added to a specification equation like (3.1), which will say, for example, that attitude a_j has a greater absolute amount of E_1 than of E_2 to begin with, before any increase in strength begins; but the ordinary factor model does not include this complication, and we can in any case avoid it by the assumption that the increase in variance of a factor has a constant ratio to its absolute level, which is not unreasonable. In that case the size of a b (a behavioral index) tells us how much the E to which it applies is contributing to the behavior a_j.

Psychologically we must assume from learning theory that this also represents how much *satisfaction* from the course of action a_j accrues in the given situation from the response a_j. For the individual would not go on making the response a_j unless it were reinforced through his getting some satisfaction from it. Or, in other words, returning to the dynamic lattice (page 24), these b values tell how much the given attitudes and its "suffixes" (as we may call the further attitudes to which it subsidiates) ultimately subsidiate to the ergic goals, E_1 and E_2.

The b's thus represent, at one and the same time, the extent to which the various ergs get satisfaction, i.e. have their tension reduced, by the given course of action, and the extent to which interest and responsiveness in that course of action will be increased by any increase in the given ergic tensions. This follows because ergic tension increase (degree of deprivation) and degree of satisfaction from action are directly correlated. The vector covering the set of behavioral indices, b's, might psychologically be most aptly called the relevance, potency, or learning vector, because it defines the potency or "bearing"

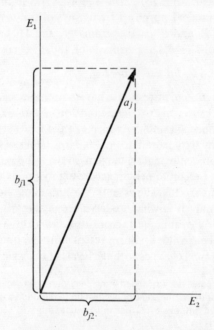

a_j Attitude strength
E_1 E_2 Ergs
$b_{j1}b_{j2}$ Behavioral indices or factor loadings representing the investment of a_j in each ergic tension

Figure 3.3 Geometrical presentation of behavioral indices as defining the contribution of an erg

of a whole series of traits upon the stimulus–response (j) in question. For easy mnemonic we will call it the *bearing vector* and code it by **B**.

Classical learning theory (whether as reflexology, or as quantity memorizing laws, or dealing with school achievement learning) has confined itself to plotting curves of change in the magnitude of the response a_j. What is now being called *structured learning theory* duly records these changes in magnitude but seeks to explain them by changes in three vectors, of which we have so far studied trait and behavioral indices. First, if the b's were to remain unchanged, a_j could increase because the vector of trait endowments, defined in the previous section, alters. (For when we set the human or animal to learn a_j je inevitably learns many other trait changing things besides.) Secondly, regardless of what happens to an individual's **T** (trait) vector, the vector of b's also changes, and this accounts also for some change in a_j.

Actually, we discover the changes in the **T** and **B** vectors by measuring people before the learning situation on a lot of attitudes, a's, and measuring them after the learning experiences on the same attitudes and making two factor analyses. Since this is a rather arduous form of experiment, it is still in its infancy, despite its theoretical importance. There are, however, pioneer studies by Hendricks, Krug, Bartsch, Vaughan, Barton, and Dielman, only one or two yet published, which show that psychologically important changes in the **B** vector actually take place.

Our first clues to changes in **B** vectors as a result of learning experiences come from Hendricks (1971) who took 193 psychology students and applied objective tests to measure the strength of the attitude-interest: "As a university student I want to learn more about psychology". Using the MAT to determine the strength of ten important dynamic structure factors [career–profession sentiment (Ca), home–parental sentiment (Ho), fear erg (Fr), narcism–comfort erg (Na), superego sentiment (SE), self-sentiment (SS), mating erg (Ma), pugnacity–sadism erg (Pg), assertiveness erg (As), and the sweetheart–spouse sentiment (SW)] he obtained the following correlations of the attitude with them for the integrated component on two occasions ten weeks apart:

	Ca	Ho	Fr	Na	SE	SS	Ma	Pg	As	SW
Occasion 1 (a_{j1})	.022	−.111	.030	.297	.141	.370	−.065	−.089	.014	−.002 (3.2)
Occasion 2 (a_{j2})	−.131	−.102	.286	.222	.159	.374	−.075	−.204	.025	−.027 (3.3)

The occasions came at the beginning of the course and after ten weeks of competitive conditions in a general psychology course. A significant difference in correlation, or b index, occurs for the erg of fear (.030 to .286) at the 5 percent level. One possible dynamic interpretation is that as the end of semester examinations draw near there is an increasing concern about the subject. The rather high correlation with self-sentiment (.370 and .374) might indicate that motivation was largely a question of "doing the proper thing", at first. Further examples of change arising from learning experience are also discussed in section 5 in our discussion of manipulation experiments.

3 Learning as change in emotive involvement in the situation

To grasp a third meaningful description and source of change in dynamic learning explored in this section it is necessary first to catch up with modulation theory, briefly introduced on page 61 above. When a state such as anxiety, arousal, fear, or sex erg tension is characteristically brought to a different level in one situation from that in another, it is said to be modulated. (Incidentally, "emotive" in this title means "moving" and is a useful term to cover both general emotional and specific ergic tensions.) One says "modulated" rather than simply "stimulated" for several reasons; first, that the affect is due to only part of the stimulus situation, second, that the vector representation makes it mathematically appropriate and third, that there are other psychological modulations in which stimulation hardly describes what happens.

A global stimulus situation, which we may designate g, typically has two parts: (1) the *focal stimulus*, h, which the individual focuses in consciousness, and which stimulates his response j (to an amount a_j throughout our formulae), and (2) an *ambient stimulus*, k, which is the background or the rest of the stimulus situation. For example, the focal stimulus might be a request to a child "Please bring my glasses" and the ambient situation a hot summer's day. We know that in this condition a_j, if measured in seconds, is likely to be longer than usual. Or if the stimulus is a whistle at the teacher, this will be differently responded to if the ambient situation is a classroom or a beach.

The ambient situation works by modulating the level of certain states, or dynamic traits (including roles) and in the standard modulation model we suppose a *modulation index*, s_{kx} (which for common situations has the same power for all people) and a specific proneness or liability in the person to a particular kind of emotion, x, which we will write L_{xi}. Then i's level on, say, the state of excitement S_x in situation k_1 will be:

$$S_{xk_1 i} = s_{k_1 x} L_{xi} \qquad (3.4a)$$

and in another situation:

$$S_{xk_2 i} = s_{k_2 x} L_{xi} \qquad (3.4b)$$

thus the general case will be:

$$S_{xki} = s_{kx} L_{xi} \qquad (3.4)$$

That is to say, his proneness or liability to excitement remains fixed at L_{xi} but s, the situational modulator, alters for each situation. His likelihood of responding in, say, a loud voice, a_j, would normally be estimated from a behavioral index, b_{jx} showing the bearing of excitement on loudness of voice, thus:

$$a_{ij} = b_{jx}S_{xki} \tag{3.5}$$

(though there would be several other—indeed a whole vector—of such terms in the full specification). This can now be rewritten, by substituting in (3.5) from (3.4):

$$a_{ij} = b_{jx}S_{kx}L_{xi} \tag{3.6}$$

That is to say, in front of the term L_{xi}, which is strictly a trait measurement, we now have the two indices, b, or behavioral index already dealt with, and s. Thus the full-fledged specification equation now changes (using only dynamic traits, i.e. E's and M's) from:

$$a_{ijk} = \Sigma b_{jx}\,E_{xki} + \Sigma b_{jy}\,M_{yki} \quad (\Sigma \text{ means "the sum of all} \tag{3.7}$$
$$\text{such terms as . . .")}$$

to

$$a_{ijk} = \Sigma b_{jx}S_{kx}L_{xi} + \Sigma b_{jy}S_{ky}L_{yi} \tag{3.8}$$

(Note: we have not cluttered the equation with the subscript h for the focal stimulus for j) where L_x's are liabilities to ergic tensions and L_y's to modulation of particular sentiments.

It will be recognized that the full specification equation now has *three* vectors in it: a *trait* vector (rewritten as characteristic liabilities); a *bearing* vector of behavioral indices showing the effect that a state has on a given action, i.e. its potency or relevance; and now a new vector of *modulators*, or ambient stimulus values, s's. The s's provoke the liabilities to yield certain state levels, and the b's then say how potent these state levels are in generating the response j from the focal stimulus h.

To keep these concepts precise we should note that the behavioral index b_{jx} refers to a focal stimulus h (not always written in) and a response to it, j, which is measured, with respect to the contribution of any trait or state x. The *modulator*, s_{kx}, on the other hand, refers to the ambient condition k, and operates in relation to the liability L_x. It would be the same regardless of what response j is to be estimated. If being in a house on fire is the ambient stimulus, the state of fear, S_{kfi}, of individual i stands at that value both on account of his characteristic liability to fear, L_{fi}, and the strong modulator s_{kf} for that situation. How strongly he will carry out any response act a_{ji} is decided quite independently by the weight of b operating upon the state strength at the time, namely, by $b_{if}S_{kfi}$, which[1] equals $b_{jf}s_{kf}L_{fi}$.

[1] Incidentally it will be noticed that an expected consequence of this model is that the average level of a given group on any emotion, such as anxiety, will retain the same ratio to the standard deviation, across all situations. This—known as the *first modulation law*—has been tested by DeYoung and found to hold reasonably well (see Cattell, 1972, page 106 and 152).

Now although our discussion has been on *one* trait liability, L_f (or L_x in general) there will, of course, be a whole series of such in the specification equation constituting a vector of modulators:

$$\mathbf{S} = [s_{k1}, s_{k2}, \ldots, s_{kx}, \ldots, s_{kp}] \qquad (3.9)$$

This description of the action of the ambient stimulus could be called either the modulation vector (in a mathematical setting), or, to give it its psychological meaning, the situation vector. For it defines what the ambient situation, k, does to the psychological readiness of the average individual.[1]

The meaning of the situation vector is what the situation typically does to the individual before he acts. Another term for it might be the "emotive vector" because it describes the stimulation of all internal emotions and motives that the situation produces. This is the "atmosphere" that for all of us clings to certain old haunts, or, for the unfortunate neurotic, the sense of stress or dread that hangs around situations he cannot bear or objects for which he has a phobia. It represents our specific emotional involvement in any situation, i.e. what it stimulates us to do.

Incidentally, in the ordinary R-technique equation, the values found by experiment are those for the general population. The instance of the neurotic, just cited, reminds us that we might want sometimes to know the *individual* situation vector values, and these would be found by resorting to P-technique. This would tell what ergic tensions or general emotions are characteristically provoked in a given individual by any situation k. Indeed the key equation in the formulation of the relation of perception to personality lies here, as is brought out more systematically later. The vector of situational modulators, multiplied matrix-wise by the individual's traits (mainly "liabilities," L's) gives in the fullest sense the perceptual meaning of that situation to the individual.

Now learning—in the full sense used in structural learning—means modifying the meaning of the situation to the individual. To a group of freshmen students the university lecture room has one emotional and motivational

---

[1] Parenthetically one may ask whether these values belong to the total, global situation $(h+k)$ or to the ambient situation alone. A theoretical purist may wish to say that a given ambient situation cannot have just the same meaning when coupled with different focal stimuli. The answer is that the definition of the ambient situation often precedes the appearance of the focal stimulus. The ambient situation might be, for example, getting oneself set to take an examination and the focal situation the appearance of a particular item. Indeed to give the ambient situation its full utility we must allow it to include incidents some time before the focal stimulus, such as some frustration that brought the subject into a bad mood.

On the other hand, an argument for the same *focal* stimulus having different meanings with different ambient situations is to be considered. It is at least in the best tradition of gestalt psychology. One replies at present that this is taken care of by allowing the ambient situation to determine the final outcome. The relation of h to k, moreover, is not simply additive $(h+k)$ in *outcome*, but a product of vectors, and therefore interactive. It remains for experiment to decide whether this fully accounts for observations or whether we need further to change b_{hjx} to b_{hjkx}, admitting that k also affects the behavioral index, b.

meaning when they first arrive and a different one after a year. This change is recordable as a change in the situation vector. There is also a change in action partly due to a change in the bearing (**B**) vector as well, but the meaning change is in the situation vector.

Thus we come to the conclusion that personality learning—which is learning in the all-embracing sense of cognitive ability learning, emotional learning, and motivational learning—requires for its adequate description a statement of changes in three vectors, as follows:

(1) *The trait vector* (also represented by **L** for liability vector)

$$\mathbf{T} = [T_{i1}, T_{i2}, \ldots, T_{ip}] \tag{3.10}$$

(The change in abilities, personality traits, sentiments)

(2) *The bearing vector*

$$\mathbf{B} = [b_{j1}, b_{j2}, \ldots, b_{jp}] \tag{3.11}$$

(The change in the bearing of traits upon the action j)

(3) *The situation vector*

$$\mathbf{S} = [s_{k1}, s_{k2}, \ldots, s_{kp}] \tag{3.12}$$

(The change in the emotive meaning of the situation, i.e. in the individual's involvement).

This is called the *tri-vector* formulation, which is an essential principle in structured learning theory. It should be noted that it is still essentially *descriptive* rather than explanatory, for it is mathematically equivalent[1] to a lot of statements about changes in single observed variables—a_{ij}, a_{ix}, etc.—over N people. But already it is on the way, in theoretical terms, from a description to an explanation. At least it introduces the tri-vector model of *structured learning* from which in subsequent analysis we shall proceed to learning laws.

---

[1] The equivalence is $\dfrac{S'S}{N} = R = V_{fp} R_f V'_{fp}$ for the mathematician, where S is the standard score change matrix of N people on n variables, R is the $(n \times n)$ correlation matrix, R_f is correlation between factors, and V_{fp} is the factor matrix from which T's and b's and ultimately s's are derived.

4 The basic theoretical model for modification of ergic tension

The reader in the happy situation of being at home with multivariate analysis may at this point have raised in his mind the alert question: "I know how you score the **T** vector, and obtain the **B** vector from factor analysis, but whence come the **S** vector values we have so freely been invoking?"

In this section, since **S** (modulator) values have to be known *for a given occasion* before their changes with learning can be used, it is proposed to concentrate on this question, and to explore some associated psychological concepts. An obvious and direct way to seek the *S* values is by the methods of classical bivariate experiment, provided we have a good test battery to measure the level of any particular general emotional state or ergic tension. Such batteries are fortunately already in existence. For example, Scheier's objective device *Eight Parallel Form Anxiety Battery* (1965) or Curran's *Eight State Questionnaire* (Curran and Cattell, 1974) (anxiety, depression, regression, exvia, etc.) permit us a wide range of state level measurement.

By such experiment we would simply expose, say, 100 subjects to situations provocative for, say, anxiety, indexing the situations (ambient stimuli) as k_1, k_2, k_3, etc. Then we would measure the mean (and sigma) of the scores in each situation. The "base line" value for such situations is the mean s value for all (S_{km}), to which the value 1.0 is assigned by using it to divide into the individual values of S for occasions k_1, k_2, etc. If we take the actual mean state score, S_{km}, S values for the situations k_1, k_2, etc., are:

$$s_{k_1} = \frac{S_{km_1}}{S_{km}} \frac{\text{(mean of situation 1)}}{\text{(overall mean)}} \text{ and } s_{k_2} = \frac{S_{km_2}}{S_{km}} \qquad (3.13)$$

and assuming the *first modulation law* (constancy of ratio of mean to standard deviation or variance) we can also calculate the variance of the *liability values*, which are actually the state values at the mean position.

Alternatively, the s values can be reached by factor analysis. There is no need to go into this here (see Cattell, in Spielberger, 1972) but we should note that the implication is that the b values as actually calculated in the ordinary way at anything but the "mean provocation" position above are actually not simple b values but products of b's and s's. Thus:

$$b_{jkx} = b_{jx}s_{kx} \qquad (3.14)$$

where b_{jkx} is literally the factor loading obtained in experiment under provocation of situation k, and b_{jx} is the standard behavioral index ("mean" factor loading) expressing how the given state, x, contributes to behavior to each and all of its levels.

Granted that the purely formal and statistical problem is solved, so that the s's for various situations can be experimentally determined, our ultimate objective is still psychological understanding. What psychological understanding do we seek? In the first place we may ask whether both ergs and sentiments modulate their levels with stimulation. It is easy to see, even without specific experiment, that ergic tensions *do* change, since we have all experienced this in everyday life. And from general observation we also have little doubt that L_x (liability) values differ from person to person, since some obviously become excessively anxious over any of several distinct anxiety-provoking situations, while others become readily amorous, and so on.

One may have more doubts about sentiments being modulable, since they are regarded as fixed trait structures, and so we will take this up in a moment as a separate issue. Meanwhile let us ask what we consider the ergic tension level of a person at a given moment is determined by. So far the answer has been simple: the provocation level of an ambient stimulus situation, s_{kx}, and the individual's liability, L_{xi}, to the ergic tension in question. But the rest of psychology suggests that L_x is itself actually many things. In general, the *stimulus term S* and the *liability term L* can lead to a breakdown adopted by Cattell in 1957, and there has since been little need (according to experiment) for modification. Thus:

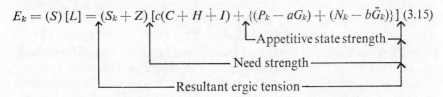

$$E_k = (S)\,[L] = (S_k + Z)\,[c(C + H + I) + \{(P_k - aG_k) + (N_k - b\bar{G}_k)\}]\ (3.15)$$

Appetitive state strength

Need strength

Resultant ergic tension

E_k is the actual ergic tension as measured at the moment k by some battery which will necessarily be through a set of attitudes embedded in the culture, as in table 2.3, page 29. Since we are speaking of any erg there is no need to add the subscript x.

S_k is the strength of stimulation by the provocative ambient situation, as usual. If this falls to zero then, unless the extra term Z is added, all ergic tension would vanish. But there is much evidence that even when stimulation is absent there is some residual ergic tension that persists. For example, in the neurological field Prosser and others (1959) have shown that nerve cells go on firing spontaneously, and in the psychological field Hebb's experiments on sensory deprivation show that gropings toward phantasy satisfactions may reach surprising proportions. Clinically it is recognized that in the absence of sexual stimulation the sex drive may issue in action on entirely non-sexual objects, and so on. The term Z represents the self stimulation which remains in any erg, and would appear in the battery measures, in the complete absence of external stimulation. $(S_k + Z)$ we shall call the stimulation level.

By definition, we shall refer to that which the stimulation level term multiplies as the *need strength*, as shown in the square brackets of equation (3.15). This is the liability or proneness term, L, for traits and states in general, as it needs to be defined specifically in the dynamic field. The internal content of the brackets is split into parenthetic groups partly for psychological meaning and partly because $(C + H + I)$ has to be scaled down by a constant c, for reasons which follow. The first group $(C + H + I)$ represents that part of need strength which is relatively permanent, C means the Constitutional, genetic component, H is the early modification of a drive that has gone on through personal History, and I represents the peculiarities associated with the Investment of the drive in the attitudes by which it is measured.

The meaning and methodology of measurement of C [by twin or MAVA (Multiple Abstract Variance Analysis) methods in behavioral genetics] can be taken as read. The effect of personal history on a drive must lean at present largely on clinical observation and psychoanalytic concepts. It is not concerned with personal history in the familiar sense of learning principles but with certain new principles that may reside in the clinical observation that a drive *as a whole* may not achieve its normal path of maturation but stay arrested at some weaker strength and relatively infantile mode of expression, in matura-tional terms. This theory is very familiar to psychologists with respect to the sex drive, being discussed by psychoanalysis far beyond any precise support by data. Nevertheless, on qualitative observation we shall take it as a reasonable hypothesis for research through equation (3.15) that consequent upon early histories of *frustration*, of *fixation* as demonstrated by imprinting (Harlow and Zimmerman, 1959; Hess, 1964) in animals, and of *hormonal upset*, the strength of a drive as a whole may become different from that genetically given in C. Conceivably all change is "damage" to a genetically given target goal, as is largely the case, incidentally, in regard to intelligence, so that H will normally be negative. The fact that it may cover two or three distinct influences, as suggested in the sentence above, need not prevent us at this stage from considering it as a single "basket" term.

The term I (not to be confused with the Integrated Component referred to earlier) is not so much an insistent concept as a concession to possibilities. If we consider the set of attitudes which define an erg and imagine two people who have equal ergic investment in them, in terms of having learnt them as a path to the ergic goal, but one is aged 30 and the other 60, may there not be a difference? The hypothesis in fact is that a difference of quality through the passage of time—a difference which we shall later discuss as a U and I component difference—exists in the response of the erg to stimuli and to other tests of "strength". In short it is likely to be necessary to add one more term, I, investment quality, to the statement of the strength of the "erg in being" at any time.

Now the *need strength*—the total value in the square brackets before any stimulation is brought to bear—can be conceived as having two parts. They are, as we have just discussed, the trait strength $(C + H + I)$ as it stands at that stage in life, and the appetitive condition at the moment, which is written $(P_k - aG_k) + (N_k - b\bar{G}_k)$. What is the latter? The first term is well known to students of animal motivation. P is a physiological condition such as hunger (low blood sugar) or sexual interest as determined by hormonal conditions (androsterone for example). The subscript k indicates the point it would have reached through the internal, cumulative "charging" processes since the last discharge. For example, k might be, as in much animal experiment, the recorded hours of deprivation since the last meal. G is a statement of the amount of gratification in the same k period. It is negatively associated, since it reduces tension and the constant a is added simply as a scaling factor, depending on the units in which P and G are measured.

To those who consider that all drives are viscerogenic (as in hunger, thirst, sex, maternal behavior) and that nonviscerogenic drives, e.g. curiosity, gregariousness are "secondary derivatives" this (P_k-aG_k) part of the appetition may seem to suffice. But the research on ergs so far presents us with no evidence for considering nonviscerogenic ergs to be "secondary". To all intents they are as innate in origin and early in appearance as, say, the sex drive. We must therefore suppose a *neural need*, N, in the central nervous system, as distinct from the viscera, which requires discharge from time to time, and, as far as we yet know, this should take the same form $(N_k-b\bar{G}_k)$ as the viscerogenic appetitive component (P_k-aG_k). It will be noted that the G is now written differently, namely, $\bar{G}$, because the gratification though conceptually similar, as satisfaction or reward, is measured in different phenomena and score units. $\bar{G}$ is now "amount of consummatory behavior" not "amount of physiological reduction" as in G.

The evidence for tension reduction by consummatory behavior alone is at present scattered and rather thin, which could well be because ideas for measuring it have been crude. Consummatory behavior could be objectively defined as that closest to the ergic goal in the dynamic lattice, and recognizable by having the highest loading (unassociated with loadings on other ergs) for the given erg on any course of action. At qualitative levels many psychologists have, however, offered evidence of this neural, N, component. For example, courtship behavior even without consummation will reduce readiness for further courtship behavior, but this issue will be developed in chapter 5.

The relative roles of the viscerogenic (P_k-aG_k) and nonviscerogenic $(N_k-b\bar{G}_k)$ components in the total appetitive state will vary greatly, as Murray, for example, would argue from a complete determination by the former, in say, hunger, to a complete determination by the latter in a nonviscerogenic drive such as curiosity, fear (escape), or self-assertion. [An additional term could be added to (3.15) to bring this out, but we shall keep the equation simpler by supposing it is taken care of in the scaling.] In either case the vital question which now arises is "Does an increase of external stimulation, S, act equally upon the fixed component in need strength $(C + H + I)$ and the changing appetitive component $(P_k-aG_k) + (N_k-b\bar{G}_k)$?"

For the present, by analogy to the trait-like component, L_x, in the general proposition on modulation, $s_{kx}L_x$, we must assume that the trait part also contributes to the rise of the ergic tension state. If a man is, for example, constitutionally of a strongly assertive disposition, then we must suppose that a provocative situation will raise his ergic tension more than in a man of lesser assertiveness. The modification by gratification, in the appetitive component, must, in short, not be confused with a modification by stimulation, which can affect both. At any rate, the model must make this investigatable, and accordingly a term c is introduced in equation (3.15) which admits that provocation may act differently on the appetitive and nonappetitive need strength components, and will, if the evidence requires, permit c to fall to zero. In any case, the actually measured ergic tension is considered a product of the inherent need strength in the individual and the strength of the external stimulus.

5   Experiments checking and extending the model for ergic tension modification

The formulation in the last section is at once a model for designing experiments, checking the theoretical analysis and hopefully for bringing out facts that will introduce useful extensions of the model. A start has been made in the form of manipulating the stimulation level—the first term in the ergic tension equation $(S_k + Z)$—and holding the need strength constant. Whilst these are early days yet in researches of this kind, some of the findings have lent support to the $E \propto S_k$ relationship and have yielded important pointers to improving experimental design. The earliest attempt was carried out by Adelson (1952) who measured the effects of water deprivation on the ergic tension level using eight subjects in a repeated measures design. Subjects were deprived of water for 24 hours before being tested, and remained in the controlled environment for a further 12 hours. About a third of the measures (chiefly the physiological ones) showed significant changes.

The basic design since this first research has been to measure the change in the dependent ergic tension variable E, using the motivational components U and I, which accompanies a manipulation of S_k. Attitudes associated with the ergs of fear, sex, and mating have been tried using an appropriately modified combination of devices from the MAT battery. By using pre- and post-test occasions for experimental and control groups, two levels of stimulation were created.

Dielman, Cattell, and Kawash (1971; see also Kawash, Dielman, and Cattell, 1972) designed three experiments relating to the fear and mating ergs. In the first, the members of the experimental group were told they would be required to deliver a short spontaneous lecture to the rest of the group. This condition was thought to be sufficiently fearful for freshmen and constitute a source of increased ergic tension. A second experiment relied on the fear of an impending electric shock from a formidable looking "electric chair" said to be part of a physiological research. In the third design the experimental group was shown publications about the increase of venereal disease in the United States, its symptoms and effects using a selection of slides and tapes. The two ergs of fear and mating were included on the assumption that the thought of contracting the disease might raise the fear ergic tension and at the same time reduce the mating erg.

The outcome of these experiments gave pointers to further research. In the first two, it was concluded that the methods needed some modification for testing the hypotheses. It is important to discuss these for the benefit of readers who may wish to engage in manipulation research in motivation. At least two problems are evident. First, one must ask if there is in fact an attitude measure within the devices of the fear erg from the MAT which is relevant to the fear of electric shock for if so the effect could be merely specific. In both the first two experiments, there was great dependence on raising the level of ergic tension by exposing subjects to specific fearful situations. Secondly, we are dealing here with highly sophisticated subjects (psychology undergraduates and graduates) who may sense what is going on. In this event, their fear will be less consistent. There may even be a reduction from the first to the second occasion because on first entering the test situation there may be apprehension which could be dispelled by the time of the second occasion. Curiously, both the control and experimental scores did, on some occasions, show a significant decline from occasions one to two. Could it be that the reduction in the fear, which might be derived from the uncertainty of the initial experimental occasion as compared with the second occasion, more than offsets the fear generated in the experiment itself? Perhaps we have underrated the impact of the first anticipated test situation as a promoter of fear in subjects.

Inspection of table 3.2 shows a compelling trend in the reduction of the fear erg from occasion one to two. If anything, the reduction in erg scores between occasions is less for the control than the experimental, but these changes are not statistically significant. One could even argue a case that the control group, whilst experiencing some reduction in fear created by the test situation itself, would be relatively *more* fearful than the experimental group in that the latter knows the worst that could happen (without accepting for one moment that it would), whereas the former having been told some tame reason for being involved in the research may have wondered whether anything more dreadful was in store for them!

Clearly, fear is not an easy erg to manipulate. All kinds of situational intrusions are possible and liable to affect the experimentally induced fear. Where a more potent fear was introduced the results have been a little more promising. In the third research of Dielman *et al.*, presentation of information about VD was sufficiently effective to produce a significant change in the fear erg as measured using the unintegrated MAT fear score. This is illustrated in figure 3.4.

Two further recent studies by Cattell, Kawash, and DeYoung (1972) have lent support to the hypotheses of the ergic tension equation. In the first, the sex erg was used as the independent variable. An experimental group of married men was exposed to erotic slides and given a specially designed MAT. Self-reports of arousal and sexual relations after the experiment were also obtained. In the second research, the hunger drive was evoked by causing an experimental group to abstain from eating from lunchtime one day until just prior to dinner the succeeding day (approximately 29 hours). The group was permitted to drink only water or unsugared tea, but other activities were carried out as usual. Results for both experiments were in the predicted direction in support of $E \propto S_k$. In the first experiment the unintegrated component once again came through as the most significant. In the second case, both the unintegrated

Table 3.2   Mean MAT Fr scores by occasion and treatment group in a manipulation experiment

Experiment 1

MAT Fr	Fear		No fear	
	O_1	O_2	O_1	O_2
Uses	2.667	2.500	2.333	2.000
Estimates	5.333	4.667	4.000	4.750
Information	1.833	1.667	1.667	1.250
Paired words	2.167	2.167	2.583	2.333
Unintegrated	8.000	7.167	6.333	6.750
Integrated	4.000	3.833	4.250	3.583
Total	12.000	11.000	10.583	10.333

Experiment 2   Means by occasion and treatment group in the four-way repeated measures analysis of variance

MAT Fr	MAT Fr scores			
	Experimental group $N = 34$		Control group $N = 19$	
	O_1	O_2	O_1	O_2
Uses	3.028	2.875	3.054	2.939
Estimates	6.476	5.986	6.039	6.072
Information	1.643	1.729	1.767	1.734
Paired words	2.775	2.528	2.834	2.306
Unintegrated	9.504	8.771	9.078	9.011
Integrated	4.417	4.257	4.600	4.039
Total	13.820	13.028	13.678	13.050

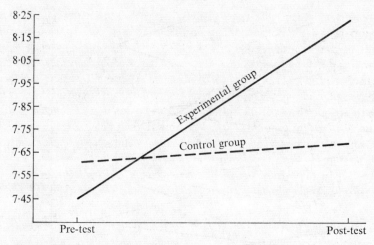

Figure 3.4   Experimental and control pre- and post-test means for MAT fear erg using unintegrated scores

and integrated components of hunger motivation increased significantly more in the experimental than in the control group.

A new, further step was taken in this research to verify the product model of $E =$ stimulation level $\times$ appetitive strength [the $(S_k + z) \times \{(P_k - aG_k) + (N_k - bG_k)\}$ of the ergic tension equation]. By forming two groups from the experimental group according to their ratings of the erotic slides—high arousal (HA) and low arousal (LA)—a measure of need strength was also secured. Means on the sex MAT battery were then found for these groups and showed that greater self-reported arousal corresponded to higher scores on the MAT. By inference, the subjects most influenced by the erotic slides were those with high sex erg level—and practical evidence of this continuing high sex erg became apparent in the analysis of behavioral data on sexual desire and relations after the testing. Thus the HA group showed significantly higher desire and relations than the LA. A result of this kind gives validity to the sex erg in showing a correlation with criterion behavior.

The relative responses scored using the U and I component scores cast some light on a basic difference between the components. It will be recalled that the integrated component relates to conscious reality whilst the un-integrated has been associated with the unconscious, unorganized aspect of motivation. Results from the above research point to a consistent, close relationship between the ratings of the slides and the U rather than the I component. We may therefore ask if the U component is a more responsive *state* measure than I. Moreover, this finding points to major research hypotheses regarding the relationship betwixt the U component and the "state-like" aspects of the ergic tension equation (stimulation and possibly gratification) on the one

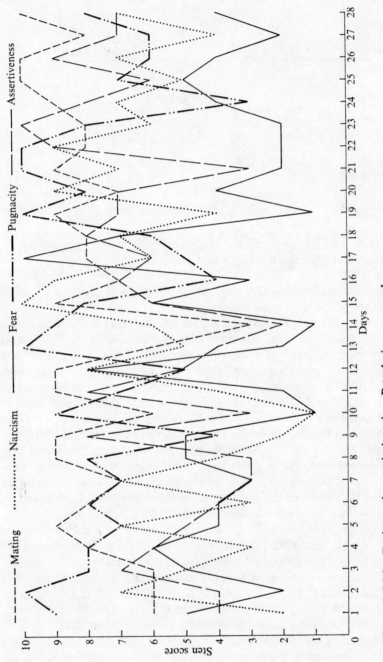

Figure 3.5 (a)   Ergic tension variations in a P-technique research
Source: Kline and Grindley (1974).

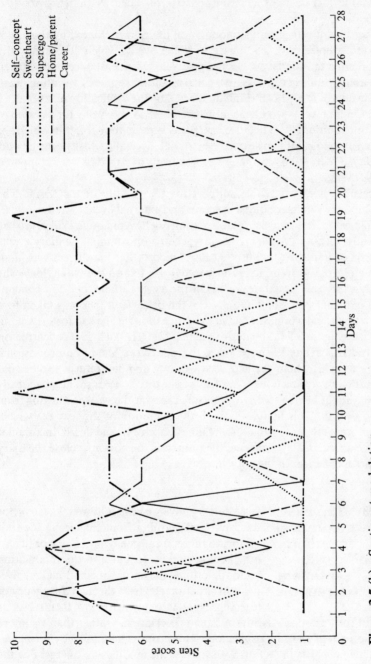

Figure 3.5 (b) Sentiment modulation
Source: Kline and Grindley (1974).

hand and the less changeable "trait-like" terms such as the $(C + H + I)$ expression on the other.

Another line of attack on the modulation of ergs is achieved by the use of P-technique coupled with a knowledge of the events which accompany the changes in ergic tension levels. Such a research has recently been undertaken by Kline and Grindley (1974). Here we had a built-in source of variation taken from the events of everyday life and unaffected by the artificiality of laboratory research. One subject, a woman, completed the MAT every day for a period of one month. Additionally, a detailed diary was kept by the subject in which she was encouraged to record any event, even trivial thoughts, which occurred during the day. Fluctuations in the erg scores from day to day were compared with these events.

The results gave remarkable support for the validity of the MAT. The relationship between fluctuations in scores and external events was very close. As an illustration, in figure 3.5 (a) the mating erg lowered quite extensively on day 14 whilst on days 25, 26, and 28 it reached a maximum. The diary events for these days, in contrast with other days, record that the subject was lassitudinous and tired—low ergic tension on day 14, but on the "high" days she repeatedly expressed sexual desire—"Oh for a wild affair" or "I'm contemplating a planned seduction". On day 25, the peak value, she was taken to a party by a boyfriend whom she had at one stage thought she had lost. A second example from figure 3.5 (a) relates to the fear erg. The high spots occurred on days 12 and 18. On day 12 she reported that she felt rejected by a professional theater group with whom she had been working and had returned to her flat crying. But more conspicuous is her fear of car travel, because she was "really distressed" about having to drive an unsafe car over the weekend lasting from day 16 to day 19. This fits ideally with the definition of the fear erg which, as we have seen, relates to avoidance of illness, accident, and death. In a similar way, Kline and Grindley elaborate their analysis to show how close the diary report mirrors changes in the ergic levels.

6   The basic theoretical model for modification of sentiment strengths

In section 3 above we have followed the tri-vector description of learning from changes in the trait vector, to those in the behavioral index or "bearing" vector, and so to those in the modulation vector describing the nature of emotional involvement in situation changes, through the agency of learning experiences, which show themselves as changes in the vector of s's. Still pursuing description—rather than the more difficult domain of learning *explanation*—we propose here to study the *modulation of sentiments* as in section 5 we studied the modulation of ergs. For the fact to be explained later by learning theory is the change in a modulation phenomenon—a phenomenon not yet in itself brought to formulation in a model.

Although the modulation of an ergic tension is readily accepted, because of our common experience of how a particular situation comes to stir up a particular tension, e.g. of apprehension in the case of a phobia, affection in the case of meeting a loved person or place, it would be easy to doubt that sentiments as such are modulated at all. However, such P-technique experiments as those of Cross (1951), Shotwell, Hurley, and Cattell (1961), or Kline and Grindley (1974) leave no doubt—as figures 3.5 and 3.6 show—that sentiments change in strength from occasion to occasion virtually as much as ergs.

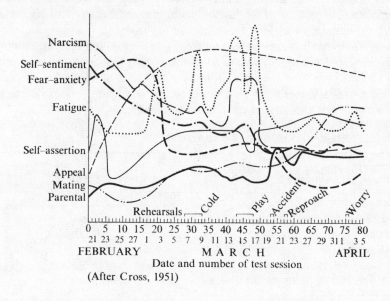

(After Cross, 1951)

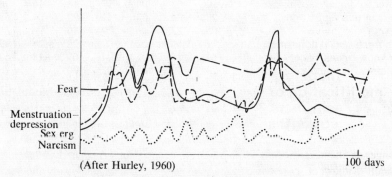

(After Hurley, 1960)

Figure 3.6 Ergic tension (and sentiment) response to stimulus (*S*), internal state (*P*), and goal satisfaction (*G*)

It is still open to discussion that the quality of modulability in ergs is what makes this sentiment fluctuation possible, rather than a quality of modifiability in some yet undiscussed component of a sentiment. But if so we should still have to account for the mixed bag of several ergs somehow managing to fluctuate together. For the capacity of a single erg characteristically to change all its manifestations at once would not suffice to explain the unitariness we now see in a mixed set.

This set can be designated easily enough, as what we have called the "ergic investment in a given sentiment". This is unitary only as a piece of accountancy, as might be, for example, "expenditures on house repair" which though a unitary item in an accountant's list, consists of diverse things done at different times. Thus if we pick out of the "factor loading matrix" in table 2.10 of chapter 2 the two attitudes which load the sentiment to career most strongly and then ask what their loadings are on the recorded ergs we would (on squaring, adding by column, and taking the square root) finish with the summed investment shown at the bottom of the ergic columns in table 3.3. Similarly for a second sentiment—the self-sentiment—we would obtain the vector of ergic investment shown in the first sum row at the bottom of table 3.3.

Table 3.3 Ergic investment in two sentiments

Attitudes loading career and self-sentiment	Factors (pattern)						
I want:	Fear	Mating	Assertiveness	Narcism	Pugnacity	Career	Self-sentiment
To control impulses	32	−07	−05	−12	14	−29	42
Never to damage self-respect	−10	−11	−08	17	−13	16	90
To maintain reputation	−22	−34	03	42	−29	−04	58
Never to be insane	05	23	06	09	14	06	84
A normal sexual adjustment	17	55	02	−07	22	28	47
To know myself better	44	13	01	−04	−09	−18	43
To look after family	23	−19	−08	−02	−00	−08	16
To be proficient in career	37	10	69	11	22	19	45
To learn my job well	04	02	25	17	00	79	08
To stick to my job	13	05	−15	−61	−11	58	−11
Ergic investment in self-sentiment	75	74	70	49	49		
Ergic investment in career sentiment	13	04	29	63	11		

Decimal place omitted.

These vector values say something about each sentiment—the amount and nature of ergic investment in it—which is important in several contexts, as discussed on page 86 below. When we add up a suitable bunch of attitude scores to give a total score estimating, say, a person's self-sentiment score on a given day, these ergic investments are necessarily included. Since this is what was done in figure 3.6 the course of the self-sentiment would necessarily vary with the sum of these ergic tensions, as a "spurious" addition. But there are technical reasons—including the fact that the ergs show different temporal courses from the sentiment—which make this explanation unlikely. There must be something in a sentiment—probably the M term itself—which fluctuates from one situation to another.

At this point we enter regions where research has not yet penetrated. The actual scores which have behaved in the ways indicated in figure 3.6 and elsewhere have actually been sums of U and I components (page 15). One seriously considered theoretical possibility is that the U component in the total for a_j in equation (3.15) represents ergic tension terms only, i.e. the E_k in (3.15) is therefore a purely U component, while the I (integrated) term represents sentiment strength expressed by M terms. Even if matters do not turn out as simple as this, we are bound to recognize that since a sentiment is learnt, by repeated rewarded responses, it should introduce elements in the motivational components by which it is measured that are more strongly represented than in ergs. Further, a sentiment should represent terms in, say, a Hullian model, that stand for frequencies of past reinforcement rather than immediate ergic tension. In our more empirical approach to motivational components there are certainly a lot of cognitive reactivities, such as word association, information, etc., in the I component, which are the kind of thing that holds a sentiment together but seem superfluous in holding an innate erg together.

Contingent on research now proceeding, therefore, we shall hypothesize that the rise of a sentiment score in response to a situational stimulus is essentially a rise in cognitive excitement in the network of ideas which constitute the cognitive part of the sentiment. The supposition is that if we have a sentiment toward, say, ski-ing, then talk about ski slopes brings to mind all kinds of associated thoughts of activities to a higher level of response potential—e.g. ideas about ski-resorts, slaloms, ski-waxes, and so on. This excitation, with its increased speed of word association and accessibility of information, spreads only as far, however, as the boundaries of the sentiment as demonstrated factorially.

The excitation does, however, include more than cognitive manifestations, for according to our model of a sentiment, a sentiment is a higher order factor containing many lower order factors ultimately going down to relatively brief mental sets, appropriate only to quite specific situations. When the concept "ski-ing" is excited, presumably it brings to a higher readiness of response even the sets associated with a swing of the hips as a "christie" is done to pass around a tree "stimulus" encountered en route. Presumably for the total excitation level of a sentiment a model can be formulated equivalent to that in equation (3.15) for the excitation of an erg, and for this the following would be consistent (k again being a specific situation-occasion).

$$M_k = (S_k + Z) [RT + E] \qquad (3.16)$$

where R is the amount of reward given with each previous exercise of the courses of action associated with the sentiment, T is the number of times the courses of action have been learnt, and E is the ergic investment (as defined in connection with table 3.3) asociated with that sentiment.

It will be understood that at present this is a theoretical model lacking the degree of experimental support available for the corresponding ergic model. But there seems little doubt that the excitation level of any sentiment alters as a whole and undergoes this modulation in relation to an external stimulus situation (an "ambient stimulus"). It is the acquiring of this power of modulation by a particular situation that has to be accounted for when structured learning theory seeks to explain the tri-vector description of learning.

7 Summary

1. Having demonstrated the existence of dynamic structures—ergs and sentiments—and our capacity to measure them, psychology has to account for their appearance through development.

2. Structured learning theory has a totally different emphasis from reflexological learning theory, and sets itself to explain structure, over and above the improvement of a single act. It is able to do so by (a) a vector of change of *trait scores*, (b) a vector of change of *behavioral indices*, (c) a vector of change of *modulators*. These together constitute the *tri-vector description of learning change*.

3. This chapter has to be primarily concerned with the first step, which is that of analytical *description* of the learning changes, leaving their explanation for later developments. Consequently it illustrates the learning process as such only in simplified form, and only on the *trait* vector—the bearing vector and the modulator vector are left to later analysis. But this suffices to show that structured learning theory deals with a "multidimensional change (in each of the three vectors) in response to experience of a multidimensional situation".

4. The multidimensional situation, for most personality learning, is implicit in a vector describing the learning change produced, e.g. in the trait vector per experience of any given experimental path in life. To connect this effectively in a learning model it is necessary to have (a) a taxonomic and coding system for describing all the possible emotional learning experiences in human everyday life behavior, this we find in the APA (Adjustment Process Analysis Chart), and (b) a learning model for bringing the characteristics of the path and the

frequency of experiencing it in relation to the trait (or *b* or *s*) gains. This we find in the Learning Summary Matrix Model. The former consists of a series of six dynamic crossroads or chiasms, at each of which several outcomes are recordable. The latter multiplies a path experience matrix by a path potency matrix to produce a learning change matrix. From this a calculation is possible of a vector (in the path potency matrix) revealing the characteristic effect of a given life experience path on the individual's vector of trait scores.

5. The second vector in the tri-vector description is a vector of change in what is best called the *bearing vector*. This consists of the *b*'s (behavioral indices) which record and express the *bearing of each trait upon performance* in the particular response being learnt.

6. The third vector in the tri-vector description is the *modulation* change vector. This sets out (using *s*'s) the changes in the emotional and motivational involvement of people in the ambient situation within which the response to the focal stimulus occurs.

7. Instances of change through learning as it appears in the trait vector and bearing vector are given, though fuller exemplification is postponed until the applied psychology results are studied.

8. The trait and behavioral index changes being well understood in principle some concentrated discussion is given to the nature of modulation itself, as a preliminary to making modulation change in learning clear. Beginning with ergic modulation, a model is presented for ergic tension in any given situation, which describes it as a product of present stimulus strength and need strength. Need strength is broken down into a trait part and an appetitive part and precise hypotheses for testing are presented by a formula. Experiments showing that at least some of these terms are calculable are described, in relation to the ergs of sex and hunger.

9. There seems little doubt from experiment that sentiments also modulate their strength in relation to situational stimulation. This cannot easily be accounted for by change only in what is defined as the *ergic investment* in a sentiment, and is presumably due to excitation in the cognitive, learnt strength of the sentiment. This excitation is hypothesized to run over the whole sentiment when any part is stimulated and to result in a heightened reactive potential in all the sets (stimulus response elements) in the sentiment. Due to research in this area being only at a pioneer stage the theoretical formula for sentiment modulation is given only very tentatively.

4 Integrative behavior and the dynamic calculus

1 Action conflict and confluence conflict Having set out the dynamic structures and discussed their origin and their variations with situational and other influences, we are well prepared to enter on a study of their manner of mutual interaction. For it is logically evident that these unitary powers can collide and conflict as well as ally themselves in joint action.

Indeed, the story of human emotional life, and the interstages in the development of dynamic structure are concerned with these conflicts of existing structures. The same is true of animal experiment on motivation which has concerned itself since the time of Warden in the 1920s with such phenomena as the conflict of two ergs. Experimentally this is generated, for example, when a rat has to cross a fear-evoking shock barrier to satisfy hunger, thirst, or sex needs. But equally definite and numerous experiments have been carried out on human conflict. Internal conflict and decision in the dynamic field constitute so substantial a fraction of our daily experiences that it is not surprising that the theme is central in psychology.

Let us first consider the very fundamental equation in factor analysis referred to as a specification equation. An equation such as (3.1) in chapter 3 or that illustrated in (4.1) below consists of two major elements in each added term. In motivation theory, the capital letters represent ergs and sentiments (E and M), whilst in personality they can be used to represent source traits. The lower case letter (b in the equations shown) signifies the factor loading which shows us the degree of involvement of each erg, sentiment, or source trait in a given performance.

In setting out a specification equation which describes how different traits add their forces to determine the amount of a particular response, it will be apparent that the weights of some could be negative, which would imply some kind of conflict. For example, if a young man takes out a girl who is not socially congenial, but who is sexually very attractive, and of whom his parents disapprove, the specification might be:

$$a_{ji} = b_{js}E_{si} - b_{jg}E_{gi} - b_{jp}M_{pi} \qquad (4.1)$$

where a is the action, E_s the sex erg, E_g the gregarious erg, and M_p the parental sentiment. If the behavior index, b_{js}, is large, or if the sex erg tension of the individual is high, the behavior a_{ji} will be positive despite b_{jg} and b_{jp} being negative. Completely to describe this conflict we should, incidentally, consider also the s's—the modulators from the ambient situation—as will be done soon.

The term conflict is, appropriately, currently applied to two quite distinct phenomena, and qualifying expressions must therefore be added. Perhaps it is hardly necessary to state that in both we are referring to *inner psychological conflict* and not, of course, to external conflict with the environment and other people, though as figure 3.1 reminds us, external conflict is very frequently the prelude to internal conflict. The first form of internal conflict is *action conflict*, leading to a *decision* (not necessarily as a conscious act of will) between two (or more) courses of action. The second has been called *confluence, stabilized indurated conflict* because when a course of action is chosen and settled down to, it is usually a compromise in which various demands have flowed together (confluence) in a course aiming to satisfy them all as much as possible. In fact, however, it commonly increases the satisfaction of some at the cost of reducing the satisfaction of others. The conflict between various ergs thus becomes accepted as a relatively permanent state of affairs—hence "indurated", though not necessarily buried.

To consider first in more detail the nature of *action or decision conflict*, let us note that it becomes possible where two or more distinct courses of action are provoked in almost equal degree in a given ambient situation, either when (a) a focal stimulus permits two or more responses or (b) when two or more focal stimuli each with its habitual response, are competing. An example of the first would be when at the sight of my friend I decide to present him with the dilemma that either we go for a swim or play tennis. This, in turn, provides my friend with an example of the second: shall he respond to the focal stimulus "swim" or the focal stimulus "tennis"? Another familiar instance of the second is when the stimuli "roast beef" and "pork chops" appear on the menu calling for competing and exclusive behaviors.

In either pattern of choice presentation involving action conflict, a specification equation can be written for each course of action, and in the basic general case when two focal stimuli and two courses of action appear in the same ambient situation, k, the choice is between:

$$a_{h_1ij_1k} = b_{h_1j_{11}}s_{k_1}T_{1i} + \ldots + b_{h_1j_1p}s_{kp}T_{pi} \qquad (4.2a)$$
$$a_{h_2ij_2k} = b_{h_2j_{21}}s_{k_1}T_{1i} + \ldots + b_{h_2j_2p}s_{kp}T_{pi} \qquad (4.2b)$$

The decision as to which action will take place will depend on whether

$a_{h_1 i j_1 k}$ or $a_{h_2 i j_2 k}$ is bigger, which in turn will depend on the b and s values and the individual's endowments in the traits. The reader may protest that a decision is not as automatic a weighing of impulsions or temptations as this. Even if we assume the reader has resolved the philosophical issue of free will–vs.–determinism in favor of scientific laws always operating, he may still want to bring more psychological forces into the arena. For instance, he may want to bring the action of the self-sentiment factor as "will", into the decision. This is sound enough, for in anything but the most automatic, unconscious or trivial[1] decisions there is referral to "Is this a proper course of action for a person like myself to take" which means that some significant b term brings the self-sentiment or superego trait to bear.

The specific importance of the self-sentiment and the superego in conflicts is a matter to be discussed later, but at this point we want to make clear only the general proposition that the outcome of a conflict, whether it reaches the level of an acutely conscious decision or is more or less automatic and sub-conscious is made simply by the relative magnitudes of the two a_{hijk}'s (with self-sentiment, etc., on the right of the equation). And theoretically (though very little experiment has been done on it) we should be able to predict what a person's decision will therefore be in any given situation, if we know (a) the behavioral indices and modulators for people in general, and (b) the strengths of the person's dynamic traits. In saying this let us note, incidentally, that "trait strengths" includes the degree of deprivation $[(P - aG) + (N - b\bar{G})$ in equation (3.15), page 73] and that the modulator indluces the strength of the stimulus [the$(S + Z)$ also in equation (3.15)].

In passing we may note that this formula for a course of action probably applies in essentially the same form for competition in recall, i.e. for what will be remembered when competing stimuli are presented. Now, as will be discussed more fully in the next section, there are two possible outcomes to what we have called a conflict: (1) one of the two habitual (or, sometimes, the innately prescribed) courses of action will eventuate and the other will be

---

[1] If space permitted a study of the taxonomy of attitudes in more detail, we should have to distinguish between major vs. trivial attitudes, also between (1) common and unique (R- and dR-analysis), (2) Active, exercised–vs–latent, and (3) Conscious and unconscious. The last is treated in chapter 8 on clinical psychology, the first has the standard trait meaning just indicated. The difference between an exercised attitude and a latent one may be illustrated by two attitudes and a fact in a syllogism, (a) I want this war to be won, (b) winning will require every man to volunteer his services, (c) therefore I wish to volunteer my services. Conceivably (a) has been an attitude repeatedly stated. Fact (b) has been known. But attitude (c) has never reached conscious realization. Since (c) is determined by other attitudes than (a) it would not follow that its appropriate strength could be fixed from (a). But taking other attitudes into consideration we can say what a person's latent attitude is likely to be on a subject he has previously not thought about. Quite conceivably the motivation components in a much exercised attitude are different from those when a person is presented with stimuli for, and measured upon, a latent attitude. For example, the exercised will probably contain more I and less U.

dropped, or (2) a third course of action is started which attempts a satisfaction of the motives involved in both, which *in toto* is greater than for either one. This latter is called a *confluent* adjustment, or confluence learning, because in one and the same course of action it tries to get to flow together the interests formerly in two courses of action.

Regardless of whether an action conflict is resolved by the first or the second outcome, it is extremely unlikely that the course of action resulting will succeed in satisfying all the drives (dynamic traits: ergs and sentiments) that are in a state of stimulation. In all but ideal, imaginary circumstances the nature of the physical and social world is such that a *conflict of integration or confluence* remains; that is to say, the chosen course of action, though the best of many that have been tried, still contains losses on some drives as a condition of gains on others. The situation remains as in the frequently empirically presented equation (4.1) above, in which there is a gain in the erg E_s but at the expense of a loss in the erg E_g and the sentiment M_p—if we take positive and negative loadings to have this meaning (see below).

This second confluent, stabilized type of conflict might also be called buried or indurated conflict because the individual accepts the course of action as the best compromise and perhaps forgets the original conflicts through which it was reached. Nevertheless, we should expect some consequences to follow from the degree of cancellation of positive by negative quantities, perhaps in the form of loss of energy.

The very existence of such empirical specification equations, however, also indicates some capacity to integrate (including what psychoanalysis calls suppression and repression). For unless the organism were able to control the expression of the negatively loaded drives they would break out and upset this compromise course of action. The integration may nevertheless not be the best that *could* be achieved and we must distinguish the *capacity to integrate*, defined as the ability to tolerate and proceed with such compromises, from the *degree of integration*, defined as the efficiency of the compromise in terms of percentage satisfaction achieved.

2 Calculation of the magnitude of confluent, indurated conflict

Closer scrutiny must be given without delay to the conception utilized in the above definitions of conflict that the *behavioral indices indicate degrees of satisfaction* and that negative values actually imply a reduction of satisfaction. Possible change in the meaning of such loadings on sentiments, as contrasted with ergs, must also be examined.

The s index (see chapter 3)—the modulation or ambient stimulation index —is a statement of how much the given situation has come to be an augmentor of ergic tension level. Its value may derive partly from innate mechanisms—

as in some sexual and fear-evoking objects—and certainly from previous learning experience as when a burnt child becomes fearful in the presence of a fire. The intensity with which a particular course of action is pursued, toward reduction of an ergic tension, will be shown by the *b* values. Granted that it is not a new but a well-learnt action, the *b* values must have reached their stable levels as functions of the amount of satisfaction (tension reduction) found from pursuing that course of action before. We are thus concluding that both the arousal in a situation (the *s*'s) and the favoring of a given course of action (the *b*'s) attain the values they have as a result of the experiences of finding rewards along the particular paths involved. Another way of stating this is to say that the strength of drive on a course of action is proportional to the satisfaction habitually obtained from it.

Now in describing the paths in the dynamic lattice as avenues to various satisfactions no mention was made at the time of the empirical fact that some loadings are negative, nor had we then encountered the arguments from conflict that such negative loadings would be expected. Further, there is no such thing as an *absolute* negative amount of satisfaction in an erg, e.g. negative loadings can only mean the reduction of a positive satisfaction. To take our instance above of a young man taking out a sexually attractive but otherwise questionable young woman, we are saying that if he does so, and in proportion to the amount that he does so, he will lose the satisfaction of his parents' approval. Is this course of action to be drawn in the lattice with some sort of *negative subsidiation* to whatever ergs (e.g. security, self-assertion) are involved in enjoying parental approval? It would seem that for mathematical consistency we must add to the lattice the concept of negative subsidiation, and draw the networks in terms of bundles of black and white threads. This does not mean that there exists "negative satisfaction", but that increasing pursuit of a course of action results (through the structure of the physico-social world) in reduction of a pre-existing positive level of satisfaction.

Granted this position, it becomes possible to write an expression for the amount of confluent (indurated) conflict in a given course of action, such as the following:

$$a_{ij} = b_{j1}E_1 + b_{j2}E_2 - b_{j3}E_3 - b_{j4}E_4 + b_{j5}E_5$$

as:

$$\text{Conflict} = b_{j3} + b_{j4} = \Sigma\bar{b} \tag{4.3}$$

where $\bar{b}$ is the sum of the negative *b*'s. In short, it is the size of the "minority" that determines the magnitude of conflict when the will of the majority prevails.

If the action a_{ij} emerges as a positive quantity then, for *people in general*, i.e. with *E*'s at their mean values, the effective intensity of the action which actually prevails is:

$$a_j = (b_{j1} + b_{j2} + b_{j5}) - (b_{j3} + b_{j4}) \tag{4.4}$$

That is to say, the negative value $(b_{j3} + b_{j4})$ has first to be "cancelled" by absorbing the equivalent amount of strength from $(b_{j1} + b_{j2} + b_{j5})$ if any positive action is to result. What is left over is effective drive, and effective satisfaction is this difference score. For some purposes it might be desirable to state the "loss in friction from the opposition" $\Sigma\bar{b}$, as a *fraction* of the *total* ergic tension involved, or the *total positive* sum of ergic tension, or the *effectively emerging* ergic tension. Indeed, there are four possible choices of indices of conflict in any given attitude, as follows:

Conflict indices:

$$(1)\ \Sigma\bar{b};\ (2)\ \frac{\Sigma\bar{b}}{(\overset{+}{\Sigma b} + \overset{-}{\Sigma b})};\ (3)\ \frac{\Sigma\bar{b}}{\overset{+}{\Sigma b}};\ (4)\ \frac{\Sigma\bar{b}}{(\overset{+}{\Sigma b} - \overset{-}{\Sigma b})} \tag{4.5}$$

These state the conflict value in principle, but in actual calculation there are unavoidable statistical technicalities. In the first place, since contribution to variance is the real criterion, we must replace all Σb terms above by $\sqrt{\Sigma b^2}$, e.g. the first and second conflict terms become:

$$\sqrt{\overline{\Sigma b}^2}\quad \text{and}\quad \frac{\sqrt{\overline{\Sigma b}^{-2}}}{\sqrt{\overset{+2}{\Sigma b} + \overset{-2}{\Sigma b}}} \tag{4.6}$$

Secondly, the above simplified presentation assumes that all ergs are equally strong. But is curiosity as strong a drive as hunger? This plunges us into two difficulties—the psychological one of operationalizing what we mean by the strength of a drive and the factor analytic one of allowing factors to take different "sizes" instead of all being artificially brought to "unit length" as in standard factor analysis. The latter has been solved by the concept of *Real Base Factor Analysis* (Cattell, 1972a) which can be set aside for reading by those going on to research. Suffice it that if we have a basis for giving different strengths to drives, the b's can be adjusted to recognize this. The different strengths question is taken up in its *psychological* meaning on page 94 below.

Thirdly, we have to recognize that the above is a statement of conflict for the average member of the population. For any individual the conflict will be greater if he happens to have a stronger endowment in the negatively loaded ergs. Thus, for the individual the simple expression $(b_{j3} + b_{j4})$ representing the tension cancelled in conflict, i.e., the amount of indurated conflict, should be replaced by:

$$\sqrt{(b_{j3}E_3)^2 + (b_{j4}E_4)^2} \tag{4.7}$$

One may also add at this juncture that the ultimate exact value for the individual is only to be obtained by P-technique, not R-technique, since the b values in the latter are "averages" for the population.

Now the above statement of amount of conflict in a single attitude course of action can be extended to apply to any larger dynamic structure. By adding the values for the weighted total of attitudes by which we estimate a particular erg or a particular sentiment, an estimate can be obtained for the amount of conflict therein. Thus such questions as "Is there typically more conflict in the sex erg, as a dynamic system, than in the parental erg?" or "Has the amount of conflict in Jim James' sentiment to his home increased or decreased in the last year?" are potentially capable of receiving a quantitative answer.

As the aggregate of attitudes increases with larger dynamic structures there obviously comes a limit in the *totality of the individual's dynamic structures.* If we agree on a list of attitudes designated representatively to sample the total dynamic structure of the typical individual in our culture, then it is possible to compare people as to the *total amount of indurated conflict* in their lives. Such an index for comparing individuals on their total adjustment is set out in (4.8b) below and followed up in the next section.

Meanwhile we must recognize two, as yet, insufficiently explored concepts in the field of conflict. First, what of the vector of modulators (s's)? These do not go negative, but only vary above or below unity. It is relatively easy to see that these should enter only as augmentors of the b values. If we return to the young man's conflict above and suppose that he is moved into an ambient situation where his attachment to his parents is modulated to greater strength, then, since it is a minority opposition force to be overcome, the task of overcoming it will be greater and the conflict more intense. Thus the more developed expression for conflict, superseding that above is:

$$C_{jk} = \sqrt{\overline{\Sigma(b_j s_k)^2}} \qquad (4.8a)$$

or
$$\text{Integration} = I = (1 - C_t) = \left(1 - \Sigma^t \sqrt{\overline{\Sigma(b_j s_k)^2}}\right) \qquad (4.8b)$$

where t attitudes are taken as the sample. And if we finally proceed to the *individual* estimate and recognize also different "sizes" (potencies) of ergic strengths, by z's, then:

$$C_{jki} = \sqrt{\overline{\Sigma^x (b_{jx} s_{kx} z_x E_{xi})^2}} \qquad (4.9)$$

The second insufficiently explored concept—the role of the negative behavioral indices on sentiments—cannot be clarified as above by logical treatment of existing experimental concepts but requires new experiment. Tentatively we are supposing that an M term represents the cognitively associated part of habit strength. It is the readiness of the system of learnt signals to invoke ergic forces in action along certain paths. Some people will be well endowed with such a system from past reward schedules, others will not. We suspect, though we have no experimental proof as yet, that the contribution of a sentiment to an attitude strength will show up more strongly in the β and γ motivation component measures (the second-order I component) and that of an erg by the U component. Nevertheless, this remains speculative, and it is still possible that what we measure as a sentiment is not just the strength (readiness) of the cognitive signal system but also all the associated ergic investment (page 84 above). In the latter case it would have to be recognized that the E's might represent original E's now depleted by the M investments, and that factoring the M's would give E's again at the higher order.

Perhaps in either case we are justified in regarding a negative loading on a sentiment as indicating that it tends to inhibit the course of action concerned. But in the former theory the sentiment is of a different "stuff" from the erg and we are adding and subtracting in a conflict index a different kind of component. Logically this would require that we consider a total conflict index and also two separate indices, one for the b's from E terms and one for the b's from M terms. The psychological meaning of the $\sqrt{\Sigma(bM)^2}$ would be an accumulation of cognitive signals for ergic response that distract and divert from the course of action in question and in favor of other responses. If the general position is correct that the M score does *not* include its ergic investment, then this conflict, unlike ergic conflict, would not have the same immediate quality of ergic dissatisfaction but rather an amnesic effect in removing ideas and stimuli from effective awareness.

3   The stabilising action of sentiments and the structure of self-sentiment and superego   At this early stage of investigation of dynamics by objective measurement and quantitative analysis the construction of a theory that will extend to explaining the total personality dynamics can be achieved only by resting inferences also upon clinical, nonquantitative observation. The theory necessarily has a patchwork quality in which concepts are justified partly by experiment and partly by clinical hunches, which latter some experimenters may prefer to call "assumptions".

If the general analysis stands firm that action conflict can have its outcome predicted by putting the specification equations in the balance—and experimental work already begins to support this—then an apparent contradiction arises with general and clinical observation. For, at least at first glance, the balancing of specification equations would seem to imply that the strengths of ergic tensions, now high now low, through stimulation by threats and temptations, would leave an individual's behavior with no "consistency of character", and at the mercy of circumstances.

Even a person of strong principles and character is "at the mercy of circumstances" in the good sense that he pursues long-term goals flexibly, with intelligent responsiveness to each set of circumstances. If we ask how it comes about that he does not respond "impulsively", as might at first be expected from the specification equation, when some one strong erg, say sexual drive, is high, we find it does not suffice to suppose that it is simply because some other ergic tension momentarily exceeds the first. Human behavior is not a see-saw between chance stimulations of different ergs. In animal experiment, as the work of Warden (1931), Stone and Ferguson (1938), Anderson (1938), and others suggests, the decision on a conflict between two stimuli, i.e. between the courses of action which each calls for, *can* usually be explained simply by the relative strengths of the drives involved, but it is reasonably clear that this is not the main basis of inhibition and decision in civilized culture.

Schneewind, Rican, Dielman, and the present writer (a team, incidentally, from four countries) set out to build up "sentiments" in rats by training and reward schedules bringing response elements into coherent patterns. The intention was to see whether the factor patterns which in man we call sentiments, and which we hypothesize to arise from such "training" by culture, could be matched by recognizably similar factors in animals which we would *know* for certain grow up by learning schedules. As chapter 5 relates, some degree of support was found for fragmentary sentiment factors in animals. Yet by and large it is surely evident that sentiment development is on an altogether lower level in animals—at least, those below primates or higher mammals—consisting perhaps of consistent reactions to a mate, an attachment to territory, a set of habits of satisfaction centering on food getting and the security of the nest or lair, and so on. It is the enormous development of culture, and habitual, balanced satisfactions of drives built by learning around specific objects, aided by the capacity to handle abstract ideas, which permits the development of so rich and strong an array of sentiments in man.

A sentiment structure of any kind acts as a check and balance to any more direct, impulsive satisfaction of ergs. It does so because any stimulus to a direct, primitive and culturally unsuitable response is likely, from past experience of long-term loss of satisfactions, to arouse also a sentiment which brings other potential directives of satisfaction into conflict with the impulse. Sentiment structures are essentially devices for long circuiting of behavior. They ensure more certain and greater total satisfaction, when weighed over any appreciable period of time. But they do so at the cost of complicating life with postponement of satisfaction, greater complication of means–end paths, and increase of what has been defined (Cattell, 1950) as "deflection strain". It is for this reason that societies have to set up the recreational and phantasy reliefs found in literature and art, and in the institution of "vacations" to "get away from it all".

The nature of this stress in control, deflection strain, etc., will shortly be studied, but here we are concerned with understanding the fact of control itself and the phenomena which constitute that consistent working for long-term goals, characteristic of man and particularly of men of character and principle.

Let us consider any fragment of everyday life behavior where some ergic impulse comes into conflict with a sentiment. The cashier at a bank, say, becomes very hungry at 10:30 a.m. and the idea occurs to him that he will break rules and walk out to an early lunch. A teacher is defied by some hulking boy and experiences an impulse to strike him. A postman delivering letters receives inviting smiles from a woman alone in her house. In each of these cases there is in the first place a sentiment connected with the ongoing activity, which could be what is set out in table 2.6, page 33, as the career sentiment. This simply means that there is a raised excitation level of a collection of mental sets and a whole series of stimuli—the bank customs, the classroom, the sack of letters to deliver, respectively in the above instances—the customary responses to which are not easily broken. In the language of the specification equation the ergic tension involved in the temptation is strong but the negative loading on the sentiment and the strength of the sentiment outweigh the impulse potential.

So far the sentiments are seen acting in the dynamics of behavior in the same way as a large fly-wheel acts in steadying an erratic engine. Rewards for long circuited behavior have built up responses to stimuli which outbid immediate appeals of a different kind and keep long-term goals in control. But these alone are not enough to account for those higher flights of rational and moral behavior which those individuals better adapted to civilization succeed in manifesting. A strong sentiment to a business career has sometimes been seen in men who, outside the immediate stimulus of the business environment, are subject to all kinds of vices of the weak-willed; an excessive sentiment for a hobby—from stamp collecting to hunting—may distort a life pattern to the point of ridiculous irrationality, and even a strong sentiment to a family has been known, in the Mafia for example, to be the root of robbery and murder.

The factor analysis of objective motivation measures on attitudes spanning the total sphere of dynamic interests has consistently turned up two patterns—here called the self-sentiment and the superego—which go far to explain the phenomena we are now discussing. In the self-sentiment (table 2.10) we see a collection of attitudes all of which have to do with that self-concept which the human level of intelligent abstraction makes possible and which we all possess. If some sub-classification of the attitudes found loaded on this pattern is pursued, it suggests (1) attitudes concerned with the preservation of the physical self and of good health; (2) attitudes concerned with good control of the self, i.e. will power, good mental functioning, avoidance of insanity, and so on; (3) attitudes concerned with the preservation of the social self, i.e. with good reputation, good economic credit, etc. These last, as we shall see, begin to verge on the moral requirements of the second structure, the superego, but are sufficiently distinguishable.

The best pre-quantitative studies of the self-concept are to be found in the persuasive writings of James and McDougall, where the various "extensions of the self" are insightfully laid out. A considerable quantitative study of the self-concept has grown up more recently in the writings of Wylie (1961), Brookover and Gottlieb (1964), Purkey (1970), and others. But much of this has stopped at the cognitive level, and the important point we have to make about the self-sentiment is that it is a *dynamic* structure—a set of attitude courses of action about the self-concept as an object, just as other sentiments have some more concrete object as the focus common to the group of attitudes.

The real problem in the self-sentiment is that of accounting for its usefulness as a means to ergic ends. Every sentiment grows up as a sub-goal, useful in a subsidiation path to ergic goals. The exceptionally powerful role that the evidence shows we must accord to the self-sentiment indicates that we have to find an exceptional accumulation of ergic subsidiations. The answer to this riddle is surely that the maintenance of the "intact" self, physically, psychologically, and in social standing, is rightly perceived as a necessary precondition for all other satisfactions. In most of the above domains, e.g. the fact that one must still physically exist to reach one's goal, this precondition is obvious. In the domain of social reputation it is brought home by increasing experience. In the extreme instance of action in this domain we know that individuals ostracized from preliterate tribal cultures, e.g. through breaking a taboo, commonly do not live long.

The self-sentiment structure must therefore be looked for toward the distal (left in figure 2.2) end of the dynamic lattice. For the sub-goal which it represents is a precondition not only of ultimate ergic satisfactions, but also of most sentiment satisfactions. A mental hospital patient cannot pursue his career, and a convicted criminal cannot set up a home. The sum total of *ergic investment* in the numerous attitudes which work for the maintenance of what the individual considers his acceptable self-image must therefore be great indeed, and explains certain capacities for inhibition we shall shortly discuss in relation to the specification equation.

The second main sentiment sharing a largely regulatory function with the self-sentiment is seen in the factor analytic confirmation of the psychoanalytic superego conception, in table 2.10 (page 39). Without space to go very deeply here into certain mysteries about its developmental origin, we would point out that it has some qualities between those of an erg and a sentiment, in that there is strong evidence (Cattell, Blewett, and Beloff, 1955; Cattell and Klein, 1973) of an appreciable genetic component in the sensitiveness to guilt which underlies this structure. After that there is evidence that its development hinges very much on an affectionate relationship to a parent with standards of moral conscience in early years. Finally, there is evidence that much of its action springs from an unconscious level, no longer open to rational or conscious manipulation in later life.

Although the pattern of the superego is evidenced from table 2.10, a glance at the broader setting at what attitudes it does and does not contain is illuminating, particularly regarding some subtle issues of the relation of superego to self-sentiment. These are also portrayed in table 2.10.

It will be seen that such attitudes as concern self-control (11), reputation (13), sanity (14), and avoidance of vice (20) have contributions from *both* self-sentiment and superego. Nevertheless, the concern of the former largely with the self-concept and its extensions, and of the latter with ethical values and a desire for moral behavior is quite clear.

In leaving these two structures primarily found in *motivation measures*, it may be well to reiterate (page 54 above) that unlike other interests and sentiments they are so broad in their effects on behavior that they also get picked up (in ratings, questionnaires, and objective personality tests) as *general personality factors*. Otherwise (page 55) the dynamic structure modality of traits is extra to (correlationally in "new space from") the general personality–temperament domain. As will be seen from table 4.1, the 16 PF

Table 4.1 The "mental interiors" of self-sentiment and superego as seen in L- and Q-data

Q_3 self-sentiment

Item no. in 16 PF	Questionnaire response	Loading* on Q_3
48	I keep my room well organized with things in known places all the time. *Yes*	.4
172A	I like to go my own way instead of acting on approved rules. *False*	.4
172B	Some people criticize my sense of responsibility. *No*	.3
67	I like to find excuses to put off work and have fun. *Rarely*	.3

G superego

In Behavior ratings (L-data): — Loadings

Characteristics

3	Wise, mature, polished vs. dependent, silly, incoherent	.35
11	Strong-willed, conscientious vs. indolent, impulsive	.33
10	Realistic, facing life vs. demoralized, artistic	−.31

In Q-data:

Questionnaire response

63	If I saw two neighbors' children fighting, I would intervene for peace. *Yes*	.48
65	I think that plenty of freedom is more important than good manners and respect for the law. *No*	.53
67	In thinking of difficulties in my work, I: (a) *try to plan ahead, before I meet them* (b) in between (c) assume I can handle them when they come	.54
69	I close my mind to well-meant suggestions of others, even though I know I shouldn't. *False*	.17

* Approximate mean loadings on the factor from several studies.

scales which define self-sentiment (Q_3) and superego (G) present a consistent picture with the approach through attitude strength and, one may add, correlate with the MAT scales (table 2.10) positively to the degree to be expected (considering attenuation and instrument factors).

4 Principles of the dynamic calculus

The interest of the psychologist is now to pursue further the study of *conflict and integration* with the aid of the structural concepts just introduced, including a modernization of the psychoanalytic ego concept that we have yet to study. But in this section we must pause before introducing new data in order to sharpen our instruments and make them more explicit. As we proceed it must be increasingly evident to the reader that a system of calculation—as in the specification equation and the above formulae for conflict—is being built up and refined in this area. For the sake of specifically designating this new development in the field of psychology it has been called the *dynamic calculus* (using calculus in a general sense, with no particular connection with "differential" and "integral" calculus).

The dynamic calculus—as far as it will be carried in this book—puts no strain on the mathematical know-how of the typical undergraduate. For it goes no further than the use of the *dynamic lattice*, the concept of *vectors* (as in trait scores, modulation indices, and behavior indices), the representation of vectors by plots on ordinary coordinate axes, and the use of linear equations in matrix algebra. A particular development of the dynamic calculus that needs to be illustrated before proceeding is that of vector summation as shown in plots. To keep illustration to two dimensions let us consider some attitudes that may be motivated by only two ergs, and which can be described thus:

$$a_j = b_{j1}E_1 + b_{j2}E_2 \qquad (4.10\text{a})$$

$$a_k = b_{k1}E_1 + b_{k2}E_2 \qquad (4.10\text{b})$$

Then these can be represented by two vectors as in figure 4.1.

The vector representation brings out still more clearly the richer meaning of *behavior response attitudes*, as defined in the dynamic calculus, compared to the sociologist's "polling attitudes" checked off as "for "or "against" in an inventory. An attitude is not just for or against. (Is one "for" or "against" say, a beefsteak or the girl one sees across the campus?) It has a complex emotional quality in relation to whatever object is involved and *this quality is representable precisely in the dynamic calculus by the direction of the vector*. The direction states the particular combination of ergic forces (and therefore satisfactions) involved in the given course of action. Thus a_j in figure 4.1 involves the same two ergic satisfactions as does a_k, but it has more of E_1 and less of E_2.

As Burt pointed out many years ago the problem which seemed to baffle most theorists of "drive strength" [as it is used, for example, in Hull and (differently) in McDougall] was that of expressing it as "directed energy". Leaving aside for the moment whether "energy", "power", or "force" is the better term, if it is the latter, then we can give direction to it just as the engineer does in his parallelogram of forces. Each vector has *direction* indicating the combination of emotional satisfactions involved, and *length* indicating its strength.

Once psychodynamics adopts such a vector representation, a whole series of useful calculations becomes possible, and it is these which constitute a major part of the dynamic calculus. For example, if we have reason to add up a series of attitudes, when some meaningful purpose belongs to the aggregate, we can do so by the familiar rules of vector summation. This is instanced in two dimensions in figure 4.1, where the *parallelogram of forces* tells us that $(a_j + a_k)$ is the sum of vectors a_j and a_k. Algebraically it tells us [if we go back to equations (4.10a) and (b)] that:

$$a_{(j+k)} = (b_{j1} + b_{k1})E_1 + (b_2 + b_{k2})E_2 \qquad (4.11\text{a})$$

Similarly, if we want to take the *difference* of two attitudes, illustrated in figure 4.1 by the dotted line vector $(a_j - a_k)$, algebraically it would be:

$$a_{(j-k)} = (b_{j1} - b_{k1})E_1 + (b_{j2} - b_{k2})E_2 \qquad (4.11\text{b})$$

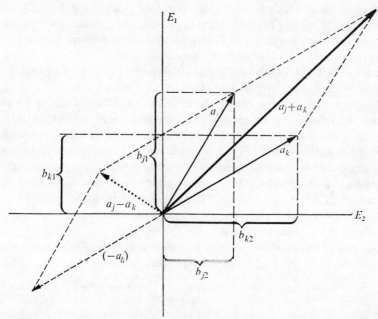

Figure 4.1 Vector summation of attitudes

Such a difference would be calculated when we want to know the particular satisfaction losses and gains from substituting one course of action for another.

Incidentally, if we wish to handle the above two transactions within the ordinary factor analytic model meaning of loadings, then we should have to renormalize[1] the final equations. This is a technicality the general reader can skip: the important psychological point is that we can conceive of a single attitude $a_{(j+k)}$ which would be a true psychological equivalent for the two previous attitudes. If the individual could find it, he could enjoy a course of action that would give him as much satisfaction as the two previous courses of action.

Much of our exploratory behavior in life is directed to finding courses of action which, in relation to the realities of the maze of the external world, will lead to *equal* satisfactions, but by a less fatiguing route, or, more commonly, to greater satisfactions, i.e. to lengthening the vector. If a *substitute vector attitude* is found as in figure 4.1 then no readjustment in all the other attitudes of the individual (those constituting the dynamic lattice) is needed. But more often the adoption of a new attitude course of action will upset the dynamic equilibrium of the whole. If an action is discovered capable of yielding an unexpectedly higher degree of satisfaction to erg E_1 then other attitudes formerly pursued to get the E_1 type of satisfaction will tend to lose some of their force. They will change their dynamic direction and may even be abandoned.

Attitude summation calculations—at present involving the large divisions of the dynamic calculus—have their principal psychological usefulness in four areas: (1) learning readjustments, as just discussed; (2) comparing the total ergic investments in particular sentiments and other dynamic structures; (3) evaluating conflict, and (4) in group dynamics.

Let us set the last aside for chapter 10 on social psychology by saying that just as the first three uses handle attitude interaction within one individual, so social psychology can utilize the dynamic calculus for adding attitudes *among* individuals, e.g. to get the common investment in a group activity. Regarding application to evaluation of conflict the main foundation has already been laid in sections 1 and 2 above. Regarding ergic investment an introduction has been given which can now be advanced. The introduction pointed out that if we take a set of attitudes, a, b, c, and d which are all well loaded on a particular sentiment, M_x, and then add up the loadings of those same attitudes on all ergs, we shall obtain values $b_{ea}, b_{eb}, b_{ec}, b_{ed}$ which may be called the *ergic investment* in the given sentiment.

The technicalities of this addition we can pass over briefly. First, if some of the attitudes are appreciably loaded on other sentiments, M_y, M_z, etc., then

[1] Renormalization means squaring and adding the behavioral indices and dividing each original value by the square root of the sum. It means that the b (and now the $(b_{j1} \pm b_{k1})$) terms must, when squared and added, come to unity. This is required because both factors and attitudes in the ordinary factor model must be in standard scores.

M_x would have to share this investment with them, for a row (attitude) in the factor matrix tells us only that the given attitude brings the given amount of ergic satisfaction and does not say to which sentiment it is attached. The best way to handle this in practice is to choose as representatives of a sentiment only those attitudes so highly loaded that no other sentiment has much role. Secondly, it will be recognized that the addition of the ergic part is a vector addition, as in figure 4.1, except that a whole bunch of perhaps 5 to 20 attitudes will be involved instead of only two. The algebra of this is simply an extension of equation (4.11) beyond two terms.[1]

What we finally have in this ergic investment vector is a *statement of the total quantity and quality of satisfaction that a person obtains through a particular sentiment object*. (Incidentally, this is what psychoanalysis used more vaguely to designate as the "cathexis" of an object.) The question arises whether we should consider this quantity as the "strength" of a sentiment, in comparison with other sentiments, or, indeed, with ergs. Certainly we can designate it the "importance" of a sentiment to the individual, and here in fact we have a real meaning for the "for" and "against" an object used rather metaphorically in the sociological "polling" concept of an attitude.

The ergic investment in an object, x, which we will designate $(EM)_x$, states how much the individual's satisfactions in life would be reduced if that object were removed. *All* the attitude courses of action satisfactions would then be cut off, and since their sum total is the quantity $(EM)_x$ this is a statement of the loss. Consequently, it is here a meaningful way of speaking to say how much the individual is *for* the object. And since some objects, e.g. dangerous, loathsome, or obstructing objects, can have a negative total, we can also score degrees of being *against* the object. As suggested earlier (page 40), the theory that the former is the total strength of being *for* an object can be tested (assuming the frustration theory of pugnacity) by the amount of pugnacity generated by a threat to the very existence of the sentiment object.

The same is not true about the object involved in a single attitude, where for or against the object is meaningless; for one and the same object is generally "used" by several different attitude courses. A man will hold many attitudes regarding his wife such as "I want to come home to my wife's good dinners", "I am proud to show my wife to friends", "I enjoy my wife's company in bridge games". Any meaning that can be given to, for, or against, a single attitude is not to an object but to the *course of action*, and there, as we have

[1] More exact expression of the general intent of the process here requires that (1) the b's be those of covariance, real base factor analysis; (2) the contributions be weighted according to the weight of each given attitude in estimating the M factor; (3) the same number of attitudes giving the same multiple r efficiency in estimating the M be used if, as here proposed, different sentiments are to be compared; (4) both the modulator, s, and the b value be considered, as pointed out on page 68 above. For if the life situation stimulates the ergic tension levels there is more to discharge, for the same b value. Thus a series of b's must be substituted eventually for the simplified b above.

seen, if we score action in a given direction, e.g. building up a bank account, the distribution of scores will range from positive to zero or to negative, some people wanting to save more and some being willing to spend more. Thus in passing we should note that the average strength of an attitude is assigned zero in a standard score, but that in a meaningful raw score the zero, in the sense of a point of psychological indifference to performing a course of action or its opposite, may fall at the upper or lower end of the distribution of people—or anywhere in between.

5   The arena of integrative behavior and the role of the self-sentiment, the superego, and the ego

The first principles of the dynamic calculus, as they concern the interaction of attitudes in conflict and confluence, the strength of sentiments, etc., have briefly been discussed. To pursue them to the topics that naturally come next will plunge us into complications of concept as well as into theories about which experimental verdicts are as yet very scanty. The integration of the human personality is complex, and consequently this is inevitably a difficult section.

In any course of action we now recognize that the self-sentiment and the superego sentiment are likely to have appreciable "loadings" for more "civilized" behavior. Let us simplify the behavioral equation by taking just one erg, E, one ordinary sentiment, M, and the two special sentiments M_{SE} and M_{SS} to represent self-sentiment and superego, though typically there would be several E's and several M's.

$$a_{jik} = b_{je}s_{ke}E_i + b_{jm}s_{km}M_i + b_{jSS}s_{kSS}M_{SSi} + b_{jSE}s_{kSE}M_{SEi} \qquad (4.12)$$

The s's—modulators for the ambient situation—are brought in for initial completeness, though in subsequent manipulations the essentials may be brought out in b's only. The subscripts have the usual meaning: j a focal stimulus with response a; i an individual; k an ambient situation, and e, m, SS, etc., fixing the values of b and s for the given trait.

Now if an individual is generally capable of resisting most impulses barred by our society, such as hitting people on the head in an argument, or sexually assaulting every attractive woman, it follows that the combined weights of M_{SE} and M_{SS} must outrank those of any single erg, however powerful. For complete control they should outweigh any combination of ergs, but fortunately the anarchic ergs, like the criminals in a society, rarely line up together. Indeed, it is difficult to imagine a stimulus situation which stimulates all ergs toward a common course of action. [A person in a manic (or a certain drugged) condition may have the equivalent of a large stimulus modulation, s, on all his ergs, but characteristically they act not together but in succession, distracted too readily by each small stimulus.]

But the essential point is that in the culturally well-raised individual the amount of learning of M_{SS} and M_{SE}, at least after about five years of age, is such that the quantity $b_{jSES_kSE}M_{SEi}$ becomes larger than $b_{jeS_keE_i}$ for the great majority of courses of action wherein the former would properly have a negative loading and inhibiting effect and the ergic course would be anti-social. If M_{SE}, say, is to do this successfully, it must either be a "big" factor in itself (large mean and variance of M), or become much stimulated when good behavior is at stake (large s's) or have large behavioral indices (b's), or all three together. Without entering into the mathematics of this we may say that (in real base factor analysis) all three are possible, but that not enough experiment has been done yet to say which is important.[1]

Parenthetically, the reader may wonder whether a self-sentiment would have much development in a person living in a very primitive society or living quite alone. However, even shorn of the substantial social portion, the self-sentiment would still have behavior-regulating value. It could be part of the self-concept of a savage that he is a man capable of leaping a brook a spear's length wide, but not one twice that width. If he gives way to an impulse to do the latter he invites disaster as surely as one ignoring the social realities of his person.

The drama of human bondage to conflict, of course, permits other arrangements of the pieces on the board than the common one just described. In general M_{SE} and M_{SS} will not stand alone against the E's but will be aided by the stabilizing effect of the established sentiments generally. And although M_{SE} and M_{SS} are generally in alliance (as table 2.10 shows by the similarity of loading signs on significant common attitudes), situations can be conceived in which they conflict. The self-sentiment is one of two distinct and powerful factors—the other being the erg of self-assertion—in the manifold phenomena which Atkinson and McClelland (1953 and 1955) have studied under *achievement motivation*. And instances occur where achievement, even in its M_{SS} component, conflicts with the superego. It happens, for example, in some instances where men capable of indispensable contributions to research accept socially more prominent and better paid administrative positions. The rich young man in the bible, who had doubtless done all the right things socially, was thrown into this conflict when Christ told him to sell all and give to the poor and "he went away sad". All careful factorings show M_{SS} to be directed to social proprieties. Compared to the superego it would not be quite correct to say "manners" versus "morals", for the self-sentiment incorporates appreciable morality, probably through its subsidiating in part to the superego, as to

[1] Also among such complex and unsettled issues remains, we must remember, the question of whether the M terms in the factoring of attitudes represent purely the strength of engrams, i.e. the cognitive excitation or signalling capacity learnt by reinforcement or both this *and* the ergic investment representing the ultimate ergic satisfaction to which the sentiment action is expected to lead. Tentatively we would represent this alternative in the model by M for the former and $(M+\overline{EM})$ for the latter, where $\overline{EM}$ is the ergic investment in the sentiment.

an erg. But its goal is the preserved and enhanced self, and addressing itself to morals only in the sense that morality is *part* of the approved self and "honesty is the best policy".

Nevertheless, in general M_{SS} and M_{SE} may be expected to be in alliance, appearing as what have been called statistically "cooperative factors". And, even if they do not always act together, there is evidence that they tend to develop together (see table 4.3 later). Incidentally, one must not suppose that their action is entirely inhibitory with respect to an opposing action by ergs. Fortunately, many ergically based performances, e.g. pity for those in trouble, self-assertiveness in pride of excellent work, are supplemented by M_{SE} and M_{SS}. It is thus that ratings of perseverance and courage in the face of failures correlate with endowment in these structures, for they keep action going when the purely ergic sources fluctuate and flag.

Now at this point in the study of total personality integration we have to introduce a new structure, corresponding to what psychoanalysis has called the ego. It has not been mentioned in chapter 2 because up to this point no one has reported finding an ego structure in the factoring of attitudes. However, in the realm of personality ratings and questionnaire items a factor of this nature was found by Cattell as early as 1946, and indexed as C. It has repeatedly been found since in questionnaire analyses down successive age levels, in the HSPQ, CPQ, ESPQ, etc., and is probably in objective tests as the factor indexed U I 16 and called Assertive Ego Strength (Hundleby, Pawlik, and Cattell, 1965). In questionnaires it loads such items as appear in table 4.2. Both the content and the numerous clinical investigations which show C to be *the* low factor universally in pathological types (neurotics, psychotics, addicts,

Table 4.2   The pattern of expression of ego strength–vs.–ego weakness
In behavior ratings (L-data):

C+		C−
Emotionally mature	vs.	Gets emotional when frustrated
Stable in interests	vs.	Changeable
Realistic, adjusts to facts	vs.	Evades responsibilities; gives in
Calm, unruffled	vs.	Worrying

In Q-data:

I feel that modern life has many annoying frustrations and restrictions. *No*	.50*
I have vivid dreams disturbing my sleep. *No*	.55
I sometimes can't get to sleep because an idea keeps running through my mind. *No*	.40
If I make an awkward social mistake I can soon forget it. *Yes*	.25
Things go wrong for me. *Rarely*	.30

* Approximate loadings on the factor to two places.

alcoholics, etc., see Cattell, Eber, and Tatsuoka, 1970) leave little doubt that what the psychoanalysts approached at the level of clinical observation is this factor now discovered and checked at the experimental level. There is also evidence that certain experiences reduce it and that therapy raises it (see page 62 above) as one would expect of ego strength.

6   Experimental evidence on the nature of the ego strength dimension

The mystery which appears at this point is why, as shown on page 99 (table 4.1), the self-sentiment and superego found in questionnaires and ratings (Q_3 and G) are picked up readily also in objective attitude measures, as dynamic structure factors, whereas ego strength, C, appears only in the former. Our theory is that C is not primarily a narrow dynamic structure factor—on investment of interests—but, like the other general personality factors, e.g. A, B, D, E, F, etc., a *way* of responding. (Temperament traits in general are abstractions from many diverse dynamic interests, a way of handling interest, often scored as a ratio, rather than an interest strength itself.)

Pursuing the indications that C is not a built up interest in some object— as M_{SS} focuses on the self and M_{SE} on value beliefs—but a way of handling drives and conflicts, we reach a theory (from clinical and rating evidence on C) that it is a *capacity for confluence learning*. That is to say, it is a capacity for finding compromises among different ergs and sentiments that will minimize the confluent or indurated conflict as expressed in formulae (4.8) and (4.9) on page 94. The high emotionality and rigidity typically rated in low C works against such efficient compromises, which require tolerant experiment. Furthermore, it seems probable that there is an innate capacity involved here determining the number of emotional needs that can be integrated. This seems to be what has been demonstrated in comparative animal psychology, showing greater capacity to defer satisfaction in higher than lower mammals.

The studies in behavioral genetics of Gottesman (1963), Loehlin (1965), and Cattell and Klein (1973) show that within the human range there is also a genetic component accounting for roughly one-third of the variance (Cattell, 1973) of ego strength. There are indications in neurology (from poor self control after injuries to the frontal cortex) that this capacity is largely determined by the degree of development of the frontal lobes. Thus the first contribution to capacity to achieve good integration (the obverse of the conflict index) issues from a greater genetic "span". The second, we shall hypothesize from the arguments above, comes from a good development of M_{SE} (G in the 16 PF) and M_{SS} (Q_3 in the 16 PF), since these represent forces which, over development, prevent the more extreme and chaotic demands on integration capacity from appearing. Lastly, of course, there would be developmental good fortune or bad fortune in regard to the consistency of parental discipline and the stresses of social environment for which Burt first made a convincing case in the *Young Delinquent* (1925).

If this theory is correct one testable inference would be that positive correlations should tend to exist between C, G, and Q_3, from their mutual aid. Now a second-order factor among them has actually been recognized for some time (Cattell, 1956; Gorsuch and Cattell, 1967), and an average pattern over seven studies and 8068 adolescents (12–18) on the HSPQ is shown in table 4.3.

Table 4.3 Pattern of the integration or good upbringing second-stratum factor in the questionnaire medium

Primary personality factors	Loadings on second stratum
A Affectia	00
B Intelligence	04
C Ego strength	(15)
D Excitability	01
E Dominance	02
F Surgency	(−51)
G Superego strength	(64)
H Parmia	−00
I Premsia	08
J Asthenia	09
O Guilt-proneness	−07
Q_2 Self-sufficiency	01
Q_3 Self-sentiment strength	(60)
Q_4 Ergic tension	−03

Mean loadings from seven samples totalling 8068 subjects, 12–18 years of age.

The experienced experimenter will note that this has good simple structure, indicating firm definition, and that the primaries (boxed) with significant loadings are C+, F−, G+ and Q_3+. There is, in short, good evidence as the theory requires that C, ego strength, Q_3, self-sentiment, and G, superego, exert positive mutual influence in development. Some investigators have conceived this (Nichols, 1974) as a secondary influence acting on all of these and considered it to be (emotionally and morally) *good home upbringing*, which would favor all three of these; this conclusion would be quite acceptable in the present framework.

A prediction which did not initially enter into our theory above, is that F−, desurgency, would also be loaded. However, it fits excellently, for desurgency (Cattell, Eber, and Tatsuoka, 1970) is a primary of *general inhibition* (from more disciplined upbringing) and it is easy to see that such inhibition is either a condition or a by-product (according to one's theory) of the learning of higher superego and self-sentiment standards.

The only other second-order in which C has a role is anxiety (see table 7.1, page 170). It would be appropriate to discuss that next, as a product of conflict and poor integration, but due to the length of this chapter, and its appropriateness to the clinical chapter it is redirected there (chapter 8). A closer issue concerns the relation of the C factor to other experimental measures of integration. Three major approaches require mention: (1) the study of Williams (1958 and 1959) directly relating C measurements to conflict–vs.–integration measures through formula (4.8); (2) the studies of Cattell (1943) and Das (1955) relating C factor to *instability* of attitudes, and (3) the studies of Cattell (1948), Cattell and Gruen (1955), Hundleby *et al.* (1965), Scheier (1965), showing that internal inconsistency of attitude measures (later called by Festinger "cognitive dissonance") correlate with low ego strength.

Williams carried out the ambitious experiment of doing a P-technique experiment (the only real basis for determining individual differences on b's) on six normals and six psychotic mental patients. The index of integration (4.8b) above was calculated and found to be (a) significantly lower for the patients, (b) positively correlated with C. Capacity for confluence adjustment is supported as a C characteristic.

Cattell (1943) and Das (1955) took a set of attitudes representative of the life interest space and readministered them to the same subjects (adults and children) after intervals from a day to a month. A score for random shift of attitude was correlated with ego strength measures and ratings. Substantial correlations of .4 to .7 (correcting almost to unity) were found between ego strength and stability. The argument is that poor dynamic integration shows itself by instability right down to specific attitudes. However, both Cattell (1943) and Wessman and Ricks (1966) have shown that a powerful contribution to changeability of interests and moods comes not only from C−, ego weakness, but also from extraversion (Wessman and Ricks) though Cattell's research pinpoints it more in the surgency (F factor) contribution to exvia.

The basis of the third approach lies in objective personality factor research, where tests were developed for poor and good dynamic integration (Cattell and Warburton, 1967). These were couched in syllogisms, such that if S endorsed premise 1 and premise 2 he should endorse a given inference. These were given in mixed order so that the inevitable connections were not apparent. Although a low score literally means cognitive inconsistency, the argument (Cattell, 1948; Cattell and Warburton, 1967) is that this inconsistency arises mostly from emotional distortion of cognitive beliefs. Festinger's later conceptualizing of this as "cognitive dissonance" regressed from this theoretical probability to a cognitive treatment. Actually the correlations of cognitive inconsistency, or low dynamic integration as defined in the personality researches, fitted the expectation of significant relation to ego strength, but also showed relations to other personality dimensions (Hundleby, Pawlik, and Cattell, 1965).

The concept of the ego strength factor which emerges here, as centrally one of dynamic integration, and the developmental capacity to acquire such integration, is thus based on an increasing experimental foundation. However, several issues call for further investigation. Three sources of contribution to ego strength and weakness have been mentioned above: (1) genes determining frontal lobe development; (2) an upbringing which by developing the self-sentiment and the superego also assists ego strength, and (3) an environment free of trauma so severe as to make integration more difficult. Now one could argue from the last that the ego might be a dynamic structure—an immediate capacity to handle impulses not an ideational referral to the self-sentiment—learnt as such from experiencing rewards for "good control in general". Is this last a specific enough line of behavior to be reinforced by rewards? The possibility surely exists that at any rate "control as such" could grow up in particular areas from reward.

The possibility must therefore exist that a factor, perhaps not of great variance, will yet be found beyond M_{SS} and M_{SE}, factoring attitude strengths connected with control, though possibly at a relatively unconscious and automatic level. The individual of strong ego strength (and delinquents are not low on ego strength, as on G and Q_3) simply has good control of impulse without reference to self-sentiment or superego. The latter, it has been suggested, are brought in deliberately when ego strength threatens to be insufficient. [This is developed (Cattell, Tatro, and Komlos, 1965) in connection with high Q_3 and low C in schizophrenics.] The development of further concepts here, and particularly the reference of the psychoanalytic concept of "the unconscious" to dynamic calculus concepts must be left to the clinical chapter (7).

7   Summary   1. Dynamic conflict exists and can be evaluated in two forms: (i) action conflict and (ii) indurated, stabilized conflict. The former reaches *decisions* on actual courses of action, which can be predicted by subtracting, one from the other, the specification equations for the two courses of action.

2. Indurated conflict exists in a single course of action which attempts to be a confluence of several desired courses and consequently works out as the best compromise possible. The conflict which remains embedded and indurated in such a course of action can be scored by several formulae involving the summation of the negative b indices (plus the ergic tension terms in the case of an individual). The success in *integration* is $(I-C)$ where C is thus the quantity of indurated conflict. It can be added across all dynamic systems to give a total score on integration for the individual, I_i. This discussion brings out that the paths in the dynamic lattice must also sustain "negative subsidiation" terms.

3. The behavior of civilized man is not a see-saw between the specification

equation outcomes of ergs erratically moved by deprivation and stimulation. It responds to these ergic ingredients in the equation, but is stabilized by sentiments which provide acceptable channels of deferred action. Ordinary sentiments would act only as "fly-wheel" stabilizers, but two in particular—the self-sentiment and the superego—act as censors and integrators in a more positive sense. Their origins are discussed, the theory of the self-sentiment being that maintenance of behavior fitting a self-concept is a precondition of most other satisfactions, so that it is the most distal structure in the lattice. Because of the breadth of their effects these two structures also show up as general personality factors and their patterns in Q-data are set out.

4. To handle the above and other problems the *dynamic calculus* has been developed over the past fifteen years (Cattell, 1958, 1959, 1965) providing concepts and calculations for summing and subtracting attitudes as vector quantities, as well as the dynamic lattice "hydraulics". Immediate uses of the vector summation part are (i) evaluating conflict of systems, (ii) evaluating alternative substitute adjustments, (iii) estimating the total ergic investment in a sentiment, (iv) (in social psychology) obtaining the investment in group life.

5. There are technicalities in using the calculus in a factor analytic framework, requiring *real base factor analysis*, which are relegated to footnotes and references. A behavioral index loading, b, multiplied by a modulator, s, defines the customary satisfaction in an habitualized course of action. Consequently, the summed attitudes in a sentiment give its ergic investment which may be said to define the total degree to which one is "for" or "against" the sentiment *object*. But in an attitude one is only for or against *a course of action* to which the object is ancillary. Among the important technical precisionings, which cannot yet be made for lack of experiment, is that concerning whether a sentiment strength should be written as M alone (the cognitive signal excitation capacity) or as $(M+\overline{EM})$ the latter being the ergic investment in the attitude.

6. Integrated behavior, productive of maximum satisfaction over a long period, results from sentiments (M's) and particularly the self-sentiment (M_{SS}) and the superego (M_{SE}). It follows that good control requires these factors to be developed to become larger in variance (real base factoring) or in b and s indices, than is the case with ergs. Examination of the phenomena of integrated behavior reveals, however, involvement of a third personality factor, *ego strength*, indexed in the 16 PF as C.

7. It is hypothesized that C has so far not appeared in factorings of attitudes because it is less concerned with any object than with a *way* of reacting on all objects. The theory is that C is the capacity to obtain the least conflictful confluences of conflicting attitudes by compromise. Its level seems to be partly due to genetic action, partly to the favoring effect of large M_{SE} and M_{SS} developments, and partly to freedom from a history of trauma. The discovery

of a clear-cut second-order personality factor, QVIII, in Q-data in which C (ego), G (superego) and Q_3 (self-sentiment) as well as desurgency, F—, are interrelated supports this theory.

8. Systematic enquiry about the association of C in personality supports the above. A low score thereon is the most universal characteristic of the pathologies; it relates negatively to actual measures of the $\Sigma\bar{b}$'s in the conflict index; it increases with therapy; and it is substantially inversely related to measures of (a) attitude fluctuation over time, and (b) scores of dynamic inconsistency in individuals, measured by logical inconsistency (perhaps "cognitive dissonance") in attitude structure.

5 Contributions from animal motivation

1 The use of animals in motivational studies
Prior to the nineteenth century, man was generally regarded as unique and unrelated in any way to the animal kingdom. Man was seen as a pleasure-seeking, pain-avoiding creature (hedonism), whilst animals were activated by instincts—inborn mechanisms which gave rise to fixed ways of satisfying their needs. Darwin's *Origin of Species* (1859) then came as a not easily accepted surprise to those who preferred to think of man and animals as unrelated. It was Darwin who gave sustenance to the notion of instincts being part and parcel of man's nature as well as that of animals. By the processes of natural selection, those animals with the most serviceable instincts would survive, propagate, and mutate (to give other orders of animals which might similarly survive their environments).

In psychology the instinct concept was given thorough theoretical treatment by McDougall and was, of course, strongly implicit in Freud, but was brushed aside by Watson's reflexological learning ideas and the cultural monomania of many sociologists. In due course psychology came back to instincts under other names—propensities, drives—and finally their existence, number, and nature were given more exact definition by multivariate experimental approaches as ergs (page 27 above).

So long as "experiment" was interpreted in the narrow classical sense of bivariate manipulative experiment (see analyses, Cattell, 1966) psychologists could not investigate instinct and drive conflict in man in any powerful degree because of ethical objections. The spearhead of research consequently tended to glance off its true target into manipulative experiments with animals, and the enormous amount of publication here has contributed much, though it always suffers in the last resort—as human psychology—by a speculative translation from lower mammals to man.

The organization of research now urgently needed may be briefly indicated as:

(1) A substantial application of multivariate research to human motivation, finding the vital structures or "significant variables";

(2) A two-handed use of multi- and bivariate designs, using manipulation on variables established in humans by multivariate analysis where manipulation is possible and finding causal relations by superior statistics where it is not. Bivariate method can supplement, for example, by examining linearity of relations;

(3) A better translation between animal and human research by paralleling the multivariate work on humans by similar methods in animal research, at present virtually unknown. For example, animal psychologists assume that unitary drives such as hunger, thirst, sex, escape exist in animals but no testing of the assumption has been made (apart from the recent Dielman, Cattell, and Schneewind work) by factor analyses such as put distinct ergs "on the map" of human motivation. The typical conceptual range of good animal experiment to date can be illustrated for example by Young's work (Young and Greene, 1953) on the distinction between palatability and appetite. He has shown, using rats as subjects, that when dietary conditions are held constant, common foods arrange themselves into a preferential order from low to high palatability. Thus the *kind* of food has no necessary connection with palatability. His conclusion was that "intake of food does not increase any single motivational factor. And a critical factor in the situation is the possibility of choice." This kind of detail plays a very necessary supportive role within the broad knowledge of the erg of hunger.

Many problems, however, if strategically attacked, require a factor analytical method as the first step. Motives rarely, if ever, operate in isolation in real life situations, and it is sometimes pointless to take one variable, manipulate it and observe another dependent variable, because the interactive effect between the essential variables of behavior is more important to an understanding of that behavior than an isolated bit of information. Commonly, a variable belongs to a functional unity of interdependent variables such that manipulation of one affects them all. This is just the kind of problem with which factor analysis can cope. We can find the functional units and determine to what extent they contribute in given circumstances. Two further reasons for resorting to factor analysis as a first stage are, first, that bivariate research can be uneconomic and time consuming when several variables are handled serially, two by two. Factor analysis can encompass all the variables in one operation. Secondly, since considerations of ethics and privacy forbid certain manipulations involving human beings, factor analytical and similar procedures offer the chance of analyzing processes in naturally occurring unmanipulated but very important human experiences.

The above three proposals for coordinated advance of human and animal motivation research belong largely in the future; meanwhile in this chapter we must extract what we can from existing research, sometimes attempting to fit it to broader theories than those in which it was conceived. Actually a greater breadth is shown in the more recent rapidly developing branch of animal psychology called ethology than in the classical experimental approach, but here we shall consider the older and more extensive work first. Here the most popular subject for animal research has been the domesticated albino rat, and the extent to which we can generalize to human beings from the results of these researches is a constant source of dispute. Rarely have the researches attempted to substantiate some of the most fundamental assumptions involved in the dynamics of basic biological or social drives (see later for a multivariate approach to this question) e.g. their unitariness, degree of independence, and validity of measurement. In fact, many of the apparently simple experiments—and conclusions—have really quite complex assumptions. One such research will be described here as a demonstration of this point.

The relationship between "drive" and learning was first looked at by Yerkes and Dodson (1908) many years ago. Would there be a straightforward increase in learning as the drive level was increased? Would a rat learn a maze more quickly as one stepped up the level of hunger? In a long series of researches they came to the conclusion that the relationship was curvilinear— at first learning improves as drive level is increased, but gradually as the drive is increased even more, learning seems to reach a peak level and any additional drive strength piled on beyond this peak *reduces* the level of learning. A generalized graphic presentation of the Yerkes–Dodson law, as it is known, is shown in figure 5.1.

The most convincing evidence of this relationship was provided by Broadhurst (1957). Rats were trained to swim in an underwater maze in the shape of a Y. One arm of the Y was lit and gave access to the open air, whilst the other

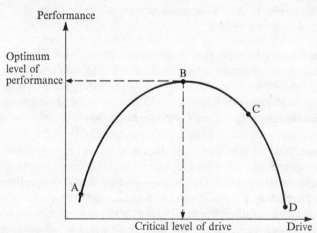

Figure 5.1 Idealized graphical presentation of the Yerkes–Dodson law

was dark and a dead-end. Four levels of motivation were created by sub-merging the rats for 0, 2, 4, and 8 seconds immediately before releasing them directly into the Y maze. The task was also controlled for level of difficulty by having three possible light intensities in the illuminated area of the maze. These were bright, moderate and very dull so that the latter was difficult (but not impossible) to discriminate from the dark arm of the maze. Figure 5.2

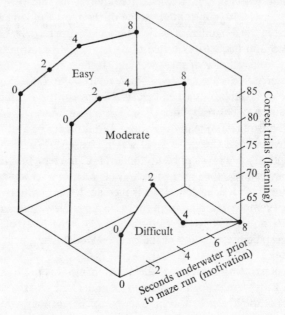

Figure 5.2 Graphical presentation of Broad-hurst's results

shows very neatly how the task performance varied with the difficulty of the task, performance being assessed by counting the number of correct trials displayed by the rats. With easy tasks, we are dealing with section AB of the Yerkes–Dodson graph in figure 5.1. Moderately difficult tasks might involve ABC and difficult tasks (where the rats had problems in trying to distinguish the closeness of light intensities) would involve ABCD or for that matter any portion of the curve beyond A.

In the light of what is becoming known about anxiety and motivation one may well question whether the Yerkes–Dodson law is conceptually correct. Complication of task often means frustration and the creation of anxiety. Cattell has suggested (Spielberger, 1972) that intensity of anxiety is essentially negatively related to goodness of most performances (motor, memorizing, deciding). Although it is known that complex performances (e.g. in intelligence tests) increase little with immediate motivation, the average performance is postulated to increase with motivation steadily, and not as supposed by the Yerkes–Dodson law. But increased motivation and increased anxiety are in most situations correlated, so, at a superficial view, it would appear that beyond a certain point increased motivation results in poorer performance. By formulae, we may say performance P is related to drive E and anxiety A, thus:

$$P = aE - bA \text{ (}a \text{ and } b \text{ being constants)}$$

But A is related to E along the lines of equations (4.7) and (4.9) above on conflict, which we may simplify to $A = EC$, where C is amount of frustration and complication producing conflict. Whence:

$$P = aE - b.EC$$

C can be independent of E, but in the pursuit of most complex goals, it is probably a function of E, which forces one onward into complexities. Consequently, the second term has really E^2, in it and a parabolic relation of performance P to ergic drive strength, E, ensues, explaining the Yerkes–Dodson curve without requiring the Yerkes–Dodson law's paradoxical quality.

2 Instincts, drives and ergs

As mentioned above, the doctrine of instincts in animals and man as postulated by McDougall (1908) has had a mixed reception over the years, especially when related to man. McDougall saw the arguments of Darwin as supporting his "hormic" or instinct theory—that animals and man are impelled by inborn urges to satisfy survival needs. These instincts were said to be innate, unlearned dispositions to behave in specific ways in response to various biological needs. The instincts characteristic of the higher animals were: food- (and water-) seeking, gregariousness, acquisitiveness, constructiveness, aggression, mating, curiosity, self-assertion, parental, repulsion, escape, and self-abasement. Later, McDougall used the term *propensity* as an alternative to instinct to avoid some of the criticisms levelled against the notion of man as a robot-like creature with little control over these innate dispositions, and various other faulty concepts. Burt (1941) elaborated the definition as a "complex inherited tendency, common to all members of a species, impelling each individual (a) to perceive and pay attention to certain objects and situations; (b) to become pleasurably and unpleasurably excited about those objects whenever they are perceived; (c) thereupon to act in a way likely in the long run to preserve the individual by so acting". Cattell's definition linking cognitive, affective, and conative innate tendencies is very similar (p. 199, 1950).

The definition of an erg

Final definition of an erg: *An innate psycho-physical disposition which permits its possessor to acquire reactivity (attention, recognition) to certain classes of objects more readily than others, to experience a specific emotion in regard to them, and to start on a course of action which ceases more completely at a certain specific goal activity than at any other. The pattern includes also preferred behavior subsidiation paths to the preferred goal.*

However, this rested on factor analytic demonstrations of the coherence, and it introduces the idea of relative ease of learning of certain connections (instead of "absolute instinct") in the concepts of *deflection strain* and long circuiting.[1] Incidentally, even in animal ethology the "instinct" is not nowadays regarded as being as rigid as when first conceived. The underlying emotional and political causes of the sociological (and reflexological) attack on innate predisposition belong to history, but in the thirty years in which "propensity" was taboo, psychologists were forced to retreat to the more concrete "bits" of behavior which they could substantiate before comprehensive multivariate methods came along to restore scientifically defensible perception of the whole. Thus Woodworth escaped opprobrium by retreating to the word "drive", defined as those internal processes (organic or physiological) which initiate, maintain, and regulate a person's actions. Another concept to do duty for propensity has been *homeostasis* (Cannon, 1932), already met with in chapter 3, relating to the return to physical and chemical stability which the body finds necessary for survival of the cells. When a deficiency occurs, as in food, air, and so on, the resulting disequilibrium from the steady state creates a *need* which (in some deficiencies) "drives" the individual to restore equilibrium. Murray (1938), from outside the experimental field, published, from clinical observation, a list of *needs*, their functional unity resting, however, on the unity of words in the dictionary. In the animal experimental domain, however, drive remained at a physiological level as the tension arising from homeostatic imbalance. We shall say more about the mechanism of this process in the next chapter when we consider the brain.

The search for basic drives (see Cofer and Appley, 1964) has taken several forms, but the three main approaches have been by biological deprivation, environmental stimulation and, in humans, the form of verbal communication. Deprivation research usually takes the form of withholding and manipulating the means whereby some characteristic biogenic activity of an organism is performed (food, water, sleep, sensory experiences, etc.) and noting the outcomes. Stimulation research involves applying pleasant or pain-producing agents (electric shocks, blast of air). The responses are frequently measured in

---

[1] Ten dynamic laws covered these relations of which the tenth is:

LAW 10. *Law of deflection strain. Modes of learned perception and response can be arranged in a gradient according to their degree of dispersion from the innately easiest path. Greater dispersion arises in alternatives established with greater deprivation and excitement in the original deprivation or blocking underlying learning, and is maintained thereafter with a greater degree of "deflection strain". This is shown, perhaps, in a permanently higher excitement level, and greater irritability, anxiety, and fatigue. The deflection strain of any given goal path must include, in any total assessment of it, the deflections and suppressions of other goal drives that this path incidentally occasions.*

terms of performance, e.g. speed and accuracy in running a maze, preferences
for different objects (food, mate) which will satisfy needs, and physiological
response measures of blood pressure, psychogalvanic reaction and observation
of behavior *in situ* (as in ethological studies).

Putting various bits of experimental evidence together in what, methodo-
logically, is still only a semi-intuitive process, the animal experimenters used
as concepts certain drives which they assumed to be common to man and
animals (many conclude the list is largely implied from common-sense obser-
vation rather than from logical integration of experiment). The major ones
stemming from biological needs are food- and water-seeking, pain avoidance,
maternal protectiveness, nesting, sucking and contact activities, respiration,
elimination, rest-seeking and mating. The work of Harlow (1959; Harlow and
Harlow, 1962) more imaginatively conceived than that of most animal experi-
menters, and extending to the primates has provided the most substantial
evidence for the nature of these drive elements in the total erg.

Several of the ergs, and of these drive elements, it will be noticed, are not
imperative for survival of the *individual* as such. Maternal activities and mating
can be, and are, completely absent in the life histories of some animals (domes-
ticated animals for instance) without causing death or injury but, of course,
normally, they are *race* preservative. A second, but less widely accepted, group
of drives are body activity, exploration, manipulation, curiosity, and orienta-
tion reaction (allied to attention) which appear to take their cue from external
stimulation. Some (Murray, 1964) have described them as intrinsic motives
because they appear to be engaged in for their own sake—they possess inherent
pleasure for the performer, but this, of course, is true of most ergs—whatever
their purpose they subjectively give pleasure. Others (Cofer and Appley, 1964)
are less certain that they can be distinguished from the basic drives alluded to
at the beginning of this section. Other possible drives or "goals" have been
posited and we have suggested several others in table 2.12 and in the research
on animal ergs to be dealt with later.

Having worked his way to the inevitable conclusion that innate drives—
elements of ergic patterns—exist, the experimental psychologist has proceeded
to numerous experiments dealing with questions of detail. Two such researches
will be briefly mentioned here to demonstrate the bivariate manipulation of
ergs. Hunger, both as a subject of research and as a means of motivating
creatures, is, of course, a well-substantiated erg. The "cafeteria" experiments
on food preferences amongst children to see if they will choose for themselves
a balanced diet and the various tests of specific hungers—deficiencies in a diet
which lead to the selective eating of foods containing the missing nutrient—are
well-known examples. Recently in a carefully devised research by Young and
Greene (1953), another factor seemed to intrude on the straightforward
specific hunger theory. Two groups of rats, who were food need-free (i.e. they
had not been starved) were given drinking tests. One group had 60 minutes in

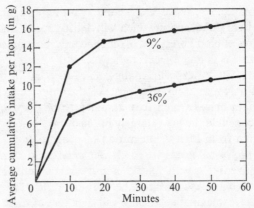

Figure 5.3 Average cumulative intake, in grams of fluid, of two sucrose solutions presented singly for a 60-minute test
Source: Young and Greene (1953).

the presence of a 9 percent sucrose solution and the other had 60 minutes with a 36 percent solution. Intake was recorded graphically. The figure 5.3 shows the results from which one might conclude that the 9 percent solution was preferred to the 36 percent solution. In fact, when the experiment was repeated by giving the rats a choice of two solutions, they invariably drank more of the 36 percent solution than the 9 percent. Young concludes that "intake depends upon at least two kinds of determinants—palatability and appetite. Hence intake does not measure any single motivational factor. And a critical factor in the situation is the *possibility of choice*" (italics by the present authors). Here by careful bivariate experiment Young hit on a truth quickly evident to multivariate methods, namely, that many bivariate experiments had been measuring a mixture of motivational components when they thought they were scoring for a single concept. A similar conclusion was reached by Haverland (1954) by factoring the hunger drive in rats, where he discovered that the most sacred bivariate "operational measure"—hours of food deprivation—was a relatively poor measure of the unitary hunger tension factor. From motivational component measures both on humans (Cattell, Radcliffe, and Sweney 1963; also Cattell and Horn, 1963) and on rats (Cattell and Dielman, 1973) this multiple expression is seen to hold not just in relation to one erg but across most, making the multivariate approach essential.

A second example is taken from the research on conflict in animals as a result of pitting one erg against another (e.g. food and water or food and fear of being shocked). Warden (1931) studied the frequency with which rats would run over an electrical obstruction (delivering an electrical shock) in order to reach a variety of incentives, namely, a litter, water, food, a mate, or exploration. Most of these were compared in twos or threes so that the number of times a mother rat with a litter would cross an electrified grid to get to her young in a given time might be compared with the number of crossings in the same time for a mate or exploration. Hunger versus sex preferences showed a higher preference for food. A tentative ranking was established of maternal, thirst, hunger, sex, and exploration. This rank has been challenged and it would seem to the authors that the only viable way of comparing these ergs is by some multivariate method whereby the strengths of the ergs can be measured in terms of the proper weights for each behavior in estimating factors of intensity of ergic tension in a proper sample of situations.

3 The search for motivation components and dynamic structure in animal behavior In chapters 1 and 2 we outlined the findings from several factor analytical researches showing that human attitudes (using attitude as a dynamic response in the new sense defined in chapter 1) are an expression of more complex, but fundamental, and dynamic structure factors which we called ergs and sentiments. Very little work objectively establishing dynamic structure has been undertaken using infrahuman subjects. Anderson (1937 and 1938) using correlation techniques attempted to find unitary ergic patterns in rats and was able to show high *correlation clusters* for behaviors involving thirst, sex interest, and curiosity (exploration), each cluster showing the unitariness of an erg. A second study by Haverland (1954) submitted rats to various interest measures applied to food and water. As might have been expected, oblique simple structure did give two substantial factors, easily recognizable as hunger and thirst drives.

Apart from these exploratory studies, there has not been a new definitive attempt until the last ten years when Cattell and his associates began to look at the motivated behavior of domesticated albino rats. The main purpose of the research was to replicate the general pattern of investigation used in human motivation experiments with the intention of seeing whether similar motivational components and dynamic structures exist in these animals. The gains to be expected from animal subjects are (a) simpler organisms are less likely to be affected by cultural influences; (b) drives in animals are more widely researched, thus if the ergs of human research can be found in animals this will lend strong support to believing in innate ergic origins in humans; (c) the possibilities of manipulating learning situations more effectively in rats could enable us to *create sentiments* by exposing the animals to prearranged environmental situations likely to enhance sentiment formation; (d) discerning patterns of sentiment structure by differential rewards, repetition, etc. It has been *assumed* that these sentiment patterns in humans—patterns which do not look innate but match the patterns of social institutions—are learned. Animal experiment would give a chance to show this in a way not possible with humans; (e) the universality of both (i) ergic dynamic structures and (ii) the motivational components by which interest strength is measured, across animals and man, can be put to the test; and (f) where cross-identification is found, manipulative designs can be carried out using animals where similar procedures could not be used with humans.

The basic design (Cattell and Dielman, 1973) was to begin with some 134 rats, all trained to a prearranged criterion in running a maze. The maze consisted of several obstacles and activities required by the rat in its attempt to reach the goal box. A plan of the maze is shown in figure 5.4 and the corresponding variables making up the equivalent of the devices used in human studies are in table 5.1. Devices include speed of running in corridors, time to force a way through a paper barrier, quickness of bar pressing, and so on. Some attempt was made to find behaviors which would parallel the human devices, for example the "Preferences" device might be choice of door or lack of errors, decision speed might be time of decision at the various door barriers. Some measures were *directly* comparable as in pulse change measures. These same devices were used for measurement across three different ergs and two sentiments. The ergs were chosen to give viscerogenic, and nonviscerogenic examples in the shape of thirst, gregariousness, and fear from electric shock. They also gave a range of aversive and attractive ergs. The learned sentiment patterns were created by extra reward and repetition (given to half the rats in particular mazes, i.e. a sentiment was a maze). Ergic tension levels were created by having two levels of deprivation in each of the three ergs and two levels of learning (of reward, of frequency, and of both). In all, there were six dynamic factors and several mazes possessing the devices of table 5.1.

The aim was now to have the animals seen at different ergic tension levels, some more, some less thirsty and similarly for fear and gregariousness. Then the 36 or more diverse possible manifestations of drive strength—speed of running, thrust against doors, speed of decision, freedom from errors in the Skinner box—were to be factor analyzed to see if distinct motivation components came out as in humans. Secondly, a search was planned to check the hypothesis about a unitary dynamic structure for each erg (thirst, gregariousness, fear) and each sentiment. To make this possible the animals in maze 1 ran under conditions of gregariousness, fear, and practice, maze 2—gregariousness, reward, and practice and maze 3—thirst, gregariousness and reward. Factor analysis to simple structure in the first domain—manifestations of motivation components strength—across three mazes followed by tests of congruence between the three occasions revealed eight of the thirteen extracted factors having consistent and replicable structure across all occasions. Four were hypothesized as "ability" however, and only four as true motivational factors. Table 5.2 portrays a summary of these eight factors as well as the outcome of a second-order analysis the results of which are interpreted as approximating to the U and I components established using human subjects.

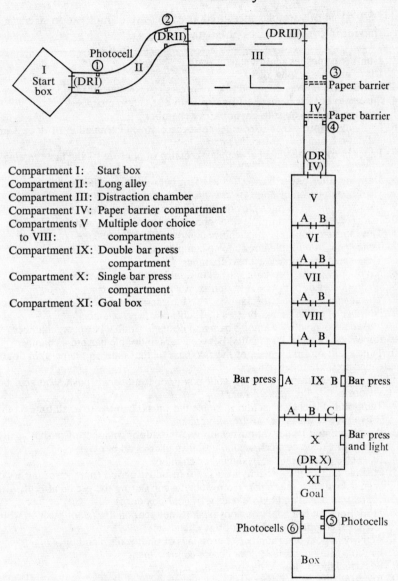

Compartment I: Start box
Compartment II: Long alley
Compartment III: Distraction chamber
Compartment IV: Paper barrier compartment
Compartments V   Multiple door choice
   to VIII: compartments
Compartment IX: Double bar press
                 compartment
Compartment X: Single bar press
                 compartment
Compartment XI: Goal box

Figure 5.4 Maze design

Source: Dielman, Cattell, and Kawash (1971).

Table 5.1 List of variables measured as expressive of motivation strength in rat behavior in complex mazes (use with figure 5.4)

1. Number of pushes against start box door
2. Running time in long alley
3. Vacillations in long alley (number of excessive crossings of photocells 1 and 2)
4. Susceptibility to distraction (time spent in distraction chamber)
*5. Pushing time on door to paper barrier chamber
6. Dallying before paper barrier (time spent between completion of door 3 and final crossing of photocell 3)
7. Paper barrier time (time between last crossing of photocell 3 and first crossing of photocell 4)
8. Dallying after paper barrier (time spent between first crossing of photocell 4 and completion of door 4)
9. Incorrect pushes in multiple door choice compartment 1 and 2
10. Incorrect pushes in multiple door choice compartments 3 and 4
*11. Time spent in multiple door choice compartments 1 and 2
*12. Time spent in multiple door choice compartments 3 and 4
*13. Time spent in double bar press chamber
14. Number of premature door pushes in double bar press chamber
15. Wrong order of bar presses in double bar press chamber
16. Wastage of time and effort between two bar presses in double bar press chamber
17. Number of excessive bar presses in double bar press chamber
*18. Impatient overactivity among bars and doors in double bar press chamber
19. Repetitious uncertainty (shifts) between bars in double bar press chamber
20. Time spent on first presses of the two bars (actual time on the bars) in double bar press chamber
21. Entirely premature pushes on goal box door (number of pushes on goal box door before first press on bar C)
22. Temporal efficiency of action in single bar press chamber (overall time on first five presses in single bar press chamber)
23. Premature and irrelevant pushes on goal box door (number of pushes against goal box door between second and fifth presses on bar C)
24. Excessive presses on bar in single bar chamber
25. Pushing and shifting activity in delayed response period (number of pushes on goal box door and shifts from door to bar during the period after the fifth press on bar C and before release of goal box door)
26. "Fiddling" on last goal box door push (time spent on final door push on which animal completed single bar press chamber)
27. Activity in goal box (number of crossings of photocells 5 and 6)
†28. Backtracking in multiple door choice compartment
29. Backtracking in double bar press compartment
30. Backtracking in single bar press compartment
31. Total grooming
*32. Total number of turn-backs
*33. Force used to open door to long alley
34. Force used to open door to goal box
35. Time fraternizing in goal box
†36. Successful removal of paper barrier

Source: Dielman, Cattell, and Kawash (1971). * and † see bottom of page 125.

The first second-order factor in each maze situation consists of the same primary components of "Goal box activity" and "Vacillation" and these have been hypothesized as motivational components. They appear to be analogous to the unintegrated motivation factor U characterized by general unorganized ergic tension. The second factor in each maze possesses (in two cases) the first-order components of "Low distractability", "Paper barrier ability", and "Discrimination efficiency", the latter two being hypothesized as ability factors. Note the negative loading of distractability coupled with high ability factors gives the impression of a generally well-integrated motivation factor not unlike the I component of human research. The remaining factors, whilst they have been tentatively interpreted (Cattell and Dielman, 1973), need to be replicated in a second factor analysis before theories are seriously developed around them.

Some support for regarding two of the above primary factors as motivational came from a further study of these data using manipulation methods. The theory accounting for the distinct motivational components in humans includes the notion that some represent primarily the component from inner deprivation and others a contribution from the strength of stimulation in the environment. The results are not yet fully analyzed but indicate that the motivational components indeed respond differently to inner and outer conditions.

Finally this extensive and novel animal experiment was planned to be factored for evidence on the hypothesized drive and sentiment dynamic structure factors, but lack of funds called this to a halt. Another aspect of the total design was an analysis of genetic elements in drive, which was catered for by having differences in the genetic strain of the animals (there being equal numbers of Sprague–Dawley and Holtzman strains). Substantiated genetic differences were in fact found, particularly in two factors, "distractability" and "purposefulness", i.e. two of the motivational factors.

Although the analysis of sentiment patterns in the above experiment is still to be undertaken, other evidence points to their existence among animals experiencing differential culturation. The work of Harlow (1959) and his associates on the "contact" comfort sought by infant monkeys demonstrates this point. He designed two substitute mothers, one a plain wire structure with a milk bottle protruding from the front, the other, made in the same shape as the first, was surrounded by a cloth cover. These were placed side by side in the cage with the young monkey. The monkeys invariably chose the cloth surrogate (substitute) mother. They would cling to the substitute and when feeding would reach across, still holding on to the cloth substitute, and feed.

---

* Deleted from maze 3 analysis.

† Due to a change in coding in the maze 3 analysis variable 36 was inserted as variable 28 in the 36 variable master list (consequently becoming variables 23 in the maze 3 list) which moves the numbering of all subsequent variables ahead by one.

Table 5.2 Second-order primary factor patterns showing agreement of patterns of motivation component expression in different mazes with different ergs involved.

Primary motivation component factors*	Maze 1					Maze 2					Maze 3				
	I	II	III	IV	V	I	II	III	IV	V	I	II	III	IV	V
M1. Distractability	06	[-49]	43	-09	-10	04	[-57]	03	08	-05	-07	[-55]	07	-01	-01
M2. Purposefulness	-10	-03	70	34	57	02	03	08	61	14	06	-05	12	77	09
M3. Goal box activity	[-47]	-10	-60	-04	-01	[-68]	09	-11	06	-40	[-30]	10	14	41	-22
A4. Accuracy in bar pressing	11	03	05	-09	75	08	06	11	-15	17	-01	07	-08	07	56
A5. Door choice accuracy	02	04	15	60	-05	04	06	56	13	06	-14	-05	-01	26	-17
M6. Vaccilation	[-57]	04	12	-03	-06	[-62]	-06	17	-11	09	[-62]	-08	-01	10	06
A7. Paper barrier ability	03	[75]	06	-10	04	02	[12]	-07	11	69	-32	[48]	09	-28	03
A8. Discrimination efficiency	-09	[28]	12	-31	-10	21	[23]	27	-09	08	05	08	45	12	-07

* The *M*'s are judged indubitably motivational in nature, but the *A*'s could be individual difference ability or temperament factors among rats.

□ Significant loadings showing similarity of pattern.

When frightened the babies would leap onto the cloth model. Harlow refers to this phenomenon as contact comfort. This is probably a compounding of the ergs of security and appeal.

However, the outcome of these researches showed that most of the monkeys subjected to this kind of rearing did not develop normal social activities. Their sexual interest was minimal and they seemed unable to carry out mating successfully. They had little or no time for other monkeys and did not play with them when in the same cage. Harlow also observed that there seemed to be a critical time in the development within which the aberrant behavior was most likely to be established. This critical period occurred between the third and sixth month after birth. Isolation with surrogate mothers only up to three months did not have a lasting effect. Actually this can be seen as an example either of the acquired sentiment formation towards fellow creatures being moulded by the circumstances and in the course of satisfying basic ergs such as food-seeking, protection, and security, or as an effect upon the inner maturation of the drive. In the equation for an ergic tension level (page 73) a term H was hypothesized from the beginning which expressed the past history of the drive (as in Harlow's experiment, or a fixation from trauma in Freudian psychology) in terms of maturational influence on the drive strength as such.

4 Ethology— The study of animal behavior in nature

The concept of instinct in animals, and to some extent in man, has persisted with least vicissitudes from Darwinian beginnings in the work of ethologists. Of all the students of animal behavior, the ethologists come closest, in principle, to an awareness of the multivariate design, even though they usually stop short of quantitative correlational analyses. Their patient observations of behavior *in situ*, i.e. in natural conditions, is alert to total response patterns in ergs such as mating or territorial and paternal protection. In such creatures as birds, for example, natural selection has favored those which have built-in instinctual responses to solve threatening situations as opposed to having to wait for learning to take place. Baby birds who did not instinctually perform the ritual of pointing upwards and opening their beaks when the nest is visited by a parent bird would die of starvation; similarly the first cries of danger must bring immediate, unlearned response from the young of many creatures for preservation. The chief characteristic of instinctive response is the rigid pattern of behavior evoked by simple stimulus.

Ethology owes much to the work of Lorenz and Tinbergen who have devoted the better part of the last forty years to the subject. Two especially important notions introduced by them are the *innate release mechanism* (IRM) and *sign stimuli*. Tinbergen defines IRM as a "special neurosensory mechanism that releases the reaction and is responsible for its selective susceptibility to a very special combination of sign stimuli" . . . Built into the stimulus–response mechanism are two further features. First is the sign stimulus which takes the form of an external stimulus possessing properties which arouse or motivate a creature to action. Well-known examples are a male robin's breast, presentation of which is used as a threat sign to other male robins in the territory. Also closely recorded are the antics of a stickleback protecting its territory against intruders. The young of the herring-gull are drawn to pick at a small red patch on the bill of the mother and this elicits a feeding response from the mother. Second, these perceptual objects are known as "releasers" (Lorenz) because the signal system releases a pattern of response of survival value. Releasers can be used by one animal (say a male of the species) in order to provoke an IRM response from another (a female of the same species).

An immediate resemblance becomes evident between the ethologist's IRM patterns and the subsidiation chain in the dynamic lattice in human behavior described in chapter 2, though the former is viewed as innate and the latter as learned from environmental experience. This is not the first instance of such parallelism, nor need it surprise us, since the acquisition by a species of an hereditary pattern by trial and error is formally similar to learning. Consequently, the same mathematical models are likely to suit both. The discovery of ergic and sentiment patterns in man has initially been by cross-sectional factoring, but the attitudes linked by loadings are actually sequential on the dynamic lattice and the factoring of animal behavior *in situ* would be expected to end up with precisely the same entities as the ethologist's IRM's. The prime example of ethologists seems to be the nest-building habits of many birds which follow a fairly set routine such as making a firm foundation of twigs, building up the sides, producing a lining and a cup at the bottom, etc. Each successive stage is dependent on the last as a trigger in the progress of the chain of events. Each stage has its own appetitive quality and consummatory act. The ergic goals in the case of nest-building are probably mating and protectiveness.

The territorial and mating rituals of the male stickleback offer a splendid example of the interplay of ergs. The following diagram gives a rough idea of the mechanisms displayed by the male and the female responses (where these are appropriate). Of special interest in this two-way interplay of innate release mechanisms following on the sign stimuli is the regularity of the process and the appearance of particular ergs as the ritual unfolds. Pugnacity and protectiveness are the key ergs in the early stage of territorial demarcation and nest-building. Then the mating urge induces the male to seek and attract a female to the nest. During this stage, there is every possibility that the male will make as if to attack the female. Thus the zig-zag dance has been described as an alternation between leading to the nest and attacking against trespassers, in this case the "trespasser" being the matured female who is ready to follow the male.

Male pattern	Female pattern

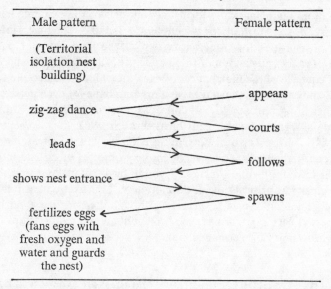

(Territorial
  isolation nest
  building)

zig-zag dance ———— appears
                    courts
leads ————   follows
shows nest entrance
                    spawns
fertilizes eggs ←
(fans eggs with
fresh oxygen and
water and guards
the nest)

Largely by analogy from these animal studies, Lorenz has built up a series of parallel IRM's in human beings. For example, the sight of a doll (sign stimulus) is seen by him to elicit maternal behavior from girls and even from women. Further, he believes that it is the pattern of stimulation which brings about the release in the form of the doll's short face, large forehead, chubby cheeks and disjointed limb movements—exaggeratedly reminiscent of a true baby's features.

The result of the independent approach to ergs by the ethologists can be represented by Tinbergen's postulation of six instinctual patterns in man, namely, patterns of locomotion, sexual behavior, sleep, food-seeking, care of the body surface, and parenthood. Lorenz would add social and aggressive drives to this list. Lunzer (1968) carries the argument a step further by suggesting that man too has an inborn set of IRM's, but that they differ from animals in being much more susceptible to modification. He has likened the process to a computer system which possesses a program of instruction for the input (stimulus reception). The "data" are not fed directly to the program, but are "read" first (the process of perception). Lunzer now hypothesizes that the program is modified in the light of the filtered incoming data. He also sees the organism as an active initiator of behavior sequences—not as passive receptors as seems to be implied by stimulus–response systems—and these sequences are programmed from birth (nervous and endocrine systems) to channel reactions to stimuli and to modify the program in the light of experience (learning). No two programs are identical (natural variation) and those "blueprints" which are very similar, e.g. in monozygotic twins at birth, can be differently modified by individual experiences. This model fits in excellently with the more mathematically formalized models of the dynamic lattice and the learning process formulated in chapters 2, 3, and 4. The blueprints consist of ergic propensities for preservation whilst the final habitual paths—the engrams—for the satisfaction of these ergic goals are developed and acquired as a consequence of the life-chances of each individual. No two life-styles are the same and the lattice thus takes on a unique shape for each person.

Another important ethological concept is that of *imprinting*. It appears in many animal species and especially birds (Lorenz, 1952, *King Solomon's Ring*; Hess, 1964). During a critical stage in the early life of the animal, it acquires a mother–child attachment to a nearby moving object. Lorenz and most of his associates have frequently "fostered" young birds by making sure they were present during the critical time of development. This fixation has not yet been evaluated in human or primate species, although the evidence so far hints at a critical period necessary for normal social contact and relationships (Bowlby, 1956; Harlow and Zimmerman, 1959).

5   Conflict in animals

Frustration and stress are experienced by animals probably at least as much as by man. However, the animal's restricted power of conceptualization, and the comparatively limited areas in which he is compelled to practice restraint, probably make long-drawn inner conflict, such as generates neurosis, less frequent. (At least Whitman, in his poem on animals, thought so!) However, the possibilities of studying conflict in animals of a restricted kind, have been extensively followed up by both ethology and classical experiment. One or two illustrations of conflict study as in watching an intruder approaching a territorial area or the experimental study of obstruction in comparing the strengths of ergs have been given. The reason for the rapid resolution of conflict in nature is probably that when territorial rights, mates, or a food find are being defended, the vanquished have learned that "he who fights and runs away, lives to fight another day".

One sees amusing to-ing and fro-ing across a defended area between adjacent animals who alternately fight and chase a neighbor from their quarters to find themselves in the territory of the opposition and thence on the receiving end of the situation. Attack and escape finally defines the boundary between neighboring territories.

Body damage is rarely the outcome of these disputes. The loser disappears before this can happen. Alternatively, some species have developed *appeasement* postures in response to threat *displays* so that the process of territorial demarcation or parental protectiveness becomes a pantomime of displays on the one hand (colour display on wings, chest, head, body movements) and appeasement postures on the other (turning away, offering the jugular vein as in wolf stocks and dogs).

Tense situations often give rise to *displacement* activities. This consists of behavior patterns suddenly introduced into a conflicting event which seem irrelevant to the immediate solution of the conflict. This we met in human conflict in discussing the Adjustment Process Analysis chart where at chiasm D one route was the psychodynamic sublimation or deflection of a desire to some alternative solution. Feeding movements in the middle of a bout of fighting occurs in sticklebacks and many birds including the domesticated hen; preening and grooming are also common displacement actions.

Nature, then, has provided many ways of resolving the important problems of self-preservation and procreation without causing excessive conflict or too great a risk of damage to individual animals. Consequently it may be the neurotic conditions amongst animals are largely a laboratory phenomenon. Such researches as those of Maier and the follow-up work on Pavlov's "experimental neurosis" do show a range of abnormal reactions to induced conflict—although the similarity to human reactions (as in the last chiasms and developments of the Adjustment Process Analysis in chapter 3) is questionable apart from the aggression symptoms in response to frustration. The technique of Pavlov, that is conditioning an animal to respond to one stimulus and to avoid a second, followed by gradually making the stimuli for the conflicting responses the same (ellipse ↔ circle) has created marked signs of stress, raised blood pressure, and produced violence. Masserman (1950) used cats to create a similar reaction in his animals; they developed symptoms of withdrawal, great stress and gastric disorders which took many months to clear after the conflict was removed. The researches of Brady (1958) into "executive" monkeys is a further demonstration of conflict producing physical symptoms. Two monkeys were saddled side-by-side. An electric shock was delivered to both of them, but one (the executive) was able to prevent the shock, provided he pressed a button within a certain time after seeing a flashing light, whereas the other had no option but to sit there and take the shocks. The outcome was an ulcerous condition for the "executive" monkey and no apparent symptom for the other monkey who had received just as many shocks as the first.

Aggressive behavior in animals is very much related to territory delineation and maintenance. The evidence for it being inborn is not conclusive, although its presence in most animal species is a fact. Aggression is also frequently shown in guarding young from predators and strangers, holding on to food (dogs with bones get very annoyed at intruders), and establishing pecking orders. Cattell has suggested with several specific examples that the tradition of using the popular, undifferentiated term "aggression" has held up scientific solutions of obscurities in the dynamic field. Multivariate experiment with humans clearly shows two distinct ergs in the domain: pugnacity, with anger as its emotion, and with destruction, or even sadism, as its goal and the self-assertive erg, with vaunting pride as its emotion and achievement and eminence as its goal. The latter, it is true, is apt to lead to situations which end in pugnacity (but also does sex and to some degree all ergs) but intrinsically it is not pugnacious and destructive. Thus when Dollard and others (1939) gave an early twist to the field with the so-called frustration–aggression hypothesis, they not only overlooked the careful analysis existing in McDougall (1926) separating pugnacity and self-assertiveness, but also set off on a wrong track in the light of the latest factor analytic findings on ergs. In any case, as Cofer and Appley (1964) point out, pugnacity is not the necessary consequence of frustration, and the lucid analysis by Cartwright and Cartwright (1971) shows why this is so. However, it seems true that the natural first provocation for pugnacity is the thwarting of any other erg in the course of its satisfaction. The provocative stimulus for self-assertiveness is very different—usually self-abasement in another person or clear evidence of superior performance in the self. Whether the result of thwarting will *remain* pugnacity or pass to anxiety, depression, phantasy, etc., depends on the lawful connections with event sequences set out in *adaptation process analysis* (Cattell and Scheier, 1961; Cartwright and Cartwright, 1971).

Psychological discussions of pugnacity have been thrust into prominence by debates between those who claim there is a natural "appetite" for war and those who see it as a socioeconomic accident of frustrations. We have already made a tentative distinction (page 119) between appetitive and nonappetitive ergs (not to be entirely aligned with Murray's viscerogenic and nonviscerogenic), and have tentatively put both fear (escape) and pugnacity among the nonappetitive. Certainly it would appear that the strength of aroused pugnacity is usually a direct function of the strength of the erg frustrated. If this is verified it would seem there is no need to assume any appetitive need to satisfy pugnacity. However, this is not much comfort to whoever wishes to deny any inevitable psychological cause for war, since abolishing frustration would be extremely difficult! However, pugnacity is only one possible end result from an initial frustration.

6   Appetitive and consummatory behavior

Three broad stages have often been posited to describe goal-oriented behavior from the stage of searching ("appetitive" behavior) through the act of satisfying the appetite (consummatory behavior) to a period of quiescence after the goal has been achieved. Food-seeking, eating, and satiation provide an obvious chain of behaviors illustrating the above. Often sub-goals are present, each having their own appetitive, consummatory, and quiescent stage, and leading to a further sub-goal. The mating of sticklebacks and nest-building in birds offer examples of releaser sequences of this kind.

Mention was made in chapter 3 that consummatory behavior may, of itself, be satisfying, even when the physiological goal, e.g. nourishment, normally present is not present. In other words, the act of attempting to satisfy a need may temporarily give satisfaction even when the objective of appetitive behavior (food, liquid, ejaculation) has not been obtained. This possibility is partly in conflict with Hull's Drive-Reduction Theory of Reinforcement (1943) which holds that the behavior of organisms only becomes repeated when it has been instrumental in satisfying needs and thereby reducing drives. A consummatory act which does not lead to need reduction is therefore less likely to be repeated. However, such acts are an inevitable part of satisfaction (eating movements, swallowing, copulation, and so forth) and always take place as part of the need-reduction process, and it seems most likely that the consummatory process itself becomes part of appetitive appeasement. For this reason, the term $(N_k - b\bar{G}_k)$ was introduced into the ergic tension equation on page 73, $\bar{G}$ being the nonphysiological, behavioral tension redirection.

Support for this latter part comes mainly from the work of Sheffield and coworkers (1951) who used the peculiar copulatory pattern of the male rat as a device. Male rats mount their females at heat, perform copulatory movements without ejaculation, and then dismount. This takes place perhaps a dozen times before the first ejaculation. Sheffield took young, maturing rats who had never copulated and placed them in a situation presenting a hurdle in order to reach a goal box. The goal box contained either a female in heat or a male companion. Copulation was permitted without ejaculation during the early stages of entry into the goal box, with the female and the male removed. Two other groups consisting of controls and noncopulators were used with which to compare the speed of running the distance from the start to the goal box. The results clearly showed that the rats who had copulated without ejaculation, i.e. had performed consummatory activity without attaining a goal, and without any previous experience of copulation, still received some reward from the act and ran faster towards the goal box. Sheffield thence concluded that the consummatory act itself was sufficient to bring about reinforcement.

An entirely different approach by Janowitz and Grossman (1949) using dogs gives less encouragement to those who support the consummatory hypothesis. They inserted a tube into the esophagus of several dogs so as to permit any food eaten to fall out before reaching the stomach. In addition, they could be fed directly into the stomach without consummatory acts of grasping, chewing, and swallowing. Starved dogs were then "fed" by food going directly into the stomach until full. The dogs behaved as if they were satisfied and did not attempt to eat food presented to them. On the other hand, a "fistulated" dog (food passes out of a fistula in its esophagus before reaching the stomach) continues to sham-eat long after it has taken in enough food to fill its stomach. Bellows (1939) carried out similar research with drinking in dogs and came up with much the same results. From this it appears that some consummatory acts in some ergs are not sufficient of themselves to reduce ergic tension. But a glance at the ergic tension equation will show (see chapter

6 also) that allowance can be made for an increase or decrease in the tension present in consummation.

On common-sense grounds one concludes there must be some fairly immediate process of feedback to the brain in order to prevent an organism from excessive consummatory activity which is unaccompanied by satisfaction. Digestion is a slow process and to wait for the blood composition to change sufficiently for the brain, i.e. the hypothalamus, to register satisfaction would take much longer than is at present apparent in normal consummatory behavior. There may, of course, be limits of consummation such that eating or drinking regularly take place over a given time during which roughly the same quantities are imbibed. With Sheffield's rats, they had never satisfied the particular sex erg involved and would not be aware of an "average" consummatory requirement. The kinds of physiological mechanisms giving almost immediate feedback include stomach distension, receptors in the throat in drinking, and ejaculation in sexual activity. These mechanisms prevent overindulgence and excessive expenditure of energy.

7   Summary

1. Although animal motivation is of scientific interest in itself the main reason psychologists have used animals in motivation research is that they are believed to have characteristics in common with human beings. The advantages of using them include the increased possibility of manipulation research in those aspects of behavior common to animals and man. By and large, however, animal motivation research started off with traditional bivariate "instrument" methods and although much knowledge has accumulated, the interactive analyses have awaited the findings which multivariate study can give.

2. The Darwinian and early ethological (McDougall) conclusions about instinct were not sufficiently experimentally documented to withstand the emotionally powerful environmentalist attack by Watson and sociologists early in this century. Concepts of propensities gave way to limited and sometimes vaguer notions of drives, a general need for homeostatic appetites, "needs", etc. Bivariate experiment with animals, observations in ethology, and multivariate experiment with humans, however, have brought back a more precise conception of ergic structures as indispensable to dynamic psychology.

3. A recent advance in animal experimentation has been the application of multivariate designs parallel to those which revealed motivation component and dynamic structure factors in man. One purpose has been to bring these under manipulative experiments should they be shown to be homologous with those in man.

4. In the motivation component field the expressions of motivation strength in rats are in fact found to parallel those in humans in number, and in being independent of the particular erg, sentiment, or drive involved. At higher order

analysis equivalents of integrated and unintegrated components in humans appear. The integrated component consisted of Low distractability, Paper barrier ability, and Discrimination efficiency. The negative loading on Distractability coupled with these other ability variables gave a general impression of integrated motivation; whereas the unintegrated component was hypothesized for the factor containing Goal box activity and Vacillation, both of which are motivation-like components and perhaps more characteristic of unintegrated, unorganized ergic tension.

5. Research on dynamic structures yielded approximately the number of factor structures expected from the drives introduced into the experiment, but the results on this large-scale experiment are still not rotated and resolved. Meanwhile, however, Haverland has shown that hunger and thirst in rats are separable as two distinct factors and that classical methods of estimating their strength are not as valid as factor score estimates would be.

6. The methods of ethology favor the holistic approach by observing animal behavior in its natural, or near natural, state in an effort to formulate patterns of behavior relating to animal ergs such as food-seeking, mating, parenthood, aggression, and so forth. Ethologists point to a parallel between the sign stimuli and Innate Release Mechanisms (IRM's) of animal species and some human activities, and it is evident that IRM's could be formally represented with precision by the same model as is used for human subsidiation chains in the dynamic lattice.

7. Frustration and conflict are present in animal life-styles, although their resolution is frequently rapid and satisfactory, i.e. neurotic conditions are probably, in nature, rare. This occurs because the processes of courtship, home-building, feeding, territorial protection, etc., are hedged in with rituals of display, appeasement, and aggressive postures which carry a well-recognized message within a given species thus obviating the need for actual combat and body damage. Laboratory-made conflict, on the other hand, tends to produce signs of stress, withdrawal, aggression, and so on, not normally found in the wild state. These have given some clues to conflict and frustration reactions in humans.

8. The cycle of appetitive, consummatory and quiescent behavior are typical of goal-oriented action. Sometimes we find complex chains of subgoals each having their own particular cluster of behaviors, but leading on, as in the IRM concept of animal life, to some final objective. The evidence for considering consummatory action without achieving a goal as being a source of need-reduction is conflicting. Nevertheless, some allowance has been made for this possibility in the ergic tension equation in the form of the $(N_k - b\bar{G}_k$ term.

6 Motivation related to physiology and neurology

1 Appetitive regulation: the hypothalamus There is a satisfying concreteness about the brain, in contrast to the mind, which has led psychologists when overwhelmed by the complexity of behavior to take refuge in physiology and neurology. Actually the refuge is illusory, since the complications are virtually as great. But in any case it behoves the psychologist and the brain and endocrine physiologist to keep close company in their investigations for each can help the other at crucial theoretical points. This was shown, for example, in a classical case in the ability field, where Spearman's statistical behavioral theory of "g" and Lashley's law of neural mass action gave evidence that both were on the right track.

Similarly in the field of motivation and emotional expression physiological psychology, as represented in animal experiments and in clinical and experimental evidence on humans, have built substantial support for concepts reached by the structural analysis of behavior. For example, it has long been known that the lower brain has centers which provoke patterns of emotional expression identifiable with those found accompanying specific ergs, and that endocrine expressions parallel those found by the factor analysis of anxiety and anger states. More recently the work of Hess, Olds, and others has located points in the mid-brain the electrical stimulation of which provokes the specific unitary ergic drives we have located at the behavioral level by multivariate experiment.

Since the student cannot be assumed to have detailed knowledge of brain anatomy or the biochemistry of hormones, our treatment must necessarily be in approximate and somewhat simplified terms. But the individual student who wishes to follow this up will find a very substantial literature on brain damage, brain, nerve, and glandular abnormalities, brain experiments with animals, subtle biochemical analyses of endocrine action, neurological studies of the vegetative nervous system, and chemical and electrical stimulation studies on the intact brain, which now integrate well with behavioral analyses in psychology (Milner, 1970; Grossman, 1973).

It has long been recognized that a part of the brain tucked away under the mass of the cortex—the hypothalamus—is especially concerned with emotional, dynamic, impulsive behavior, and that the cortex, particularly the connections with the frontal lobes, exercise some control over these expressions. Thus damage to the frontal lobes leads to less control of hypothalamus behavior, in both senses—lack of emotional control and lethargic lack of "prodding" to act when external stimulus is lacking. Various clues suggested the origins of drive actions, in response to body needs—food- and water-seeking and sex activity—are also located here. As long ago as the 1930s, Hess (1931, 1936) inserted electrode probes into the anterior regions of the hypothalamus to discover localization of certain body functions such as rest, recovery, digestion, and elimination. Figure 6.1 shows a side view of the brain with the approximate location of the hypothalamus in relation to other well-known parts.

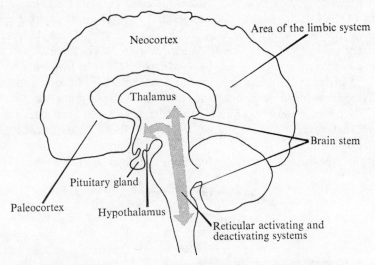

Figure 6.1   Brain areas important in emotional motivation
Source: Murray (1964).

Hetherington and Ranson (1940, 1942) using a fine cutting instrument, were able to produce lesions in the ventromedial nucleus of the hypothalamus. This resulted in the animals (rats in this case) becoming obese because the satiation response region of the hypothalamus had been destroyed by the lesions and the animals therefore ate relentlessly. Return to normal, presumably by new areas taking over, is possible, but very slow, taking several months. On the other hand, if this region is momentarily stimulated with an electrical probe, the animal, if it is feeding, will immediately stop, thus fortifying the view that it is a satiation structure. There appear to be several routes by which the hypothalamus can be stimulated. One theory (Mayer's glucostatic theory, 1953) maintains that feeding control occurs via changes in glucose concentration in the blood stream operating upon the hypothalamic neurons, although this process would be slow in comparison with the usual time it takes for a person to feed and feel satisfied. Stomach response (by distension) and the consequent transmission of impulses to the hypothalamus is another possibility. There may also be a relationship between brain temperature, which accompanies the intake of food, and satiation (Brobeck, 1957).

Another part of the hypothalamus, the lateral hypothalamus, if destroyed will give rise to the condition known as aphagia. The animal is unable to eat or drink and ultimately will die unless force-fed (Anand and Brobeck, 1951). We have, then, a feeding centre which, like the ventromedial nucleus, receives stimulation from the changes in blood sugar concentration and decreases in the brain temperature. There is, therefore, good reason to believe that eating is very much controlled by a dual system of acceleration and braking in two regions of the hypothalamus—the "appestat". A region in the lateral hypothalamus has also been linked with a "drinking centre" where destruction leads to adipsia (inability to drink). The evidence for a chemical as well as a neural component was presented by Andersson (1953) in Sweden who injected a 5 percent solution of salt into the hypothalamus of goats. The goats quickly began to drink large quantities of water. The reasoning was that the salt solution had in some way affected the delicate balance of salt surrounding the hypothalamus (through the bloodstream) and it caused responses typical of water deficiency.

But the hypothalamus has wider functions still (figure 6.2). Benzinger (1962)

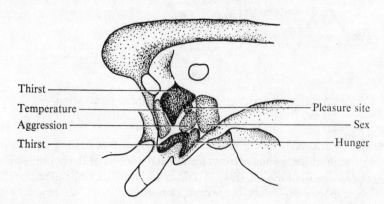

Figure 6.2 A fore-and-aft cross-section of the hypothalamus, showing the locations of particular functions. One of the regions of the brain thought to be different in men and women lies near the temperature control site
Source: Calder (1970).

has shown it to act as a thermostat in body temperature regulation. The posterior hypothalamus seems to function as a heat-maintenance unit whilst the anterior of the organ is a heat-loss unit (i.e. controls body temperature in warm surroundings).

Towards the rear of the hypothalamus (figure 6.2) is a "sex" site which when electrically stimulated produces sexual excitation in animals. Also, there is a connection between the hypothalamus and the pituitary gland. This latter secretes gonadotrophic hormones necessary for sexual motivation, and the neural connection, in fact, represents a control of pituitary functioning by the hypothalamus. This is achieved not by direct neural stimulation but indirectly. Nerve processes in the hypothalamus (Everett, 1964) initiate the release of chemicals into the vascular system connecting the organs and these chemicals are responsible for the release of gonadotrophic hormones. These bring about the secretion of gonadal hormones which in turn stimulate, via the blood vascular system, the anterior hypothalamus. Sexual behavior is thence elicited by the agency of this anterior site.

The parental protective erg has also been shown to draw its motivation from the hypothalamus and hormones. Injection of the male hormone testosterone into rats, first attempted by Hess, produced not sexual but maternal behavior. A female placed in the cage alongside an injected male was picked up by the scruff of her neck and carried, like a baby rat, bemused, to a corner of the cage. This action was repeated each time the female tried to move away from the corner. The experimenters soon realized they had hit on a method of eliciting parental behavior and placed small pieces of paper in the cage whence the male rat proceeded to convey them to a corner and make a nest.

We have reason to suppose that the hypothalamus has also an "aggression" center. Hess, using electrode probes, touched on an area in the hypothalamus of cats (since repeated with other creatures) which made them vicious, attacking anything which came near. Delgado, as a result of a long series of researches, was able to control the aggressive tendencies in such animals as bulls. Apparently, he was able to stage a mock bullfight in which a treated bull (electrodes passing into the hypothalamus under remote control) was made to stop or start charging at the turn of a switch.

The evidence thus far presented gives a very formidable argument for asserting that brain and chemical mechanisms play a substantial role in the genesis, control, and maintenance of animal and, by implication, human ergs. Within the hypothalamus alone we have located sites of appetite and satiation linked with food and drink and other sites connected with body temperature control, sex, paternal behavior, and aggression.

2 Hedonic centers and the definition of satisfaction

The idea of man as a pleasure-seeking, pain-avoiding animal has been a common belief for many years. Even as a psychological concept it has waxed and waned in popularity for centuries. Thorndike, in the formulation of his Law of Effect, states that when satisfaction follows a response there is more likelihood of a firm connection being made between the situation and the response such as to encourage repetition of the response, but "satisfaction" is an uncertain term. Actually the initial aversion to the hedonistic principle in psychology came from moral philosophers who maintained that man was more than a pleasure-seeking animal. But within psychology McDougall, for one, criticized it as oversimplified and pointed out how, for example, an animal mother defending her young will suffer extreme pain rather than let them come to harm. The debate is entangled in the semantics of terms like "pleasure", happiness, hedonism, and satisfaction. Dynamic psychology is governed not by pleasure-seeking or even by a long-sighted goal of happiness, but by *satisfaction* of innately given drives, a satisfaction which is perhaps so different for each drive that a general term is inappropriate. However, psychologists swing toward a general term *drive reduction*, without often seeing the implication that all drive tensions must have something in common and indeed, mutual exchange rates, if solution of conflict among drives is to be explained.

In chapter 4 we have faced the full challenge of alternative models here and have hypothesized that drive-reduction theory as used in the past is not enough to explain the observed phenomena. Instead we posit two components—drive tension and excitement level—which, over the ergic goal-seeking process, follow courses controlled by different conditions but which also permit a generation of ergic tension from the excitation ingredient. The confirmation (Cattell and Miller, 1952; Cattell, Horn, Radcliffe, and Sweney, 1964) of the reality of such ergs as exploration (curiosity), escape (fear) and constructiveness, in which the classical form of need reduction is most clearly inapplicable, and where motivation strength often increases with passage of time, supports the need for this two factor theory. So also does Sheffield's work with rats mentioned in the previous chapter where the animal actually seeks stimulation that might raise drive tension. Young's showing that drinking preferences are less determined by physiological levels than by taste preferences might also argue against drive reduction being the whole story.

In the present state of experimental knowledge, e.g. the recency of distinguishing measures of drive tension and excitation in man, there are plenty of riddles. For example, is there a common second-order ergic tension factor to each of the measurable ergic tensions? And is this common factor something like unpleasure–distress–versus–pleasure and delight? Here the physiological is ahead of the behavioral-analytic evidence for Olds clearly finds evidence for a neural center of general pleasure, and Young feels he can interpret his experiments by recourse to such a notion.

The latter is less convincing but can be briefly stated: Young (1961) postulates a "hedonic continuum" from extreme negative affectivity (extreme distress) to extreme positive affectivity (delight or pleasure) with indifference at the mid-point of the continuum. This he simply substitutes for the drive-reduction continuum. Thus as action proceeds (food or thirst drive depletion), he posits a change on this hedonic continuum from a negative state towards the center of the continuum (a "decreasing negative" change or affectivity). He believes this provides an explanation for the possible occurrence of "increasing positive" change accompanying exploration or curiosity, though just what causes it is not clear.

Basic physiological evidence for the existence of "pleasure" or "pain" centers came in 1954 when Olds was experimenting with implanting electrodes in rat brains. He inadvertently stimulated hypothalamic regions which made the rat return, to the very spot where the stimulation had occurred. It soon became apparent that the rat was searching for the source of its pleasant experience brought on by brain stimulation (technically referred to as intercranial stimulation or ICS). A further step was taken by employing a T maze in one arm of which was food. Just before reaching the food, a stimulus was given to the rat. On repeating the T maze task, rats preferred to stop at the point in the maze where they had experienced the stimulation. The most widely known of Olds experiments involved placing ICS rats in a Skinner-type box where the lever was connected to the stimulation control. In other words, the rats were now able to control for themselves the pleasant stimulation as and when they felt the need for it. In these circumstances, the rats were quick to learn that they could bring on the pleasure state by pressing a lever which turned on the current and they repeated this with increased rapidity.

About the same time Delgado and others (1954) were able to show areas for "aversive behavior" in the hypothalamus of cats, stimulation of which provoked fear and escape behavior (a further erg now established and clearly related to biological mechanisms of animals and man). Research has also embraced experiments using human subjects. Naturally they were patients undergoing brain treatment, surgery, or therapy. Delgado and others (1956) report that patients have recalled feelings of pleasantness and well-being during certain kinds of brain stimulation, whilst Bishop *et al.* (1963) have induced psychiatric patients to press a lever to receive a pleasant sensation much as in the rat research of Olds.

The "pleasure" areas appear to be more widely distributed than over the hypothalamus alone. Portions of the brain surrounding it (such as the hippocampus, septum and cingulate region) are also involved. "Aversion" areas are less widely dispersed being found in the thalamus as well as the hypothalamus. But in returning to the ergs of hunger, thirst, and sex, it does seem that there is anatomical correspondence between their hypothalamic sites and the pleasure or reward sites, the latter being, however, more extensive. The neural stimulation, as might be expected, has its effectiveness partly determined by general physiological and endocrine state. When rats or cats have been deprived of food for varying periods of time, the rate of bar pressing to receive stimulation is proportional to the extent of deprivation (Brady, 1958). The same relationship holds true for water deprivation. In the case of the sex erg, Prescott (1966) found a connection between self-stimulation and variations in the sexual potency (heat-cycles). The existence of the pleasure areas in anatomical contiguity to quite different ergic drive areas suggests that factor analytic study of several ergs together might isolate a second-order factor corresponding to this pleasure determiner. Indeed this may already be waiting to be identified in one of the motivational components (page 14) common to all drives.

If we are justified in transferring these findings to human functioning, and the parallel research conducted so far lends total support to this assumption, there are a number of points which are important to the theoretical formulations of chapters 2 and 3. So far, the neurophysiologists have managed to isolate hunger, thirst, mating, aggression, rest, escape, and parental protectiveness as under the direction of brain and chemical control. Table 2.12 will be found to contain all these (and more which we will discuss presently) as a result of factor analytical research in motivation.

The appetitive term in the ergic tension equation (3.15), i.e. $(P_k - aG_k) + (N_k - b\bar{G}_k)$ presents a model which fits very well the findings described above. The first bracket deals with difference of need and satisfaction (G = gratification) in purely physiological terms, the second with the corresponding difference in regard to consummatory behavioral expression. If P, the physiological term, is measured in the direction of deficit, e.g. shortage of blood sugar, then G is any increase in blood sugar from feeding activity. It is now clear that certain neural areas in the hypothalamus may be considered the machinery of this action and determiners of the constant, k, which defined the sensitiveness of this reaction. [More will be said about the expressions $(N_k - b\bar{G}_k)$ in the next section, but for the moment it is necessary to point out that the whole term for appetitive state strength is multiplied by another expression $(S_k + Z)$ which represents the stimulation level.] The findings of Sheffield and Young described above tell us that ergic tension is not necessarily reduced as a consequence of relevant activity in the pursuit of a need. An increase (increasing positive affectivity) in pleasure (and therefore no immediate drive reduction) occurs in exploratory behavior. This can be accounted for in the ergic tension equation by assuming that the stimulation level S_k probably increases (multiplying the other terms—C, H, etc.,—in the ergic need equation, page 73) without any corresponding change in aG_k (and hence $P_k - aG_k$), thus giving an overall *increase* in the strength of ergic tension.

3   Arousal and related states   A concept that has come increasingly into dynamics in the last decade or so is that of the state of *arousal*. This began more as a neurological than a psychological concept, being associated with the discovery of nerve tracts in the rubro-spinal area through which any kind of incoming stimulation apparently activates a system called the reticular system, having to do with waking up and with excitation level of consciousness. In due course it was found that other manifestations, such as alpha waves in the EEG and electrical skin resistance, associate with reticular activity, and from this Duffy (1962) and others have developed our knowledge of the natural history of arousal. Actually, the beginnings go a long way back, since the concept that low skin resistance is associated with high alertness and arousal was developed and substantiated in experiments by Cattell in 1928.

At any rate, the concept was handled operationally mainly by the EEG, skin resistance, and signs of afferent activity in the reticular system. The EEG—electroencephalograph—is an instrument capable of sensing the electrical potential changes in the cells of the cortex when electrodes are held on the scalp. The amplitude and frequency of the waves generated, is recorded by a pen moving across a rotating paper roll. Nowadays, the waves can be analyzed by a computer after being recorded on magnetic tape.

In deep sleep, the cells of the cortex tend to change in potential simultaneously thus giving a regular, steady wave pattern as shown in the illustration under "relaxed" and "sleep" conditions. Excitation, on the other hand, involves desynchronization of electrical discharges, consequently the wave pattern is irregular in both frequency and amplitude—and what is called the "percent time alpha" is reduced. The amplitude is larger for relaxed than for excited conditions. These differences can be seen clearly in figure 6.3. Although the EEG is picking up the electrical activity of the cortex, we are only seeing the end product of interaction with deeper centers in the brain such as the hypothalamus and reticular formation (to be described shortly) which determine the cortical activity level. Once again, the hypothalamus plays a substantial part in this case as a control center for wakefulness. Ranson in 1939 showed that lesions in the posterior hypothalamus produced permanent sleep or drowsiness. Hess and Akert (1955) found that electrical stimulation created alertness. Furthermore, as the pituitary gland is, as we have already mentioned, under the direction of the hypothalamus, the latter is paramount in the control of the chemistry of arousal. The pituitary guides the release of hormones from other endocrine glands such as thyroxin from the thyroid to regulate metabolism, adrenalin from the adrenal cortex to stimulate body activity, and the secretion of sex hormones from the gonads of both sexes.

So far we have pursued brain anatomy only as far as the cortex and hypothalamus, but the third area we have named must now be described. This is located (see figure 6.1) as a complex network of white and grey matter at the top of the brain stem and leading into the hypothalamic region. The functional concepts for this area at present assign to it three important operations. In the first instance, the major nerve trunk routes are directed through the ascending afferent pathways towards the cortex. They also send out collateral roots to the reticular system so that any message received by the cortex is also transmitted into the reticular formation. These latter transmissions activate the reticular formation such that arousal messages are also sent to the cortex from it (see figure 6.4). Note too that sense organs also operate through the ascending pathways so the reticular formation is a main trunk route for sensory as well as visceral transmissions. Depending on the information received by the cortex, the reticular formation is instructed by the cortex to continue to arouse or suppress the activity. The network of connections between the body sensory and visceral organs, the cortex, the reticular formation, the hypothalamus, and

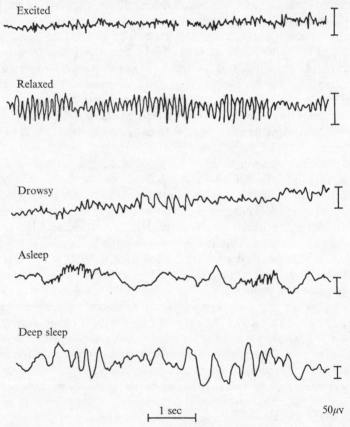

Figure 6.3   Various human EEG patterns under several arousal states
Source: Jasper (1941).

so on, mediate in determining the degree of arousal of an organism to external and internal stimuli. Interaction between the reticular formation and the cortex mainly controls the extent of arousal according to the level of stimulation received.

Three important questions arising from arousal theory based on this model require brief discussion here (a) are there noticeable differences in personality as a consequence of inherent differences in the functioning of the reticular activating system and visceral brain? (b) In what ways does performance in various fields relate to level of arousal (see the next section)? (c) what is the relation of arousal to anxiety and to ergic tension levels on various specific ergs? In regard to arousal and personality two rather different hypotheses have been put forward respectively by Eysenck (1967) and by Cattell. The former uses the concept of extraversion (exvia–vs.–invia) and has an elaborated physiological model showing a distinction between the ascending reticular activating system (reticular formation) itself and the "visceral brain" (i.e.

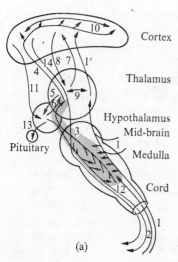

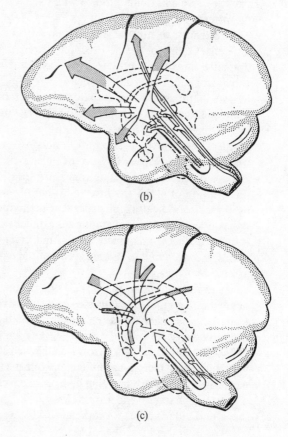

Figure 6.4 The reticular formation and some of its relationships. (a) general demarcation and location of the formation; (b) ascending reticular activating system (ARAS); (c) corticoreticular influence upon reticular formation and ARAS

Source: Lindsley (1951, 1957).

the limbic system—hippocampus, amygdala cingulum, septum, and hypo-thalamus) and the differential thresholds which exist in these. The loop des-cribed above, the information-processing loop, is thought by Eysenck (1967) to provide the physiological basis for differentiating inviants (introverts) from exviants (extraverts). Through the braking action in extraverts he suggests that arousal is finally higher in inviants than exviants under identical stimu-lating conditions. Certain experimental checkable conclusions follow from the theory. First, since anatomical structure is involved, the exvia–invia difference should prove to be largely genetically determined; secondly, the inviant person should show less retroactive inhibition whilst performing a task than the exviant. Further, tasks requiring concentration and vigilance should, by and large, be better adapted to the introvert arousal system than to that of the extravert. Eysenck has also hypothesized a relationship between visceral brain, ascending reticular activity, and his personality dimension of neuroticism which according to psychometric evidence (Cattell, 1973) is essentially anxiety. If there is a link via the collaterals between the visceral brain and the reticular formation, any excessive emotional arousal will also tend to affect the normal output of the latter.

The theory of arousal and personality put forward by Cattell is totally different. Of the four largest second-order personality factors known in ques-tionnaires and objective tests—exvia–invia, anxiety, cortertia, and independence—he associates cortertia, not invia, with high proneness to arousal. First let us note that for every one of these traits a corresponding state pattern has been found. The cortertia state pattern is in every sense one of alertness and arousal. In the questionnaire it loads harria (the negative pole of I), praxernia (M—), an alert concern for practicalities, and A(—) a guarded attitude to human weaknesses. Correspondingly in the objective test battery for cortertia (U.I.22) it loads quickness of reaction time, quickness of reversible perspective, much interruption of alpha rhythm, and other measures which have been regarded as the chief indicators of arousal. Furthermore, Curran and Barton have independently shown that among state dimension changes this cortertia pattern is quite distinct from anxiety, stress, and exvia–invia state dimension. The last finding seems fatal to Eysenck's requirement of high association between arousal and exvia.

As to the relation of the arousal dimension as a state, e.g. as measured and defined in the multistate batteries of Barton and of Curran, with a personality trait, there is a very great similarity of pattern both in questionnaires and objective tests between the arousal state pattern and QIII (equals I.U.22) defined as cortertia above. However, Nesselroade (1966) has brought out the very interesting fact that although any one person fluctuates on cortertia level, e.g. as he wakes in the morning his arousal level rises steeply, he tends to adopt a personal characteristic arousal level through most of the day. Each person has a particular "notch", on the arousal state scale to which he settles down.

(That of neurotics as a group, is significantly low, Cattell and Scheier, 1961.) By this theory and its associated observations, therefore, arousal, determined in part by neural structure, is both a state and a trait, in that for some (possibly anatomical) reasons some individuals can operate continuously and characteristically at a higher level than others. The personality associations and performances of persons high in cortertia are documented in Hundleby, Pawlik, and Cattell (1965) and in the 16 PF Handbook in chemical and occupational relations of QIII.

4 Activation theory and ergic states One of the main riddles now facing researchers in this area concerns the relations of what are called the general psychological states, appearing on the factored dimensions of anxiety, stress, depression, regression, exvia, and arousal, to the specific dynamic states of ergic tension— fear, sex, curiosity, etc.—as discussed above. The area is going to yield its secrets only to subtle concepts, but at least it is evident from adaptation process analyses (Cartwright and Cartwright, 1971) that the general states can arise from adaptation problems in any one of the specific ergs. For example, anxiety, elation, arousal, depression can appear from success, failure, or prolonged

Table 6.1 Factor pattern of cortertia trait and P-technique (U.I.22) state

Verbal fluency	(High)
Reversible perspective	(Fast)
Tempo of arm–shoulder circling	(Fast)
Electrical skin resistance	(Low)
Reaction time	(Short)
Flicker fusion test rate	(High)
percent alpha on EEG	(Low)

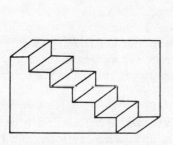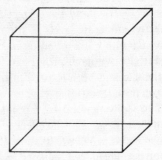

Illustration of the reversible perspective item.

conflict alike with sex, security, assertiveness, or curiosity as the operative dynamic system.

Just as we have suspected that the anatomical pleasure and unpleasure centers are set to operate in relation to any specific ergic center, so we may suspect in regard to arousal level that rise in arousal is a concomitant of rise in excitation of each and all ergic processes. Factor analyses, skilfully applied, should be able to check on this concept of arousal as a second-order factor among all ergic tensions, thus relating behavioral patterns to neural patterns.

Exploration of the relation of dynamics to physiology requires relating behavioral functional patterns not only to neural anatomical discoveries but also to general bodily reactions, as expressed through the autonomic nervous system and the endocrine glands. At first these reactions were seen largely as a "general commotion" associated notably with fear and anger. From early in this century, there has always been a small band of psychologists prepared to claim a connection between emotion and general body mobilization. Cannon (1929) held a general energizing view of emotion (emergency theory), i.e. mobilization of resources for emergency action, and Duffy (1934) even suggested abandoning the term "emotion" and thinking more in terms of excitation in an organism. Substance began to be given to these views in the early work of Hebb, Malmo, and Lindsley. Lindsley (1951) outlined an activation theory of emotion using the variations in encephalographic traces with behavior patterns. The tying together of activation theory and emotion has not the same appeal nowadays as it had twenty years ago as we shall see in some recent theorizing by Eysenck later in the section, but there is, nevertheless, a strong movement in support of activation theory. The term is sometimes used synonymously with arousal, although some (e.g. Eysenck) prefer to use these terms in distinct ways.

The first hard evidence came in 1958 when Fuster trained rhesus monkeys to discriminate between two geometric shapes by rewarding them when they picked up the correct shape (food was hidden beneath the correct one). With normal animals as controls he compared their performance with another group having electrode attachments to the reticular formation. The electrical stimulation was varied and the correct responses noted at different levels of stimulation. At moderate levels of stimulation, the percentage of correct responses improved with corresponding increases of stimulation up to a point beyond which the percentage progressively deteriorated. Two things had happened. First, a site had been located in the brain which offered a means of effecting changes in the arousal level of the animal and, secondly, this had been manipulated to show that up to a point alertness improved performance, but too much "alertness" had the effect of confusing rather than clarifying the quality of performance. We are dealing here with arousal and not anxiety or conflict, but the parallel in the U-shaped relationship between these independent sources of variance and performance is unmistakable.

A general drive state has also been a central tenet in Hull's theory of learning in which he proposes an all-purpose source of energy which is mobilized for the satisfaction of particular ergs as the occasion arises. In his now famous formulation

$$_sE_R = {}_sH_R \times D$$

where $_sE_R$ is excitatory potential, $_sH_R$ is habit strength and D the general drive condition compounded from one or more of the basic human drives or ergs, we see the potential for action as dependent on the existence of drive motivation D. It is this hypothesis of generality of "drive" across ergs that now needs to be factor analytically tested.

The relationship between the general arousal state and the tension created by body needs for ergic satisfaction is not clear. Can the separate ergic drives be subsumed, at a given time, to give the total drive potential of an organism? Is it, in fact, an additive model of energies or a multiplicative model? Hull's Theory implies a multiplicative system, whilst Spence's modification of Hullian Theory favors an additive solution. Parenthetically, it is common practice in scientific exploration to adopt the most parsimonious model first and only to discard it for a more complex model in the light of evidence. Thus in the theory outlined earlier, we have stuck to an additive model for this very reason and regarded the ergic tension as a summation of competing ergs.

There is now appreciable support for believing in the functional unitariness of each ergic tension—as a change in level, not merely in individual difference terms—in the work of De Young on sex, Kawash on hunger, Krug (1971) on other ergs. Krug chose two dynamic traits, one toward doing well at school (school sentiment), the other to avoiding war, violence, and sickness (fear erg). To create a manipulated situation, the achievement sample was divided to give an experimental group which received poor reports on their achievement scores—below their personal expectation level (fictional in most cases), whilst the control received scores at or slightly above the personal expectancy. The experimental fear group saw a movie called "Toys"—a Canadian film with a powerful message against war and violence. The control group in this case was shown a fairly dispassionate film about a pig farm. Direct analysis of differences between means on the possible dynamic factors showed the experimental group to be: (1) in school achievement significantly higher on the unintegrated, pugnacity erg and significantly lower on the integrated school sentiment than the control group, and (2) in the fear research, the experimental group to be significantly higher on the unintegrated fear erg than the control group. In fact, the fear erg is more convincingly a functional unity in so far as an experimentally induced fear towards war and violence was sufficient to bring forth a general response affecting the entire fear erg measure of SMAT which includes fear of quite varied objects.

How far these ergic tension levels change with the general arousal state is, however, still an unanswered question. Let us return to this in terms of the neural and physiological correlates. The neural analyses suggest that when falling asleep, but still conscious, we experience both stimulation through the sensory pathways and engage in "spontaneous" behavior. The evidence for spontaneous neuron activity is now well established (see Bullock 1959, for a description) and, in any case, the encephalograph portrays quite convincingly the incessant changes of electrical potential in the electrical discharges of brain cells. However, for normal waking functioning the brain actually seems to need sensory input. With regard to this need for stimulation, Bexton, Heron, and Scott (1954) employed university students to lie in a cot housed in a sound-proof room with normal lighting. The students wore translucent glasses, gloves, cardboard cuffs up to the elbows, and nested the head in a U-shaped foam pillow to lower tactile stimulation to the head. A short time was allowed out in each 24 hours for food and toilet needs. Few students could endure the intolerable inactivity for more than two or three days—forfeiting the princely sum of $20 a day for doing nothing! Immobility and boredom sometimes led to hallucinations and feelings of nausea. Spontaneous neural activity has been assumed to occur as shown in the ergic tension equation (chapter 3) as the term $(N_k - b\bar{G}_k)$ where N_k is the neural need of the central nervous system to discharge periodically.

Throughout the previous discussion, the terms activation and arousal have been taken to mean the same. However, Eysenck (1967) has argued that we should keep a distinction between them. Arousal, produced by the loop described above, is immediately connected with sensory stimulation, intellectual activity, and symbolic processes—to wit, they are "cortical" in nature. The illustration of someone sitting quietly in an armchair and reading brings to mind a situation of low arousal with reticular and cortical activity. On the other hand, the second loop incorporating the visceral brain and the reticular formation, whilst it has an arousing effect in the same fashion as the first loop, is responsible for emotional expression via the limbic system (which has control over the pituitary body and thus the hormonal secretions associated with emotional behavior). For this second kind of expression, Eysenck reserves the term *activation*. Cattell, in recognizing the need for two distinct concepts nevertheless believes that the evidence for the nature of this limbic–hormonal activity is that it corresponds to *anxiety*, already recognized and measurable in response patterns QII (in questionnaires) and U.I.24, in objective behavior and physiological tests.

The difference of arousal from activation or anxiety can be described by considering our reader in his armchair. He will certainly be at some level of arousal in order to receive sensory stimuli from the pages of his novel or newspaper, but he may not necessarily be activated emotionally. This will depend on the reading matter. Activation, however, always leads to arousal through the autonomic nervous system.

Cattell (1950) factor analyzed the extensive research data of Wenger on diverse manifestations of autonomic-endocrine activity and discovered three factors (see table 6.2)—the previously suspected sympathetic system and parasympathetic system patterns, plus a *general* autonomic system factor, affecting such variables as metabolic rate, pulse and breathing rates, skin conductivity, etc. The same patterns have been found by P-technique on fluctuations within the individual (Williams, 1954). Later research on anxiety shows that this general autonomic activity factor is closely tied to anxiety and may be considered *the* physiological expression of anxiety (from which Cannon's adrenergic response and the parasympathetic system response are quite different).

Now, speculating, we might expect this general autonomic activation via the limbic system to correspond to the general unspecified drive stimulation level hypothesized above. But it must be remembered that unused drive, frustrated by lack of a clear course of action, quickly turns to anxiety, according to the theory set out in detail elsewhere (page 173 here, and Spielberger, 1972). Although the transformation from drive to anxiety is commonly conceived as occurring through several steps in the adaptation process analysis scheme it is conceivable that unused drive from the beginning is expressed physiologically as the general autonomic activation factor. Indeed, there are studies (Herrington, 1942) of ratings of individual activity level which correlate substantially (Cattell, 1950) with autonomic activity measures.

Although the general autonomic activity factor, with its combination of neural and endocrine activities, undoubtedly correlates substantially with anxiety, the possibility must remain open for the present as to whether it also correlates with a general ergic activation level which need not immediately transform into anxiety. Agreeing with Eysenck that arousal as measured in our factored texts is cerebral and not ergic (but locating it as QIII, cortertia, not QI, exvia) we postulate that the general autonomic physiological activity factor is initially an expression of general ergic activation level, but that since the latter almost invariably "degenerates" into anxiety, substantial correlation is found between the general autonomic factor and the anxiety factor (QII and U.I.28). The possibility must also be seriously considered that this general ergic activation, prior to anxiety, is measured by the general unintegrated (U) component in motivation strength.

5 The role of emotion in motivation

In the early introspective phase of psychology, chapters on emotion played a prominent part in textbooks, e.g. in William James, Titchener, and others; but nowadays the experience of emotion as such is seen almost as an epiphenomenon in dynamic processes. It is something which is not motivation and drive itself, but which colors the quality of each particular erg, and which comes into prominence mainly when all does not go well with the drive. Nevertheless there may be important physiological associations, e.g. of increased fatigue or stress response through long exposure to the physiological effects of emotion.

The first surprise on looking at our knowledge today is that in spite of all the early emphasis by early writers—James and Lange, for example, and the early breakthrough by Cannon and Rosenbluth re fear and anger—no precise information exists about the differences of physiological response patterns corresponding to the introspected differences. Our language is full of expressions describing the conscious sensations of visceral change accompanying an emotive experience. Joy, fear, despair, pity, disgust "a sinking feeling", "a rising gorge" are expressions attempting to capture the conscious manifestations of internal body processes. We have already indicated in chapter 2 some of the more common emotions associated with the ergs, e.g. sex, loneliness, pity, curiosity, fear, pride, and sensuousness are emotional reactions to the ergs of mating, gregariousness, parental protectiveness, exploration, escape to security, self-assertion, and narcistic sex.

The classical interpretation of emotional activity and response was that after a stimulus has been received (or some internal visceral activity, including thinking, occurs) which is threatening or enticing, the body reacts through the autonomic nervous system and endocrine secretions to give rise to feelings of emotion. Fear, for example, is apparent when heartbeat and breathing becomes faster, the mouth becomes dry, hair stands on end and the face becomes white (contraction of the blood capillaries). As mentioned in the previous paragraph, what makes the judgment that one is experiencing fear so difficult is that these body changes are not—as Cannon showed discernibly—all that far removed from those which accompany anger. Bridges (1932) postulated a differentiation of emotions starting with general body excitement at birth and quickly growing into pleasure reactions (delight, elation) or displeasure reactions (distress, anger, disgust, fear) as shown in the figure on page 154. There is a strong similarity between this and the hedonistic categorization of motivational origins.

As is well known, Lange and James (1922), independently in the first instance, took issue with the then widely held assumption that the emotions generated action, like drives. They revised this, making emotion a side-effect

Table 6.2 Factor analysis of manifestations of autonomic-endocrine activity

General autonomic Activity Factor 1	Approximate loading
Large PGR deflection magnitude	0.70
High ratio of emotional to nonemotional words recalled	0.70
High pulse and blood pressure	0.60
Rating of "sociable"	0.50

Table 6.2 *cont.*

High basal metabolic rate	0.50
Rating of "vigorous"	0.50
Large ratio of pupil to iris diameter	0.50
High skin resistance	0.40
High critical frequency of flicker fusion	0.40
Brief duration of after-images	0.40

Factor 1 closely resembles Herrington's general autonomic activity factor mentioned above. The ratings of 'sociable' and 'vigorous' however, suggest a reaction formation to anxiety rather than anxiety itself.

Sympathetic adrenergic activity

Factor 2	Approximate loading
Low skin resistance (high conductance)	0.70
High pulse pressure	0.60
High pH (alkalinity) of saliva	0.60
High irritable emotionality	0.60
Large performance upset by noise distraction	0.50
High glucose concentration in blood	0.50
High lymphocyte count	0.40
Long dark adaptation period of eye	0.40
High pulse rate	0.40
Moderately large PGR deflections	0.40

Factor 2 seems to be a more complete and, it might be argued, more carefully rotated, picture of the sympathetic, adrenergic factor in the above reported studies. Among the P-technique studies a third clear factor occurred, as follows:

Parasympathetic activity

Factor 3	Approximate loading
High skin resistance	0.60
Rating "relaxed" (and large skin resistance rise in relaxation period)	0.60
Low cholinesterase in the blood	0.60
PGR response magnitude	0.50
Briefer dark adaptation period of the eye	0.50
Frequency of urination (and volume of urine)	0.45
Small difference in upward and downward flicker fusion frequency	0.40
Slow pulse rate	0.40
Low blood sugar (glucose)	0.40

Factor 3 seems to be substantially what is generally described as the parasympathetic or vagotonic factor, some aspects of which have already appeared in the factorizations with fewer variables mentioned above.

or epiphenomenon, saying "we are afraid because we run; we do not run because we are afraid". However, Cannon's more functional theory of emotion, that the body is mobilized for fight or flight by the concomitant emotional changes in the body, became more widely accepted, though it still leaves the introspective feeling of the emotion with little function but to act as a symbol and referent in emotional learning, e.g. of control. What functions such emotions as pity or pride play in a physiological sense is still obscure. Whilst there is a Darwinian appeal about the survival utility of emotive body responses, the argument cannot be applied consistently across the spectrum of emotional reactions. It is possible that more understanding of the different qualities of emotion could be given in terms of the three-factor theory—that of sympathetic, parasympathetic, and general autonomic response components.

For the student who has not taken a course in physiological psychology it is probably desirable to take a closer look at the classical picture of the sympathetic and parasympathetic nervous systems in the total autonomic setting. As the term "autonomic" implies, the system was thought to be self-controlling and beyond the reach of man's conscious control. However, this is now shown to be false and it is possible, by operant conditioning, to lower such activities as heartbeat by consciously "thinking the heartbeat rate to a lower level", reinforcement coming from seeing an oscilloscope or hearing a buzzer sound when the rate is falling. The organs innervated by the ANS are the heart, lungs, stomach, intestines, bladder, and duct glands (tear and salivary). Both

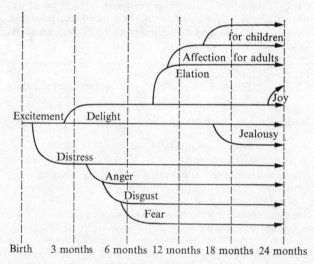

Figure 6.5 Differentiation of emotions during early development. Observations of infants and young children show that specific emotions are formed by a differentiation of more generalized reactions

Source: Bridges (1932).

the sympathetic and parasympathetic systems innervate these organs; the sympathetic, amongst other things, enables increased activity by providing more oxygen in the blood (increased breathing), excess blood supply to the brain, slowing down of digestive system, and the release of glycogen from the liver as a source of "fuel" for muscle activity. The parasympathetic section innervates the same organs, but has the reverse effect by acting as a braking system against excessive activity. It is, nevertheless, important to remember that the emotional process is also dependent upon glandular hormonal secretions[1] as well as the nervous system. Experiments where the nerve connections to some of the viscera are severed show that the latter still respond to emotion-provoking stimuli as the outcome of hormone action through the bloodstream.

The distinction between emotion and conation, i.e. drive to act, has thus long been made introspectively and it seems to be true also in neuro-anatomy that the centers for impulse are not identical with those of emotion, though emotion develops in the course of action, as when a cat is incited to attack another by implanted electrodes. The function of emotion, we have suggested above, is partly like that of imagery, to supply symbolic reference to behavior whereby behavioral learning can occur ("Last time I panicked I got into more trouble than if I'd controlled my emotion"). Probably, however, its greater function is to reinforce action by bringing about the appropriate bodily adjustments to favor execution of the stimulated erg.

This manipulation of bodily chemistry by the emotion, however, has its drawbacks as well as its gains, particularly in a civilized society where the age-old emotional response patterns are superfluous. Duodenal ulcers are a very common side-effect from excessive worry. A famous research in America (US Army Medical Department) producing gastric ulcers in unsuspecting monkeys by giving them nerve-racking responsibilities has already been alluded to in chapter 5.

6 Summary   1. The study jointly of physiology and neural anatomy in relation to dynamics in animals and man has proved very rewarding, the behavioral and physical analyses often given mutual guidance in reaching vital concepts. In neural anatomical terms it has long been recognized that the cerebral cortex enters only in a learning

[1] In particular, the endocrine (or ductless) glands which secrete hormones directly into the bloodstream regulate several body functions. The pituitary gland, already mentioned as a most important companion to the hypothalamus, is a linchpin in the control of the other endocrine glands by liberating hormones which activate them; the thyroid (in the front of the neck) secretes thyroxin which aids in growth and metabolic control; the adrenals (near the kidneys) secrete adrenalin and noradrenalin—the former has been associated with fear and the latter with anger (a fragment of evidence supporting chemical differentiation of emotive states); the gonads secrete hormones relating to secondary sexual characteristics and sexual activity.

and controlling role, and that drive and emotion are functions of the underlying mid-brain and particularly of the hypothalamus and the limbic system. These centers also coordinate, via the autonomic nervous system, the endocrine and other adjustments in the body associated with drive action.

2. Distinct centers are found in the region of the hypothalamus which activate each erg and its corresponding emotion, though complete parallelism of these with the functional unities—the ergs—found by factoring behavior has not yet been explored.

3. In addition to these drive centers for coordinating the ergic processes in hunger, sex, etc., anatomical areas which evolve general pleasure and unpleasure have been located. Theoretical connections are suggested between this finding and the study of appetites in animals, on the one hand, and the search for a general drive factor (second order to the separate ergic tensions) in man.

4. The notion, however, of a single hedonic level being responsible for motivation seems inadequate, even in the modified form of a "drive-reduction" theory, and when physiology is more fully explained it seems likely that (in arousal, ergic activation, anxiety, etc.) we shall find concepts, parallel in physiology and behavior factors, presenting a better fit to the observed complexities of the drive process.

5. Analysis of general states has shown the distinction of arousal, depression, anxiety, exvia, regression, etc., in questionnaire scales and objective tests. Eysenck relates arousal to exvia, QI, but in pattern, as Cattell has alternatively suggested, it is much closer to cortertia, QIII, and Nesselroade has shown that individuals operate at a characteristic cortertia level. This characteristic or trait level is marked by EEG and skin resistance levels as well as reaction time and flicker fusion speeds. It is to be conceived as connected with the operation of the reticular system and thus hypothesized to have substantial physiological and genetic determination.

6. Although a general factor of ergic tension level has not yet been isolated there are indications to suggest a hypothesis that this activation level is different from arousal, as Eysenck also argues. Physiologically it is supported by the finding of a general autonomic activity level (different from the sympathetic and parasympathetic patterns) and the fact that this correlates substantially with anxiety is met by the observation that undischarged ergic tension commonly transforms into anxiety. However, it is also possible that ergic tension activation and anxiety will prove separable though both correlate with autonomic activity, and that the unintegrated component in motivation will prove the same as the general ergic activation level factor.

7. Although neurons fire spontaneously, the general integrated operation of the mind requires that a minimal arousal level be maintained by sensory input. The arousal in the reticular system normally passes over to stimulation of ergic tensions in the hypothalamus and limbic system. The simple notion

that an ergic process starts at a high ergic tension (activation) and follows behavior paths which reduce tension is inadequate. Our hypothesis is that both arousal (excitement) and ergic tension (activation) drive the behavior onward. The normal course of events actually increases excitement and this transforms to ergic tension, which is continuously reduced by profitable behavior and increased by excitation. The relevance of this for learning is discussed elsewhere (structured learning theory, Cattell and Dreger, 1975).

8. The mutual relations of physiology and emotion have long been intensively studied (though the specific physiological patterns of different emotions are still only fragmentarily understood), but the relation of emotion to drive is less clear. In general, emotion has been shifted from central importance as a motivator to an associate of motivation. It functions to adjust the physiology of the body to the particular ergic course of action operating, and in so doing can also produce physiological stresses. The particular introspective quality from a unique physiological pattern, due to autonomic and endocrine combinations, may also help as a symbolic referent in emotional learning.

The dynamic calculus and clinical psychology

1 The two kinds of diagnostic relevance of dynamic trait measures Clinical psychology concerns itself with (1) diagnosis (implying prognosis), (2) treatment. Since enlightened treatment requires insightful diagnosis, we shall begin with the latter, and proceed later to questions of treatment.

Diagnosis has been conceived in clinical psychology, as in medicine generally, in two ways: (a) assignment of the patient to a recognized disease category, and (b) recognition of the existence of a particular disequilibrium. Clinical psychology has experienced unstable swings of the pendulum between these, partly associated with changes of philosophy. The "dynamic" theorists have thought of pathology not as specific diseases, as in germ disease, but as deviance or maladjustment in essentially normal processes, as in, say, diabetes. It has then seemed to them pointless to "pigeon hole" patients in classical syndromes, which further, they associate with leaving the patient without treatment. Instead, they want to look at the particular conflict or even attack just the special symptom. A proper perspective on this is surely that *both* approaches are helpful, and not mutually inconsistent. To place a patient in a category as a neurotic or schizophrenic is useful even when one looks also at the specific conflict, because past experience of the "type" or syndrome offers prognosis of what is likely to happen and what treatment is likely to be effective. Consequently we shall consider diagnosis both in terms of finding a "diagnostic category" and of exploring the nature of the dynamic maladjustment.

Psychological testing of personality, state, and dynamic trait strengths has been a valuable aid to the psychiatrist, and in many mental hospitals nowadays the psychiatrist depends as much on the psychologist's test evidence as on all the rest of the data together. In the Handbooks of the 16 PF test, the MMPI and the Clinical Analysis Questionnaire, for example, there are well-validated profiles of scores for the typical anxiety neurotic, the psychopath, the schizophrenic, the "acting out" delinquent child, etc., which provide an objective basis for diagnosing any given patient—a basis needing to be supplemented, of course, by more qualitative sources. The question naturally suggests itself to the progressive clinician, "Could not this profile on general personality source traits be usefully supplemented by one on, say, the ten dynamic factors in the Motivational Analysis Test (MAT)?" Such an extension would represent a genuine increase of information because, as we have seen (page 52), it has been demonstrated that the dynamic structure factors are out in "new space" relative to the general temperament factors. That is to say (with the exception of the superego and self-sentiment factors, which are measured afresh in the new medium) the ergs and sentiments in the MAT are *further* concepts— distinctive, independent types of trait—relative to the general personality temperament factors of the 16 PF, CAQ, HSPQ, etc.

Whether these ergic tension levels and sentiment development levels will prove to have some sort of characteristic pattern for each of the syndrome categories recognized by the psychiatrist remains to be settled by experiment. Some psychoanalytic theories would suggest that relatively constant differences should be found on drive levels, e.g. on narcistic compared to heterosexual drive in the schizophrenic. More general dynamic theories might suggest that the score on integrated pugnacity–aggression would be higher relative to the unintegrated in the criminal who is expressing it in actual violence than in the normal law-abiding citizen who fantasies in "who-done-it" detective stories, and so on. Distinctive patterns of dynamic need might also be expected in, say, alcoholics and drug addicts. And though this wanders somewhat outside the narrower clinical domain, we might surely expect some characteristic levels of satisfied and unsatisfied ergic tension in particular occupations and social status positions (see chapter 9).

On the other hand, since the ergic tension levels fluctuate in themselves, and since the validity and reliability of the MAT and SMAT scales are not yet at the levels of the 16 PF, etc., scales, it is likely that the differences in profile in dynamic traits will be less clear and emphatic, and more blurred by fluctuation (unless based on averages of repeated measurements) than for general personality traits.

2 Indications of the characteristic dynamic diagnostic syndrome profiles for clinical types

Locked into the particular testing practices current at the time of getting degrees, a sadly large proportion of clinical psychologists has failed to recognize the radical advances in practice offered by the systematic advances of the last fifteen years in objective measurement of dynamic traits. And since a practically useable test for adults, the MAT, has been available for barely a decade, and the child test, the SMAT, much less, the available data for this section is sparse indeed. What follows here is especially indebted to the alert pioneer work of Professors Sweney, Horn, Delhees, Krug, Lawlis, May, Caffelt, Kunzman, Davis, and Mays (see summary in Sweney, 1969).

These investigators, despite restriction to few and small psychiatrically diagnosed groups, have given a partial answer to our question above, in that their results do indicate some fairly marked differences of dynamic trait profile among diagnostic groups. We shall not examine these in statistical detail, but consider them only as preliminary illustrations for discussion of issues which,

Sten mean conflict	Sten mean total	Dynamic areas	Standard ten score (sten) 1 2 3 4 5 6 7 8 9 10	Centile rank conflict	Centile rank total
7·0	4·5	Career sentiment		77·3	30·8
4·5	4·0	Home–parental sentiment		30·8	22·7
7·0	7·0	Fear erg		77·3	77·3
6·5	2·5	Narcism comfort erg		69·2	6·7
6·0	5·0	Superego sentiment		59·9	40·1
7·5	5·0	Self– sentiment		84·1	40·1
7·0	2·0	Mating erg		77·3	4·0
4·5	4·5	Pugnacity–sadism erg		30·8	30·8
3·5	4·5	Assertiveness erg		15·9	30·8
5·5	2·5	Sweetheart–spouse sentiment		50·0	6·7

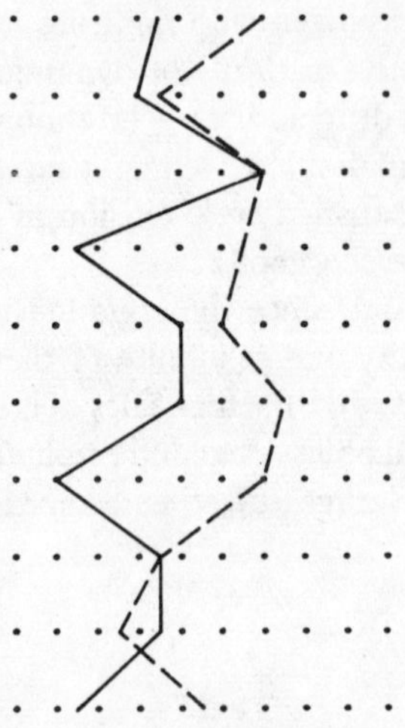

Conflict sten mean — — —   Total motivation sten mean ———

Figure 7.1 Dynamic structure profile (total strength and conflict level) for criminals convicted of crimes of violence (*N* = 19).

Source: Caffelt and Sweney (1964) from the Preliminary Descriptive Manual of the MAT (1969).

by the time this book is published, are likely to be illustrated by results on more substantial samples and a broader array of diagnostic syndromes.

Figure 7.1 represents a profile from Caffelt's work (Caffelt and Sweney 1965) on criminals, starting with a small sample of 19 convicted of crimes of violence. The results are given by both sten point scores and by centile ranks. The separate analysis of the integrated and unintegrated components has proved extremely useful in all the profiles here considered, though for reasons of space figure 7.1 does not cover it directly. Instead this offers in the thick continuous line the *total* dynamic strength, and in the discontinuous line the *difference* of U and I scores, since, as discussed below, (U—I) may be considered a measure of conflict. The conflict level in figure 7.1 is higher than average, especially in regard to career, sex, the self-sentiment, and the need for security. In the major sentiment areas this type of individual is seriously frustrated, though the frustration of need for security is probably connected with his own violence. The interesting finding here is that he is not experiencing frustration or conflict about the expression of aggression itself, as shown by the (discontinuous) line for pugnacity and assertiveness scores. In this domain he has

Sten mean conflict	Sten mean total	Dynamic areas	Standard ten score (sten) 1 2 3 4 5 6 7 8 9 10	Centile rank conflict	Centile rank total
5·5	4·5	Career sentiment		50·0	30·8
5·5	4·5	Home–parental sentiment		50·0	30·8
6·5	5·0	Fear erg		69·2	40·1
8·0	2·5	Narcism comfort erg		89·4	6·7
6·0	5·0	Superego sentiment		59·9	40·1
7·5	5·0	Self– sentiment		84·1	40·1
6·0	2·5	Mating erg		59·9	6·7
5·0	5·0	Pugnacity–sadism erg		40·1	40·1
4·0	4·0	Assertiveness erg		22·7	22·7
6·0	4·0	Sweetheart–spouse sentiment		59·9	22·7

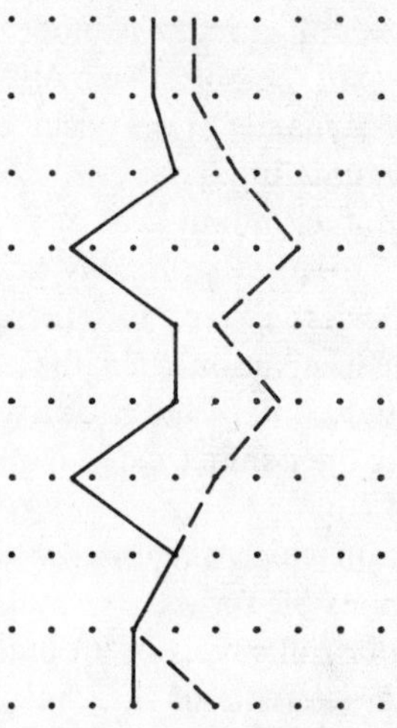

Conflict sten mean — — —   Total motivation sten mean ————

Figure 7.2 Motivational pattern for individuals convicted of "crimes of stealth" (mainly theft) ($N = 19$).

Source: Caffelt and Sweney (1964) from the Preliminary Descriptive Manual of the MAT (1969).

expressed himself, and exchanged conflict within himself for conflict with society.

It is interesting to compare with this Caffelt's finding on the criminal who works by stealth—theft rather than robbery—as shown in figure 7.2. Again there is trouble over the self-sentiment—the individual's behavior is not what he would like it to be, and again he is in a state of fear and insecurity, presumably through the kind of life he leads. But now the strongest conflict has shifted to the narcistic erg. This says that the individual is not able to "support himself in the style to which he is accustomed", or, more exactly, that his desires for the luxury, ease, and self-satisfaction which constitute the narcistic erg are beyond his realistic capacities to gain such levels of satisfaction. Here at least is one understandable motivation for stealing.

By contrast with the above we set out in figure 7.3 Davis's results (1966) for students in a seminary, for ministers of a certain denomination. In this case the striking feature is the absence of such discrepancies of U and I scores as have characterized the above. [Actually the profiles are for the U and I, not for the (U+I) and (U−I) in figures 7.1 and 7.2, but the highest conflict measure as set out separately in Sweney (1969) is in the sixties rather than in the eighties (percentiles) as for the two varieties of criminals.] Both the superego and the self-sentiment, in the integrated mode of measurement, are above average for these men aiming at the career of a minister, and it is only in regard to the mating erg that the conflict index is moderately high—in the sixties (Sweney, 1969). Thus once again the objective motivation devices applied to factorially discovered unitary dynamic traits yield criterion relations consistent with psychological understanding.

By contrast one must admit that at present the profile for thirty schizophrenics in figure 7.4 is not so readily understandable—at least in terms of psychoanalytic theories. Except for interest in home–parental, career, and superego values the motivation strengths are all below average, which does fit the notion of reduced total libido, but why home–parental, superego, and career? And why is the conflict index high on parents, superego, and sex, as shown in figure 7.4?

The overprotection which is reported with undue frequency in schizophrenic homes may be responsible for the parental dependence and the conflict therefore being high, while difficulties over obtaining and holding a career position are also highly characteristic of the clinical reports. Next to these the most frequently reported deviation is in maintaining normal sexual roles. So perhaps the MAT profile is not as strange as it at first appears. Furthermore, a marked deviation of profile from that of the general population, which runs down the center much as in figure 7.3, is an indication that should be expected from an effective instrument applied to so severe a form of mental disorder.

Actually, the new objective test devices in the MAT and SMAT dynamic structure tests are not yet as effective as a psychometrist could desire. To get

Sten mean conflict	Sten mean total	Dynamic areas	Standard ten score (sten) 1 2 3 4 5 6 7 8 9 10	Centile rank conflict	Centile rank total
5·1	5·2	Career sentiment		42·1	44·0
5·0	5·0	Home–parental sentiment		40·1	40·1
4·3	4·8	Fear erg		27·4	36·3
5·7	6·2	Narcism comfort erg		54·0	63·7
6·0	6·0	Superego sentiment		59·9	59·9
5·4	6·7	Self–sentiment		48·0	72·6
5·8	5·5	Mating erg		56·0	50·0
5·3	5·4	Pugnacity–sadism erg		46·0	48·0
5·2	5·1	Assertiveness erg		44·0	42·1
6·3	5·5	Sweetheart–spouse sentiment		65·5	50·0

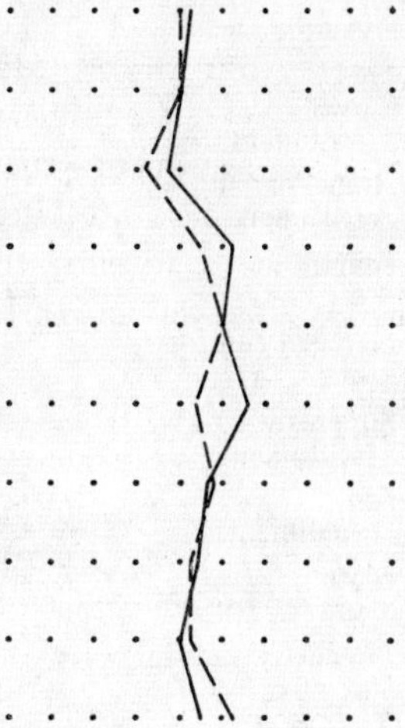

Unintegrated sten mean — — —   Integrated sten mean ———

Sten mean conflict	Sten mean total	Dynamic areas	Standard ten score (sten) 1 2 3 4 5 6 7 8 9 10	Centile rank conflict	Centile rank total
5·7	4·5	Career sentiment		54·0	30·8
6·2	4·3	Home–parental sentiment		63·7	27·4
5·3	3·8	Fear erg		46·0	19·8
5·4	5·7	Narcism comfort erg		48·0	54·0
6·0	6·2	Superego sentiment		59·9	63·7
4·7	6·2	Self–sentiment		34·5	63·7
6·0	5·2	Mating erg		59·9	44·0
5·9	4·8	Pugnacity–sadism erg		57·9	36·3
6·1	4·3	Assertiveness erg		61·8	27·4
6·5	5·7	Sweetheart–spouse sentiment		69·2	54·0

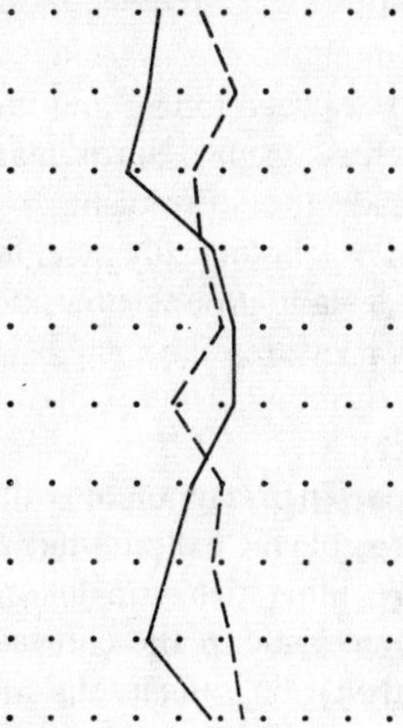

Conflict sten mean — — —   Total motivation sten mean ———

Figure 7.3 Patterns of unintegrated and integrated motivation in dynamic structure factors for seminary students ($N = 267$).

Source: Davis (1966) from the Preliminary Descriptive Manual of the MAT (1969).

Sten mean conflict	Sten mean total	Dynamic areas	Standard ten score (sten) 1 2 3 4 5 6 7 8 9 10	Centile rank conflict	Centile rank total
5·8	8·2	Career sentiment		56·0	91·2
6·5	7·0	Home–parental sentiment		69·2	77·3
5·2	3·5	Fear erg		44·0	15·9
4·2	3·2	Narcism comfort erg		25·8	12·5
6·3	7·5	Superego sentiment		65·5	84·1
7·0	4·4	Self– sentiment		77·3	29·1
7·8	4·6	Mating erg		87·5	32·6
5·6	2·0	Pugnacity–sadism erg		52·0	4·0
6·0	4·7	Assertiveness erg		59·9	34·5
2·5	5·2	Sweetheart–spouse sentiment		6·7	44·0

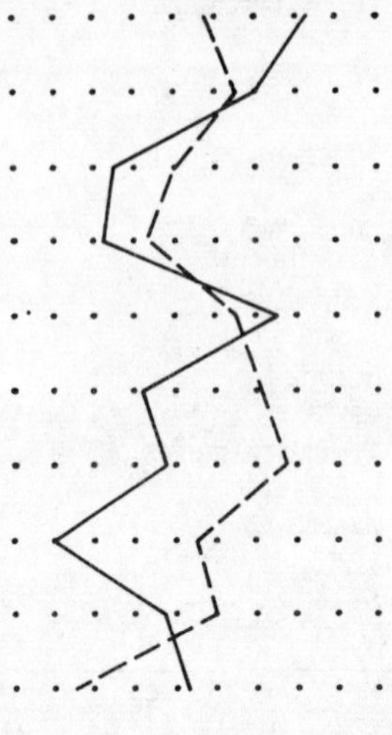

Conflict sten mean — — —   Total motivation sten mean ———

Figure 7.4 Diagnostic pattern for the schizophrenic syndrome ($N = 30$)

Source: May and Sweney (1965) from the Preliminary Descriptive Manual of the MAT (1969).

sufficient reliability we need longer and more developed tests (B forms to add to the A forms) such as Sweney, Burdsal, and others are now researching upon. But it is surely already a very promising future that is indicated by the statistically significant and psychologically meaningful differences of profile for clinically and socially deviant groups now indicated by these ergic tension and sentiment strength measures.

3 The coming use of P-technique in "quantitative psychoanalysis"

In chapters 2 and 6 a method of experiment called P-technique—correlational analysis within the single person—has been described. Its purpose was explained respectively as checking how much the dynamic structures of individuals depart from those of the average man, and what the dimensions of *state* variation, as distinct from trait differences of level, actually are. The answers were unequivocally that ergs and sentiments vary functionally over time in the same patterns as are found by individual difference research (chapter 2) and that in addition to these ergic tension and sentiment arousal states there are general states like anxiety, depression, general excitement, etc. (chapter 6). In this section we shall concentrate on P-technique mainly in the dynamic area leaving to later sections the relations of ergic tensions to the generalized states.

It has already been pointed out that the dynamic specification equation (e.g. equations (3.1) or (4.1), pages 65 and 89) for a particular act or symptom, a_j, is nothing less than a "quantitative psychoanalysis". It tells us what ergs and sentiments habitually gain satisfaction through the act of symptom, a_j, and the behavioral indices—the b's—tell us in fact *how much* a unit increase in the given drive strength produces increase in the symptom—granted the habit connections that have been established. Each b states how much the particular drive, self-sentiment, superego factor, etc., is *involved* in the given behavior.

For the clinical psychologist who is interested in developing his practice further along psychoanalytic lines, or even the lines of general dynamic determinism, one would expect the appearance of this technique to have much the same impact as the appearance of the steam engine in the days of the stage coach. Four circumstances, however, seem to have hidden the remarkable implicit possibilities from the general clinician. First, when only the R-technique results were available, he would correctly say that the analytical values apply to the *average man* and are not applicable to the given patient, belonging therefore to social rather than clinical psychology. Secondly, when P-technique demonstrated that the values could be found for a given individual, bringing out the roots of motivation for his own particular symptoms and conflicts, it did so at the cost of requiring a testing session a day for about a hundred days— and what clinic could afford such time? Thirdly, in the decade (1950–1960) after P-technique was demonstrated, clinical psychology as a whole was swinging from psychoanalytic to behavior therapy approaches, including both "group therapy" and "desensitization". It had tired of the guesswork of the psychoanalytic couch and turned to more positive if cruder methods—alas just when more positive aids were coming to assist in the growing and subtler regard for the comprehensive dynamics of the patient. Fourthly, one must in realism also record that apart from any swings of fashion the training and interests of the clinician are such that he is singularly ill-prepared to recognize a mathematical argument, or to subject his intuitions to the harsh check of a computer finding.

Yet of all four of these reasons only one would affect a professionally keen psychologist, namely the fact that P-technique is expensive of time, and some intensive technical research might well remove this impracticality, as it removed the impracticality of early photography or aviation. The direct attack on the symptom—in behavior therapy—is impressive to those tired of the guesswork of armchair dynamic analysis, but dynamic understanding is going to be necessary in the long run for insightful therapy, and a radical new avenue to its realization has been offered by P-technique. Let us therefore move on from the bare statement of it as a research method (page 82) to see in more detail how it needs to be developed as a clinical method.

It is necessary first to have repeatable measures of the major ergic tension factors, such as sex, fear, pugnacity, gregariousness, etc., and of the arousal level of various sentiments, especially the self-sentiment and the superego. Few such dynamic traits are covered by objective batteries in one hour in the MAT test. But one would want 100 equivalent forms of MAT for a clinical run, and so one must look to other objective devices, e.g. reaction time, GSR response, fluency count, etc., that can be used again and again, as Cross did in her pioneer study (Cattell and Cross, 1952, page 83 above). Against the background of these basic ergic tension levels one builds in special measures, also by objective test methods of the strength or activity level of the symptoms or attitudes central in maladjustment. For simplicity let us restrict discussion to one symptom, such as an overwhelming sense of dread, or an obsession to argue with superiors, or an inability to sleep. On each occasion—commonly on each day—of testing the symptom also will be quantified. Eleven columns of scores—the ten dynamic traits and the symptom—will thus be generated as the diagnosis runs over the hundred days (rows in the score sheet).

Now life can usually be depended upon to provide the stimuli or hard knocks that will cause the ergic tension levels to change from day to day, and the sentiments to reach various levels of arousal. However, clinical experience may suggest that the method can be improved by the psychiatrist bringing certain pressures to bear deliberately to provoke, for example, the arousal of the self-sentiment. No matter which, the dynamic calculus theory would predict that when an attitude or symptom is an expression of drive X, a stronger stimulation of X, or a more general blocking of its satisfaction, will result in a rise of the given symptom. Thus if we take our 100×11 score matrix above and correlate the symptom with the drives we shall obtain a specification equation—in fact a multiple correlation, as follows:

$$a_j = b_{j1}E_1 + b_{j2}E_2 + \ldots + b_{jk}E_k + b_{jm1}M_1 + \ldots + b_{jmn}M_n \qquad (7.1)$$

where there are k ergs (E's) and n sentiments (M's) measured by the battery. [The b's are derived from the r's (correlations) in the usual way in multiple correlations. They may also be obtained as factor pattern loadings from a factor analysis. But once the repetitive MAT battery has been set up establishing what the ergs are and how to measure them there is no need to do a factor analysis for each patient. An 11×11 correlation matrix suffices.]

The dynamic specification equation in (7.1) is different from that in (3.1) because it is peculiar to the person rather than general to our population. The b's tell us what that particular symptomatic behavior, a_j, means for *him*, and what the relative contributions are for different drives and sentiments. Furthermore, since the test would yield both U, unintegrated, and I, integrated, component scores for both ergs and the symptom, additional understanding comes from these qualities in the connection.

The question of where we go in treatment once this dynamic analysis is reliably made has been answered already by psychoanalysis, on the assumption that it knew the structure reliably, which is very doubtful. Even if its answers were given to the present firm basis, they might not be correct, and we must recognize that the new precisions of the dynamic calculus in P-technique are now capable of providing new precisions of generalization about the effects of various treatments. But those generalizations and principles can emerge only after the dynamic calculus has been applied for some years in clinical psychology.

Meanwhile we must also recognize the economic realism of the second obstacle above, and that advance in clinical understanding from a wide use of P-technique is unlikely to occur so long as P-technique is so time demanding. One can only point out here that in science, whenever the principle has been sound, technologists have sooner or later found some way of overcoming the impracticalities of the basic invention. Surely a clinical task force with sufficient funds and ingenuity will find ways of cutting down the testing time from an hour to ten minutes, and with sufficiently sensitive measures it may not be necessary to wait for a whole day's change. Thus the series of 100 testings might perhaps be condensed from 100 days to 2 days. The ensuing calculations are insignificant to a computer, and we may yet live to see a self-recording testing booth transmitting data to a computer which, a few minutes later, will send back a "quantitative psychoanalysis" showing the origins of symptoms, the locations of conflicts, and the indications for points of attack by relearning and behavior therapy procedures.

4 Evaluating the intensity of conflict at loci and foci In the above section on applying the dynamic calculus by P-technique it is assumed that once the clinician, knowing the dynamic structure in a positive way, has brought the patient to realize connections which produce the symptoms, he can re-educate him to express his ergic needs more appropriately. What psychoanalysis brought out, even for those who think it brought out nothing else, was the extreme complexity of the tangles into which humans are led by their personal history. Part of that tangle is that motives become unconscious—not in the ordinary sense in which most of us are not clear on our real motives, but in the sense of an absolute repressive barrier to our recognizing certain memories and motives as our own.

So far the dynamic calculus has not been pursued here into the concept of the unconscious, though we have pointed out that there is some parallelism between the U (unintegrated) and I (integrated) components in motivation measures and the unconscious and conscious in psychoanalysis. Probably the unconscious is a subdivision within U, namely, the epsilon component (page

14) showing high GSR response with low reminiscence and retarted word association; but this needs crucial research.

Such research must relate the measures of response to some stimulus to a course of action, as revealed by positions on the Adaptation Process Analysis chart, set out in figure 3.1 (page 60). The APA chart is a device for bringing some order into the tangle of motive and counter-motive we have discussed above. It recognizes that the individual's desires and interests have gone through a history of stimulation and frustration involving critical events at what we have called (figure 3.1) "dynamic crossroads" and "chiasms". The dynamic crossroads with which the clinician is concerned are those toward the end of the run, in the branch which starts with irremediable and inexorable frustration at crossroads D, which generates a state of conflict and anxiety. From this state of conflict and anxiety there are three main possible attempts at solution at choice point E, namely, phantasy and related defenses, attempted repression and regression of the ergic expression. If repression is attempted without complete success then the consequence at F is neurosis in some form: conversion symptoms, psychomatic symptoms or anxiety depression symptoms (figure 3.1).

If we are to understand the rise of anxiety and neurosis it is important to be able to measure the intensity of conflict and plot it over the sequences in the C, D, E, and F crossroads. In 1964 Cattell and Sweney considered all the manifestations of conflict listed by clinicians, such as mistakes in memory, vacillation in decision, overweighting of emotional responses, muscle tension, seeking social support, slips in performance, etc. Sweney found that these expressed themselves in some six factors as shown in table 7.1. It should be noted that in this research the concepts of *loci* and *foci* of conflict were introduced. The first is a sociological or environmental concept and defines the *area* of conflict, e.g. between family and religion, peer group and parents, leisure and money, etc. The second defines an internal psychological parameter, between erg and erg, erg and sentiment, sentiment and sentiment. Conceivably the manifestations of conflict could be characteristically different with a different sociological locus, or internal psychological focus, so the research by Cattell and Sweney (1964) planfully varied these. As the three columns on the right of table 7.1 show, there is a rather remarkable degree of constancy across these loci.

These patterns tell us that intensity of conflict needs half a dozen independent scores to encompass it. One expresses suppressor action with cognitive disturbances, another heightened sensitivity with attempt to restrict any reference to the problem, another fantasy, another the familiar increase in tension and impulsivity, etc. Although this study did not include anxiety measures, other studies amply show that anxiety is a usual expression, as also is effort stress (Cattell and Scheier, 1961).

It would be fair to say—in view of the Sweney research being ten years in the literature without replication—that clinicians are not yet seriously appre-

Table 7.1 Dimensions in which conflict is expressed (children)

		Highest loading variables of primary conflict factors			
	Description of conflict factor	Behavioral expressions involved in factor. Note adjectives already adjusted to sign of loading	Loci of conflict*		
			A	B	C
Factor I	Suppressive action with cognitive disturbances				
	1	Many mistakes in performance: cancellation	+33	+26	+59
	3	No vacillation of decision: few erasures	−50	−35	−17
	21	Much displacing conflict into motor performance: cancellation—strikes done	+35	+27	+44
	2	Much interference with attention-memory: newspaper articles	+25	+28	+16
	4	Uneven sensitivity to insults on alternative choices: con minus pro (B−A)	−28	−12	+11
Factor II	Restriction by the presence of possibilities of provocation versus heightened responsiveness to conflict issues				
	6	Reduced perception of conflict-evoking stimuli: scrambled sentences	−64	−43	−41
	8	Rejection of humor on the topic: jokes	−54	−45	−28
	5	Acceptance of more compliments on one side: compliments, pro minus con (A−B)	+32	+10	+24
	7	Restriction of matter perceived cognitively relevant to conflict: matching words	−21	−20	−32
	14	Little belief in possibility of a confluent (compromise) solution	−08	−14	−20
Factor IV	Fantasy from perplexity or frustration versus unconcern over solutions				
	12	Much inclination to fantasy easy solutions	+42	+40	+39
	10	Paralysis of actual decision: many middle category responses	+45	+33	+05
	3	Vacillation on decision: many erasures	+20	+50	−05
	11	Much susceptibility to influence: shift toward authority	+21	+28	+05
	13	More peripheral, subconscious attention to possible solutions: noticing relevant facts	+25	+09	+22

Table 7.1 *cont.*

	Description of conflict factor	Behavioral expressions involved in factor. Note adjectives already adjusted to sign of loading	Loci of conflict*		
			A	B	C
Factor V	Invoking ego action in person versus ignoring conflict				
	6	Enhanced perception of conflict-evoking stimuli: scrambled sentences	+26	+34	+51
	15	Enhanced sense of compliments being paid to either solution: compliments, pro plus con (A+B)	+27	+37	+40
	14	Greater belief in possibility of a confluent (compromise) solution: guessed success	+43	+31	−01
	13	More peripheral, subconscious attention to possible solutions: noticing relevant facts	−07	+31	+46
	4	Uneven sensitivity to insults on alternative choices: pro minus con (A−B)	+20	+30	+08
	23	Little internal inconsistency of action preferences	−34	−27	+06
Factor VI	Expression in tension sensitivity				
	16	More mistakes in immediate memory: coding errors	+37	+42	+20
	17	More pugnacity–anxiety over choices: controlled muscle-tension change	+40	+29	+41
	18	Enhanced sensitivity to insults to either viewpoint: insults, pro plus con (A+B)	+26	+28	+29
	15	Enhanced sense of compliments being paid to either solution: compliments, pro plus con (A+B)	+34	+08	+32
	3	Vacillating decision: many erasures	+24	+33	−12

Note: Factor III, which may be anxiety, is omitted because considered later.

* The loci of conflict were A, reading funnies versus going to Sunday School; B, looking after younger sibs versus pets; C, pleasing peers versus pleasing parents.

ciative of what the measurement of intensity of conflict could do for their science and their practice. Incidentally, this is part of the general failure of newcomers to science to realize how inexorably all advance in sound theory hinges on advance in clarity and precision of measurement. The questions persist "Are these seven or eight distinct directions of expression of conflict (including anxiety, effort stress, and, ultimately, depression) the full span of expressions?" And "What is the meaning of their distinctness?" In response to the latter one might theorize that each represents a different chiasm on the APA (Adjustment Process Analysis) chart (page 60). This is persuasive, for example, with regard to effort stress (chiasm B), anxiety (chiasm C) and depression (chiasm D), as responses to a conflict situation which moves into increasing insolubility, as shown. On the other hand, one might theorize that they represent the effects of frustration on each of the distinctive *motivational* components (α, β, γ, etc.). But since a well-checked theory is not yet in our possession regarding the latter this does not immediately help us. On the model expressed in equation (3.15) (page 73)—that these components represent respectively a stimulation effect, a gratification effect, a past history, a physiological state, etc.—we should simply suppose that each represents a high tension on the given component. These approaches are speculative, but meanwhile the facts are sufficiently checked by the three loci studied above; that when conflict over behavioral expression arises it takes the form of specific expression in cognitive avoidance of the topic, hesitating behavior, physical signs of tension, fantasy over solutions, tendency to make mistakes in current activities, and anxiety. And as far as experiment yet goes these kinds of independently developed expression run across all sociological loci and psychological foci of conflict.

5   The nature of anxiety and its relation to conflict and drive strength   When Freud said that "anxiety is the central problem of the neuroses" he was making a sound observation which, however, nowadays must be extended to include the additional dimensions of conflict just discussed. The question in clinical psychology that we are approaching is "How do these measures of conflict—in suppressor action, restriction, impulsivity, vacillation, anxiety and effort stress—relate to our measures of motivation strength and to the indices of conflict worked out in the motivation domain?"

A fairly common and uncritical assumption is that anxiety is itself a form of motivation. Several experiments in Spencerian learning theory have been carried out using anxiety scales as measures of motivation strength. And it is a common expression of the man in the street that he is "anxious to do so and so". Yet the opposing theory will be developed here that anxiety is not a *primary* source of motivation, but only a derivative, and that in some cases it is the merest debris of motivation, exercising a disorganizing rather than strengthening action on performance and achievement. In saying this one must emphasize the difference between fear and anxiety [which Freud labored over semantically in *"Furcht"* and *"Angst"*, and which Cattell and Bartlett (1971) have brought out factor analytically]. The drive to the goal of security (fear) is simply another erg, like sex or self-assertion, and as such is a real source of energy and reactivity. The introspective resemblance of anxiety to faint fear we shall seek to explain below.

To proceed it is necessary first to define anxiety. Between 1960 and 1970 tremendous strides were made in locating the unique pattern of anxiety as a trait and a state, and in separating it from other states, such as stress, depression, arousal, and regression. The research concerned was done in the frame of reference that we can distinguish *general states*, on the one hand, such as anxiety, arousal, depression, which are not bound to the action of any one drive, from specific *ergic tension states*, on the other, such as hunger, fear, lust, pity, etc., clearly related to particular ergs and primate behaviors. It is also an historical fact that research on these two areas proceeded with some independence of method and personnel. Anxiety, and the general states were investigated by questionnaires, physiological batteries, and clinical signs and by both psychometrists and clinicians whereas the ergic tensions were investigated by objective devices (in the motivational components) and by experimentalists and psychometrists. It is the concepts from these two streams that we are now aiming to bring together.

The steps for "zeroing in" on the anxiety concept and its measurement can be condensed as follows:

(1) Among objective measures of personality, e.g. enterprise in performance, emotionality of comment, accuracy/speed ratio, a single factor indexed U.I.24 (Hundleby, Pawlik, and Cattell, 1965) was discovered (Cattell, 1955) which fitted the common clinical properties of anxiety.

(2) A second-order factor among questionnaire primaries, covering C−, H−, L, O, Q₃− and Q₄, was well replicated (Cattell, 1956; Cattell and Scheier, 1961) also having the properties of anxiety, as shown by clinical associations. This factor QII proved to align with the objective test factor U.I.24 (Cattell, 1955) and to be different from U.I.23, regression (Eysenck's "neuroticism") and from depression and other "neurotic" states.

(3) When research proceeded from traits to states, by shifting from R (individual difference) to dR (difference over time), a corresponding state pattern was found (Cattell and Scheier, 1961) in both Q and T media differing little in pattern from QII and U.I.24.

(4) This state pattern has been shown to behave with situational changes (Cattell and Scheier, 1961), with tranquilizing drugs, etc. (Cattell, Rickels *et al.*, 1966), as such criteria would require. Anxiety as trait plus state has also been shown to correlate negatively with school performance (Sarason *et al.*, 1960;

Cattell and Butcher, 1968) *et al.* These general extensions of content and criterion relation for the anxiety factor (QII–U.I.24) can be read in Spielberger (1972).

(5) A more complete characterization of the anxiety state, by differentiation as a factor from stress, arousal, regression, depression, etc., has been made by Curran (1968), Bartsch and Nesselroade (1973), and Barton (forthcoming), and included as a measure in the *Eight State Battery* (Curran and Cattell, 1974).

Thus both conceptually and in terms of uncontaminated measurement, anxiety advanced between 1954 and 1974 in precision and applicability. Conceptually it has the property on the physiological side of *generalized autonomic* excitation. A refactoring of Wenger's data on autonomic variables (Cattell, 1950) and a repeat with broader data (Cattell and Luborsky, 1950) showed that it resolved into sympathetic and parasympathetic system factors plus a *general* autonomic factor loading such variables as pulse rate, blood pressure, body temperature and metabolic rate, large GSR response, large ratio of pupil to iris, high critical flicker fusion frequency, and ratings of higher activity level. Later research has emphasized in the physiological response pattern also faster respiration, low skin resistance, excretion of ketosteroids in urine, more and more acid saliva, etc. The difference from various specific drives is obvious: the difference from arousal is that arousal is more cortical whereas anxiety is a general autonomic expression, and so on. Introspectively anxiety is experienced as a restlessness, hesitation, lack of confidence, and inability to cope. It seems to be a by-product of any high drive stimulation where the appropriate specific coping responses cannot be made.

The quality of attenuated fear must be presumed due to our capacity to become afraid of loss and deprivation. Any threat to the satisfaction of any drive can evoke anger, but because of our capacity to react to symbolic dangers it also evokes degrees of fear. Expectation of a deficient future satisfaction thus evokes anxiety, but it is suggested also that *uncertainty*, making any drive-reducing course of action difficult to choose also converts ergic tension into anxiety. A precise model has been developed by Cattell regarding the relation of anxiety to dynamic drive strength out of the above considerations. It supposes (Spielberger, 1972, page 173) that there are three contributors to the level of anxiety, which may be placed in an equation thus:

$$A = a_e + a_c + a_p \qquad (7.2)$$

The component a_e is the contribution from the ergic tension, E, of the drives being excited, but its effect is augmented by the degree of uncertainty, U, about the best course of action for satisfaction as well as the individual's temperamental proneness to fear, F, i.e. his susceptibility to threat. Thus:

$$a_e = E.\,U.\,F \qquad (7.3)$$

(This has constants and some elaborations in the Spielberger presentation.) The second component, a_c, is what Freud described as the threat to the ego, and which we may operationalize as fear of loss of control, with whatever painful consequences have come from that before. If we consider the personality factors C, ego strength, G, superego, and Q_3, self-sentiment, to represent the individual's sources of control then:

$$a_c = \frac{1}{(C + G + Q_3) - ka_e} \tag{7.4}$$

where k is a scaling constant. That is to say, this component of anxiety increases as the ergic tension source of anxiety climbs closer to the strength of the controlling forces.

The third component is theorized to be the threat of definitely known and expected loss or deprivation. One might argue that this is only disappointment or depression, not anxiety. If a man knows for certain that he will have a tooth removed tomorrow it could be that he will experience no anxiety about it, and if we argue that he is anxious because there is *always* an element of uncertainty in life then this formula would merely return us to the a_e component. Social psychology measures, however, tell us that anxiety is higher in people of lower economic resources, and it seems reasonable to add a term for low gratification as a *certain* loss of satisfaction, thus:

$$a_p = a_e - G \tag{7.5}$$

where G is the amount of habitual gratification from a course of action. The resulting formulation from substituting in (7.2) looks complex (though it is simpler than the earlier formulation it replaces in Spielberger):

$$A = 2\,E.U.F - G + \frac{1}{(C + G + Q_3) - k(E.U.F)} \tag{7.6}$$

In general terms this is saying that anxiety is a function of the stimulated drive level, of the fear of deprivation, of the degree of cognitive uncertainty regarding suitable action, and of certain personality traits which magnify any fear response, and of others which determine degree of control. The relation of anxiety to motivation is that it is a complex by-product and not the whole of motivation. It would indeed be a dreary philosophy that all our acts are generated by anxiety. Much behavior is directly motivated by the need to satisfy hunger, assertion, gregariousness, sex, curiosity, etc., i.e. the basic ergs, and it is only the complexity of our culture which forces some of this motivation to be held up, transformed into anxiety, and directed into a somatically exhausting form of expression.

Now it turns out that the other forms of expression of conflict studied by Sweney may have a similar relationship. The fact that the number of conflict primaries found by Sweney matched exactly the number of motivation factors found in several earlier researches suggested to Cattell that the possibility of identity should be examined. Krug (1971) included the motivation and conflict measures in one factoring, and found indeed that the markers appeared on the same factors. This suggests that these conflict expressions, like anxiety, have much of their variance determined by strength of motivation. Nevertheless, if the above theory and model for anxiety is correct, dynamic strength is not the *only* determiner of the variance, and probably, as with anxiety, we can look for a second-order pattern in personality factors that will contribute over and above the motivation primaries, to their expression in particular conflict forms. Thus there seems no longer any doubt that for a given intensity of ergic arousal, and a given degree of thwarting of expression and requirement of control, individuals of low ego strength (C−), high threctia (threat susceptibility, H−), high guilt-proneness (O), and poor self-sentiment development (Q_3−) will show more anxiety.

Manipulating human drive levels, and frustrating their expression, in experimental situations, is one of the hardest areas of psychology in which to work. The above theory suggests that the state levels on anxiety and the other conflict measures should, however, be a function both of the level of such stimulation-with-nongratification, in so far as it can be produced, and the individual's trait levels on C, H, O, Q_3, etc. The derivation of quantitative laws in this area, roughly on the model of (7.6) above, would certainly be a great contribution to clinical psychology.

6   The action of the self-sentiment and the superego

It is in clinical psychology that the main attempts have been made in the past to develop dynamic principles to the point where the miracle of the integration of the self might be understood. Regardless of clinical psychology the dynamic calculus would ultimately have to face this issue, but the problem is met centrally in mental disorder and its treatment, and it is in this chapter that we can appropriately study it.

Actually the necessary factual findings and conceptual ingredients for the present synthesis have been set out three chapters back in "Integrative behavior and the dynamic calculus" (chapter 4). But the presentation was so unavoidably condensed that it is appropriate to review the foundations and extend them before proceeding.

Apart from hypothesizing a stabilizing effect of sentiments upon ergs generally, i.e. the provision of learnt appropriate channels for discharge of stimulated ergs, the theory stated that integrated behavior is assisted by three structures: the ego (C factor), the superego (G factor), and the self-sentiment (factor Q_3).

The self-sentiment, which can be measured both as a personality factor in questionnaires, and as an attitude sentiment structure by objective motivation tests (tables 4.1 and 4.2), hinges on the existence of a cognitive conception of the self which the paths of action on the sentiment are concerned to preserve. The attitudes clearly show a foresighted subsidiation to the end of preserving the physical, social, and moral self, with the emphasis on a useful social image and a firm basis for self-respect. The superego—G, in questionnaires, SE, in the attitude factor pattern—is an uncompromising demand for morality, and even all these years after Freud's attempts to explain its origin we are still in appreciable doubt about the ergic goals which sustain it. If we accept the theory that the loading of the strong attitudes in a sentiment on ergs tells what investment or cathexis that sentiment has on ergic goals then (Cattell, Horn, Sweney, and Radcliffe, 1964) we find the superego *negatively* loaded on self-assertion, and narcism, and little positively on anything (except the self-sentiment, which by theory is subsidiated to the superego). The psychoanalytic theory is perhaps not too crudely stated by saying that the superego attitudes are generated in the first few years of life to satisfy affection and fear. Are we perhaps to consider that "imprinting" acts so powerfully in these first years of parental exposure that the superego virtually becomes functionally autonomous—so much a force in itself as to constitute factor analytically an "erg" on its own, with its connections with fear, dependence, libido, etc., no longer demonstrable? In terms of *correlations with other factors*, not loading on attitudes shared with other dynamic structure factors, the evidence has been reasonably consistent that superego strength correlates negatively with strength of the sex, fear, self-assertive, and narcistic ergs, and positively with strength of sentiment to the parental home. Whether one can argue from this that some higher order factor has somehow robbed these ergs of their motivation and transformed it into superego strength remains to be seen.

Intensive studies were carried out both by Gorsuch (1965) and Horn (1961) to trace the structural connections of the self-sentiment and the superego (and, more incidentally, of the ego) because it has been a favorite theme of theorists, such as Allport and, more precisely, McDougall, that the ultimate integration of personality brings the self-concept (or sentiment) and the superego into a functional unity. Factor analytically this amounts to the expectation that although G and Q_3 are distinct as primaries they will prove to possess a single second order that will account for most of the variance of both. Parenthetically, this would satisfy not only many clinicians, but also the almost obsessional liking of many old style factor analysts for a hierarchy capped by a single monarchical factor at the second or third order.

But that is not the way the careful factor analyses of Horn and Gorsuch came out. Instead they agreed in showing the self-sentiment and the superego persisting in their independence right through the third order. They also showed a substantial negative relation at the second and third order, not suspected before, between anxiety and a higher order integration of superego manifestation across (a) diverse instrumentalities (SE in the MAT and G in the 16 PF) and (b) a very wide array of superego value areas tried by Horn. If psycho-analysis is right in finding anxiety raised by the demands of the superego, then this must be a peculiarity of the neurotic path. For across the general population the gross balance sheet is clearly that the stronger superego is associated with reduced conflict and anxiety. One may speculate that this means that the person of strong superego never gets into such temptations, or such predicaments from having succumbed to temptations, as beset the life of the person of weaker superego.

The second-order factor that one *does* find in this area, and which has been repeatedly replicated, and indexed as QVIII is, as described in table 4.3, page 108, one which loads G substantially (perhaps more than half its variance) and Q_3 quite moderately, but also desurgency, $F(-)$, moderately, and ego strength, C, slightly. What can be made of this theoretically? The most probable explanation is that which has been embodied in the tentative title for QVIII, "integrative upbringing". That is to say it is a pattern which develops to the extent that a child is brought up in a family giving concern to moral upbringing in a stable psychological background. This, we hypothesize, favors particularly (1) the early superego development; (2) produces also a reduction in the general happy-go-lucky impulsivity of surgency (an aspect of maturity in as much as surgency declines normally fairly steeply with age); (3) provides a favorable atmosphere for a consistent self-sentiment (Q_3) to emerge; and (4) also helps, though only slightly, and probably through the anxiety reduction, in the growth of ego strength. But to say that all of these are subject to such an upbringing influence is not to say that they are functionally bound together, though on other grounds—the theory of subsidiation in the dynamic lattice—we would expect some functional relation of the self-sentiment to the superego, in as much as it has to subsidiate to it—among other goals.

One would naturally hope to supplement the cross-sectional correlation evidence so far considered by developmental evidence, which can only be meaningful, however, if it traces the development of an *identifiable factor pattern* across several strategically planned cross-sections. There are not lacking any number of theories about developmental stages, such as Kohlberg's (1964) stages in the superego and Loevinger's (1969) about the development of ego strength. The agreement of Kohlberg's theoretical patterns, which pass from a purely practical "Shall I get punished?" first to a regard for group opinion, and ultimately to the internalized superego we describe in G, with cross-sectional factor evidence is scarcely to be seen. Questionnaire investigation has shown the G pattern in adults, in sixteen year olds (Cattell, Wagner, and Cattell, 1970), in ten year olds (Schaie and Cattell, in preparation), and as far as can be seen from the content the pattern is remarkably constant, showing from at least seven years the "categorical imperative" character which Kant and Freud have always maintained. However, data from objective motivation measures is still lacking below twelve (the MAT stops at 18, and SMAT at 12) and the more refined developmental analyses are still to come. Meanwhile one must suspect that the armchair analyses of the superego which speak of a progress from responsibility to group reputation to responsibility to an "inner voice" are confusing two patterns—the self-sentiment (Q_3) and the superego (G)—which are simultaneously present all along, though in different proportions in different people.

It has perhaps already been made sufficiently clear that G and Q_3 are what is technically called "cooperative factors". That is to say they are distinct influences which nevertheless overlap much more than would be statistically expected in the variables they affect. Thus the analyses of Cattell, Horn, Sweney, and Radcliffe 1964) show them to share loading on "I want to control my impulses", "I want to maintain a good reputation", "I want to reduce vice in society", and so on. The factors themselves, however, are essentially uncorrelated, which suggests that any subsidiation of the self-sentiment to the superego, such as we have considered above, is trivial. The self-sentiment is concerned with self-preservation, for which good self-control and a good social reputation are important. The superego desires these for more idealistic reasons. It is concerned with the preservation of society, not of the individual, and is so handed down. The two get confused when clinical insight fails to distinguish the different roots of "prizing a good reputation" and when psychometrics mistakes a correlation cluster (which the above attitudes undoubtedly form) for a factor, which better methodology would resolve into two uncorrelated factors.

7   The quantitative, experimental concept of the ego structure and its integrative action

The triumvirate of powers—C, G, and Q_3—most discussed as integrators by psychologists, is at present more clarified experimentally in regard to the relation of superego and self-sentiment than the relation of ego strength to these. The C factor of ego strength has been well located in questionnaires, and tolerably in objective tests, but not at all in the factoring of attitudes measured by objective motivation devices, such as have revealed superego and self-sentiment. The perhaps obvious reason is that SE and SS (Q_3 and G) are concerned with the "what" of motivation, i.e. they have content, whereas C is concerned with the "how", and has no specific content.

As discussed so far the nature of the C factor has been documented as a capacity to control impulse in the interests of the best overall, long-term satisfaction. Low C loads items such as "inability to cope", "dissatisfied emotionality", "dissatisfaction with the self", "inability to maintain a steady line of action", and "being at the mercy of one's own emotionality". Low C correlates so substantially with high ergic tension, Q_4, and high guilt-proneness or inadequacy, O, that factor analyses are still published (e.g. Comrey and Duffy, 1968; Howarth and Browne, 1971) which fail to separate them. Descriptively this says that inability to arrange for effective expression of one's drives, leading to high accumulation of ergic tension, is correlated with and easily mistaken for, the sheer ergic tension accumulation itself. Just as a poor engineer might fail to distinguish the pressure on a dam resulting from heavy rains from that due to blockage of the turbines. Actually the second-order personality factor which most involves $C(-)$ brings in not only O and Q_4, but some $G(-)$ and much $H(-)$, L, and $Q_3(-)$. This factor which is clearly recognizable by many associations as anxiety will be discussed in a moment in connection with the combined action of C, G, and Q_3.

Meanwhile, in seeking to understand the nature of C, ego strength, we have pointed to something analogous to it in animal experiment when the animal is required to learn to defer and control the response he is immediately being stimulated to make, in the interests of getting fuller satisfaction to that impulse. Our central theory of ego strength is that it is a capacity which shows itself in (1) the ability to learn to delay gratification for increased gratification just instanced, and (2) the ability to compromise between two contending stimulated emotional impulses in such a way as to maximize joint satisfaction. We hypothesize that both of these depend on the same power which is partly genetic and partly acquired. It is partly genetic because animal psychology reveals substantial differences between species in this "deferment" capacity, and among men it is associated with differences in intact frontal lobe anatomy. The acquired component has presented us with a puzzle already discussed—namely, that the action of reinforcement is generally specific, whereas here, to account for the general C factor, it is necessary to suppose that control "in the abstract" is increased by reward for specific action of control.

A full discussion of this would take us too far afield into diverse experimental and clinical areas, but we shall hypothesize that there *is* a generalized reward from acts of self-control (partly due to the teaching agencies—parents and school—pointing out the connections and generalizations) and generalized punishment, partly through the existence of the self-sentiment, occurring at each loss of control. (Evidence of growth of ego strength through reduction of emotional upsets is offered by Cattell and Rickels, 1968.)

In advanced cultures the nature–nurture ratio for the development of ego strength is high presumably because our culture requires people to operate close to the upper limit of their powers of self-control. Learning influences favoring control are strong, but the individual encounters conflict beyond an endurable point in terms of biological limits. One outcome of extensive use of the 16 PF, with its defined ego strength factor, has been the finding that no other factor has its property of being low universally through all forms of clinical disorder, neurotic and psychotic. In the neuroses this is not so severe and is partly accounted for by height of the second-order anxiety factor, which contains C(−); but in the psychoses it is the cardinal feature, along with the general psychoticism factor. The latter, common to six different directions of psychosis, may represent that cognitive confusion, hallucination, etc., which is a primary statement of loss of reality contact. But low ego strength is also a part of loss of the reality principle in as much as the individual is no longer able to defer and compromise over emotional drive satisfaction in a way realistic for his greatest satisfaction. Although the question cannot be pursued far here, one naturally enquires what the cause of ego strength weakening or poor development may be. As argued below, within certain ranges a high anxiety level may be. As argued above, failure to establish rewarding integration, through traumatic experiences of being emotionally overcome, may contribute, and though the Rickels–Cattell evidence (Cattell, Rickels, Weise *et al.*, 1966) from tranquillizers, above, has not yet been put to experiment again, it is at least suggestive. Obviously, injury to the frontal lobes, though uncommon except in the portion of the population with severe atherosclerosis, weakens ego strength. Finally, and more systematically, we would revert to the experiment of J. R. Williams (chapter 4, page 109) showing that psychotics have higher *indurated conflict* scores than controls, i.e. that their behavior generally has reached poorer confluence of drives and has tied up more dynamic energy in internal conflict. One may at least hypothesize that ego strength is an inverse function of the $\Sigma \bar{b}^2$ value (page 93), and the evidence of Das (1955) on C factor and attitude inconsistency, and of Cattell (1943) on C factor and fluctuation of attitudes fits in with this.

The position we are taking here is that all three structures play a part in what is commonly evaluated clinically as control and integration. The evidence for this springs not only from direct evidence of control, but also from indications of interaction, e.g. in the genesis of anxiety, and also in a few peculiar observations. An instance of the latter lies in the finding that Q_3 is high in schizophrenics, in whom C is low, and has led to the suggestion (Cattell and Tatro, 1966) that, at least in disorders of slow onset, there is an attempt to substitute behavior control through the self-sentiment for the disappearing control from the ego structure, much as a ship falls back on hand control of steering when power control fails.

The theory that all three of the "controllers" we have discussed—C, G and Q_3—operate upon the same control problems is supported also by the repeatedly replicated pattern of the second-order anxiety factor, and by the Gorsuch and Horn findings of increased anxiety at lower superego strength. G must operate at a different level in as much as its negative loading on anxiety is small, and the negative correlation is with anxiety as a whole, between third-order factors deriving from QII, anxiety, and QVIII, integrating upbringing (G, F−, Q_3). Presumably the person of high G succeeds in avoiding situations of maladjustment, which are the root of much anxiety, from the beginning. But once one is in an anxiety-generating situation, then the story is better told by the loadings of the second-order anxiety factor, QII. The roles of H, L, and O need not be pursued in this dynamic context, since they seem to be temperament factors which magnify whatever dynamic effect exists, but the loadings in C($-$), $Q_3(-)$ and Q_4 (ergic tension) are very relevant to our present enquiry into control systems.

Surely the most likely hypothesis here is that ego weakness with its poor control of impulse, and an ill-organized and poorly formed self-sentiment, $Q_3(-)$, making the directions of required control unclear, combine to leave a disturbing accumulation of ergic tension, Q_4, undisposed of. This in turn threatens the already weak ego, leading to a "spiral of anxiety" as set out in the theory of QII elsewhere (Cattell, 1973). Conceivably also the QII correlations are telling us that additionally a high anxiety level is developmentally inimical to the growth of C, though this would lead us into the question of the still scarcely attacked issue of the effect of prevailing state levels upon a dynamic learning process.

Integration is definable as the making of correct decisions in the context of the total and long circuited satisfaction of the dynamics of the individual, and, therewith the reduction of that "degraded" energy which appears in anxiety, and the other signs of conflict. In chapter 4 the dynamic calculus of a decision has been set out as the calculation of the difference between two specification equations, representing the strengths of two competing attitudes (courses of action) $a_{h_1 i j_1}$ and $a_2 \hat{h}_{i j_2}$ thus:

$$a_{h_1 i j_1} = \overset{e=r}{\underset{}{\Sigma}}\ b_{j_1 e S h_1 e} E_{ei} + \overset{m=p}{\underset{}{\Sigma}}\ b_{j_1 m S h_1 m} M_{mi}$$

$$a_{h_2 i j_2} = \overset{e=r}{\underset{}{\Sigma}}\ b_{j_2 e S h_2 e} E_{ei} + \overset{m=p}{\underset{}{\Sigma}}\ b_{j_2 m S h_2 m} M_{mi}$$

where h_1 and h_2 are two stimuli occurring at the same time stimulating respectively actions j_1 and j_2. The E's are ergic tensions that gain satisfaction through these courses of action and the M's are excitation levels of sentiments in which these attitudes have been incorporated.

If the actions are such as to involve moral conflict then one of the M's heavily involved will be the superego sentiment (SE or G). And if additionally the behavior contemplated is such as to involve the person's self-regard, in regard to community reputation and his own self-respect, the self-sentiment (SS or Q_3) will also come in strongly. Most likely, as we have seen, they will act with the same sign, but they need not do so, as with Savonarola, when G mastered Q_3 or many a politician, when status needs overcome conscience.

A typical integrative challenge is where $a_{h_1 i j_1}$ has heavy loadings on E's compared with M's and the individual himself stands at high ergic tension levels, while $a_{h_2 i j_2}$ has loadings mainly on the self-sentiment and superego sentiments. It has been suggested earlier that integration requires that the loadings (b's—but also the s's) shall be higher for the SE and SS factors than for most ergs on most attitude-actions. But now, through the above dis-cussion of ego strength, we see the necessity for something more. For what if all the accountancy of dynamics comes down in favor of the decision for action (1) rather than (2) but the individual finds himself unable to sustain the defer-ment of satisfaction which action (1) requires? To revert to the earlier distinction of G and Q_3 on the one hand, from C on the other, *what* is best to be done, in the interests of maximum satisfaction, has been decided by the dynamic calculus, but *how* the decision is to be effected remains for the ego to show. Some theorists may regret that the simplicity of the accountancy in the dynamic calculus is upset by this new dimension of determiners, but completeness requires them. These determiners have to do with an ego strength term, with terms for relative length of deferment of satisfaction in the two courses. Prob-ably this will lead to a specification equation for the act of decison itself, in-volving measures of ego strength. Until this is developed the integrative process will not be fully encompassed.

8   Summary   1. The contribution of the dynamic calculus to clinical psychology is considered in relation to (a) diagnosis–prognosis, and (b) insightful explanation and treatment. In pursuing the latter it is essentially continuing the study of the higher levels of the dynamic calculus, in the domain of integration, approached in chapter 4.

2. Diagnosis is first aided by study of profiles of patients, delinquents, addicts, and other deviants in regard to statistically helpful differences on profiles on the ten ergs and sentiments measured in the MAT, SMAT and other objective dynamic structure probes. Analysis in terms of comparison on inte-grated and unintegrated components, as pioneered by Sweney, has been particularly enlightening. Excess of the unintegrated component has proved an almost invariable indicator of maladjustment or conflict.

3. A second contribution to diagnosis is the use of P-technique yielding information on the individual foci of conflict and aspiring to a "quantitative psychoanalysis". Reasons for the delay in developing the method in clinical practice are examined in terms of technical difficulties, cost, and the temporary retreat of clinical psychology from understanding the patient as distinct from removing a symptom.

4. Progress in clinical laws requires a capacity to quantify degrees of con-flict. A comprehensive array of dynamic conflict indicators has been factored, consistently yielding the same six or seven dimensions across different socio-logical loci of conflict. However, there is strong evidence that these dimensions are nothing other than the seven primary motivational components, but measured in a domain of conflict indicators, so that we are saying that conflict intensity is, first, simply proportional to the strength of the motives in conflict.

5. Anxiety, and perhaps other "general states" such as stress, regression,

depression, must also be considered derivatives of conflict. In the case of anxiety, measurement has reached such relative precision that equations can be hypothesized expressing the relation of anxiety to the strengths of motives involved. Here the known correlations with personality factors demonstrate, however, that additional terms to those of motivation strength are required to account for the severity of conflict, such as cognitive uncertainty, ego weakness, guilt-proneness and (negatively) strength of the self-sentiment.

6. The superego and the (ideal) self-sentiment have often been theorized to integrate but the evidence is clear that they remain independent factors at all levels of factor analysis. They are also persistently negatively related to anxiety. The virtual absence of intercorrelation suggests that not much of the self-sentiment is subsidiated to the superego, but that its concern with "ethical" behavior is social. Both dynamic structures, however, "cooperate" in strengthening attitudes of self-control, regard for social reputation, etc. Certain stages in the development of superego, ego, and self-sentiment can be speculatively set out, but positive evidence on pattern change is still lacking. The most reliable evidence indicates pattern persistence from 7 through 22 years of age.

7. Although behavior in the area of control, integration, and ethical standards is clearly effected by a triumvirate of discoverable structures—C, G, and Q_3—the nature of the ego strength factor is very different from the other two. Partly built up by reinforcement of diverse specific integrative successes and partly determined by genetic limits, ego strength appears as a capacity maximally to find realistic expression for ergs, by deferment of satisfactions, compromises of drives in confluent behavior, etc. All three structures combine in decision-making, as is shown, for example, by anxiety and other conflict signs being negatively associated with the strength of each. The superego and self-sentiment, having content, determine more the "what" of action; the ego the "how". Thus comparing two specification equations (and the individual's endowments) may indicate what the outcome should be in terms of a satisfactory choice, but ego strength measures may indicate how feasible it is to make the decision.

8 Motivation in education: the dynamics of structured learning theory

1 Psychological aspects of predicting school achievement Education is involved both in teaching and assessing the effects of teaching. From a psychological point of view the former rests on learning theory (and classroom group dynamics) and the latter on psychometrics. In the former the recent advances in motivation research promise revolutionary developments in learning theory. The impact in regard to assessing and predicting examination achievement, on the other hand, can be more readily contained within classical psychometrics. Accordingly we plan to begin with this simpler problem and advance to the radical changes in learning theory thereafter.

Assessment may be thought of as having two stages: (1) Selection of those who will best profit by a given form of education. This we may call prediction of potential, and (2) Assessment by examinations. Beyond the classroom and lecture hall stand employers and professional bodies who require accurate and dependable assurances that a satisfactory level of competence has been reached. Certainly industry and the professions such as medicine, the law, and teaching need to know, in the interests of economy and safeguarding the public, that the majority of their trainees are capable of reaching the required standard.

Let us take dependable exams for granted, as beyond present interests, and ask what the psychologist does to predict individuals' performance. All the emphasis until this decade, both in selection and counselling, has been upon intelligence tests. In Great Britain, tests of verbal and numerical ability were for many years the major criteria for placing school children at age eleven into different kinds of schools said to be best suited for the intellectual prowess of the children. However, all these attempts at prediction have been marred by the limitations of the instruments in measuring the range of characteristics. Measures of human ability give only part of the picture of human potential and when these have been extended to include self-rated interest in different occupational horizons the procedure has become unreliable.

The literature of attempts to relate predictors of achievement to the criterion —actual performance—is quite extensive (for example, see Lavin, 1967; Cattell and Butcher, 1968; Fiks, 1969; Dielman, Barton, and Cattell, 1971; Sumner and Warburton, 1972) and are popularly considered under the four major domains of cognitive, temperamental, dynamic, and sociological determinants, e.g. biographical inventory data. Even physical characteristics such as hyperuricemia have been associated with achievement (Dunn *et al.*, 1963; Brooks and Mueller, 1966; Anumonye *et al.*, 1969; Katz *et al.*, 1973). The research findings at graduate, college, and school levels have regularly shown the most reliable measures of ability account for about 25 percent of the variation in academic performance, i.e. the correlation centers on 0.5. But, our day to day observations have taught us that intelligence is not enough to account for the variations and irregularities in task performance. Adequate performance obviously depends also on the degree of interest and the attitudes of people, i.e. upon their motivational condition. It is probable also that specific broad surface personality attributes are potent, and, as we shall see later emotional stability and the source traits of superego strength (G), self-sufficiency (Q₂), submissiveness (E−), and reservedness (A) are vital in affecting academic performance.

Social variables also have some effect on performance. Apart from the obvious consequences of socioeconomic background, there is ample ground for believing that role relationships, both inside and outside school or college, can affect the attitudes of students and hence their achievement. In part this belongs in the domain of motivation in so far as the individual's acquired attitudes towards academic work, will be part and parcel of his sentiment structure, especially to his school, his self-concept, and his superego sentiment. As we shall see, other things being equal, a high measure of self-sentiment correlates with school achievement. The n'Ach or "need for achievement" motive of McClelland is also closely related to this self-sentiment. The pupil who is high on superego tends to be conscientious and hence more likely to settle down to the dogged task of studying.

Much progress has been made in "sizing up" the relative contributions of these four sources of variance to scholastic achievement. But since the values alter with the age, social status, educational level, etc., there is need for continuing research. A general additive behavioral equation has already been given in chapter 2 having the following form:

$$\text{Achievement } P_j = b_{ja}A + \ldots + b_{jt}T + \ldots + b_{jd}D + \ldots \qquad (8.1)$$

The b terms are behavioral indices and A, T, and D have their usual meanings. The dots after each term are a recognition of the fact that there are several abilities, temperament or dynamic traits involved. Objective tests of abilities and temperamental traits having high validity and reliability have been with us for some time, and values can be inserted for A and T terms; only in the last decade have we seen sufficient advance in motivation measurement to enable us to obtain some idea of what the D terms do. This has come about particularly through recent developments in the measurement of motivation, in particular the appearance of such objective measures as provided by the MAT and SMAT scales.

However, before outlining some of the research which brings together these sources of variance, we must first say a word about the method expressing the contribution of each to the total achievement. The most popular procedure is to square the correlation coefficient obtained between the trait and the measure of achievement in order to obtain the variance. Thus if the correlation between intelligence and achievement in a given school subject is .6, the variance contributed by intelligence will be $(.6)^2 = .36$. In other words if all people taking the exam were exactly equal in intelligence we should expect the variability of exam marks to be reduced by 36 percent. (Expressed as a percentage we simply multiply the squared r by 100.) The result also says that 64 percent of the variance in achievement is not attributable to intelligence and this tells us that we must look elsewhere for the remaining source of variance.

The earliest attempts to involve all three modalities (Cattell, Sealy, and Sweney, 1966; Cattell and Butcher, 1968) and compare their predictive powers revealed immediately that they are of about the same order of magnitude. Although psychologists had confined their predictions for fifty years to intelligence tests the evidence is that temperament tests and dynamic motivation or interest tests are about equally important. Let us scrutinize the experimental results more closely.

2   The nature and magnitude of motivational effects

The strategy in the studies here briefly surveyed has been to measure all three modalities of predictors in the student (holding the fourth—his present environment—out of the calculation), namely, ability, personality, and motivation. In this way their relative magnitudes can be easily compared, and any statistical interaction effects among them studied. The main studies today using this combinatory tactic and with meaningful unitary traits as predictors are those of Barton, Butcher, Cattell, Dielman, Sumner, and Warburton.

Table 8.1 shows results from Cattell and Butcher's (1968) study with high school students and table 8.2 shows studies with somewhat younger children. Results have also been obtained on personality factor predictions at the University level. The remarkable characteristic of these results is the similarity of the predictive weights: (a) across all main areas of school performance, and (b) across different ages, though here there are some interesting differences

Table 8.1 Multiple correlations between tests of personality, motivation, and ability and measures of school achievement (144 seventh- and eighth-grade pupils)

Test of personality, motivation, and ability	Number of predictor variables	Criteria	
		Standardized achievement test	Average of school grades
SMAT	15	.522 (.282)	.482 (.164)
*HSPQ (less factor B)†	13	.520 (.329)	.597 (.462)
HSPQ + SMAT	28	.688 (.367)	.717 (.449)
HSPQ + SMAT + IQ	29	.854 (.734)	.813 (.650)

Source: Cattell and Butcher (1968).
* HSPQ = High School Personality Questionnaire.
† Factor B is a measure of intelligence.
Figures in parentheses are the multiple correlation coefficients corrected for shrinkage.

Table 8.2 Prediction of school achievement from ability, personality, and motivation measures (sixth and seventh grade)

Model	Percentage variance							
	Social science		Science		Mathematics		Reading	
	6th	7th	6th	7th	6th	7th	6th	7th
1. HSPQ + CFIQ + SMAT vs. O	54	51	46	55	61	69	69	76
2. SMAT vs. O	38	39	32	43	38	45	58	64
3. HSPQ − B vs. O	23	20	16	21	19	27	28	25
4. CFIQ vs. O	19	22	15	29	36	43	27	42
5. I vs. O	35	34	29	41	32	41	55	58
6. U vs. O	4	8	4	9	7	13	10	23
7. HSPQ + CFIQ + SMAT vs. CFIQ + HSPQ	12	13	9	11	9	14‡	19‡	17‡
8. HSPQ + CFIQ + I vs. CFIQ + HSPQ	8*	8	6	9*	5	8*	15‡	14‡
9. HSPQ + CFIQ + U vs. CFIQ + HSPQ	4	6	3	2	3	6	8†	6*

Source: Cattell, Barton, and Dielman (1972).
* Significant at the 5% level.
† Significant at the 1% level.
‡ Significant at the 0.1% level.

too. Since prediction, as such, is not our theme, but only prediction from dynamic, motivational traits, we shall dismiss intelligence and personality by allowing the figures themselves to tell the tale. Before turning to the motivation effects *per se* let us note, however, the general magnitude of the overall prediction.

Across all four subject areas of Social studies, Science, Mathematics, and Reading in table 8.2 we find a range of total variance predicted from 46 percent (sixth-grade Science) to 76 percent (seventh-grade Reading). These figures represent multiple correlations of .68 and .87 respectively. In general the predictive power of the measures is greater for the seventh grade than the sixth. The overall contribution of ability, personality and motivation thus approaches the hypothesized value of 75 percent although, as we shall see, the contribution of each modality fluctuates with the school subject. The models in rows 2 to 6 show the effectiveness of the three tests taken singly. In model 3 we have extracted the influence of factor B in the personality test because it is a measure of intelligence. Thus HSPQ–B becomes a thorough-going measure of personality variables. The CFIQ is especially potent in Mathematics and Reading where the values reach 43 percent in the seventh grade.

In the realm of dynamic traits alone, models 5 and 6 represent the integrated and unintegrated aspects of the motivational components. The effect of SMAT as a predictor is quite substantial particularly in Mathematics and Reading where the variance ranges from 38 to 64 percent. Of particular interest is the differentiation in the contributions arising from the isolation of the I and U components. It would seem entirely in line with prediction that the integrated component, contributing values between 29 and 58 percent, is substantially more significant than the unintegrated component, having values mostly less than 10 percent. The integrated component has been defined above as reality tested, systematically adopted, conscious motivation and we would therefore anticipate a higher correlation between this component and achievement than the unintegrated (similar in some ways to the psychoanalytical concept of unconscious motivation) component, which is vacillating, unattached and probably more state-like. The latter even seems in some cases (sex and pugnacity) to have an inhibiting influence in school achievement but this is still a matter for research.

The above results find support in the work of Cattell, Sealy, and Sweney (1966) who showed the variance contributions for the separate modalities were 21 to 25 percent for intelligence, 27 to 36 percent for personality traits and 23 to 27 percent for motivation (I + U). The total variance amounted to between 70 and 75 percent. As can be deduced from the first six models (rows) of table 8.2, these values are, if anything, surpassed particularly in the case of Mathematics and Reading.

The specification equation indicates by its weights the contributions of the separate factors to achievement, but it is also of interest to analyze according to the separate modalities as set out in the last paragraph for the earlier results. Table 8.2 also contains the result (row 7) of finding the amount of variance in achievement scores which can be accounted for by the motivation variables of SMAT beyond that accounted for by the other major variables. The figures in the table for models 7, 8, and 9 are the result of comparing the variance due to motivation (Total, I and U) over the other variables in answer to the question "To what extent do motivation variables add to those of personality and ability in the prediction of achievement?" Clearly, in Reading achievement the motivation variables make a significant contribution. In the seventh-grade research the prediction of mathematics achievement is also improved by the motivation variables. It is worth noting the difference in magnitude of the contribution of integrated and unintegrated motivation (models 8 and 9) where five out of eight of the former values are statistically significant. Dielman, Barton, and Cattell in another study (1973) substantiated the overriding influence of the SMAT I component in other school subjects such as Art, Music, and Spelling. Intriguingly, the one subject to which neither SMAT I nor U contribute is Physical education.

Most educationists have operated on the principle that achievement is more than a question of intelligence. Now by the use of systematic experiment we can turn these intuitions into reality, for the evidence supports the hypothesis that personality and motivation in addition to ability make independent contributions to the variance found in achievement scores. Further, whilst the relative importance of these factors varies according to the subject area considered, the overall effect approaches 70 to 75 percent of the total variance.

3 Unraveling the causal connections in school achievement

The above section discusses findings regarding correlation of achievement with characteristics of the individual (learning in the classroom and at home aside). But it is a familiar truism that correlation does not establish the direction of causation. Do personality and motivation influence achievement, or, in addition, is there some effect of successful achievement in turn upon these? Common sense says there must be, and Tsushima (1960) by feeding back (for a short time) false information about students' degrees of success or failure was able to show that anxiety and other motivation changes resulted from the success or failure the individual thought he was achieving. Cattell, Sealy, and Sweney (1966) also studied over a one year interval the correlations of *changes* on achievement with changes in personality and motivation in the hope of establishing by sequences the causal directions. Their results were inconclusive except in supporting in general a bidirectional action.

However, we can at least examine some hypotheses about connections, and in doing this we may be helped by examining findings for *particular subjects* and particular *ergs, personality traits, and sentiments*. There are intuitive reasons for believing that constructiveness, curiosity, submissiveness, or assertion would be essential to achievement, and some research (see Cattell and Butcher, 1968)

Table 8.3 Correlations between motivation variables and achievement

Grade 6 ($N = 169$)

ETS Achievement tests	Motivation variables (SMAT)														
	Assertiveness			Sex			Fear			Narcism			Pugnacity		
	U	I	T	U	I	T	U	I	T	U	I	T	U	I	T
Social studies	02	19*	13	15	16*	13	03	20†	14	−01	07	04	−05	36†	20†
Science	00	07	14	00	20†	13	15	17*	22†	08	11	12	−09	22*	07
Mathematics	−03	09	03	00	20†	13	06	14	14	−14	13	−02	−14	34†	12
Reading	−03	19*	09	10	19*	20	15	29†	30†	14	23†	23†	−18*	36†	09

	Protectiveness			Self-sentiment			Superego			School sentiment			Home sentiment		
	U	I	T	U	I	T	U	I	T	U	I	T	U	I	T
Social studies	00	08	04	−10	30†	12	02	40†	26†	−07	23†	08	08	13	14
Science	−07	14	02	00	37†	24†	−02	31†	18*	−02	27†	15	−05	12	02
Mathematics	06	17*	15	−07	29†	13	−04	32†	17*	−01	24†	13	−13	21†	01
Reading	10	15	17*	−09	49†	26†	−01	43†	26†	05	33†	24†	−08	17*	03

Grade 7 ($N = 142$)

ETS Achievement tests	Motivation variables (SMAT)														
	Assertiveness			Sex			Fear			Narcism			Pugnacity		
	U	I	T	U	I	T	U	I	T	U	I	T	U	I	T
Social studies	04	19*	15	−07	23†	12	21†	05	20†	01	25†	17*	−02	25†	15
Science	00	23†	15	01	27†	20†	19*	15	24†	04	17*	14	−11	28†	10
Mathematics	08	27†	23†	00	42†	30†	19*	13	22†	04	24†	18*	00	28†	19*
Reading	−03	27†	15	−13	43†	22†	29†	16	32†	02	31†	22†	−24†	28†	00

	Protectiveness			Self-sentiment			Superego			School sentiment			Home sentiment		
	U	I	T	U	I	T	U	I	T	U	I	T	U	I	T
Social studies	08	20†	18*	03	33†	24†	−06	32†	17*	08	30†	24†	−15	25†	−00
Science	12	31†	28†	−01	31†	19*	−02	34†	20†	13	32†	29†	−18*	24†	−03
Mathematics	19*	20†	28†	04	32†	24†	−15	23†	04	11	32†	28†	−22†	25†	−06
Reading	21†	20†	30†	−63†	41†	24†	−02	42†	25†	15	39†	35†	−23†	34†	−03

Source: Cattell, Barton, and Dielman (1972).
* $p < .05$.
† $p < .01$.
Note: Decimals omitted.

has indicated correlation between these. More recent and detailed evidence which allows for both the objections of using an all-inclusive measure of achievement and the unrefined version of SMAT is found in the work of Cattell, Barton, and Dielman (1972) where both U and I erg and sentiment scores were compared with four separate achievement scores in social science, science, mathematics, and reading. Table 8.3 demonstrates a convincing pattern of correlations between integrated motivational factors and achievement with over 75 percent in both grades showing better than 5 percent significance.

Another pressing question is the extent to which each of the separate dynamic trait structures makes an independent contribution to achievement, particularly beyond that of IQ. In a study using the Culture Fair Intelligence test alongside SMAT, Dielman, Barton, and Cattell (1974) found several consistencies. The integrated superego structure was a firm predictor across most areas of achievement. In the sixth-grade study the integrated self-sentiment was another significant predictor (except in Physical education). This is in keeping with a view expressed earlier that the "achievement motive" (see McClelland *et al.*, 1953) springs from at least two dynamic sources, namely, self-sentiment and superego. Some have claimed that self-assertion also contributes to n'Ach, but, as we shall explain later, the evidence in this and other similar studies suggests that though self-assertion is a striving for eminence it is actually, alone, not a potent influence (beyond a culture fair intelligence and other tests contributing). Certainly the correlations for assertiveness in table 8.4 are generally low as compared with the self-sentiment, superego and school sentiment.

The place of the assertive erg may thus still be in question, but the potency of self-sentiment and superego is very clear. Educational systems, certainly in Western cultures and probably to an increasing extent in the East, are geared more and more to a meritocratic model which rewards those who attain well in conventional school and university examinations. It is not surprising that those who score highly on self-sentiment, i.e. those who are well disposed to socially acceptable behavior, tend to have elevated achievement scores when we control for differences in intelligence (table 8.4). It also stands to reason that those high on superego, being a measure of expedience–conscientiousness, will tend to perform better at school, other things being equal. These two factors are also found in the 16 PF, and wherever the latter has been used with achievement, similar results have been obtained. The 16 PF scores of G and Q_2 in Cattell, Sealy, and Sweney (1966) are both positively correlated with achievement (+.26 and +.24 when corrected for attenuation).

The characteristic profile of the high achiever compared with the low achiever offers some preliminary approximations to a specification of the qualities which assist in scholastic attainment. Figure 8.1 is a rough diagram showing the relative importance of some motivational factors. The self-sentiment and superego figure prominently as indicated above. The self-sentiment is an acquired structure related to self-assertion in creating and maintaining self-respect and social status. In an essentially achievement-oriented society—as all societies important in cultural history have been—there is little wonder that achievement and self-sentiment are correlated. However, even the lonely savage presumably experienced pride and self-congratulation when he jumped a wider brook or threw a straighter spear at his prey.

Table 8.4   Multiple regression analysis of SMAT U and I factors and achievement

	English	Art	Maths	F ratios Music	Spelling	Soc.sci.	Science	Phys. Ed.	Grade avge.
Sixth grade	$(N=169)$	$(N=80)$	$(N=169)$	$(N=131)$	$(N=169)$	$(N=169)$	$(N=169)$	$(N=169)$	$(N=169)$
IQ+Self S (U)	2.20	0.65	5.43*	0.40	5.89*	2.29	4.80*	6.44*	4.99*
IQ+Self S (I)	15.67‡	7.39†	9.49†	12.69‡	16.70‡	21.27‡	27.19‡	0.88	15.33‡
IQ+Super E (U)	0.64	0.12	0.60	4.42*	1.95	0.60	0.08	1.61	1.40
IQ+Super E (I)	7.13†	3.59	4.95*	10.14†	4.36*	8.28†	13.73‡	2.59	8.39†
Seventh grade	$(N=99)$	$(N=79)$	$(N=118)$	$(N=81)$	$(N=108)$	$(N=75)$	$(N=142)$	$(N=142)$	$(N=142)$
IQ+Self S (U)	0.35	0.04	0.10	0.00	1.96	0.29	0.29	0.83	0.07
IQ+Self S (I)	9.73†	2.26	3.32	0.40	0.99	5.95*	0.86	1.75	0.00
IQ+Super E (U)	5.39*	0.57	1.50	4.27*	0.37	6.03*	0.03	0.59	0.06
IQ+Super E (I)	5.96*	1.27	9.28†	3.00	1.98	9.15†	6.95†	1.03	4.11*

Source: Dielman, Barton, and Cattell (1973).
* Significant at the 5% level.
† Significant at the 1% level.
‡ Significant at the .1% level.

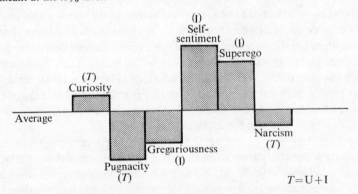

Figure 8.1   Profile showing relationship of dynamic structures to achievement

In contrast to the self-sentiment, the superego has probably its roots in unconscious influences. Parents and school have the important role of establishing nonconscious motives of service and high moral standards. Pleasing others in the reference group (parents, other relations, close friends, teachers) spills over into school achievement. The much quoted work of sociologists in the field of social class and educational opportunity repeatedly shows the crucial impact of the home in which little encouragement (often outright antagonism) is offered to continuation into higher education. Both self-sentiment and superego stand to suffer by this subjection to parental attitudes antagonistic to further education.

We have already noted the connection between the above factors and need for achievement. It is sometimes popularly held that self-assertion is directly related to n'Ach, but this is an oversimplification. Assertiveness is a purely instinctive erg which shows itself in competitiveness, pride, and so forth, and appears in all human activity involving mastery of nature. Some small part of this ergic tension is involved in self-sentiment, but it is really the latter acquired sentiment which is connected with achievement.

The reason for the appearance of curiosity as a positive factor in high achievement is self-evident, but the negative correlation for the integrated measure of the gregariousness erg may not be so obvious. However, inspection of table 2.14 soon reveals a positive correlation between gregariousness and the personality factors A (sociable–outgoing) and F (loud–happy-go-lucky). These qualities also constitute part of the second-order factor of exvia–invia, an important variable in school and college achievement. Given children of similar scholastic potential, it seems plain that those who are reserved, sober, less social would tend towards solitary pursuits such as study, reading, and writing. The case for good students, especially in higher education, tending to be less gregarious than others in the same age group is a strong one.

The negating effect of pugnacity is a little more difficult to explain. It may be that we have a hen–egg problem of whether pugnacity is a quality which leads to low achievement or whether low achievement leads to the high frustration and consequent outward show of aggression so typical of young people who are failing in school work. The latter is far more probable. One is reminded of the Adjustment Process Analysis chart (figure 3.1) where prolonged failure can lead to persistent nonadjustive pugnacity at chiasm C. In the case of the narcism correlation it is relatively clear that we are dealing with an effect *on* achievement *by* narcism. The broad interpretation of narcism is of a factor displaying self-indulgence, avoidance of work, selfishness and rejection of moral standards. The implicit distractions from achievement towards self-love have been suggested as the source of the negative correlation. The negative correlation with superego ties in with the pattern of figure 8.1.

The place of submissiveness, constructiveness and the sex erg is less clear. Some studies have given a negative correlation for sex and achievement

(Cattell and Butcher, 1968, although Cattell, Barton, and Dielman showed positive values) suggesting either that high sex drive constitutes a source of distraction from school or college work, or the Freudian psychoanalytic generalization of sublimated sex drive by which individuals who experience high levels of sublimation (i.e. have reduced the level of the sex erg by redirecting their energies) will do better because they have greater resources available for attainment. At first sight submissiveness (i.e. conformity to the expectations of school and college systems) and constructiveness would make favorable qualities in academic work. Occasionally, both have been found to correlate with school attainment, but no consistent pattern has emerged so far from the several researches mentioned above.

4   Motivation and learning in structured learning theory

One could describe the essence of teaching as an attempt to bring about change in the learner's behavior in a premeditated direction, and learning itself as the process of change.

Since the time of Pavlov, Watson, Thorndike, and in the work of the more recent reflexologists, such as Spence and Skinner, teachers have dutifully looked to conditioning as a possible fount of new knowledge for their art. But mainly they have looked in vain, for most of classical and operant conditioning was already more or less explicit in the common-sense practice of the classroom, e.g. in Montessori, etc.

Meanwhile a radically new development called *structured learning theory*, has appeared in psychology which we have described in introductory fashion in chapter 3. It is a development with several facets, however, and so we shall recapitulate some of the main points in chapter 3 as we proceed. It promises a learning technology at once broader and more subtle not only for cognitive, academic school learning, but also for personality and character development. It is perhaps most effectively reintroduced in a short space by considering the four main innovations that can be recognized in chapter 3.

The first innovation is in *describing* the changes with which learning theory in any comprehensive sense has to be concerned. In the past it has concerned itself almost entirely with a measurable change in some one act—a reflex response or an intellectual performance such as memory recall. This we can symbolize as $(a_{jt_2} - a_{jt_1})$ where the act a_j is measured at two occasions, t_1 and t_2, before and after learning. A series of a_j measures at $t_1, t_2, t_3, \ldots, t_n$ may be plotted to give a learning curve, and so on. But in everyday life we are more concerned with changes in broad unitary abilities—recognized in a whole pattern of acts—or personality or dynamic traits as a whole. Structured learning theory concerns itself with changes in the total profile on the unitary personality, motivation, and ability traits that personality measurement is mainly interested in.

However, if we consider an act that can change through learning, and express it in our usual specification equation, it becomes evident (see chapter 4, page 89) that to account for the change in the act it is necessary to consider something more than change in the traits alone. Let us write the specification including what were defined on page 68 as the modulator indices—s's—thus:

$$a_{hij} = b_{j1}sh_1T_{1i} + b_{j2}sh_2T_{2i} + \ldots + b_{jk}sh_kT_{ki} \tag{8.2}$$

with k traits (T's), k behavioral indices, b's, and k modulator indices, s's. Earlier we distinguished traits and states, introducing modulation as a response characteristic of states. But since then it has become clear in several researches that most traits also modulate, i.e. become more strongly activated with the impact of a suitable *ambient stimulus*. This is especially evident in the effects of stimulation and gratification upon ergic dynamic traits and of excitation and arousal upon sentiment dynamic traits.

Thus the first innovation we must recapitulate from the introduction (chapter 3, page 71) is the *tri-vector theory* of change description, which, as the reader will remember, says that the change under learning requires three vectors (profiles or ordered series of numbers) for its description. These are (1) the *trait vector* of T's, (2) the *bearing vector* of b's (so called because it describes changes in the bearing of traits upon behavior), and (3) the *modulation or involvement vector*, s's, which describe how much the individual's drives have become involved.

The second innovation in structured learning theory is that all traits and states in the individual are recognized as taking part in determining the learning gain (whether measured as $a_{jt_2} - a_{jt_1}$ or as tri-vector gain). That is to say, the learning experience alone does not determine the learning. Thirdly, any experience affects all traits and all traits (or other vectors) are affected by any one experience. This leads to a third innovation: a mathematical way of analyzing the potency of "learning paths" by what is called matrix calculation. Recognizing that most real life learning is "a multidimensional change from experience of a multidimensional situation" structured learning theory finds through matrix operations the profile (vector) of changes on many traits through a given type of experience. What is called *adjustment process analysis* (page 60) provides a systematic basis for coding these life experience paths.

Finally—and it is here that our present study of motivation makes its largest contribution—structured learning theory formulates the reward ("reinforcement") by which "operant conditioning" works as a *specific* set of tension reductions instead of a "general drive reduction". Actually, neither with animals nor with humans has classical reflexology been able to give valid quantitative values to ergic tension levels or the reward assumed to occur through reduction of ergic tension levels. It has measured reward, e.g. in the rat by amount of bran mash supplied to assuage hunger, or, e.g. in the human, by length of time deprived of this or that. These are the external physical manipulanda, not the reward to the ergic tension itself. In structured learning theory, as will be brought out in more detail in the next section, the reward can be more explicitly quantified, but the central term therein is (E_1-E_2), i.e. the difference in ergic tension at the time of meeting the learning situation and at the goal of action. Since there is a whole series of drives—fear, sex, hunger, curiosity—and any experience in human life will normally present a complex satisfaction of several drives, reward itself must be recorded as a vector of values. To the mathematician of psychology this again means matrix methods and computer aids.

5   Explicit principles in structured personality learning   Structured learning theory is at once flexible enough, and precise enough, to encompass all types of learning experience from the simplest repetitive cognitive performance in the classroom or laboratory to the deepest emotional learning in life, such as modifies the whole personality. It is able to do so because in the first place it has vector representation covering all the terms that might enter into the description of any change. These terms, as the tri-vector model states, describe, first, the change in well-known traits, next in behavior indices, and last in modulators.

Regarding the first, several illustrations have been given. For example, as Graffam's results (1967) show, a young man becomes more radical, more dominant and less certain in superego values $(Q_1+, E+ $ and $G-)$ through being an undergraduate, compared to his peer who does not go to a university. Or as Barton's results show (with Cattell 1972) the "path" of marriage (compared to staying unmarried at the same age), decreases surgency (F) and increases conservatism (Q_1-). Such experiences as successful job promotion (Barton and Cattell, 1972b) and the bereavement of a close relative have also been shown to produce statistically significant changes in the vector of personality source traits. So also does clinical therapy, as shown in the work of Hunt (page 61), or of May (1950) specifically on shock therapy. Some of these profiles of change in the trait vector are likely to be quite subtle. As more evidence accumulates we are likely to find that they are also highly characteristic of particular school or adult life experiences.

The changes in the *bearing vector* (the *b*'s), when they occur in abilities, reflect changes in ways of doing things and *could* occur without any change in the level of performance, i.e. in a_j, itself. When they occur in the dynamic field, with respect to attitudes, they tell us about a change in the dynamic lattice itself occurring as a certain "attitude-course-of-action" comes to subsidiate more to some ergic goals and sentiments and less to others. For example, if someone has been in the habit of attending dances for satisfactions which are subsidiated in part to the gregarious and in part to the mating erg, and then finds the right girl, instead, say, at his job, the interest in the dance course of action is likely both to become weaker and to change in ergic composition. That is to say, the bearing vector for dancing changes—by lesser loading (b) on the mating erg and other changes. The work of Laughlin (1974), of Hendricks (1971), and of Vaughan (1973) has produced confirmation that the changes in the bearing vector values supervene in ways that would be theoretically expected from applying common understanding of psychological satisfactions in life to the concept of the lattice and the dynamic calculus. Change in the bearing vector, as found by comparing two successive factor analyses, is thus a powerful and precise means of investigating that learning which consists of motivation acquiring more complex or different motivation.

The general meaning of changes in the situation or involvement vector—the vector of modulators (s's)—has already been defined (page 68). In some respects it accounts for more of what is commonly thought of as emotional learning (or dynamic development) even than changes in the bearing vector.

But perhaps the form of emotional or personality learning of which the average man is most aware is that which the dynamic calculus encompasses in the calculation of the involvement vector. This has to do with the modulators, and tells us what the feeling tone or emotional provocation of a particular situation is. The city that meant for a certain person just one more colorless city becomes, through certain experiences, enriched by a particular mood which it now always provokes. Or the girl who was to the male student just one more classroom co-ed takes on an altogether embarrassing capacity to evoke complex emotions. Or, in the domain of animal experiment, the rat who went slowly and with many reversals down a maze path now twitches his whiskers excitedly at the familiar odors and plunges with high motivation and velocity down the alley way.

The vector of s indices—modulators—thus describes what particular ergs, sentiments, and emotional states are provoked by the general situation (or "ambient stimulus"). And a change in the s—the involvement vector—tells what learning has taken place in terms of new patterns of emotional involvement.

Up to this section it has been enough to explain what the bearing and involvement vectors mean (what the trait change vector means is obvious). But the student is now perhaps ready to wonder how the quantities are actually obtained. The actual calculations are too much to consider here, but the principles should not be left blank. The changing b values—expressing the extent to which the given course of action has been learnt as a way of reaching various ergic satisfactions in various degrees—are obtained, as just mentioned, by comparing factor analytic loadings (on the given attitude course along with many others) before and after the period of learning. If the investigation is concerned with only one attitude then a factor analysis is unnecessary; one simply correlates scores on the given attitude (across, say, 300 people) with scores on the ten dynamic entities (five ergs, five sentiments) in the Motivation Analysis Test. The correlations are roughly loadings—*b* values—and tell (on the before and after occasions) how much these important ergs are utilizing the given course of action for their satisfaction.

The calculation of the *s*'s is more recondite. A large *s* value for a particular emotion in a particular situation (s_{hx} in equation (8.2) where *x* is the given emotion $(1, 2, 3, \ldots, x)$ and *h* the given ambient situation) means that both the mean and the standard deviation—the variability among people—of the emotion are increased. For example, if h_1 is being in a house on fire or a vital exam tomorrow, and h_2 is lying on a sunny beach, then $s_{h_1 x}$ will be much larger than $s_{h_2 x}$, where *x* is the state of anxiety. Thus $s_{h_1 x} L_x$ (from the equation for a dynamic state on page 69) will have a higher level for everyone in a house on fire, and also a bigger variation. The problem in calculation is that ordinary factor analysis brings all factors artificially to the same mean and standard deviation, so we have to go to *covariance factor analysis*. And therein one will have to compare factor analyses over many different *h* situations to see how factor levels and sizes change. Alternatively, the reader may think of it as a bivariate problem—if the state factor can actually be measured with a scale—in which means and standard deviations for that state are measured for a typical sample of people over many situations and the *s* indices calculated directly.

Experimental examples of changes in the *s*'s—the involvement vector—are as yet hard to come by, since *real base factor analysis* is so new. Research with the bearing vector is more abundant as in the work of Hendricks (1971) in which psychology students were tested with the MAT at the beginning and after ten weeks from the beginning of their university careers. This has already been examined in chapter 3. Here we saw some significant change in the fear erg probably brought about by the impending semester examinations. In the same chapter, discussion also centered on the researches of Dielman, Cattell, Kawash, and DeYoung using R-techniques with laboratory modulation of dynamic traits. Also, the significant P-technique investigation of Kline and Grindley (1974) added further weight to the argument that natural events bring about modulations within each person from day to day and these are reflected in changed dynamic scores. Vaughan (1973) designed a manipulation research with high school pupils to test the general hypothesis of the practicality of manipulation and the more particular hypothesis that those subjects who are highest on given dynamic factors will show the most change as an outcome of manipulation. His findings only partially supported the first hypothesis, i.e. two of the manipulations, those relating to attitudes towards the army and marriage, caused attitude changes. On the attitude to the army, subjects who were high on the dynamic factor of assertiveness (U) showed more attitude change than subjects low on the factor. However, apart from the pioneer classroom studies of Barton and Dielman showing new ergic tension levels developing through exposure to certain themes, there is very little research which makes a direct attack on bearing or situation index manipulation in educational settings.

6 Dynamic learning laws and the rise of unitary traits

The reader may be willing to grant that structured learning theory is capable at a *descriptive* level of getting closer than Pavlovian–Skinnerian reflexology to what education is really about, but he has still to be satisfied that it can also account for the changes described. Descriptively it is more powerful in that it deals with the structural unities which we know to *exist*, in ability and personality traits. In terms of broader educational goals and the philosophy of education, moreover, it performs the service of reminding us, in schools which all too readily shrink to more concrete *cognitive* aims, that education of the emotions and the building of character are probably the more important half of education.

Incidentally, even in the cognitive exercises of education there has recently been a revolt against the purely reflexological principles now incorporated in electronic teaching machines. Not so much on any grounds of their being wrong as because they simply are not enough. Thus the followers of Piaget have attacked the followers of Skinner on the grounds that discovery is a vital experience in education, and that the insightful perception of relations does something to intellectual growth that the operant conditioning learning of the right answer cannot produce. This argument moves toward our position that change in a whole trait is more important than change in a single reflex act. When we say that descriptively we have numerical ability, verbal ability, spatial ability, and other unitary source traits it becomes evident that what learning has to account for is not particular isolated responses but the emergence of these unitary patterns.

In an account of the emergence of *anything*, structured learning theory has the advantage that it can measure the ergic tension level of particular drives. As pointed out above this brings the gain that (a) one does not have to depend on the questionable notion of "general drive", and (b) one can measure tension reduction reward directly without having to assume that "grams of bran mash" or "hours of sexual abstinence" actually define the tension level. In this final section we propose to attack two major learning problems: (1) the relation of the observed, described, and measured learning gains in the vectors above to reward and other parameters of the learning experience, and (2) the reasons for unitary traits emerging at all from the seemingly atomistic process of learning.

The concept of reward (we prefer to discriminate clearly conceptually between *reward* as a dynamic experience and *reinforcement* as an increment in response potential) cannot be defined as comprehensively as we would wish until the researches of Barton, Bartsch, Nesselroade, Sweney, and others have clarified a little further the relation of ergic tensions to general states.

Meanwhile our position is that ergic tensions and general arousal or excitement are different but related things and that in the course of pursuit of some goal ergic tension does not simply begin high and decline as the goal is reached but begins high, drops suddenly at certain sub-goals, and is stimulated afresh by new features of the environment.

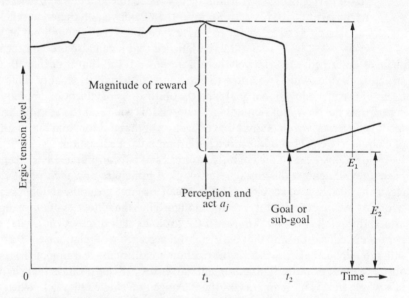

Figure 8.2 Ergic tension change in learning

There are still obscurities here, which may require the concept that, in the goal path, excitement (arousal) can mount, but ergic tension generally declines. Meanwhile we shall begin with the simplest model, in figure 8.2, which supposes that some response to a stimulus seen at t_1 occurs at t_1 and is rewarded at t_2. Figure 8.2 shows the decline of ergic tension from E_1 to E_2 which occurs at t_2. It now hypothesizes that the amount of learning—as an increment on future occasions in the strength or earliness of act a_j is a function of (a) the tension reduction (E_1-E_2), and (b) inversely of the time between act and reward (t_2-t_1). The latter is explained by the hypothesis that any cognitive act "reverberates" in a linear (or more complex) falling curve of cognitive activity and that the amount of memorizing achieved, as brought out in figure 8.3, is a function of the magnitude of the residual cognitive reverberation at that moment of reward and of the magnitude of reward. If some constant k expresses this decline of reverberation then the memory creating capacity (engramming) of the experience is:

$$M = (E_1 - E_2)[x - k(t_2 - t_1)] \qquad (8.3)$$

where x is the cognitive excitation level at the time of the perception which led to the right response.

If we would preserve the perspective of multiple determination of learning we can now add (8.3) into earlier equations of school achievement (learning) which rest only on the person's traits and states, thus:

$$(a_{ij_2} - a_{ij_1}) = \Sigma bsT + \Sigma bsL + \Sigma(E_1 - E_2)\,[x - k(t_2 - t_1)] \qquad (8.4)$$

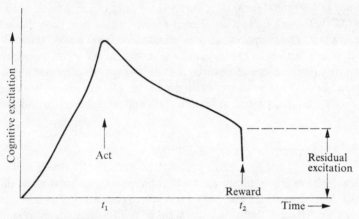

Figure 8.3 Engramming magnitude as a function of residual cognitive excitation (reverberation) and reward magnitude

where the Σ simply reminds us that a whole series of T's (traits), L's (state liabilities), and E's (ergs) are involved, not just one. This equation is directed to changes in traits or elements in traits. More complex derivatives would be wanted to explain the changes in b's or s's. But the principle would be the same.

The second problem—that of accounting for traits growing in a unitary fashion, giving factor structures rather than chaos—suggests two hypotheses in the learning area. (Here we set aside genetic explanations, *outside* the learning area, which could account for some unitary growth as common *maturation*.) The first feature of equation (8.4) that could account for a whole set of $(a_{j_2} - a_{j_1})$ terms increasing together would be if some already existing unitary trait loaded highly on all these gains. This is illustrated in the growth of the crystallized general intelligence factor which appears as a single factor partly because the fluid general intelligence factor loads a whole set of gains in complex learning.

The second feature that could accomplish this would be a learning "schedule" which caused all the variables in the unitary pattern to be equally rewarded and subjected to an equal amount of repetition (for a given person, and a different amount across all variables for another person). There are several institutions in our society, e.g. going to school for longer and shorter periods, that could give equal repetition. These have been explored in more detail by Cattell, along with cognitive transfer effects, in *Abilities: Their Structure, Growth and Action* (1971). But of greater interest here are the *motivation* conditions that might establish higher rewards for person X than person Y simultaneously on a whole series of variables—those which yield a unitary factor trait.

A clear example of this occurs where an individual belongs to an important institution, such as a church, where a whole series of attitudes and activities are rewarded in proportion to the total ergic satisfaction he gets out of it and the frequency of his attendance. Here surely is the root of the growth of the sentiments (M's) of which quite a number of examples have now been unearthed by factor analysis. The common sub-goal constituted (part way to the ergic goals in the dynamic lattice) by the object of the sentiment generates a uniformity of motivation and therefore of rewards for the constituent attitudes and courses of action. Doubtless, however, other instances of creation of unitariness in traits by coordinated reward to learning will appear as investigation proceeds.

7   Summary   1. School achievement clearly depends on more than just cognitive ability. Teachers and psychologists alike have grown to appreciate that temperamental, dynamic, physical, and sociological variables also play a crucial part as determinants of academic performance. Three of these, namely (1) the cognitive—human ability measures using IQ tests, (2) temperamental—using personality measures, and (3) dynamic—using the motivation analysis tests, are discussed in some detail. The conclusion from several researches analyzing the variance involved has led to the hypothesis that approximately 25 percent of the variation in performance is ascribable to each of these three domains. The remaining variance is assumed to be accounted for by individual differences in home and social experience and, of course, by error variance inherent in the test materials.

2. The tactic of combining all three predictors in one and the same major research is surprisingly recent and novel (Cattell, Sealy, and Sweney, 1966). An important starting point was to pin down achievement in particular subject areas—rather than obtaining some all embracing measure of school achievement—and to study the predictive power of the three psychological domains for each of these. In Social studies, Science, Mathematics, Reading, English, Art, and Physical education, a surprising uniformity emerged, lending support to the 25 percent hypothesis mentioned above. The overall contribution of 75 percent variance was the most consistent finding throughout these researches.

3. On breaking down the dynamic component into integrated and unintegrated contributions, the former was, understandably, the most significant because it represents the real, systematic, conscious effort to satisfy dynamic ergs through achievement in an essentially achievement-oriented society. The pattern of higher I than U involvement occurred for all the school subjects except Physical education.

4. The specific dynamic trait structures which figured most prominently with the criterion of high achievement were integrated superego and integrated self-sentiment. The concept of achievement motive (n'Ach) expounded by McClelland and associates has a similar structure. The characteristics of high disposition to seek social prestige and status coupled with high conscientiousness are ready-made for the demands of our Western educational systems. Other dynamic traits of the high achiever are high curiosity and low pugnacity, gregariousness, and narcism. A thumbnail sketch of the stereotyped successful scholar, with an insatiable appetite for probing new fields, diligently undertaken in secluded places (laboratories, libraries, private studies, etc.) in anything but comfortable conditions does not seem too far removed from the profile obtained for high school achievers.

5. In recapitulating the structured learning theory laid down in chapter 3, closer attention was given to the reward mechanisms as seen in the reduction of ergic tension levels. Hypotheses were presented by which quantitative methods could be applied to learning situations as total, and not bivariate, events. Some fundamental research was described in which the bearing vectors had been manipulated, but there is much to be done in the field of situation (involvement) vector manipulation. Ergic tension changes in learning which accompany reward were considered and added into the basic equations for achievement to account for changes in traits. A more complex equation was envisaged to explain comparable changes in the b's and s's.

9 The dynamics of daily work and occupation adjustment

1 The Group-sociological and individual-psychological approaches to human enterprises

From the beginning of this book the writers have sought to cater for the span between two extremes of reader: the pure theoretical scientist in psychology and the practical clinical, educational, or industrial psychologist who aims at practical results from dynamic principles in everyday life. The latter, who has born the abstract thinking of the initial chapters may now seek his practical reward. The former will find further food for thought in these practical findings, fragmentary though they are at this early stage of application.

Attention has been given to educational and clinical applications and some approach has been made to industrial psychology—the third major applied field—in our discussions of group dynamics and administration in organized groups. However, the last is only one segment of the spectrum of occupational activity by which men live in modern society. As Cattell has pointed out in more detail in *Beyondism* (1972b) the evolution of social groups, proceeding through the survival of the fitter, has produced societies with ever more complex roles and service institutions. Through the work of sociologists and social psychologists such as Sorokin (1937), Bronfenbrenner and Devereux (1952), Boulding (1953), Borgatta, Cottrell, and Meyer (1956), Merton (1957), Singer (1965), Emmet (1966), and others, we are beginning to get a more precise taxonomy of institutions and some glimpses of their interactive dynamics. The dynamic interaction of groups and institutions, in psychological terms, is a study in itself (Cattell, 1950a, 1961; Borgatta and Cottrell, 1956; Alker, 1964; Rummel, 1972) and, of course, passes into the domains of political science. Here we must take the group structures—home, government, school, church, and business—for granted, and restrict ourselves to the satisfactions and frustrations of people in that framework.

Lest undue expectations be raised it must be reiterated at the outset that those in social-industrial psychology have only just begun to nibble at these problems. They have written freely on all; but the use of precise, objective and structured motivation measures is so recent that the selection of topics here can have no pretence to being representative of what should properly be covered eventually in a well-balanced chapter. Fortunately, one of the most central issues—the development of interests in a career sentiment—has received psychometric attention and with this we shall start.

2 The career sentiment A method for evaluating the relative strengths of sentiment structures, in terms of the total of ergic satisfactions which occur through them, has been set out on pages 84 and 85. Although it has not yet been applied to comparisons of important sentiments, e.g. to family, religion, recreations, the self, and occupation, one can be reasonably certain that in the mature individual—though not in the late adolescent, uncertain of field of choice and not entirely ready for the harness of civilization—the career sentiment is a powerful and pervasive one. It is easy to see that in terms of ultimate satisfactions of basic ergs subsidiation chains that pass through career activities are numerous indeed. For example, a career provides money which buys food, security, social status (improved self-sentiment), and the opportunity for acquisitiveness; work enables social interaction and the satisfaction of the gregariousness erg; work can satisfy the need to be constructive; in addition to social status through financial gain (in the community at large) the work group most frequently provides opportunities for satisfactions (self-assertion, dependence, status) within its structure of managers, foremen, shop stewards, school principals, fellow workers, and so on. If we draw out the threads of the career dynamic lattice from the plexus of attitudes and sentiments which could exist in the total picture (a fragment is shown in figure 2.2) we would have a representative model resembling that shown in figure 9.1. Parenthetically, the situation at the sentiment level is made complex by the interplay of such significant sentiments as sweetheart/spouse, self-sentiment and superego as we shall discover in the next few sections.

The thorny problem of the factors which actually go, and which should go, into making a career choice has not really been solved. In broad terms we are aware that personality characteristics, motivational factors, job availability, and social structure play some part. Native endowment, initially, sets the scene for the potential within which an individual could reasonably expect to cope with a particular job. For example, one could not expect to see a person of low intelligence in a learned profession. Job availability plays a crucial role in determining the selection level and prospects of workers. Certain areas, because of physical conditions (resources, topography, climate), only offer certain jobs and those unable or unwilling to move are thereby obliged to make Hobson's

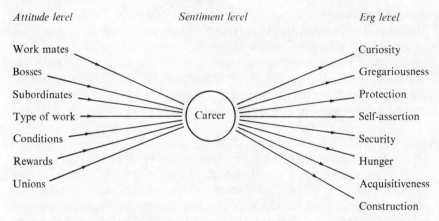

Figure 9.1   A simplified dynamic lattice associated with the career sentiment

choice. Further, the social structure, with its stratification system, values, economic hazards, and technical ability, imposes strictures or opens up vistas of work opportunities. The situation is perhaps not quite as bad as the philosopher Pascal made out when he said that a correct choice of career is the most important thing in an individual's happiness, yet that the actual choice is usually sheer accident. Most human beings have reasonable flexibility and reach a position whence they gain substantial satisfactions from what they have to do. But though adjustment occurs, and subsidiation chains establish themselves like roots seeking water, there remain many maladjustments. And although we are becoming aware of the main ergic satisfactions in the typical career sentiment, and realize that it is one of the strongest of sentiments, we are still almost completely lacking that valuable practical quantitative information which defines the typical profiles of ergic satisfactions characteristic of the main kind of occupations.

3   Motivational patterns in diverse occupational groups

If research and organization of services were seriously undertaken to work out the selection methods with regard to abilities, personality traits, and dynamic interest structure, it would be possible to eliminate most unnecessary vocational dissatisfaction within a decade. The means of measuring interest structures objectively are catching up with those for ability and personality, and sufficiently delicate psychometric–statistical methods are being developed.

Broadly and briefly the evaluation of a person's fit to an occupation—in any traits, physical or mental—can follow either the *adjustment* or the *efficiency* principle (Cattell, Eber, and Tatsuoka, 1970). In the former we have to find the central pattern among those who are adjusted (reasonably content and functioning) in each occupation. In the latter we discover the specification equation which predicts the main criterion performance required in the occupation most accurately. Of course, in both methods the psychologist realizes that only part of the endowment is genetic, and he can take account of how much change may be expected with time and circumstance. The need to consider this is particularly great in dynamic traits, but even here there is much evidence that environmentally produced traits do not alter much after about 30 years of age.

Implicit in the "adjustment" technique of selection is the assumption that different occupations are distinguishable by different profiles in their followers. Evidence for fairly stable patterns of personality and ability being associated with particular job descriptions is quite firm. Work with the 16 PF (Cattell, Eber, and Tatsuoka, 1970) gives detailed evidence also for replicable specification equations by the efficiency method, though at present it offers more occupational profiles for the adjustment method. Much less investigation has taken place using the MAT or SMAT, but this section will be devoted to pulling together the few researches extant. The outline of a dynamic lattice in section 1 makes it evident that persistent attitude and erg connections form the substrate from which work interests and satisfaction are moulded. We should not, therefore, be surprised to find characteristic patterns of ergic tension levels and sentiment strength emerging from particular and well-defined occupational groups. To this date, we have information, however, on such widely diverse callings as business executives, servicemen, student priests, criminals, nurses, foresters, and doctors.

What dynamic qualities of ergs and sentiments best describe the top male executive in America? Several studies, as yet unpublished and confidential to the firms involved as regards the place and detail of the findings, do give a statistically different pattern from the average man, according to the norms. The young, successful executive (Noty, personal communication) tends to be the man who has high career drive in the early stages of his climb up the ladder (figure 9.3). But the well-established executive does not display a similar high career sentiment, possibly because he has already "arrived" and therefore has less need to overtly or covertly express a strong attitude towards career. The high ambition linked with the bright young man in a career may sober with success and experience. Interestingly, the college student is typically high on unintegrated, but low on integrated career scores. Thus if we accept the tentative interpretation of U and I scores (page 15) one explanation is that a conflict exists at this stage between drives and outlets in reality.

Sentiment towards home/parents is generally lower than average possibly reflecting growing independence from parental affiliation and a more satisfactory adjustment. However, even at later ages the men of high achievement show less attachment to the home as such. But as regards *parental* home attachment the high achiever pattern (Sweney, 1969) appears to be a moderate

Standard ten score (sten)

→ Average ←

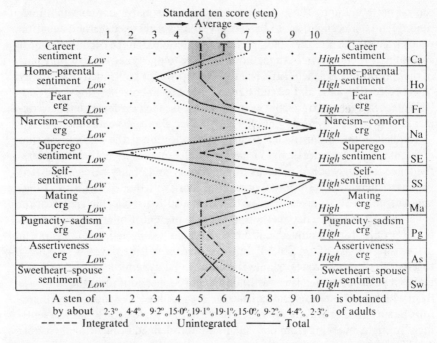

A sten of   1   2   3   4   5   6   7   8   9   10   is obtained

by about   2·3% 4·4% 9·2% 15·0% 19·1% 19·1% 15·0% 9·2% 4·4% 2·3% of adults

- - - - - Integrated   · · · · · · · · · Unintegrated   ——— Total

Figure 9.2   Average scores for top executives (20 presidents of insurance and service organizations)

Source: Unpublished work by C. Noty.

integrated and low unintegrated score indicating a low need for parental home dependence. Figure 9.2 shows this very clearly.

Attachment to a wife or sweetheart, portrays a need for affection beyond and apart from sexual or gregarious needs. The top executives seem well balanced in U and I as well as total motivation except that the conflict score (obtained from the difference between U and I) is on the high side and shows a denial on their part of indulging the need for close attachment to, or affection from, a member of the opposite sex. It is, of course, easy to see in many high achievers in history, such as Napoleon, the great religious leaders, Newton, and others, that there may be a cynicism towards romance and domestic affection and these latter have played a small part. It is interesting to see that in lesser ranges of achievement, measurement bears out this pattern as well as a high rating on conflict (and low on total motivation). It reappears in several professional (or potentially so) groups, such as doctors and college students. The riddle of this connection between professionalism and high conflict with low total spouse sentiment has not been disentangled and is ripe for research. One speculation is that a professional's work makes demands of him similar to those of "affection"—in other words he becomes attached to his work in a way which depletes the affiliatory energies available for his wife and children.

Not unnaturally, high self-sentiment prevails in executives and leaders. For being good at one's job, maintaining high social standing, and so on, are positive needs of the situation. A carefully planned life in terms of getting a good education, seeking social position, and developing social skills are part and parcel of an executive's bid to fulfil his aspirations. Noty (see figure 9.3) in a series of studies of businessmen, reports them to be high on integrated self-sentiment and lower on the unintegrated scale—a well-balanced combination (Sweney, 1969).

Interpretation of the superego scores fits well into popular beliefs about those in positions of responsibility in industry and commerce. Low U scores probably indicate a preoccupation with materialistic and secular affairs. The extremely low score obtained by top executives (figure 9.2) suggests a misanthropic tendency and reminds us of the findings of Rosenberg (1957) and others, that the student of management says he is most frequently "material" (or thing) oriented rather than "person" oriented when asked about those things he values most in his work. On the other hand, at least outside of business, leaders tend to be significantly higher than their followers on superego strength (Cattell and Stice, 1960).

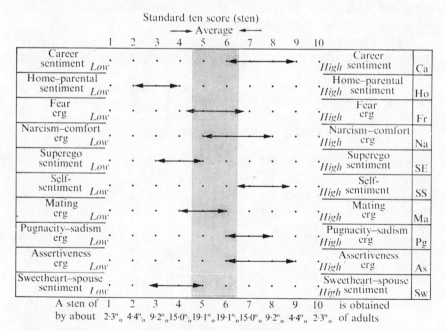

Figure 9.3   Profile of the typical successful businessman
Source: Unpublished work by C. Noty.

Of the five basic ergs the two most noteworthy for the executives are narcism and mating. Predictably, the executive has a marked liking for creature comforts. The personal investment of time and effort which goes into any professional training seems very likely to stimulate, exponentially, high self-concern. The physicians profile in the next section shows the same trend. High scores on both U and I scales, found particularly in affluent societies, is often associated with the "bon vivant" who with insatiable appetite seeks higher and higher levels of comfort. The mating erg appears high on the U score, but average on the I. This pattern is characteristic of unfulfilled sexual tension—a case of unrequited sexual drive. Have we here a classic example of the Freudian concept of "sublimation" in which sexual energy is being deflected to, and dissipated at, work?

So far we have leant on the adjustment principle of vocational guidance which requires as its target the profile of the adjusted job holder. But Noty has also done compilational studies, which yield a specification equation for an efficiency prediction. Here he correlated each dynamic trait level with performance as measured, in salesmen by actual sales figures over three years, and by compounded company ratings on a merit system. As Tatsuoka and Cattell (1971) have shown, a translation can be worked out between a specification equation and a mean profile, and since so far we have dealt in profiles the results in figure 9.3 are similarly expressed. It will be seen that the two approaches (9.2 and 9.3) give reasonably concordant results.

Another area in which statistically valuable results are beginning to come in is the field of military service. Using the MAT factor measures Skelton (1968)

Table 9.1   MAT results for officer cadet candidates and biserial correlations with selection criterion

MAT Scale	Total group ($N = 52$)		Selected ($N = 17$)		Rejected ($N = 20$)		r_{bis}
	M	SD	M	SD	M	SD	
Career	17.2	2.4	18.3	2.5	16.6	2.4	.33*
Home/parental	17.4	2.5	16.8	2.2	19.0	2.3	−.41†
Fear	11.3	2.4	10.0	2.1	12.0	2.6	−.39†
Narcism	11.2	2.7	10.4	2.5	11.4	2.7	−.18
Superego	31.9	3.8	31.4	4.5	33.0	3.4	−.20
Self-sentiment	51.1	4.8	52.2	5.0	51.5	4.5	.07
Mating	13.2	2.9	13.4	2.5	13.7	3.5	−.05
Pugnacity	12.8	2.5	13.0	2.3	13.3	2.6	−.06
Self-assertion	14.1	3.4	15.3	3.2	13.3	3.8	.28*
Sweetheart–spouse	14.2	2.4	14.2	2.6	13.7	2.1	.10

* Significant at 5% level.
† Significant at 1% level.
These *r*'s are over the total group.

examined the scores of officer cadet candidates (OCS), NCO's coming forward for warrant officer promotion and a regular army recruit group. Two findings are worth noting. First, the OCS group was divided according to whether they had passed or failed the Selection Board and their total MAT scores compared. Table 9.1 displays four significant differences all of which would be in accord with the conventional criteria used in army officer recruitment. The chosen candidates for officer training were significantly higher on career sentiment (highly ambitious) and assertiveness, but lower on sentiment to home/parents (independence from apron-strings—suited to a job away from home) and fear (a little less concerned about personal safety). These would seem to fit the stereotype of the army regular.

When we come to the differences between the three groups (raw recruits, OCS and NCO's) we find the more experienced NCO's ahead of the other two on narcism and pugnacity and lower on superego (showing less regard for organized religion—men of the world, presumably). The officer cadets were lower on fear than the others. Recruits are lowest on career, probably because there is less definition of their future roles than either of the other groups, and highest on sentiment to sweetheart and spouse. T. E. Lawrence's record of life in barracks—*The Mint*—supports this well at a literary level, except that the excess of pugnacity in recruits above the general population seems more emphasized there.

Of the groups so far studied (see Sweney, 1969, for an up-to-date record), the socially, clinically or physically disabled (unemployed, criminal, schizophrenics,

Table 9.2 MAT scores for recruit, officer cadet candidates selected and non-commissioned officer course groups

MAT scale	A Recruits (N = 138)		B OCS selected (N = 17)		C NCO course (N = 35)		t		
	M	SD	M	SD	M	SD	A−B	A−C	B−C
Career	16.4	2.7	18.3	2.5	17.6	2.0	2.82†	2.93‡	.98
Home/parental	17.7	3.5	16.8	2.2	17.5	3.4	1.30	.31	.88
Fear	12.7	3.1	10.0	2.1	12.3	2.6	4.09‡	.53	2.46‡
Narcism	10.5	2.7	10.4	2.5	12.5	2.6	.24	4.00‡	2.44†
Superego	29.7	4.6	31.4	4.5	27.6	4.4	1.44	2.47†	2.81‡
Self-sentiment	49.5	6.2	52.2	5.0	49.4	4.1	2.02	.11	1.95
Mating	14.7	3.6	13.4	2.5	13.1	2.5	1.86	2.96‡	.34
Pugnacity	12.8	3.5	13.0	2.3	15.2	2.8	.31	4.62‡	2.18*
Self-assertion	12.6	2.9	15.3	3.2	13.5	2.6	3.29‡	2.30	1.77
Sweetheart-spouse	16.2	3.7	14.2	2.6	14.5	3.0	2.78†	2.21*	.32

* Significant at 5% level.
† Significant at 2% level.
‡ Significant at 1% level.

orthopedically disabled) have been instructive in pointing up the motivation measures which accompany maladjustment. Lawlis (1968) made a detailed study of 75 chronically unemployed males (had at least six jobs in the last six months and left before completing any assignment) and compared them with the same number of employed males matched for age, IQ, race, and general educational level. The general profile for U, I and total scores is given in figure 9.4. High ergic tension on fear (presumably due to economic insecurity) and low assertiveness (little interest in economic or other competition) mark the chronically unemployed, while, naturally, the integrated career sentiment is low (but the wishful unintegrated is high). Especially revealing are the MAT conflict scores (excess of U over I scores usually expressed as sten scores). High conflict exists in the sentiments of career, superego, self and sweetheart/spouse. A high frustration index amongst the unemployed comes as no surprise and the nonfunctional guilt-proneness—a vague intention to be more dependable and conscientious, unimplemented by habits—may explain the high rate of job change typifying this group. The need for affection suggests that conflict occurs between man and wife probably because of the instability created in the home by the frequent unemployment and shortage of money. Finally, the high self-sentiment conflict is very common amongst those whose self-concept is beset

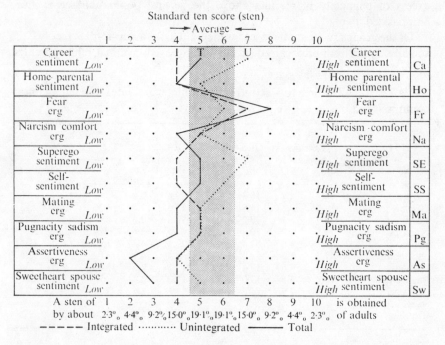

Figure 9.4   Motivational patterns of the chronically unemployed
Source: Lawlis (1967).

with failures because they are not reaching the goals they have regarded as appropriate for themselves. This conflict is sometimes referred to as the *loser's syndrome* (Sweney, 1969) about which more will be said later.

Comparing the employed with the unemployed we find several important differences noted in table 9.3. The reasons for the significantly higher career conflict and lower self-sentiment have already been speculated about in the pre-

Table 9.3 Comparison of MAT scores between chronically unemployed and employed

| | Mean | | S.D. | | | |
	Empl.	Unempl.	Empl.	Unempl.	F	t
Assertiveness (total score)	5.59	3.49	2.40	2.35	1.02	5.40
Self-sentiment (I)	5.72	3.65	1.59	1.37	1.16	8.53
Career (conflict)	5.97	7.51	2.43	2.22	1.09	4.04

Source: Lawlis (1967).

vious paragraph. Lower assertiveness seems logical if we recognize that assertion is concerned with "status seeking" and this cannot be too high in men who are moving from job to job without ever completing a set task. This explanation may be contrasted with that for doctors where the low level is not ascribed to low endowment in assertiveness, as here, but to high satiation. It is, presumably, the man who builds up confidence and a reputation in a career who is most likely to have pride (high SA score) about his status.

4 Dynamics within the occupation: the prescription behavior of doctors

Difference of occupational demand and adjustment are of major interest to those in vocational guidance and industrial selection; but the particular mechanisms operating within occupations and administrative groups are important to the sociologist and even the economist. Discussions of the motivations in dealing with bosses and assistants, of accepting rules, of handling clients, of bargaining for wages, etc., are as long as the longest library shelf; but studies with objective, structured motivation measures, pursued in depth, are at this time so rare as to be almost nonexistent. For this reason we are compelled to take for illustration a somewhat unusual theme—the reasons why doctors prescribe as they do—which is nevertheless near to most of us!

In this study a prominent pharmaceutical house obtained the cooperation of some 200 doctors, whose prescriptions recorded at the local pharmacists were analyzed over most of a year in relation to personality and motivation measures on the doctors.

Among the practical questions posed were (1) what are the typical motivation and personality profiles of medical practitioners as compared with the general population; (2) what kind of doctor is more active in general in utilizing the resources of the pharmocopeia; (3) is there a discernible special motivational and attitude pattern in willingness to use the new psycho-active drugs; and (4) are there correlates of general professional work habits and MAT variables? To answer these, the sample (after losses) of 135 doctors from two distinct areas were tested on the 16PF questionnaire and the MAT objective dynamic structure factors. Additionally, a biographical questionnaire was completed by the doctors as a background of information on domestic and professional activities.

The first step was to determine the means of the 26 dimensions of the MAT (10) and 16PF and to see if the profile significantly and typically differed from that of the general American population.

The less than average score on both home and spouse is, as we have noted before, a sad but true feature of individuals whose professional or creative work makes heavy demands on them. The greater superego strength is surely to be expected in a profession which takes the Hippocratic oath and has such traditions of service. The same, together with the wide community relations to numerous patients and institutions surely accounts for the more intense concern with the self-image in the self-sentiment. What at present is puzzling is the high narcistic need. Unlike a business man the professional man has his chief capital in himself. His survival depends on his powers of remaining intact, and he has invested a great deal in his education. It is perhaps not surprising that

Table 9.4 Dynamic, motivation structure measures for doctors*

Dynamic trait	U	I	Total	Direction in which doctors differ from general population (Total)	Significance of difference (Total)
Career	6.10	4.75	5.75	—	n.s.
Home	4.16	4.29	3.16	Less	$p < .01$
Fear	4.72	6.56	5.72	—	n.s.
Narcism	5.76	7.48	7.48	Greater	$p < .01$
Superego	5.96	5.80	6.36	Greater	$p < .01$
Self-sentiment	5.83	6.81	6.99	Greater	$p < .01$
Mating	5.41	6.00	5.41	—	n.s.
Pugnacity	5.38	5.92	5.76	—	n.s.
Self-assertion	4.98	5.85	4.83	Less	$p < .01$
Sweetheart–spouse	6.58	3.50	4.08	Less	$p < .01$

In general a difference of 0.39 has a $p < .05$ and 0.49 of $p < .01$, for groups of these sizes (135 and the standardization pool).

* These measures have the added reliability of being averaged over two occasions 6 months apart.

he "takes care of himself" (the narcistic erg) more than most, as a surgeon, for example, may insure his hands—a thought which scarcely occurs to the average man.

In the ergic tensions we note no other departure except that in the self-assertive need. The fact that the latter occurs entirely at the unintegrated level is appropriately interpreted to mean that the doctor gets such ample discharge in his work for the need for pride, and for high regard from others, that his self-assertive needs are satiated.

Conflict scores obtained for each dynamic interest, besides the narcism already discussed, are those of interest in wife and interest in career. A higher unintegrated score (as already suggested) is commonly interpreted (Sweney, 1969) as an indication of a greater interest than can be discharged in the available circumstances, i.e. conflict and tension are caused by frustration. It suggests that the doctor's emotional need in respect to his wife is not a subnormal one, but that time and the demands of an exacting occupation prevent his giving this the real expression and interest attentions which it might otherwise receive. We noted the same state of affairs for top executives. Similarly we would have to infer that in the career field his interest is kept stimulated at a higher level than he is able concretely to express in sufficient reading, attendance at meetings, attention to patients, etc.

A brief consideration of the 16PF findings—by comparing the doctors with norms (established from an approximate sample of 3 600)—is instructive.

Table 9.5 Personality measures of doctors compared with general population

	Personality factor	Sten score	Direction in which doctors differ	Significance of difference
A	Cyclothymia	5.4	—	n.s.
B	Intelligence	7.0	Intelligent	$p < .01$
C	Ego strength	5.4	—	n.s.
E	Dominance	4.5	Unassertive	$p < .01$
F	Surgency	5.5	—	n.s.
G	Superego strength	5.1	Expedient	$p < .05$
H	Parmia	5.4	—	n.s.
I	Premsia	5.5	—	n.s.
L	Protension	5.2	Relaxed	$p < .05$
M	Autia	5.5	—	n.s.
N	Shrewdness	5.7	Shrewd	suggestive
O	Guilt-proneness	5.5	—	n.s.
Q_1	Radicalism	5.5	—	n.s.
Q_2	Self-sufficiency	6.5	Self-sufficient	$p < .01$
Q_3	Self-sentiment	6.3	Controlled	$p < .01$
Q_4	Ergic tension	4.9	Composed	$p < .01$

A $p < .05$ value is $> .36$ stens; a $p < .01$ value is $> .47$ stens.

If, as was claimed in the assembling of the sample, that these constitute a good stratified sample of general practitioners concerned with possible drug prescription to anxious and neurotic patients, we can make certain definite generalizations about the personality involved. Part of this generalization fits the public stereotype; that the doctor is a person well above average intelligence (B), self-sufficient (Q_2), controlled (Q_3), and composed (Q_4). More surprising is the low dominance, i.e. (E). This might be interpreted as meaning a lack of really fundamental intellectual and social independence and a strong tendency to conventionality. It must be remembered that, unlike the researcher, and more like the soldier, the doctor has to act obediently to many practical rules which he has absorbed in a long and rigorous training (physiology, anatomy, symptoms, cures, etc.). A man at leisure in a study can question all things; but one facing life and death emergencies is considered better trained if he responds with accepted habits. At a lower ($p < .05$) significance we notice some tendency also to the expediency associated with lower superego strength (G). This is surprising because in general samples there is a substantial correlation of 16PF and MAT scores on superego strength. However this does agree with an indication of shrewd (N), self-advantage orientation.

In addition to the standard MAT questions, several items were included to measure the sentiment towards selected drugs (prescription attitude measures), for example, "I believe in the use of drugs for remedying psychological conditions, i.e. additionally to psychotherapy", "I want to use new drugs as psychotherapeutic agents", "I believe in using tranquillizers rather than hypnotics of the old type". These attitudes were also measured by objective, not questionnaire, devices.

Systematic relations have been found between actual prescribing behavior and more major dynamic structures in the personality of the doctor. Stronger measured self-sentiment development, which is associated with success in college achievement (over and above intelligence), correlates here significantly with greater general prescription of ataractic drugs. We can suppose either that this means connection with greater general success in practice or with more enlightened and up-to-date use of new drugs.

There is a distinct possibility—speculative though it may be from the significant connections found—that specific directions of prescription are determined by the doctor's own empathic sensitivity. At any rate those high on pugnacity (and by implication frustration) prescribe more hypotensives, and those with high undischarged sex interests prescribe more muscle relaxants.

Strength of fear or apprehension about dangers in the real world (not anxiety in the neurotic sense but ergic tension as "need for safety", tend to be associated with sparing use of ataractic drugs. The erg of fear may well prove to be in general one of the roots of conservatism and avoidance of the new and strange.

Level of tension on the self-assertive erg is also significantly correlated with low prescription in general. Is it possible that pride in personal medical skill causes some doctors to "pooh-pooh" the power of ataractic drugs, and to believe they already possess in their personal prestige enough power of suggestion to influence adequately the patient's psychological deficit.

Prescription of a tranquillizer is specifically associated with attachment to wife and family (but not parental home) and devotion to career, but negatively to superego strength. Again, it is with hesitation and due caution that we make a theoretical speculation about this finding, but once more it suggests that the doctor who is "comfortable in himself" is more concerned to see his patients the same, by regular prescription of tranquillizers if necessary. The negative correlation with superego strength suggests what is seen also in other "straws in the wind" in the form of smaller correlations found elsewhere in this study, that there persists some unspoken, lingering moral objection to tranquillizers. Such objection has, of course, been explicitly made by some religious leaders. But evidently the doctors with stronger guilt development in superego can have scruples which tend to reduce his prescription of these drugs. This was supported by the reduced prescription with higher guilt-proneness in the personality factors.

Another pattern which stands out clearly empirically is that of the physician who believes in the role of private enterprise in the realm of drug research. Psychologically, he is temperamentally more independent, and in motivation more aggressive and also more narcistic. This type of individual "projects" himself in the sense that he believes in self-motivated action with rewards accruing to the self.

The fourth and last question above was directed to the relationship of professional habits in general to MAT and personality variables. Using correlational techniques the following relationships emerged. There was some tendency for married doctors to be lower on dominance and tough-mindedness, and higher on self-sentiment and introversion than their unmarried colleagues. In motivation they have stronger interest in their parental homes. Number of children is also related positively to self-sentiment strength and to intelligence, but negatively to the personality factor N (shrewdness, sophistication). Time spent with hobbies correlates .26—low but significantly—with strength of sex drive suggesting that hobbies are in part a substitute for sexual satisfactions. Amount of group sociability (as a recreational alternative to individual hobbies) correlates negatively ($-.28$) with a self-sufficiency score, and $-.22$ with strength of superego motivation. Perhaps the person with a strong superego feels guilty of time spent in "nonconstructive" sociability and gossip.

Turning to behavior closer to leadership and learning in the field, we find that more buying of books and journals correlates positively (but slightly) with intelligence, negatively with ergic tension (Q_4: presumably the tense cannot sit still and read!), significantly with narcism, and somewhat with superego and career interest strength. It will be remembered that narcism must not be thought of as only concern with personal pleasure: it also encompasses general concern about, and investment in, the mental and physical self. Consequently, if the importance of a man's library and other beloved possessions are seen as an extension of himself, higher narcism would be expected to generate more activity in collection. Narcism also ($r = .24$) seems to motivate expansion of the self by participating and taking active roles at conferences. Pugnacity (.29) also seems to motivate frequency of attendance at conventions. The most direct measure of leadership was taken to be involvement and high activity in professional medical societies, etc., and it correlates with pugnacity (.21), nonsusceptibility to fear (.22) and interest in wife (.21). It is noteworthy that "interest in wife" behaves here as elsewhere, as one more predictor of "interest in other people". Number of officerships in societies correlates positively with intelligence (.16) and extraversion (.21), the latter being a second-order 16PF.

Finally, another type which emerges pretty clearly is that of the busy (or overbusy) doctor contrasted with the more absorbed and detached who defends his leisure, taking time (according to behavior records) for both vacations and hobbies and for reading. The former has stronger superego development, is more "grown out" of his parental home attachments, is less narcistic, less interested in radicalism *per se*, and less polished.

Some social-psychological aspects of commerce also emerged from this extensive motivation study. For the doctors' motivations and attitudes were actually measured twice, six months apart, with pharmaceutical advertising for a particular product turned upon them throughout the interval. Relating to the control group, without advertising they showed some interesting changes both in (a) the absolute strengths of certain attitudes, and (b) the way in which attitudes subsidiated to further goals, as shown by the factor analytic loading of the attitude on the dynamic structures. Because of limitations of sample size the changes of the second type did not reach satisfactory statistical significance. However, even indications are worth mentioning, for this is one of the few available experiments to throw a precious illumination on the possibilities of the new tri-vector description of learning within structured learning theory. According to this theory (pages 71 and 195) a learning experience should change not only the attitude level, but also its loadings on certain ergs and sentiments, showing that certain subsidiation paths have been strengthened and others reduced in strength.

Among the interesting changes found through this exposure to persuasions about the value of a particular therapeutic drug were first, the most obvious one—an increase in interest in using the particular product—but with the new scientific finding that this occurred in the *objective* motivation devices. Secondly, it was found that "stimulus generalization" occurred. Since in the doctors' minds this drug was logically one of a class of drugs, the increased interest spread to the whole class. However, the firm's advertising efforts were not entirely cancelled, for this gain was less than for their own product.

As to the changes in subsidiation strength, as shown by loadings, they turned out to be emphases of the original lines of dynamic reward. The relation to superego was originally negative and it became more negative. Thus one can understand in terms of the argument above together with the well-based theory that the superego is peculiarly rigid and immune to later attack after childhood, (the Jesuit educational maxim "Give us a child until six . . ."). The man who believed it wrong to prescribe psycho-active drugs originally felt so still more strongly after being "tempted". The negative loading in the narcistic and sex ergs, which also increased, awaits a theory. In the career sentiment and sentiment to wife a curious difference of U and I exists, the former being negatively related. As to career, the doctor with stronger conscious interest in his professional life may see this new drug as fulfilling further his technical competence, so that he learns more rapidly to incorporate it in his practice than does one whose integrated career interest is weaker.

It is easy to see that this aspect of the dynamic calculus which has to do with the relation of propaganda or educational changes to the original endowment strengths and the points at which rewards are applied has tremendous relevance to politics, advertising, religion and many other areas of social psychology. The recent studies of Nichols (1974) and of Laughlin (1973) show that a true science of emotional learning is arising through this use of the dynamic lattice and the dynamic calculus, but that the sensitivity of our instruments is not yet sufficient for statistical significance unless large samples are used.

5 Adjustment and satisfaction at work The activities and influences of a man's work pervade his whole life-style. It could hardly be otherwise when such activity occupies at least a third of most days in his adult life. The psychology of job choice and satisfaction has received much attention, though only with verbal self-report until quite recently, and the low validity of such measures permits little superstructure of dependable analysis and prediction. The issues studied are, for example, whether individuals given vocational guidance experience greater satisfaction (Thorndike and others find better than chance; others question it), and whether certain systems of wage change, incentives, promotions, and management are superior. Much of this verbal enquiry has concentrated on the professions (groups more easily defined) rather than on manual workers because the intellectual demands, conditions of work, financial returns, pathways to elevation, and means of attaining job satisfaction are more easily defined.

The definition of "job satisfaction" might be that it is a measure of strength of the positive attitudes one has towards work roles. Obviously, these attitudes are the rudiments of the career sentiment and load most heavily on that factor. But less obviously, as we shall see, most other dynamic structures are to some degree involved. To know what these other oblique satisfactions are one needs to use—along with objective measures of the given work attitudes—a test of the main dynamic structures, such as the MAT. Such precise work is quite recent and scarce, and in what follows we must often lean on questionnaire devices, etc.

The kinds of considerations necessary when we do look at job satisfaction will be seen to have at least two important aspects; first, there are the extrinsic factors which make work attractive or intolerable—such as the supervisor, agreeableness of work mates, hours and wages, the demands of the job, and promotion prospects; secondly, we have the intrinsic factors of personality and motivation.

The influence of the supervisor was the subject of Putnam's (1930) research at the Hawthorne works (Western Electric Company). Whilst the evidence was widely criticized for not taking into account the effect of a novel experiment itself on the morale and productivity of employees, it must be said that many replications of the research generally support the findings which showed the primary importance of the supervisor's relationship to his charges. The emphasis in more recent work has been to determine the leadership qualities of supervisors. We shall see in chapter 10 in the section on the dynamics of leadership that the effective leader first and foremost has to provide a framework within which individuals can satisfy their role needs. He must resolve their differences, raise their total reward because they are in the group, and be seen to be fair-minded. The attributes of the supervisor as leader are therefore critically relevant.

Mayo (1945) made much of the influence of fellow workers in satisfying the needs of individuals. This fits the findings (page 244) of a "Morale of congeniality" factor. In the study of group "synergy" in chapter 10 we have pinpointed particular qualities and conditions of the group which augment this and have shown that a group will last as a group only as long as the individuals gain real satisfaction from group membership. In dynamic terms the group, be it at work, in the home, in sports teams, a trade union or a native tribe, will survive as a group in the face of attempts to disperse it only in so far as individuals get some personal need reduced. The higher this satisfaction, the greater is likely to be the contribution of each person in a group and therefore the greater will be the group energy (synergy).

The quality of work, be it intellectual and physical, monotonous or varied, delicate or crude, is widely held to contribute to job satisfaction (Walker and Guest, 1952; Herzberg *et al.*, 1957, 1959). But the multivariate nature of all these external influences is brought home in the work of Walker and Guest who found aversion to the repetitive nature of production line work to be easily counterbalanced by the economic benefits which industries can bring to bear— particularly of course, higher hourly pay than many other jobs. Another solution to production-line monotony has been tried in recent years at a SAAB motor works in Europe. Here the workers share in the various tasks necessary for the assembly of components and can move around from one task to another as the mood strikes them. The success of this venture is still not certain because some jobs essential to the finished article are universally disliked and there is still a tendency for people to find a "cosy little corner" of a job for themselves and to stick to it.

Some of the connections between job efficiency and individual differences in personality and ability are well documented (Eysenck and Eysenck, 1964; Cattell, Eber, and Tatsuoka, 1970). Provided job efficiency, the criterion, can be accurately adjudged, it is possible to build up specification equations displaying typical weightings of ability and personality traits for a given occupational task.

Of course, the job efficiency specification equations we discussed above (page 206) are not analyses of what satisfaction a person gets from his work. A bright man could be outstandingly efficient in a routine task and loathe every minute of it. We have, on the other hand, a need to determine the characteristics of those *best adjusted to a job*, in other words the satisfaction gained from doing a particular job. For this we may assume that those who have stayed with a job are more likely to be adjusted. Naturally, some people are trapped in jobs for life because of circumstances beyond their control, but by and large one would expect the profile of the "stickers" to typify the best adjusted. Figure 9.5 shows two profiles—note how different they are. These profiles would not necessarily be identical to those constructed for the most efficient clergyman or doctor— although finding suitable efficiency criteria for these two occupations would present a challenge!

As yet, the equivalent research into the detection of motivation profiles is fragmentary and much more tentative. However, the compilation of table 9.6

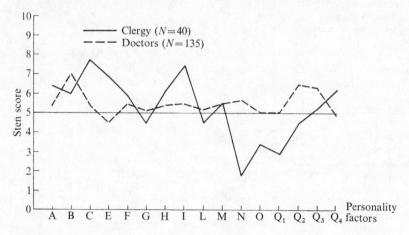

Figure 9.5 Comparison of personality profiles for clergy and doctors

represents a beginning based on adjustment (long-term) criteria. More in the spirit of enquiry than of stating fact, we shall point out some similarities and differences between the groups in table 9.6.

Amongst the sentiments, notice the low interest in parental home of professional groups such as teachers, physicians, and executives. The unusually high sentiment strength of schizophrenics to home and to career is not easy to explain except that the former could represent high dependence, or the fact of being institutionalized for an indefinite period may enhance their longing for the parental home. The figures here are pooled integrated plus unintegrated; separate U and I scores might tell us more. A curious feature not particularly noted clinically is the very high superego strength of the schizophrenics. This indication fits the observation of high religious interest among schizoids (Kretschmer, 1931) and certainly calls for a follow up in dynamic measurement studies. Incidentally, it contrasts particularly with the rationalizing expediency implied by the low score of business executives. The difference between superego and self-sentiment is illuminated here by the fact that those who have high professional investment (education, training) have larger self-sentiment scores than others. In fact, the college students, and disabled who have not yet been

Table 9.6 MAT sten scores (rounded) for various occupational groups

Occupation	N	Career	Home	Fear	Narcism	Superego	Self-sent.	Mating	Pugnacity	Assertion	Sweetheart
Army Officers	44	6	4	5	8	4	5	6	7	5	6
Theological seminary males (clergymen)	279	5	4	4	6	6	6	5	5	4	6
Teachers	64	5	3	5	3	5	7	6	5	5	6
Physicians	112	6	3	6	8	6	7	5	6	5	4
Executives	20	6	3	5	10	1	10	8	4	5	6
Disabled workers	34	6	5	6	5	6	4	5	5	4	5
Construction workers	17	8	4	5	6	4	5	4	7	7	6
Engineer supervisors	27	7	5	5	5	5	5	5	5	5	5
Engineers	23	7	5	5	5	5	5	5	5	6	6
College students	100	5	4	5	3	4	4	3	4	4	4
Chronically unemployed	75	5	4	8	4	5	5	4	4	2	3
Violent criminals	19	5	4	7	3	5	5	2	5	5	3
Nonviolent criminals	19	5	5	5	3	5	5	3	5	4	4
Schizophrenics	30	8	7	4	3	8	4	5	2	5	5

put in a position to realize their potential are low on self-sentiment. Although the table does not show I and U scores, it is known (Sweney, 1969) that patients in mental hospitals, students who are failing, and prisoners all have high *unintegrated* self-sentiment scores. A glance at table 9.6 reveals lower total scores and therefore we may assume that the conflict scores are high. We shall look at this point later when discussing the "loser's syndrome".

The ergs display intriguing differences. The chronically unemployed and violent criminals manifest high fear scores; caution and insecurity dominate the minds of these high scorers. At the other extreme we find the clergy and schizophrenics both unaffected by the threats of life, though perhaps for different reasons.

Narcism scores show a striking regularity in that the executives, army officers, physicians (all rewarded by high status in society) are high on narcism whilst college students, the unemployed, and criminals score low. It seems that those who have experienced the fruits of status, comfort and perhaps luxury value them still more highly than before. The mating erg seems to be a measure of availability—the established worker, especially the financially well-placed, scores high, but the institutionalized student (mostly unmarried anyway) and criminal score low. This is seemingly in the integrated component. Pugnacity is high in Army officers—a professional virtue—though why it should be high in construction workers is not clear. Schizophrenics, meanwhile, give abnormally low scores which show an unwillingness to meet reality head-on. Criminals are moderately high, but it would be most valuable here to classify according to types of crime.

A distinction was made earlier between efficiency and adjustment in a job and a method was suggested by which to obtain an individual's fitness to a job in terms of each. An interesting and instructive side-step is to look at the profiles of those who are selected or rejected using well-defined criteria. Skelton's work (1968) with officer selection has already been mentioned (page 21). An extreme of "job adjustment" comparisons is reached when we compare, as in the study of Lawlis (1968) already mentioned, those chronically unemployed with a matched control group of employed people. Putting these researches side-by-side indicates three dynamic factors which significantly differentiate those doing a good job from those who fail or have no job at all.

Dynamic factor	Direction of difference for those satisfactorily in a job (*in both studies*)
Career	Higher
Fear	Lower
Self-assertion	Higher

The lack of an immediate outlet, lesser enthusiasm and feelings of failure may all contribute to the direction of the difference. Understandably there are higher feelings of insecurity in the unemployed. The reader speculating incidentally about the relation of fear to anxiety will find that although the evidence is clearly that they are not identical as patterns (Cattell and Bartlett, 1971; Cattell in Spielberger, 1972), there is evidence of substantial correlation of the U component in the ergic tension of the fear erg with anxiety (Sweney and Rich, 1966; Spence and Sweney, 1966). Thus the "unsuccessful" seem (see anxiety) to be higher both on straight insecurity and on general anxiety. Self-assertion is correlated with a high need to succeed. Could it be that those who do not pull off an attempt to be appointed are showing less enthusiasm and lower status motive? These questions must await more detailed research.

In the Lawlis study, the scores for the dynamic traits were correlated, using the point-biserial, with employed versus unemployed. Table 9.7 presents the relationships. Lawlis concludes that the chronically unemployed person feels

Table 9.7 Simple correlations of unemployability with motivational variables

Dynamic factor	Unintegrated	Integrated	Total
Career	−.040	−.482‡	−.381‡
Home–parental	−.186	−.075	−.209
Fear	.309†	−.041	.160
Narcism–comfort	.088	−.380‡	−.220
Superego	.102	−.178	−.040
Self-sentiment	−.068	−.570‡	−.403‡
Mating	−.155	−.406‡	−.355†
Pugnacity–sadism	.069	.094	.116
Assertiveness	−.250	−.309†	−.403‡
Sweetheart–spouse	−.135	−.397‡	−.333†

Source: Lawlis (1971).
Note: The point-biserial correlation.
* $p < .05$ level uncorrected for multiple comparisons.
† $p < .01$ level uncorrected for multiple comparisons.
‡ $p < .001$ level uncorrected for multiple comparisons.

fearful of expressing himself. This is indicated by his lower assertiveness. The lack of assertiveness extends to a lack of career motivation—work presents an unwanted opportunity to expose his inadequacies. Courtship and marriage are likewise difficult because his lack of a job places him in a vulnerable position with respect to his wife, or to courtship. The role of assertive male would not come easily to him. These observations also tie up with the lower self-sentiment he displays. Thus the use of objective measures of dynamic traits brings out the way in which particular frustrations and life situations produce ramifying effects throughout the whole spectrum of needs.

6   The associates of social status: winners and losers

The personality and ability associations of social status have long been investigated with reasonable adequacy; but the dynamic structure associations have not. Social status from the standpoint of structure proves to be largely a single factor dimension, loading such measures as years of education, economic success, intelligence, size of house, and, until recently perhaps, smaller family size (Cattell, 1943). But it has been interpreted from a more individual point of view by many psychologists, notably in Sweney's "winners and losers" concept, when the area and kind of success are viewed more locally. However, intellectuals, artists, alienated subcultures, and saints aside (who after all are a small group), the definition of "success' in society falls along the social status axis.

The personality and ability researches on social status show a correlation of about .3 with intelligence (Vernon, 1950; or about .2, Cattell, 1971, with culture fair intelligence tests) and correlations also with higher emotional stability, C factor, surgency F, dominance E, harria I($-$), and lower ergic tension, $Q_4(-)$. Recently (Cattell, 1966b) it has become apparent that diverse "dropouts" from the culture, e.g. delinquents, persons chronically on welfare payrolls (relief), drug addicts, alcoholics, tend to have a certain communality of deviations on personality factors, such as lower B (intelligence), C (ego strength), F (surgency) and higher ergic tension (Q_4) and anxiety (QII). Moreover, this pattern turns out to have marked resemblance to the lower social status pattern in our culture. Consistent with this, lower status is associated with higher incidence of delinquency, drug addiction, mental defect, schizophrenia and various psychopathologies. These findings hold in societies with free upward mobility, and in the name of scientific caution, we should not conclude they hold in strict caste societies.

The question of how far the traits accumulated toward the top and bottom of the ladder are those arising from selection by promotion, and how far from the effect of holding a given status has begun to be investigated by examining what traits lead to promotion. Doubtless, each career structure demands its own idiosyncratic personality factors, but there may be a case for believing that some factors are, in general, more potent than others. To this time, the research has been largely a matter of recording the attitudes and actions of the promoted compared with others. The anomalous results (see Vroom, 1964) are largely due to inadequate devices and the only research so far to use an objective measure has shed light on the personality rather than motivation dimensions in predicting promotion prospects.

Barton and Cattell (1972b) took high school graduates and ran two testing sessions with the 16PF, once at school and again five years later when they were at work. The sample was divided according to whether they had been promoted or not during the interim period. This repeated measures method enabled a base-line to be produced from which change scores could be computed. An analysis of variance for main and interaction effects showed some prominent differences as shown in figure 9.6.

The most striking thing about the overall picture is the change which has accompanied the promotion of individuals from a basic situation where, in most cases, the mean score was the same. An important question springing to mind for some future research is the nature of the change—is it a change deliberately "cultivated" to enhance promotion prospects (some people are here assumed to be cleverer than others at spotting the qualities of the promoted), or are the qualities there ready to be brought out and developed as part and parcel of the demands of promotion. Compared to the nonpromoted, the promoted show a decrease in dominance (E), guilt-proneness (O), and ergic tension (Q4). The two last findings agree with other results of success, but the dominance is

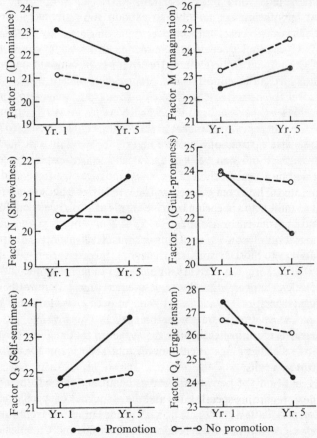

Figure 9·6 Promotion versus no promotion, occuring between year 1 and year 5 of testing.

Source: Barton and Cattell (1972b).

anomalous, since, even in animals, Mowrer and others have shown that dominance increases with success. Perhaps in humans, and at this late adolescent age, things are more complicated, and there arises an Adlerian overcompensatory power seeking in those who fail. Imagination (M), shrewdness (N) and self-sentiment (Q_3) increase to become significantly greater amongst promotees after five years. All but dominance commence at means which are not significantly different. This is not recorded in the figure, but a main effect was that promoted subjects had and maintained higher scores on factor A, (warmheartedness), and were consistently lower on factor Q_2 (self-sufficiency). The combination of warmheartedness and group dependence seem curiously advantageous factors—at least in the early stages of a career. We might imagine the willing, "gets on with fellows", cultivator of advantageous friendships catching the eyes of those responsible for promotions.

Several hypotheses are possible to explain the differences observable in figure 9.6, but it should be remembered that these are only speculations. The curious dominance effect could arise either as an overcompensation as above, or through dominant behavior being increasingly redundant once promotion has been achieved. The nonpromoted subjects become less practical (or down-to-earth) over the period and since the whole sample was a noncollege group, the jobs they would have are more likely to require relatively more practical skills than imagination. The increased shrewdness of the promoted individuals involves the development of a more polished and socially aware outlook—an obviously useful tool when having to lead others. The decrease in guilt-proneness may well be a concomitant of increased feelings of security and well-being when promoted. The increase in self-sentiment (high in the case of professionals as we saw in table 9.6) appearing here is consistent with the general observation that the self-sentiment builds up with success and prestige and disintegrates with failure. That ergic tension, being a measure of general frustration level, should increase in those who achieve their goals is inconsistent with the meaning given to this factor. The stability offered in staying with the same job in a position with some responsibility and greater financial rewards should decrease such frustration. Incidentally, if we score the second-order personality factors on change, it turns out that anxiety (QII, covering C—, H—, O, Q_3— and Q_4) reduces significantly more among the promoted. This fits the general observation of higher anxiety with poorer school performance and with lower social status in adults.

A coherent body of knowledge is thus beginning to be formed in the personality field, regarding social status and the associates of specific occupational success and failure. But the separation of positional *effects* from *causes* of promotion, by such studies as those of Barton, Bartsch, and Cattell is only beginning. One would hypothesize from the known nature of the factor, incidentally, that increased surgency (F) with success and status is an illustration of the *effects* of position.

Meanwhile, however, the relation of status to *dynamic* factors, as measured in the MAT and SMAT, is virtually an uninvestigated realm, except in so far as the self-sentiment and the superego occur also (as Q_3 and G) in the questionnaire medium too. However, the pioneer work of Sweney (1967) on various deviant groups allows us inferences on what dynamic trait differences may be associated with social status. His findings with the MAT concern partly the average scores, but mainly he claims greatest differences with regard to conflict scores. He discovered a cluster of motivation traits which consistently showed high conflict measures amongst deviant and disadvantaged groups such as juvenile delinquents, criminals, unemployed, and disabled. Table 9.8

Table 9.8   Summary of losers' syndrome on the MAT

Groups	Size	MAT (stens)			
Losers	N	Conflict career	Conflict superego	Conflict self-sentiment	Total conflict
Juvenile delinquents	126	6	9	9	10
Chronically unemployed	28	9	9	8	9
Schizophrenics	30	5.8	6.3	7.0	6.8
Criminals (violence)	20	7	6	7.5	7.0
Criminals (stealth)	20	5.5	6	7.5	7.5
Orthopedically disabled	34	6.5	6.4	7.2	7.4
Compared to norm		High	High	High	High

Source: Sweney (1967).

shows the high conflict scores in career, superego and self-sentiment structures (others are not so clearly significant). The theory behind the conflict score (Williams, 1959; Delhees, 1968; Horn and Sweney, 1970) is that where the unintegrated component (U) motivation score is high, relative to the integrated (I) this tension of unexpressed drive arises from repression or frustration, depending on the direction of control required. For example, if a person is knowingly inhibiting the expression of a dynamic urge, and therefore not satisfying a basic need, U being then greater than I, the conflict will be typical of repression. If, however, the inhibition is imposed by the society (or some source external to the individual) or by lack of opportunity, the situation is more likely to be one of external frustration, i.e. conflict with the environment. The free and successful expression of an erg will be reflected usually in higher scores on the integrated component factors (devices of: information, word association, memory, etc.), but if the need is at once stimulated and blocked it will show in higher scores on the U component (the unintegrated factor measures: autism, phantasy, projection, "I want . . ." statements as in inventories, etc.). The conflict score $(U-I)$, has been shown to correlate with other manifestations of the presence of conflict (page 223).

With these definitions in mind, it is not difficult to see how it is that career, superego and self-sentiment are so markedly affected in the deviant and disadvantaged. The term *loser's syndrome* has been applied by Sweney to this collection of conflict symptoms. The losers in table 9.8 are defined by being chronically unemployed or having character or physical defects which make an ordinary earning status difficult to achieve. There is therefore little wonder at the high career conflict. The commonest cause is high aspiration for success in a career in the absence of opportunities to achieve this success. The pressures in our culture to do a "fair day's work for a fair day's pay" are sufficient, we would suspect, to create a strong urge to work which is frustrated in all these unfortunate cases.

A healthy superego sets up firm guidelines for behavior, but where conflict exists as defined here, it means that the original endowment in this structure has not succeeded in expressing itself in rewarding, stable habits and values. In the case of delinquents, criminals, and possibly the unemployed, the sources of conflict are self-evident. For the disabled there may be a case of irrational self-blame through not being able to live a full life.

Most clear, and of most interest to general personality theory, is the deformation which arises in "the loser" in relation to the self-sentiment. The self-sentiment (Q_3) has been defined (page 35) as the set of subsidiated satisfactions which take place through having a well-formed, self-concept and the accompanying stable habits of expression. The unfortunate "loser" type is the victim of a vicious circle in which his failures do not permit him to form a satisfying self-image, and the lack of a definite concept in turn causes his behavior to be less integrated and satisfactory in society. The need for a self-sentiment exists as an adequate U score shows, but as table 9.8 brings out, the integrated, I, measure falls far short in all these types and particularly in the delinquents.

7   Summary   1. Occupation and industrial psychology has to be considered from two approaches for adequate understanding: (a) that of the dynamics of social institutions and their functional requirements, and (b) that of the dynamics of the individual in adjusting to them. Our concern here is the latter.

2. The career sentiment was established comparatively early as a factor among the major dynamic structures. The chief attitudes which subsidiate to it are known, and, as would be expected, they have great diversity of ergic goals—food, sex, self-assertion, etc.

3. Two methods are known to psychometrists for vocational guidance or selection (a) the efficiency criterion, which uses a specification equation against a success criterion, and (b) the adjustment criterion, which measures the similarity of the individual's profile to the mean of those who stay in the job.

4. Appreciable progress has been made along the latter approach since personality and ability factor profiles have been established, notably with the 16PF test, for many important occupations, but the discovery of profiles of strengths on dynamic structures, by use of the MAT and SMAT, is only in its infancy. Nevertheless, profiles for employed and unemployed groups have been obtained, notably for the professional and for executives in the former. The efficiency criterion is also known for some groups, e.g. the Army officers specification equation shows positive loadings on strength of career sentiment, and the self-assertive erg, and negative on attachment to home and parents and on need for security (fear).

5. This dynamic specification, as well as that for doctors and the adjustment pattern for others still leaves us at present, however, uncertain about the direction of cause and effect. For example, is the doctor's lesser attachment to wife and family a cause or consequence of his greater professional performance? The discrepancies of U, unintegrated, and I, integrated, components in various dynamic structures also show interesting work associations. In any case the career relates to more in dynamics of personality than to the career sentiment alone.

6. As an example of the dynamics of discharge of tasks within any one occupation we have taken the prescribing behavior of doctors. In regard to the (at the time) controversial psycho-active drugs (tranquillizers) psychologically meaningful personality and dynamic trait associations to interest in prescribing such drugs were found. Also propaganda was found to produce dynamically measurable changes both in the strength of attitudes and the loadings which show the nature of their subsidiations. For example, high superego led to cautious use of such drugs, and propaganda for them led to stronger opposition from this source. The wide political, commercial and religious applications of the dynamic calculus are stressed.

7. Theoretically the whole important question of job satisfaction can now be examined more objectively and more analytically since U and I measures of separate dynamic structures became available. Exploratory studies, showing different characteristic sentiment levels and ergic tension levels in different occupations should be productive of good theory. At present, however, the uncertain roles of strength of stimulation and level of gratification in determining U and I levels leave doubt about interpreting the values of the job satisfactions directly from these profiles.

8. Success and failure in a broad sense in society, in occupations and in other fields, can be considered in most a condensed fashion in terms of association with social status and with local observations on "winners" and

"losers". Studies with the MAT of delinquents, unemployed, handicapped, and other groups indicate a discernible common pattern of personality and dynamic structure in more versus less "successful" individuals, while longitudinal records throw a little light also on which is cause and which effect. In any case there are significant associations of failure with subnormal scores on the career, superego and self-sentiment factors, especially in the sense of the integrated component being less than the unintegrated. This is interpreted as evidence of major conflict in these areas, associated with occupational or social failure.

10 The dynamic calculus of group life

1 The definition and nature of a group

Men—except for a few Robinson Crusoes—survive by, and have many of their most important emotional relations with, a variety of groups to which they belong. Economists and sociologists have done their bit to help us understand the life of groups. But in the last resort the roots of understanding of the family, marriage, the adolescent peer group or gang, social classes, and the culturo-political life of national groups lie in human motivation. In this chapter we shall hope to show that the same dynamic calculus principles as have enlightened individual motivation and conflict can give us a new grasp of the dynamics of groups.

To enter this field we must master certain new concepts about groups themselves. A group is sometimes defined as a set of people with similar qualities (in the sense of a mathematical group) or subscribing to some common principle; but the basic definition is a dynamic one: *a set of people held together by the existence of that group contributing to the satisfaction of each.* The "similar interests" definition fails, for a man and his dog get very different qualities of satisfaction from the symbiosis—the only thing in common is the wish that the togetherness continue. Nor can we accept the requirement of a common conscious recognition of who is in and out of the group or what the group is for, because many satisfactions are unconscious, and though a year old baby is undoubtedly a member of the family he is certainly not aware of what the family is.

A taxonomy of groups could and has been made many times, classifying the varieties of groups (Cattell, 1948a; Hemphill and Weste, 1950; Stogdill, 1952; Borgatta and Cottrell, 1956; Roby, 1957; Guetzkow, 1958). There are neonate groups, consisting of individuals brought together for the first time in a group without organization, there are traditional groups, heavy with laws, precedents, and rituals; there are groups with many structured roles and others with few; there are groups low in a group hierarchy and others near the top in decision-making, and so on. Brevity compels us in this chapter to consider three widely representative examples: (1) the small (eight to twelve people) neonate group with an elected leader; (2) the family, and (3) the vast, multi-roled cultural group we call the nation.

Any group that lasts more than a matter of hours acquires recognizable role positions—a leader, followers, a secretary, an executive committee member, etc.—and therewith certain rules and expectations of conduct. As soon as it begins to act *as* a group it acquires characteristics measurable in a world of groups. It is an aggressive group, or an uncertain group torn by dissensions, or a high or low productive group, and so on. Just as the most systematic scientific way to find the unitary traits of people is to factor analyze many performances of many people, so the unitary dimensions for measuring groups *of a certain type* can be found by taking, say, 200 groups of that type, e.g. football teams, and correlating say 50 kinds of group performance across these 200 groups.

When Cattell and Stice (1960) did this for ten-man neonate groups, over some 40 performances they found twelve distinct dimensions necessary to describe small groups, two of which can readily be related to individual dynamics in ways soon to be seen.

Granted that a series of scores can be given to describe any particular group on the typical "source traits" of that species of group—just like the source traits of human beings, such as intelligence, ego strength, surgency, etc.—we can speak of the *syntality* of a group just as we speak of the personality of an individual. Syntality is therefore to be analogously defined as *that which determines what a group will do in any defined stimulus situation*. Like a given personality it will be measured by a profile ("vector") of scores on the source traits existing in groups of that type.

Finally, we should recognize that groups are not self-contained and mutually exclusive in membership as we would like for simplicity, but have overlapping membership. A man belongs to a family, a recreational club, a church, a nation and often he has difficulty in sorting out his loyalties and rendering to Caesar what is Caesar's. It is easy to see that many, but not all, of the structures we have studied in previous chapters as *sentiments* are dynamic loyalty systems built up to particular groups, and that the *self-sentiment* is the coordinating self-concept system in the individual which regulates rivalries among these sentiments for the greatest good of the individual. Such implications from previous analysis of individual dynamics may be already clear, but for the rest we enter new ground.

2 Group syntality and synergy

One must never overlook the fundamental fact in the relation of individual to group dynamics that someone belongs to a group only if he gets some satisfaction from it. Thus a group is a tool to the ultimately biological needs of individuals, just as impersonal things may be tools. And, of course, a group will disintegrate when it ceases to provide whatever satisfactions of sex, security, etc., needs it originally provided.

The need satisfactions may sometimes be obscure, especially in groups that seem to do nothing. But in any group whatever, we can commonly recognize the remaining satisfactions of the gregarious and self-assertive ergs, as in a man who is made treasurer-commodore of a yacht club but does not know a sheet from a halliard, and quite dislikes being afloat.

Now any attitude vector, for a well-established attitude, records in its ergic and sentiment loadings the habitual rewards which the given course of action brings to a man. By testing the attitude "In my present life situation I want to continue to belong to this club", and factoring it in the context of a set of ergic tension measures, such as is provided by SMAT and MAT, it is possible to get a specification equation—embodying a particular vector of loadings on ergs and sentiments, which tells us objectively the nature of the satisfactions which the individual gets from belonging to that club.

Hitherto it has been shown how *different* attitude vectors, e.g. those all belonging to a given sentiment or erg, can be summed *within one individual* to give, for example, his total sentiment strength, or level of ergic tension. But at this point we introduce the reciprocal design of summing the *same* attitude across a set of different people. In effect we propose to take all members of the group and add the measures of their attitude strengths on the attitude "I want to continue in this group". Properly this would be a vector summation, to yield a group vector expressing the quality of the interest along the various ergic dimensions. Thus added we reach what we shall define as the *synergy* of a group—the total response energy which keeps it going.

Since individuals in different roles get different satisfactions out of their activities in the group this total synergy may not resemble particularly any one person's vector. And there may be *negative* satisfactions on *some* ergs in the synergy vector just as in any individual vector, though no individual can have a wholly negative vector, since he would then drop out of the group. For example, the positive gregarious and superego satisfactions of belonging to a good police force may be partly offset by the negative satisfactions of the individual's need for security, in a dangerous calling.

Now the synergy of a group, measured in appropriate units, tells us much about the dynamic life of a group, and is to be considered, in the mathematical model, as a sub-space of the *syntality*, as previously defined. That is only saying, in mathematical terms, that the dynamic roots of a group issue in vectors that form part of the total dimensional description of the group, just as the ergic tensions and sentiment strengths of the individual are a section of the dimensions which describe him, along with the general personality dimensions.

To indicate this briefly in formulae, we would say that the performance, X, of a small group, e.g. in a tug of war, or in reaching an accurate conclusion in committee, or in scoring goals in a football game, can be represented by a specification equation like that for an individual, thus:

$$X = b_{a1}A_1 + \ldots + b_{ap}A_p + b_{t1}T_1 + \ldots + b_{tq}T_q + b_{d1}D_1 + \ldots + b_{dr}D_r$$

$$(10.1)$$

where the A's are ability factors, T's temperament-like traits and D's dynamic traits. For there is no reason to expect that the syntality of a group will have anything different from the three *modalities*—A's, T's and D's—that we find in individual behavior. The D part of this syntality vector is what we have just defined as synergy.

It will be recognized that the response or performance X in (10.1) is the performance of the group *as* a group, not the mean performance of the population. These could be very different. For example, in two groups of equal population mean and sigma on intelligence, if decisions are made in the first by equal weighting of votes and in the second by a role structure which puts decisions more in the hands of the upper half of the population by intelligence, the more intelligent decisions will be made by the second group, as a group. What we may call the *structure* of a group, R, defined by the role and rule structure within it, intervenes between the population characteristics as such, P, and the syntality, S, the final determiner of group action. The population vector is defined as simply the mean (and sigma) of the characteristics of the members, e.g. their average intelligence, education, emotional stability, superego strength, the ergic tension, and sentiment strength levels, etc. The basic formula relating population, P, structure, R, and syntality, S, characteristics (as vectors) is:

$$S = (f) P R \qquad (10.2)$$

where (f) simply indicates some function we do not yet know and the juxtaposition of P and R does not mean that they are multiplied but only that both are considered. Thus it says essentially that the syntality of a group is a function of the characteristics of the population and of the traditions and roles which describe the pattern in which people are arranged in the group. In this total framework our concern here is with the relation of dynamics of the population to dynamics of the group.

3 Experimental evidence on the structure and sources of synergy and morale

The measurement of the attitude "I want so much to belong to this group" is strictly the measurement of a sentiment, for it sums all the attitude satisfactions that a given individual gets in relation to a group, e.g. "I enjoy the company of the members", "I enjoy the power I have as committee member", "I am proud to tell people I belong to the group", "I like meeting the attractive young women who belong to the club".

Like any sentiment vector this total interest in belonging will have a particular ergic quality. Gregariousness, assertiveness and security satisfactions will usually be large, but sex, curiosity, parental–protective will also appear, e.g. respectively in a dance club, a scientific society, and a missionary charity society. It will also vary in magnitude (length) from society to society, since the satisfactions obtained in, say, the family, the trade union, or the nation, are greater than those from, say, a car-pool group or a stamp collecting society. The total synergy of a group—the amount of energy and loyalty it has to draw upon—is thus in general proportional to the size of the average sentiment vector and to the number of people in the society.

This synergy may be thought of as the *dynamic income* of a group, and since in social psychology we are approaching the boundaries where psychology and economics meet, it is often close to being the same thing as the monetary income. People are prepared to pay larger subscriptions to family, professional union and nation than to lesser societies, because they get vaster psychological satisfactions, e.g. of affection, status, and security from them. Synergy and group income are closely related in those groups which handle relations in terms of economics. Parenthetically, we should also recognize that as each individual belongs simultaneously to a dozen or more groups, yet has only a limited total dynamic energy, there is typically competition among groups for people's interest-energy. The dynamic equilibrium which ensues is decided by the sustained expectations of individuals about the satisfactions they get from the various groups—since groups, as we have said, are tools toward individual satisfactions.

This defines the group income; but what about the group's expenditures? In the disposal of synergy a distinction has been made between *maintenance* and *effective* synergies, though it is only one of several analyses that can be made. The maintenance synergy is that which is absorbed simply in performing the functions that keep the group in being—collecting the taxes, preserving order and the rules, assuring the succession in roles, etc. The effective synergy is that which performs the functions for which the group was brought together—the fighting effectiveness of an army, the missionary endeavor of a missionary society, the research advances made by a laboratory. Recent investigations of certain charity organizations which display heart-rending pictures of starving children, remotely abroad, showed that most of the money collected went in salaries providing jobs to the organizers. This painfully illustrates the distribution that can occur of total synergy between maintenance and effective synergy.

This is as far as group dynamic conceptual analysis can be pursued in one chapter and we must turn without delay to empirical evidence, scant as yet, illustrating these conceptions. (For further pursuit of theory, see Stogdill, 1952; Borgatta and Cottrell, 1956; Cattell, 1948a, 1951, 1953, 1961; Roby, 1957; Guetzkow, 1958.) The research here necessarily began with studying the total syntality of small groups, out of which evidence on synergy, especially in relation to leadership, emerged. Incidentally, since correlations must be obtained across a sufficiency of groups—80 to 100—this research is arduous, for, with ten man groups, one is recording interactions in groups of 800 to 1000 men.

The opening researches on small group syntality began with Cattell and Wispe (1948) on 20 groups and continued to 80 neonate groups (Cattell and Stice, 1960). Some fifty group performances of a most varied kind, that could be objectively measured, were devised. Men who had never met before were measured on the 16PF test and then assigned to groups of ten. The group synergy derived basically from the fact that being a member of the group was an avenue to earning possibly $100.

As to structure, three leadership criteria were used to form distinct sections to the investigation, namely (i) a leaderless group with no formal leader, (ii) leader having defined powers was elected, and (iii) an elected leader was retained from a previous session. [These are the R's in equation (10.2).] Measures of 32 population (personality and motivation) dimensions (P's), 45 group internal structure variables (sociometric, interactional, and immediate observer assessment) (R's) and 34 group performance (S, syntality) variables were obtained. Measures were designed. The latter included mechanical construction work, committee-like procedures requiring decisions based on inadequate data, code cracking as a group exercise, reaction to panic-producing situations as produced by severe electric shock in a rope-pulling experiment, arriving at group decisions as to what line of action the group should take in regard to satisfaction of interests, and the honesty of the group in dealing with other groups in competition. The groups worked as teams during three periods of three hours each. A reward system was instigated—$100 was to be awarded to the best *group* performance, stress being placed on the fact that it could be earned only by group and not individual activity. Ultimately, the scores from the three sessions were used to provide three different factor matrices all containing the population, structure, and syntality variables. Robustness of factors was judged from their recurrence in two or all three analyses.

Thirteen identifiable syntality factors resulted. Of these most would be considered of A or T modality, but there were at least four which appeared as major synergy dimensions falling specifically as dynamic aspects of group life. All four described aspects of group morale or synergy and clearly portrayed ways in which dynamic cohesion is maintained in the small groups. Note that the popular usage of "morale" assumes only one dimension whilst here the evidence is that at least three and probably four directions which morale might take to provide synergic drive.

The four most consistent factors in all three sessions were labeled *synergy through leadership*, *immediate (gregarious) synergy through group membership*, *reward morale*, and *effective role interaction*.

Leadership synergy (Morale 1) is a score which expresses interest in the existence and purpose of the group through the stimulation and organization of the leader. The chief loadings of the factor are the sociometric count in group unity, optimism for the future of the group, a sense of common purpose, high confidence in the leader and high feeling of freedom to participate.

Immediate (or gregarious) synergy (Morale II) through group membership is reflected in persistent high loadings on such variables as high degree of group organization, interdependence, cohesiveness, orderliness of procedure, some high ratings of leadership, strength of motivation of comrades, and actual good group performance. (The last is somewhat surprisingly absent in the loadings of Morale I.) The motive force in this kind of synergy derives from the satis-factions gained from group membership. The congeniality of fellow members gives rise to a sense of high spirits and to good performance. Deutsch (see Cartwright and Zander, 1953) similarly found high cohesiveness in a group where the goals were clearly defined and when all had agreed to aim for these goals, especially where the individual's goals coincided with the general aims of the group. Performance was also enhanced in these circumstances. Deutsch also showed there to be less synergy in internally competitive conditions than in internally cooperative conditions.

Reward Morale (Morale III), or personal gain synergy, depends upon the energy put into group activity and seems to arise from a sense of individual personal gain (either material or mental). Whilst the pattern is not quite as firm as in the previous factors, there are some regular features in there being little group argument or time spent in getting to a solution. At the negative pole there is little unanimity, dissatisfaction with the group leader, not much forti-tude to shock treatment and a high sense of frustration when the group is decidedly unsuccessful. The fourth synergic factor, effective role interaction (Morale IV), had been postulated (Cattell, Saunders, and Stice, 1953) to spring from satisfaction in one's personal role, i.e. in employing skill and thereby gaining status which enables the individual to play a specific role in the group. Loadings were high on some population variables, e.g. cyclothymia (A—out-going, participating) and alaxia (L—trusting and easy to get on with). This is associated with accuracy in group judgments (i.e. freedom from prejudices) and fairness. There was also evidence of susceptibility to immediate emotional appeals in a jury-type judgment. This response to emotional appeals rather than to logical thinking is typical of the cyclothyme.

Support for the existence of these synergic dimensions comes from several sources. Katz (1949) in his analyses of industrial settings found higher satisfaction where: (a) there were feelings of gregariousness or "belonging" gained from group membership; additionally, small groups had higher morale than large ill-defined groups (Morale II); (b) satisfaction was gained from clear-thinking management and leadership (Morale I); (c) proper pay and promotion prospects listed (Morale III); (d) there was pride in personal skills (intrinsic job satisfaction) and a sense of personal worth (Morale IV). Rosenberg (1957), in his work on occupational value complexes, found three major complexes (since confirmed using factor analytical techniques) which he called extrinsic reward, intrinsic reward and people-orientation. These three factors came in response to questions about the opportunities which an ideal job should offer. The link between extrinsic reward (good money, status, prestige) and Morale III, intrinsic reward (self-expression in using special abilities or being creative and original) and Morale IV, and people-orientation (liking for working with people and being helpful to them) and Morale II is clear. Wilson, High, Beem, and Comrey (1954) found four factors: leader–nonleader rapport (Morale I), congenial work group (Morale II), informal control (also linked with Morale I) and group unity (Morale II). Festinger (1950) located three basic reasons why people join groups—either for prestige gained by membership (Morale IV), to help the group reach a goal (Morale II), and because they value their association with the group (Morale II).

While the empirically reached group dimensions in these large researches converge with acceptable precision on these four morale-synergy patterns, the theoretical interpretation of the latter remains to be checked. Our own theory is that Morale I, synergy of leadership, represents the extent to which the leader is able to stimulate interest in the group by making clear that it will satisfy the needs felt by individuals. Morale II, gregarious synergy of congeniality, expresses the extent to which individuals enjoy and trust other members, and is therefore loaded on some population characteristics. Morale III is less clear, but may represent the smoothness of internal functioning and the absence of causes of strife. Morale IV, role morale, is the increment of synergy in the group which comes from the psychological gains which individuals experience in their role positions. What some group dynamicists have called "cohesiveness" is a product of all these, though particularly obvious in Morale II. The fact is that when all four sources of interest and satisfaction in the group—its purposes as clarified by the leader, its congeniality of comrades, its smoothness in achieving goals, and its conferring of role status satisfactions—add to zero, the group dissolves and "cohesiveness" vanishes.

4 The dynamics of leadership

The positive correlations of rated goodness of the leader in a group with the dimensions of group morale offer at once a clue to the dynamic functions of the leader. He has to show and persuade the members that their needs can be met through the group (Morale I); he has in fact to deliver the goods (this may be a hidden part of Morale II); he has to settle and smooth out clashes of interest among members in a just way (Morale II) and he (or tradition) has to provide the framework in which individuals can get their role satisfactions.

In this section we propose to look at the personality qualities of leaders which facilitate these dynamic procedures, and—although nondynamic population characters are not our primary interest—to note that personality-temperament traits of the group members also facilitate dynamic developments.

A generalization which quickly emerged from the studies of Cattell and Stice, as well as that of Gibb (1949) and others, was that leaderless groups placed in competitive intergroup situations nearly always quickly decide that they want a leader, and elect one. By their mode of action some three types of leaders have been recognized: (1) *Popular elected* leaders, who are individuals with the highest popularity (by sociometric count and voting as likable); (2) *Effective* leaders, selected from among the above as being rated most effective in actual leadership, regardless of their popularity; (3) *Technical* leaders—individuals not necessarily in the actual leadership position, who have the highest score on having found solutions to problems faced by the group. In connection with these operational distinctions, incidentally, Cattell has proposed the most objective definition yet offered of a leader—apart from that of his being explicitly recognized in the group as occupying that traditional role—namely, that the *leader is the group member whose removal brings about a greater change in syntality values than that of any other member.* This radical definition has still to be put to experiment. Other classifications, e.g. by sociologists, have approached these, e.g. in the authority figures speculated by Weber (see Bendix, 1960) who supposed that, apart from those whose authority has been invested in them by virtue of their birthright or hierarchial position in an organization (Kings, Lords, the church, etc.), we have (i) the legal-rational leaders who by the bureaucratic process are given leadership, and (ii) the charismatic leaders who by dint of compelling personal qualities attract the support of the group. However, in the present case the types are defined by actual experimental observations.

Table 10.1 shows the actually obtained personality differences between leaders and nonleaders for each of the three types of leaders. First, there are three personality traits recurring for all three criteria, namely, venturesomeness (H+), confident adequacy (self-assurance, O−), and high self-sentiment (self-disciplined, Q_3). Two out of three criteria (elected and effective leadership qualities) give also high superego (G+). For the elected leaders we find, in

Table 10.1 Differences between leaders and nonleaders using the 16PF

Personality factor	18. *Observers' leaders* (effective)				19. *Elected leaders* (popular)			
	L	Non-L	d	C.R.	L	Non-L	d	C.R.
A	18.3	19.7	−1.4	—	18.6	17.4	1.2	—
B	12.5	11.7	0.8	—	10.9	10.3	0.6	—
C	36.1	34.2	1.9	2.2*	34.8	34.0	0.8	—
E	27.0	26.0	1.0	—	25.2	24.4	0.8	—
F	26.1	26.2	−0.1	—	26.4	22.5	3.9	4.6
G	22.4	21.3	1.1	—	22.4	20.8	1.6	3.6
H	39.8	35.8	4.0	3.4	36.6	33.2	3.4	3.2
I	9.8	10.6	−0.8	—	10.0	10.6	−0.6	—
L	16.8	17.8	−1.0	—	17.9	18.6	−0.7	—
M	18.6	19.8	−0.8	—	18.6	20.2	−1.6	2.5*
N	23.0	22.2	0.8	—	21.4	20.7	0.7	—
O	11.3	13.6	−2.3	2.4*	13.0	15.9	−2.9	2.7
Q_1	21.5	21.2	0.3	—	19.7	19.8	−0.1	—
Q_2	15.9	14.5	1.4	—	13.6	14.6	−1.0	—
Q_3	26.7	24.6	2.1	2.2*	26.0	23.6	2.4	2.1*
Q_4	12.0	15.0	−3.0	2.2*	14.7	16.0	−1.3	—
N	43	100			92	233		

Personality factor	66. *Frequency leadership acts* (*technical*)					
	High L'ship	Mid L'ship	Low L'ship	d_1 (H−L)	(H−M)	(C.R.)
A	17.8	17.9	17.5	0.3	−0.1	—
B	11.4	10.4	9.7	1.7	1.0	4.2
C	35.1	34.1	33.6	1.5	1.0	—
E	25.6	24.4	24.0	1.6	1.2	—
F	26.9	25.6	25.0	1.9	1.3	2.5*
G	22.1	21.0	20.6	1.5	1.1	3.1
H	36.7	33.3	32.9	3.8	3.4	3.1
I	9.8	10.7	10.7	−0.9	−0.9	—
L	18.1	18.6	18.4	−0.3	−0.5	—
M	19.0	20.1	20.1	−1.1	−1.1	—
N	21.9	20.4	20.6	1.3	1.5	—
O	13.3	15.4	16.2	−2.9	−2.1	2.2*
Q_1	19.9	20.3	18.8	1.1	−0.4	—
Q_2	14.1	14.1	14.1	0.0	0.0	—
Q_3	25.8	24.3	23.2	2.6	1.5	3.4
Q_4	14.7	16.3	16.4	−1.7	−1.6	—
N	90	140	90			

Source: Stice (1951).

* Significant at 5% level. All other critical ratio C.R. figures shown are significant beyond 1% level.

addition to the above, surgency (F+), and practicality (M−). These are all obviously serviceable qualities for a leader. He must be visible and make easy contacts. A timid, withdrawn schizoid (H−), an anxious, worrying (O+) and undisciplined (Q₃−) person is not likely to inspire enthusiasm and confidence in his followers. Secondly, he must offer that promise of justice among members, and of selfless persistence for the group good which are possible through high superego strength.

Two further points are worth noting from the table 10.1. The few differences between the results for the three leader criteria suggest that selection by syntality change (frequency of leadership acts) tends to favor those of high intelligence (B+), character strength (superego, G+) and high self-sentiment formation (Q₃+) to a higher degree than for selection by sociometric devices. Since problem-solving is a major function of the leader, it is undoubtedly a great mistake to confuse leadership with mere popularity as has been done by depending exclusively in many so called leadership researches on sociometric counts. The reappearance of superego and self-sentiment amongst leadership traits will remind the observant reader that these two personality factors were seen at the crossroads of the temperamental and dynamic patterns discussed in chapter 4. There it was asserted that the pattern of attitudes underpinning self-sentiment is concerned with self-preservation (physical, mental, and social), self-control and will power. Similarly, the contribution from the superego comes from a preoccupation with high moral standards, fair play, and dependability. Together G and Q₃ are admirably suited, and provide powerful motives, for fulfilling leadership roles.

The tabular evidence in table 10.1 can be shown somewhat more clearly, for the purposes of differentiating, in the conventional profile diagram in figure 10.1. The general pattern displayed has been confirmed in the work of Carter (1951), Haythorne (1953), and Mann (1959). Correlational studies between personality traits and effective leadership persistently show that intelligence (B+), self-confidence (O−), and enthusiasm to participate (G+) (Hare, 1963) are vital qualities.

By piecing all this evidence together it soon becomes possible to build up a specification equation of the typical leader. There is much more work still to be done in this respect, but tentative equations have been calculated from the 16 PF and these are incorporated in figure 10.1. The overall picture may finally be summarized as follows. The problem-solving type of leader tends towards higher intelligence (a quality not always apparent in elected leaders); emotional stability, both in the leader and as a syntal property of the group, is a benefit; elected leaders (rather than effective leaders) are high on surgency; leaders of all three kinds are more conscientious (high superego strength) than followers; those high on parmia (adventurous, "thick skinned") generally feel free to participate and attract more attention from group members; individuals high on autia (imaginative, bohemian, M+), whilst they make leader-like sugges-

Figure 10.1 Sten profiles and specification equation weights for three leader types

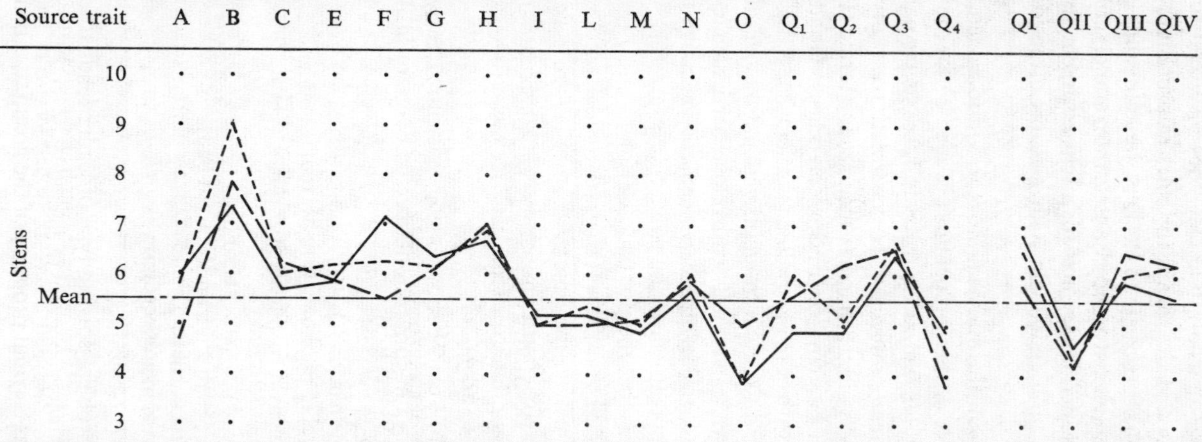

Stens scale (10, 9, 8, 7, Mean, 5, 4, 3)

Profiles

	N		A	B	C	E	F	G	H	I	L	M	N	O	Q1	Q2	Q3	Q4	QI	QII	QIII	QIV
Elected leaders	92 M	——	6·0	7·3	5·7	5·8	7·1	6·3	6·7	5·2	5·2	4·8	5·7	3·9	4·9	4·9	6·4	4·9	6·8	4·6	5·9	5·6
Effective leaders	43 M	— —	4·7	7·8	5·9	5·5	6·1	7·0	5·0	5·0	5·1	5·9	5·0	5·6	6·2	6·5		3·8	5·8	4·2	5·9	6·2
Technical leaders	90 M	----	5·8	9·0	6·0	6·1	6·2	6·1	6·9	5·0	5·3	5·0	6·0	3·9	6·0	5·1	6·6	4·5	6·5	4·2	6·0	6·2

Sten weights

	A	B	C	E	F	G	H	I	L	M	N	O	Q1	Q2	Q3	Q4	Constant
Elected leaders	-0·14	0·62	-0·97	0·00	0·39	0·26	0·09	0·04	-0·06	0·06	0·03	-0·99	-0·44	-0·07	0·26	0·02	10·45
Effective leaders	-0·33	0·68	-0·52	0·10	-0·05	0·07	0·65	0·01	0·05	-0·16	0·00	0·64	-0·31	0·18	0·14	-1·01	4·73
Technical leaders	-0·05	0·93	-0·69	0·07	-0·10	0·20	0·21	-0·01	0·12	-0·03	-0·05	-0·55	-0·18	-0·19	0·32	-0·11	6·11

Source: Based on data from males alone taken from Cattell and Stice (1954).

tions, ultimately find their suggestions are rejected—they also tend to show
dissatisfaction with group unity and the regard for rules of procedure—thus
we find the more practical (M—) being elected as leader; the self-assured (O—)
personality is preferred to the apprehensive and insecure; the routinely effective,
perhaps even more so in the elected leader, has high self-sentiment strength
(Q$_3$—controlled, socially precise, etc.); people with high ergic tension (Q$_4$)
rarely become leaders.

As part of the understanding of the dynamics of morale and leadership we
should turn finally to the effects of the personalities of members—the popu-
lation characters. High synergy of leadership, Morale I, seems virtually un-
related to member qualities; it can presumably be generated in any group by
showing them that the group will give them what they need. Morale II—that
of congeniality—on the other hand has many associations. "Good com-
panions", as table 10.2 shows, are low in protension (suspiciousness, L), low in
worrisome ergic tension (Q$_4$ and O), high in emotional stability (C), and in
group dependence (Q$_2$—). The other variables which load here, such as "high
degree of 'we' feeling", "high degree of interdependence", "effective leader-

Table 10.2   Morale II: synergy of congeniality

Variable matrix no.	Descriptive title	Factor loading
9	PTM Relaxed security (L)	−.85
75	*or* High degree of leadership	.63
76	*or* High degree of group orderliness	.53
79	*or* Low degree of frustration	−.53
78	*or* High degree of 'we' feeling	.50
16	PTM Low ergic tension (Q$_4$)	−.49
3	PTM High level of emotional stability (C)	.47
12	PTM Low level of worrying, suspicious anxiety (O)	−.46
92	*or* High level of motivation	.46
73	*or* High degree of group organization	.42
71	Dynamometer: High score on sustained pull	.40
14	PTM group dependency (Q$_2$)	−.35
80	*or* High degree of interdependence	.31

Definition of immediate high synergy–vs.–low motivation. Essentially here we have a
collection of observer ratings such as would be implied by our hypothesis of synergy. The
group appears highly motivated, cohesive, and desirous of a high degree of leadership.
"Sustained pull" is perhaps the performance which would be expected most directly to
reflect simple high general motivation.

Again, however, the highest loadings are in population characters and on general principles
we would therefore expect these to be the "cause" of the associated group performances.
Personality factors of warmheartedness (L, freedom from protension), emotional maturity,
and freedom from anxiety and nervous tension are here thrown together, possibly as a
second-order factor.

ship", etc., are presumably the dynamic effects of these favorable personality environments.

A well-supported finding is that a high level of neuroticism in members admitted to a group tends to destroy group morale. Likewise, introvert tendencies in a group sometimes militate against successful group life. This generalization, of course, must be punctuated with qualifications about the nature of group leadership and the purposes of the group because the research from which the above information was culled involves neonate groups having several goals to achieve. In well-established groups with clearly defined goals, it may well be that the nature of the task, or mutual understanding, is sometimes aided by introvert characteristics; in academic research groups there may be trends towards introversion. It has been shown elsewhere that groups engaged in "creative" tasks are at an advantage if there are introvert tendencies there.

We see from the foregoing a very practical sense in which the population variables contribute towards the syntality of a group. With more reliable personality measures now at our disposal it is entirely conceivable that we could create groups with prescribed tendencies by selecting a biased membership in terms of population means, i.e. by considering the standing of each individual in relation to population parameters and choosing those with the required bias (see Cattell and Stice, 1954; Katz, 1949, for examples taken from military and industrial settings). The idea of forming groups from individuals having similar personality profiles is by no means new. The pious hope of selecting the right people for various occupations using an interview as a substantial criterion has a long history. But this crude and notoriously subjective method cannot be depended on as a way of selecting groups with prescribed characteristics (Kelly and Fiske, 1951; Eysenck, 1953).

Available results give us largely the relation of group dynamics to characters of members and leaders. But this leaves untouched the *situational* effects, e.g. of group success and failure, accord and discord, upon the nature of the vectors of individual group interest and the total synergy. Certainly it has been good strategy first to find out about the taxonomy of groups and their populations. But a whole world of new laws about relations of individuals and groups now opens up with the provision of objective measurement devices, and the formulations of the dynamic calculus.

5 Intra-familial attitudes and family as group The second type of small group at which we promised to glance is that of the family, with its enormous importance both for the sociologist and for the psychologist studying child development or marital compatibility.

As to marital compatibility there seem—strangely—to be no experiments yet undertaken using the MAT to see how the need strengths of husband and wife interact and how they differ in successful and unsuccessful marriages. Parallel data, however, are now available on several samples with the 16 PF and the clear evidence is that partners in successful marriages are more alike (higher positive correlation) on virtually every personality source trait than are those who break up (table 10.3). One can only hypothesize (with some support from Lowell Kelly's research; see Cattell, 1957) that the same will be true of interests.

One may safely hypothesize that the same or an even greater degree of resemblance would exist on the sentiment strengths on the MAT, since common interests are vital, but it is not so clear what might be expected on the ergic

Table 10.3 Correlations of husbands and wives in stably and unstably married couples

	Stably married	p	Un-stably married	p	Z (of differences)	p value (two-tailed)	p value (one-tailed)
A. *First order*							
A (Affectothymia)‡	.16	n.s.	−.50	< .01	3.61	< .001	< .001
B (Intelligence)	.31	< .01	.21	n.s.	.53	n.s.	n.s.
C (Ego strength)	.32	< .01	.05	n.s.	1.44	n.s.	n.s.
E (Dominance)	.13	n.s.	.31	n.s.	−.94	n.s.	n.s.
F (Surgency)	.23	< .05	−.40	< .05	3.27	< .01	< .001
G (superego strength)	.33	< .01	.19	n.s.	.78	n.s.	n.s.
H (Parmia)	.23	< .05	.12	n.s.	.60	n.s.	n.s.
I (Premsia)	−.15	n.s.	−.13	n.s.	−.09	n.s.	n.s.
L (Protension)	.18	n.s.	−.33	<.05	2.60	< .01	< .01
M (Autia)	.22	< .05	−.01	n.s.	1.16	n.s.	n.s.
N (Shrewdness)	.18	n.s.	.27	n.s.	−.50	n.s.	n.s.
O (Guilt-proneness)	.11	n.s.	.36	< .05	−1.35	n.s.	n.s.
Q_1 (Radicalism)	.27	< .01	.34	< .05	−.40	n.s.	n.s.
Q_2 (Self-sufficiency)	.15	n.s.	−.32	n.s.	2.41	< .05	< .01
Q_3 (Self-concept control)	.27	< .01	−.02	n.s.	1.47	n.s.	n.s.
Q_4 (Ergic tension)	.16	n.s.	−.11	n.s.	1.35	n.s.	n.s.
B. *Second order*							
I (Exvia–vs.–Invia)†	.22	< .05	−.30	n.s.	2.69	< .01	< .01
II (Anxiety)	.31	< .01	.23	n.s.	.45	n.s.	n.s.

$N = 102$ couples, stable group; 37 couples, unstable group.

† (Exvia and anxiety are fairly uniformly negatively correlated, averaging —34 for the four possibilities.)

‡ The following terms give a superficial description of the source traits measured by the 16 PF : A : outgoing, warmheated; emotionally stable; F: happy-go-lucky, enthusiastic; H: venturesome, socially bold; I: tenderminded, sensitive; L: suspicious, self opinionated; M: imaginative, bohemian; Q_4: tense, driven, overwrought.

Data on a further sample, fully supporting the above, are available in Barton and Cattell (1972 and 1972a).

tensions. Presumably positive correlation would be found in the more stably married on the strength of the sex drive, but perhaps the principle of complementariness would hold for self-assertiveness or for security-seeking (fear).

Although no data on compatability and the MAT have yet been gathered like the above, some indirect findings exist and a study is now nearing completion by Bolz (in press), in which a couple is being measured on the MAT on the same days over 50 or more occasions, i.e. it is like the longitudinal studies of Cross (page 83) and Kline (page 82) except that two interacting people are involved. Unfortunately, the experiment is not yet analyzed, but one can see that *dual dynamic P-technique* as we may call it has tremendous possibilities in establishing laws of human dynamic action, especially in such common role relations as husband and wife, mother and child, psychotherapist and patient, and so on. Some technical difficulties, as yet only partly overcome, remain to be met in repeatedly giving the same MAT or SMAT over a hundred occasions, but as the work of Cross, Kline, and others shows the difficulties are not insuperable.

Meanwhile what we have just called indirect data exists in the study by Barton, Kawash, and Cattell (1972) which obtained accounts from married people about various activities or conditions in their marriages, and related them to MAT scores of husband and wife as shown in table 10.4. It is noteworthy that husband and wife with high narcism scores do not have (respectively) high frequency of going out together, or any sense that they want to spend more time together. It also fits the concepts involved that high frequency of sex relations is impeded by superego, self-sentiment and narcism or that high assertiveness tension in the husband goes with more disagreements over child rearing. It should not be difficult to proceed from these rough approaches regarding the ergic contributors in various attitude vectors to calculations on the synergy in the married couple or family group, and to indices of morale consistent with those above for small groups.

The full dynamics of the family can be profitably studied, however, only when an adequate model concerning intrafamilial attitudes has been worked out. Then we should expect relations between the dimensions of families in terms of "family atmospheres", such as Baldwin *et al.* (1945) have worked out, and some function of these attitudes. Similarly we can hypothesize that there will be relations between the dimensions of child upbringing practices, such as Dielman (1974) is measuring in the CRPQ (Child Rearing Practices Questionnaire) and the particular constellations of intrafamilial attitudes (Dielman and Cattell, 1972).

Let us therefore consider how constellations of intrafamilial attitudes may be approached. Figure 10.2 reminds us of the sets of attitudes that exist in the "full" family, i.e. with mother, father, two sons, and two daughters. Let us next consider what a measurement of each such attitude, e.g. my attitude to my brother means. This attitude measurement, if taken as a single total attitude, is actually a *sentiment*. There are indeed dozens of attitudes, as separate courses of action, involving the object "my brother". For example, "I want to go fishing with my brother whenever possible", "I want my big brother to protect me from enemies", "I want to get more time on the bicycle I share with my brother", "I wish my brother would stop telling tales about me to the parents", and so on.

Here there exists the typical relation of a set of attitudes about one sentiment object to the final strength of the sentiment. According to the model argued for on page 48 above, we should expect the sum total of the vectors of these attitudes to yield a single vector, "I want this sentiment object to go on existing" which expresses as a single vector all the different types of ergic satisfaction occurring in the actions which involve the object. When we ask "What is the (total) attitude of X to his brother?", it is this sentiment that we really mean.

Table 10.4 Relation of ergic tension and sentiment measures (in the MAT) to marital behavior

Behavior	Erg and sentiment scores related	Total prediction (multiple R)	
		U	I
High frequency of disagreements	Negative with (I) self-sentiment (H); with (U) sentiment to spouse (W) and (I) strength of career (W)	.28	.35
High frequency of going out together	Negative with (U) narcism (H)	.27	.33
Spends as much time as he or she wants with spouse	(U) Assertiveness (H); (U) career (H), (I) fear, (H), (I) narcism (W)	.33	.43
High frequency of desiring sex relations	(U) Sentiment to spouse (H); (U) narcism (H), (I) career (W)	.33	.34
High frequency of having sex relations	(U) Negatively self-sentiment (H) (W); (I) negatively narcism (H); (I) career (W); negatively (I) superego (W)	.40	.39
High frequency of doing something pleasing together	(U) Mating (H); negatively (U) assertiveness (W); (U) fear (W); (I) self-sentiment (W); negatively (I) career (H)	.43	.42
High frequency of common pastimes	(U) Self-sentiment (H); (U) mating (H)	.34	.34
Differences over child rearing	(I) Assertiveness (H)	.34	.36

Source: Barton, Kawash, and Cattell (1972).
    (U) or (I) before each indicates whether it is a measure by unintegrated or integrated; (H) or (W) afterwards indicates whether for husband or wife. Only those with significant r's (in .20 to .31 range and $p < .05$ through $p < .01$) are recorded. Correlations at right are mean for husband and wife.

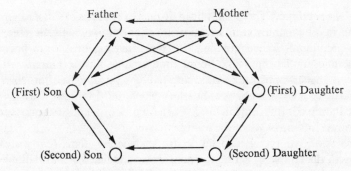

Considering son to father attitude as generic, regardless of which son, and brother to sister similarly rankless, it will be seen that there are eight relations to be considered, each reciprocated, giving fourteen "types" of attitude, e.g.

Father to son   Brother to sister
Son to father   Sister to brother
Brother to brother   Daughter to mother
Sister to sister   Mother to daughter

Figure 10.2   Types of intrafamilial attitudes needing to be incorporated in an intrafamilial dynamic measurement scheme

The usual ambivalences arising from negative values in particular action attitudes will result in some cancellation of total ergic involvement, but a negative total corresponding to "I wish my brother did not exist" will be uncommon.

Ideally, the psychologist concerned with the dynamics of the family would like to know the sentiment vector of each family member to every other (the single action attitude vectors would usually be too numerous to bother with). But when we set up a specific attitude measure corresponding to the sentiment, using the devices valid for the integrated and unintegrated components, the score is typically a single value, and the *ergic composition of the attitude is the same for everyone.* Thus one might get a score of sten 7 for Jim on "I want to see more of my brother" (which is essentially the central sentiment expression) and it will be understood from the R-technique factoring that this attitude has the specification, say:

$$I_b = .4E_s + .3E_g - .2E_a$$

where I_b is the total interest in wanting his brother, E_s is the erg of need for security, E_g is the gregarious erg tension and E_a the self-assertive ergic tension.

But what we would actually like is the *weights peculiar to Jim*, as from a P-technique study, not the R-technique common loadings, if we would say "Jim's satisfaction in his brother is so much to the need for security, so much gregariousness, and so on". To get the total score without this possibility of analysis is not good enough, yet the ordinary way of scoring an attitude will give only the total score and permit us to evaluate the kinds of satisfaction only according to the common trait specification equation, i.e. with the same total score all individuals would get the same ergic investment scores. Since a P-technique analysis is impossible because we assume that the family attitude battery will be administrable only once, a special construction has been attempted in what is called the FAM battery (the Family Attitude Measurement Battery: Parent Form, Barton and Cattell, 1974; Child Form: Burdsal, Sweney, and Cattell, 1974).

The solution would seem to lie in so constructing items that instead of dealing with the course of action as such, they tie the action and the object to the ultimate ergic goal. Thus, if we were dealing with questionnaire items instead of objective devices there would be items like "I am glad of my brother because he protects me from bigger boys who might attack me" (fear erg investment), or "When I am lonely it is good to know that I can play with my brother" (gregarious erg). In this design (using objective measures, of course, such as autism, word association, information, etc.) the measurement of the sentiment strength is divided from the beginning into sub-sets corresponding to each erg. Thus in factor structure the set of, say, 30 sub-test items might be divided into five for each erg involved, each set checked as covered by one ergic factor, while a general factor, corresponding to the sentiment object (brother, sister, mother, etc.) would run across the lot. Each of the six sub-scores would thus indicate how far a given erg is being satisfied through the given object.

As soon as the FAM measures are more widely taken up in experiment, we shall see how far the syntality and synergy of the family can be explained as the sum of intrafamilial attitudes.

6   The dimensions and dynamics of national cultural groups

The step from the family or small peer group to the complex "traditional" group we call the nation is a big one, and our glance at its dynamics—while still retaining the synergy and leadership concepts—must avail itself of different kinds of data.

It has already been pointed out that the sentiment patterns in individuals would be expected to reflect the institutional structures in the culture. However, many of these are so universal—extending even to preliterate cultures—that the number and nature of sentiments might be expected to be similar. For example, we may reasonably expect sentiments to father and mother, to the family as such, to the peer group, the "profession", the religion, and the tribe or nation.

What is new, in dynamic terms, is the type of general adjustment that must occur to different levels among nations on the dimensions of syntality. National syntality has now been reasonably well investigated and checked by the factor analysis of 50 to 100 variables over 80 to more than 100 countries by Cattell (1949, 1950a), Cattell, Breul, and Hartman (1952), Alker (1964), Rummel (1972), Sawyer and LeVine (1967), and others.

Among the major dimensions which emerge are those one would naturally expect, such as size and affluence, but also "morality level" (Cattell and Gorsuch, 1965); a dimension of "vigorous order", to which McClelland's "achieving society" is very similar; and an intriguing pattern called "cultural pressure", the chief items loading on which are shown in table 10.5.

Table 10.5 Items having high loadings on the "culture pressure" factor

Cultural pressure
High ratio of tertiary to primary occupations
High frequency of political clashes with other countries
High frequency of cities over 20000 (per 1000000 inhabitants)
High number of Nobel prizes in Science, Literature, Peace (per 1000000 inhabitants)
High frequency of participation in wars (1837–1937)
High frequency of treaties and negotiations with other countries
High expansiveness (gain in area and resources)
Many ministries maintained by government
High creativity in science and philosophy
High musical creativity
High death rate from suicide
High incidence of mental disease
High horsepower available per worker
High percentage of population in urban areas
High cancer death rate
High divorce rate
More severe industrial depression in world depression
High total foreign trade per capita
Numerous patents for inventions per capita
Higher number of women employed out of home
More riots
Lower illegitimate birth rate

Source: Cattell (1966c.).

This pattern has three major areas of expression: (1) cultural complication, as shown by high urbanization, etc., (2) pugnacity and maladjustment as shown by wars, riots, suicides, etc., and (3) creativity, as shown by Nobel prizes, musical productions, inventions, etc. The theory proposed by Cattell here is that the onward rush of complication is essentially frustrating to immediate ergic satisfactions, even though it makes life safer and longer. To this frustration people react with aggression (war, riots), or withdrawal (alienation, counter-cultures) or, if they are stable enough to sustain sublimation, by creativity (which, however, continues the spiral of complication).

If this theory is correct we should expect to see a correlation across countries

Table 10.6 Cross-cultural personality profiles (sten mean and standard deviation)*

		Sex	Norm popt	N	A	C	E	F	G	H	I	L	M	N	O	Q1	Q2	Q3	Q4
Australian	Mean*	f	C	579	5.2	6.2	5.1	6.0	5.6	4.8	5.6	5.4	4.9	6.2	5.9	5.7	6.2	6.0	5.0
					1.9	1.9	1.9	2.0	2.0	1.9	1.9	2.0	2.0	2.0	2.1	2.0	2.0	2.0	1.9
Australian	S.D.*	m	C	694	5.1	5.6	5.2	5.6	5.1	4.5	5.7	6.1	5.3	6.1	5.9	5.6	6.6	5.4	5.5
					2.0	2.0	2.0	2.1	2.0	1.9	2.0	2.0	2.0	2.0	2.0	1.9	1.9	2.1	2.0
Brazilian		f	GP & C	828	4.8	5.2	6.0	4.6	4.8	5.5	6.0	7.6	7.1	5.3	6.1	7.4	6.6	5.6	5.6
					1.9	2.2	2.3	2.3	2.2	2.3	2.3	2.1	2.0	2.2	2.4	2.4	2.1	2.4	2.0
Brazilian		m	GP & C	1406	5.6	4.7	4.8	3.7	5.6	5.3	6.4	7.6	7.2	5.0	6.5	6.1	6.1	5.5	6.0
					2.1	2.5	2.4	2.4	2.1	2.0	2.2	2.0	2.1	2.2	2.5	2.2	1.9	2.3	2.3
British		f	GP	1005	5.1	4.9	4.9	5.5	4.9	5.1	5.2	6.2	4.7	5.9	6.0	5.6	5.9	5.6	6.1
					1.7	1.6	1.9	2.3	1.9	2.0	1.8	1.9	1.7	2.1	1.8	1.9	1.9	1.8	1.8
British		m	GP	1004	4.6	4.5	5.0	4.9	4.7	4.9	5.3	6.6	4.6	6.0	6.0	5.8	6.2	5.4	6.2
					1.9	1.7	2.3	2.5	2.0	2.0	2.0	1.8	1.8	2.2	1.8	2.0	2.0	2.0	2.0
Canadian		f	C	167	5.6	5.6	6.3	5.6	4.3	5.6	6.2	4.9	6.6	4.5	5.0	6.7	6.4	5.0	5.5
					1.8	1.8	2.0	1.8	2.0	1.8	1.8	1.8	2.0	1.9	2.0	1.7	1.8	2.0	1.8
Canadian		m	C	201	5.1	4.7	5.7	5.6	5.2	5.1	5.0	6.2	6.0	6.2	5.7	6.1	6.6	5.4	5.7
					2.1	2.2	2.0	2.0	2.2	1.8	2.2	1.9	1.9	1.9	1.9	1.9	2.0	2.0	2.1
Chilean		m	C	321	5.7	4.8	5.0	3.6	4.6	4.1	6.7	7.1	7.3	5.4	6.0	5.8	7.1	5.5	5.8
					1.5	2.7	2.5	1.7	2.0	2.0	1.1	2.2	5.7	2.2	1.2	1.9	1.6	1.7	1.8
Chilean		m & f	GP	291	5.1	5.9	5.9	5.0	4.6	5.2	5.9	7.8	6.2	5.5	6.5	6.3	6.8	5.1	5.7
					1.9	2.1	2.6	2.1	2.1	2.1	2.6	2.0	2.2	2.2	2.1	2.1	1.9	2.2	2.1
Chinese		f	C	385	4.2	3.9	5.1	3.6	4.4	4.4	4.6	7.8	5.9	4.7	5.4	6.4	6.4	6.1	5.0
					1.8	1.9	1.9	1.9	2.0	1.9	1.8	1.9	1.9	1.9	1.9	1.9	1.8	2.0	2.0
Chinese		m	C	425	5.4	3.9	3.9	3.8	5.1	4.8	6.1	7.0	6.5	4.6	5.5	6.0	6.2	6.7	4.8
					1.9	2.0	2.0	1.9	1.9	1.9	1.9	2.0	1.9	1.9	1.9	1.9	2.0	2.0	2.1
French		f	GP	79	5.3	4.9	5.1	4.9	5.1	5.1	5.3	7.0	6.0	5.3	4.9	6.9	5.4	4.9	5.4
					1.4	2.2	1.8	2.0	2.3	1.5	1.9	1.8	1.6	2.0	2.0	1.9	1.8	2.1	2.0
French		m	GP	377	5.5	4.8	4.8	5.0	5.3	5.0	6.4	6.7	5.6	5.8	5.4	6.3	5.5	4.7	5.7
					1.8	1.9	2.0	2.1	2.2	2.0	2.0	1.9	2.1	2.0	2.0	2.0	2.1	2.0	2.1

Table 10.6 cont.

	Sex	†	N														
German	m	GP	1000	5.7/1.7	6.1/1.9	4.9/1.8	5.5/1.8	5.5/1.6	5.4/1.7	3.6/1.8	5.7/1.9	4.9/1.7	6.6/2.1	5.7/1.8	6.5/1.0	5.3/1.8	7.1/1.7	4.4/1.8
Indian	f	C	100	3.0/1.9	3.0/1.5	3.6/1.8	2.6/1.7	4.5/1.6	4.2/1.6	0.6/2.6	5.1/1.9	3.8/1.6	3.0/2.5	4.8/2.1	5.4/2.3	5.0/1.7	5.2/2.4	3.9/1.9
Indian	m	C	100	4.6/1.6	2.6/2.1	3.4/2.3	3.5/1.5	5.0/1.9	4.8/1.8	2.4/2.2	5.5/1.8	5.0/1.8	4.2/1.9	4.6/2.1	5.3/2.3	4.7/1.7	4.6/2.7	3.9/1.8
Italian	m+f	GP	200	5.3/2.1	6.3/1.3	6.7/1.5	5.1/1.6	6.1/1.8	5.8/1.7	4.8/1.5	7.0/2.2	7.0/1.9	7.7/1.5	6.0/1.9	7.4/2.1	6.2/1.8	6.3/1.5	4.1/1.7
Japanese	m	C	300	4.2/2.0	3.3/1.8	5.3/1.9	3.2/1.9	4.5/1.8	3.8/1.7	6.0/2.0	5.9/2.1	7.2/2.1	5.7/1.9	6.7/2.1	7.3/2.2	6.8/1.8	4.6/2.0	6.6/2.0
Mexican	m	GP	138	5.6/1.7	6.6/2.2	4.4/2.0	4.7/2.0	5.8/1.7	5.7/1.9	4.7/1.6	5.9/2.0	7.2/2.5	5.4/2.5	6.1/2.1	5.6/2.1	6.3/1.9	6.9/2.0	4.3/1.6
New Zealand	f	HS	521	5.1/1.8	5.4/1.9	5.6/2.1	5.5/2.0	4.6/2.1	5.1/1.9	5.2/2.0	6.0/2.0	5.9/2.1	5.4/2.0	5.7/1.9	6.4/2.0	5.9/2.0	5.6/2.1	5.5/1.9
New Zealand	m	HS	611	5.2/1.9	5.4/2.0	5.5/2.1	5.3/2.1	4.6/2.0	4.9/1.9	5.0/2.0	5.9/1.9	5.8/2.0	5.8/2.1	5.5/1.9	6.4/1.9	6.0/2.0	5.8/2.0	5.8/2.0
Philippine	f	C	2468	5.0/1.3	4.8/1.8	6.0/1.4	3.5/1.4	6.1/1.6	4.7/1.5	6.0/1.7	6.8/1.6	6.1/1.5	5.7/1.7	6.5/1.4	5.6/1.8	5.4/1.7	6.8/1.8	5.4/1.3
Puerto Rican	m & f	GP	341	5.9/1.7	4.4/2.0	4.7/2.1	3.8/1.9	6.2/1.9	6.1/2.0	7.0/2.4	5.9/2.2	4.1/2.1	6.0/2.0	5.5/2.2	4.4/1.8	5.5/1.8	7.5/1.9	4.6/2.0
Venezuelan	m	GP	1144	5.9/1.8	5.3/2.1	4.9/1.9	5.9/2.0	4.7/3.1	5.0/1.9	5.2/1.9	7.2/2.0	4.5/1.9	5.8/2.1	6.5/2.0	4.9/2.0	4.6/2.0	5.3/2.0	5.5/2.2
Venezuelan	f	GP	67	6.0/1.8	6.8/2.1	5.2/1.3	6.4/1.8	5.8/1.8	7.2/1.6	4.8/1.9	6.6/2.0	4.2/1.8	5.7/1.9	4.3/1.9	6.0/1.8	4.7/1.6	7.2/2.0	4.1/1.3
Yugoslavian	m	C	387	5.0/1.8	4.2/2.0	4.7/1.7	4.6/1.7	4.7/1.9	5.6/1.7	5.6/1.9	5.6/1.9	5.6/1.7	3.0/1.9	6.8/2.1	7.4/2.0	5.5/1.7	6.5/1.9	5.6/1.6

Source: From *Handbook of the 16PF* which records the sources of data Cattell, Eber, and Tatsuoka (1970).

* In all cases, mean scores on factor B have not been reported here. Translators have frequently reported difficulties in doing the B scale. Consequently, it has not seemed desirable to include the results here.

† Symbols in this column indicate the norm tables which were used in converting the raw scores to stens. GP represents general population norms, C represents college student norms, and HS represents high school student norms. In each case, raw score profiles were converted to stens on the basis of the most appropriate norm table.

between mean population MAT scores and the syntality scores on the above dimensions. Collecting such data is so arduous that at present practically none exist, though the next best thing—16 PF profiles—are now available for comparable groups in ten or more different countries. These results are of a good consistency and show quite substantial differences, as shown in table 10.6.

The explicitly dynamic variable obtainable from this data is the anxiety level (second-order factor QII, covering C—, H—, L, O, Q_3 and Q_4 primaries). A rank order on anxiety worked out by Lynn (1971) from data by Cattell, Eber, and Tatsuoka (1970) and others is shown below. Lynn shows that higher anxiety among these nations is associated with higher suicide, alcoholism, traffic accident rate, and economic growth rate, but lower food intake.

High anxiety	Medium anxiety	Low anxiety
Austria	Belgium	Sweden
Japan	Denmark	USA
Germany	Switzerland	Australia
France	Norway	Netherlands
Italy	Finland	Canada
		New Zealand
		United Kingdom
		Ireland

As they stand these variables may not be too intelligible, but anyone familiar with the culture pattern dimensions of cultural pressure, affluence–education and morale–morality can see that they fit the theory of high culture pressure, low affluence and low morale. The action of the two last is relatively straightforward, low affluence and the disorder of low morale increase anxiety by creating insecurity. If our frustration–pugnacity–sublimation theory is the central dynamic experience in cultural pressure then this also would generate anxiety at the crossroads between pugnacity and sublimation (Cartwright and Cartwright, 1971).

Measures of the mean population levels on the ergic tensions of the MAT, as well as the comparison of U and I components, and the general degree of inherent conflict, will undoubtedly open up to the social psychologist and cultural anthropologist of the future new laws and generalizations on the dependence of culture pattern upon dynamics toward which we are now only able dimly to grope.

7   Summary   1. A group is properly to be defined dynamically as a set of people for whom the existence of the group machinery is a means to originally individual ergic satisfactions.

2. To describe a given group three "panels" must be covered: (1) mean population characteristics, (2) structure, in terms of agreed internal, traditional

behavior, defined by roles and rules, and (3) syntality—analogous to personality, and enabling us to predict what the group as a single entity will do in a defined situation. The vector of syntality values includes the vector of synergy values, which parallels the dynamic modality of traits in personality.

3. The synergy of a group is theoretically the sum of the vectors of attitudes for all members "I want this group to continue to exist". Like any single attitude or sentiment it will have a specific ergic quality as shown by the satisfactions along the vector. Groups overlap and compete for synergy, and vary greatly in their total synergy. One useful division of synergy from a group functioning standpoint is into effective and maintenance synergy.

4. When the syntality of small groups is examined by factor analysis four of the twelve or so dimensions found appear to be synergy dimensions. They are theorized to be (1) synergy of leadership—the extent to which the leader can show the group how to satisfy needs; (2) synergy of congeniality—the gain from gregarious satisfaction through mutual liking; (3) synergy of harmony—the gain through low incidence of internal disputes and from a sense of justice maintained; and (4) synergy of role satisfactions—through individuals gaining expression and satisfaction in suitable roles. These may also be called Morale I, II, III, and IV, and some of them, notably II and III, are found to load mean personality trait scores for the group members.

5. No scores are yet available on the ergic tension levels of leaders in relation to followers, but as to sentiments it is shown by the 16PF that elected leaders are high in the superego sentiment and self-sentiment, as well, of course, as intelligence and the extravert factors which help make them visible and approachable. The function of these qualities can be dynamically interpreted in that the dependability and positive values of the superego and self-sentiment make for group harmony and reduction of injustices, while the extravert qualities aid communication of values.

6. A group of special interest is the family, concerning which we already have evidence on the principle of congeniality and of compensation, as shown by personality trait correlations. However, the main understanding of family dynamics is likely to be gained through objective measures of intrafamilial attitudes. The construction of intrafamilial attitude batteries so as to yield a score both for the total sentiment strength and for the particular ergic investments in the object is described.

7. Dimensions have been discovered and checked for the measurement of national culture patterns. Though the systematic relating of these to dynamic traits in the population and to structural features has barely begun, a definite dynamic theory has been proposed fitting the phenomena of the cultural pressure dimension. Measures of anxiety levels may relate to this positively and to affluence and moral level negatively. Meanwhile substantial national differences on the 16 PF traits have been demonstrated and need to be related to measured differences in national syntality.

APPENDIX I
Factor Analysis

To convey the full meaning and value of factor analysis would require far more space than is available in a text of this kind. For an introduction to factor analysis for those who are not too handy with mathematics, readers might like to try *The Essentials of Factor Analysis* by Child, 1970. For those who want more depth, still at a readable level, *Factor Analysis* by Cattell, 1952, Gorsuch, 1973 or the relevant chapters in Cattell (1966c), should fill the bill.

For the time being, we will give here a superficial explanation of some basic terms met with in this book and hope that the student will spend some time expanding on this thumbnail sketch.

The basic premise of factor analysis is that when several variables consistently intercorrelate, that is their magnitudes grow, diminish or disappear together, there is an underlying reason. When plants begin to sprout in the Spring, trees show their leaves and hibernating or migrating animals return and propagate, these simultaneous events are caused by an underlying factor or factors, e.g. the sun and its position relative to that region on the earth. The purpose of factor analysis is to show us which variables do, in fact, interrelate and the extent of this interrelationship. From the factors we may wish to deduce causal relationships. The correlation coefficient is the statistic used.

Using the oxygen deficiency example quoted in the text, a reduction in the oxygen supply to organisms brings about corresponding or "concomitant" changes in body functions. Observations soon show that mental and physical activities degenerate, blood color and constitution change, breathing rate is affected, heartbeat changes, feelings of tiredness creep on, etc. One or several of these symptoms might occur in response to some other abnormal condition, but some unique blend of these symptoms will be characteristic of oxygen deficiency. Factor analysis can tell us which symptoms are especially involved *and* the extent to which each is involved.

Suppose we observed six variables in a particular situation—a great advantage when we want a more rounded notion of how various aspects of behavior interact in a real life situation—and label them *A* to *F*. The table below is a hypothetical arrangement of the solution using factor analysis.

Variables (tests, devices, items, etc.)	Factors		
	I	II	III
A	52	12	08
B	40	02	02
C	35	−10	11
D	35	15	71
E	10	45	50
F	05	70	00

First of all, notice there are three *factors*. Sometimes factors are given alternative names such as *components* or *dimensions*. Using well-defined criteria, it is possible to specify the number of factors which will tell us all we want to know about the interrelationships of the variables. The term we use for this process is *extracting* factors. Note the way the figures appear. They are, in effect, correlations which we call *loadings* and can have values between +1 and −1, so that all the numbers in a factor *matrix* such as ours begin with 0.. Therefore, the correlation of *A* with factor I is really +0.52, but we have omitted the 0. because we can take it as read. Plus signs are also taken for granted, but negative signs, as for the correlation of *C* with factor II, are recorded.

The important figures to look for are the high ones. The sample size, amongst other things, is a determinant of just how big the loadings must be to become significant, but as a rough guide values less than 15 (± 0.15 remember) are rarely entertained and more commonly they would need to be greater than 25. All the high values have been blocked off for the three factors. Variables *A*, *B*, *C*, and *D* have something in common and contribute to factor I (we ignore *E* and *F* in discussing factor I except to say that they do not figure in it if there was some previous case for believing they were involved). *E* and *F* in factor II have something else in common. Observe in factor III the inclusion of two variables *D* and *E* already involved in the other factors. Obviously, it is quite possible for a variable to have something in common with more than one factor. Using the oxygen deficiency example again, if *D* was breathing rate and *E* a questionnaire carefully designed to discover the conscious experiences of the subjects, *D* would certainly correlate with, or *load on*, the first factor which, shall we say, is the factor containing the symptoms of oxygen deficiency, i.e. *A*, *B*, and *C*. But it might also load on factor III because of a relationship between breathing rate and conscious effort to breathe faster in order to increase oxygen supply. This is an illustration of the way in which factor analysis subtly teases out dual functions which might never have appeared in bivariate analysis.

Depending on the methods adopted, the factors may be unrelated or partly correlated. The former, i.e. unrelated, procedure is called an *orthogonal solution* (or at 90 degrees) and the latter an *oblique solution*. Most of the analyses mentioned in this book, unless otherwise stated, are oblique. Whilst orthogonal solutions have their uses, they do tend to ignore the simple fact that most aspects of human behaviors are related to some extent and this accounts for the adoption of oblique solutions. The term *rotation* occurs from time to time and this is the method by which we arrive at the final oblique solution to give us the figures such as in the above table. The graphs in figure 1.1 have axes which are not quite at 90° because the factors in table 1.3 were slightly correlated.

APPENDIX II
Elementary Matrix Algebra

In the little space available we can do no more than introduce readers to some of the commonest terms used in matrix algebra which appear in the text. For a short introduction, readers might try M. M. Tatsuoka, *Significance tests: Univariate and Multivariate* (No. 4 of Selected Topics in Advanced Statistics), Institute of Personality and Ability Testing, Champaign, Illinois, 1971, or A. G. Hammer, *Elementary Matrix Algebra for Psychologists and Social Scientists*, Pergamon, Australia, 1971.

An arrangement of numbers in a square or rectangular form as in the illustration below is called a *matrix*. There are several partial examples in this text, but a complete one appears on page 63 in chapter 3. For convenience, a matrix is commonly given a symbol or capital letter in bold type to represent it. **A** below is a square matrix of numbers and **B** is a rectangle of symbols as shown:

$$\mathbf{A} = \begin{bmatrix} 6 & 4 \\ 2 & 1 \end{bmatrix} \qquad \mathbf{B} = \begin{matrix} \\ 1 \\ 2 \\ 3 \end{matrix} \begin{matrix} 1 & \quad 2 \\ \begin{bmatrix} b_{11} & b_{12} \\ b_{21} & b_{22} \\ b_{31} & b_{32} \end{bmatrix} \end{matrix}$$

The individual entries in the matrix are called *elements*. Reading across a matrix (6, 4 or b_{31}, b_{32}) we have a *row*. Reading down (b_{11}, b_{21}, b_{31}) is a *column*. In **B** the rows and columns have been numbered which will help to demonstrate how we locate an entry. The rows are always numbered from top to bottom and the columns from left to right. A complete row or column is sometimes referred to as a *vector*.

To find the position of an element within a matrix we note the row number first then the column number. In **B** the element in the bottom right-hand corner is b_{32} because it intersects at row 3 and column 2. Where we have large matrices as often happens in factor analysis, we may want to refer to an element *in general* in which case we suffix the element with ij, that is, the element at the intersection of the ith row and the jth column. (It could have been any other two letters of the alphabet.) Frequently in the text we have referred to attitude-interest strength as a_{ij} for the very reason that we wanted to develop a general argument. It serves the same purpose as x or y in algebra.

Matrices cannot necessarily be dealt with using the four rules of number. As it will be seen in the texts recommended above, there are some exceptions to the normal rules when applied to matrix problems. The addition of matrices involves adding the elements in identical positions in each in the following way:

Let
$$C = \begin{bmatrix} 1 & 4 \\ 2 & 5 \end{bmatrix}$$

then A + C gives
$$A + C = \begin{bmatrix} 6 & 4 \\ 2 & 1 \end{bmatrix} + \begin{bmatrix} 1 & 4 \\ 2 & 5 \end{bmatrix} = \begin{bmatrix} 7 & 8 \\ 4 & 6 \end{bmatrix}$$

Subtraction of A and C gives
$$A - C = \begin{bmatrix} 5 & 0 \\ 0 & -4 \end{bmatrix}$$

(Note that we must always have the same number of rows and columns in the matrices, i.e. the matrices must be of the same *order*.)

Multiplication of matrices is a little more complex. Taking a simple "1 by 3" matrix (as usual, rows first, columns next), let

$$D = [2 \quad 4 \quad 1] \quad \text{and} \quad E = \begin{bmatrix} 3 \\ 4 \\ 2 \end{bmatrix}$$

We have written the D vector in a row and E as a column, because as we shall see presently, when there is more than one row or column in the matrix, we multiply rows in the first matrix by columns in the second, so it is much more convenient to have the vectors already arranged in that way. To find the resulting matrix we multiply the first number in the first row of the D matrix by the first number in the first column of the E matrix ... and so on along the row and down the column. The products are added together for each row × column as shown.

$$D \times E \text{ (or DE)} = 2 \times 3 + 4 \times 4 + 1 \times 2 = 6 + 16 + 2 = 24$$

$$AC \text{ would be } \begin{bmatrix} 6 & 4 \\ 2 & 1 \end{bmatrix} \times \begin{bmatrix} 1 & 4 \\ 2 & 5 \end{bmatrix}$$

$$
\begin{aligned}
6 \times 1 + 4 \times 2 &= 6 + 8 &&= 14 \text{ (1st row in A with 1st column in C)} \\
6 \times 4 + 4 \times 5 &= 24 + 20 &&= 44 \text{ (1st row in A with 2nd column in C)} \\
2 \times 1 + 1 \times 2 &= 2 + 2 &&= 4 \text{ (2nd row in A with 1st column in C)} \\
2 \times 4 + 1 \times 5 &= 8 + 5 &&= 13 \text{ (2nd row in A with 2nd column in C)}
\end{aligned}
$$

giving the resultant matrix

$$AC = \begin{bmatrix} 14 & 44 \\ 4 & 13 \end{bmatrix}$$

The general case using matrices **F** and **G** would be

$$\mathbf{F} = \begin{bmatrix} f_{11} & f_{12} \\ f_{21} & f_{22} \end{bmatrix} \quad \mathbf{G} = \begin{bmatrix} g_{11} & g_{12} \\ g_{21} & g_{22} \end{bmatrix}$$

As before,
$$\mathbf{FG}_{11} = f_{11}g_{11} + f_{12}g_{21}$$
$$\mathbf{FG}_{12} = f_{11}g_{12} + f_{12}g_{22}$$
$$\mathbf{FG}_{21} = f_{12}g_{11} + f_{22}g_{21}$$
$$\mathbf{FG}_{22} = f_{12}g_{12} + f_{22}g_{22}$$

Thus

$$\mathbf{FG} = \begin{bmatrix} f_{11}g_{11} + f_{12}g_{21} & f_{11}g_{12} + f_{12}g_{22} \\ f_{12}g_{11} + f_{22}g_{21} & f_{12}g_{12} + f_{22}g_{22} \end{bmatrix} = \begin{bmatrix} (\mathbf{FG})_{11} & (\mathbf{FG})_{12} \\ (\mathbf{FG})_{21} & (\mathbf{FG})_{22} \end{bmatrix}$$

With a regular matrix, it is important to state the precise arrangement of matrices to be multiplied, because **AB** does not necessarily equal **BA**. A simple illustration should suffice.

Let $\mathbf{H} = \begin{bmatrix} 1 & 2 & 3 \\ 2 & 1 & 4 \end{bmatrix}$ and $\mathbf{I} = \begin{bmatrix} 1 & 2 \\ 1 & 1 \\ 2 & 2 \end{bmatrix}$

$$\mathbf{HI} = \begin{bmatrix} (1+2+6) & (2+2+6) \\ (2+1+8) & (4+1+8) \end{bmatrix} = \begin{bmatrix} 9 & 10 \\ 11 & 13 \end{bmatrix}$$

However $\mathbf{IH} = \begin{bmatrix} (1+4) & (2+2) & (3+8) \\ (1+2) & (2+1) & (3+4) \\ (1+4) & (2+2) & (3+8) \end{bmatrix} = \begin{bmatrix} 5 & 4 & 11 \\ 3 & 3 & 7 \\ 5 & 4 & 11 \end{bmatrix}$

Clearly, $\mathbf{HI} \neq \mathbf{IH}$.

Bibliography

Adelson, M. (1952). A study of ergic tension patterns through the effects of water deprivation in humans. Unpublished *Ph.D. Thesis*: University of Illinois.

Alker, H. R. (1964). Dimensions of conflict in the General Assembly. *Am. pol. sci. Rev.*, **58**.

Anand, B. K. and Brobeck, J. R. (1951). Hypothalamic control of food intake in rats and cats. *Yale J. biol. Med.*, **24**, 123–140.

Anderson, E. E. (1937). Interrelationship of drives in the male albino rat: I. Intercorrelations of measures of drive. *J. comp. Psychol.*, **24**, 73–118.

Anderson, E. E. (1938). Interrelationship of drives in the male albino rat: II. Intercorrelations between 47 measures of drives and learning. *Comp. Psychol. Monogr.*, **14**, 119–241.

Andersson, B. (1953). The effects of injections of hypertonic NaCl-solutions into different parts of the hypothalamus of goats. *Acta physiol. Scand.*, **28**, 188–201.

Anumonye, A. *et al.* (1969). Plasma uric acid concentrations among Edinburgh business executives. *J. Am. Med. Assoc.*, **208**, 1141–1144.

Atkinson, J. W. and Birch, D. (1970). *The Dynamics of Action*. Wiley: New York.

Baldwin, A. L., Kallborn, J., and Breese, F. H. (1945). Patterns of parental behavior. *Psychol. Monogr.*, No. 58.

Barton, K. and Cattell, R. B. (1972). Marriage dimensions and personality. *J. person. soc. Psychol.*, **21**, 369–375.

Barton, K. and Cattell, R. B. (1972a). Real and perceived similarities in personality between spouses: test of likeness versus completeness theories. *Psychol. Rep.*, **31**, 15–18.

Barton, K. and Cattell, R. B. (1972b). Personality factors related to job promotion and turnover. *J. counsel. Psychol.*, **19**, 430–435.

Barton, K. and Cattell, R. B. (1973). Personality factors of husbands and wives as predictors of own and partner's marital dimensions. *Can. J. Behav. Sci.*, **5**, 83–92.

Barton, K. and Cattell, R. B. (1974). *The Family Attitude Measurement Battery: Parent–Child.* Institute for Personality and Ability Testing: Champaign, Illinois.

Barton, K., Dielman, T. E., and Cattell, R. B. (1972). Personality, motivation and IQ measures as predictors of school achievement and grades: a non-technical synopsis. *Psychology in the Schools*, **9**, 47–51.

Barton, K., Kawash, G., and Cattell, R. B. (1972). Personality, motivation and marital role factors as predictors of life data in married couples. *J. Marriage Family*, **1972**, 474–480.

Bartsch, T. W. and Nesselroade, J. R. (1973). Test of the trait-state anxiety distinction using a manipulative, factor-analytic design. *J. person. soc. Psychol.*, **27**, 58–64.

Bellows, R. T. (1939). Time factors in water drinking in dogs. *Am. J. Physiol.*, **125**, 87–97.

Bendix, R. (1960). *Max Weber: An Intellectual Portrait.* Doubleday: New York.

Benzinger, T. H. (1962). The thermostatic regulation of human heat production and heat loss. *Proc. 22nd Int. Congr. Physiol. Sci.*, **1**, 415–438.

Berlyne, D. E. (1960). *Conflict, Arousal and Curiosity.* McGraw-Hill: New York.

Bexton, W. H., Heron, W., and Scott, J. H. (1954). Effects of decreased variation in the sensory environment. *Can. J. Psychol.*, **8**, 70–76.

Bishop, M. P., Elder, S. T., and Heath, R. G. (1963). Intercranial self-stimulation in man. *Science*, **140**, 394–395.

Bolz, C. (In press). A study of P-technique of the mutual ergic adjustments of a young cohabiting couple.

Borgatta, E. F., Cottrell, L. S., Jr., and Meyer, H. J. (1956). On the dimensions of group behavior. *Sociometry*, **19**, 223–240.

Borgatta, E. T. and Cottrell, L. S. (1956). On the classification of groups. *Sociometry*, **18**, 665–678.

Boulding, K. E. (1953). *The Organizational Revolution.* Harper: New York.

Bowlby, J. *et al.* (1956). The effects of mother–child separation: a follow-up study. *Br. J. med. Psychol.*, **29**, 211–247.

Brady, J. V. (1958). Emotional behavior and the nervous system. *Trans. N.Y. Acad. Sci.*, **18**, 601–602; Brady, J. V. (1958a). Ulcers in "executive monkeys". *Scient. Am.*, **199**, 95–103.

Bridges, K. M. B. (1932). Emotional development in early infancy. *Child Dev.*, **3**, 324–341.

Broadhurst, P. L. (1957). Emotionality and the Yerkes–Dodson Law. *J. exp. Psychol.*, **54**, 345–352.

Brobeck, J. R. (1957). Neural control of hunger, appetite and satiety. *Yale J. biol. Med.*, **29**, 565–574.

Brogden, H. E. (1940). A factor analysis of forty character tests. *Psychol. Monogr.*, **234,** 35–55.

Bronfenbrenner, U. and Devereux, E. C. (1952). Interdisciplinary planning for team research on constructive community behavior: the Springdale project. *Hum. Relat.*, **5,** 187–203.

Brookover, W. B. and Gottlieb, D. (1964). *A Sociology of Education* (2nd ed.). American Book Co.: New York.

Brooks, G. W. and Mueller, E. (1966). Serum urate concentrations among university professors: relation to drive, achievement, leadership. *J. Am. Med. Assoc.*, **195,** 415–418.

Bullock, T. H. (1959). Neuron doctrine and electrophysiology. *Science*, **129,** 997–1002.

Burdsal, C., Sweney, A. B., and Cattell, R. B. (1974). *The Family Attitude Measurement Battery: Inter-Sibling.* Institute for Personality and Ability Testing: Champaign, Illinois.

Burt, C. (1925). *The Young Delinquent.* University of London Press: London.

Burt, C. (1941). Is the doctrine of instincts dead? A Symposium. II. *Br. J. educ. Psychol.*, **11,** 155–172.

Burt, C. (1955). The permanent contribution of McDougall to psychology. *Br. J. educ. Psychol.*, **25,** 10–22.

Caffelt, D. and Sweney, A. B. (1965). Motivational dynamics of violent and nonviolent criminals measured by behavioral tests. Paper given at *Southwestern Psychological Association*, Oklahoma City.

Calder, N. (1970). *The Mind of Man.* BBC: London.

Cannon, W. B. (1929). *Bodily Changes in Pain, Hunger, Fear, and Rage* (2nd ed.). Appleton: New York.

Cannon, W. B. (1932). *The Wisdom of the Body.* Norton: London.

Carter, G. C. (1951). A factor analysis of student personality traits. *J. educ. Res.*, **44,** 381–385.

Carter, H. D., Pyles, M. K., and Bretnall, E. P. (1935). A comparative study of factors in vocational interest scores of high school boys. *J. educ. Psychol.*, **26,** 81.

Cartwright, D. S. (1974). *Introduction to Personality.* Rand McNally: Chicago.

Cartwright, D. S. and Cartwright, C. F. (1971). *Psychological Adjustment, Ego and Id.* Rand McNally: Chicago.

Cartwright, D. S. (1974). *Introduction to Personality.* Rand McNally: Chicago. Evanston, Illinois.

Cattell, R. B. (1928). The significance of the actual resistances in psychogalvanic experiments. *Brit. J. Psychol.*, **19,** 34–43.

Cattell, R. B. (1935). The measurement of interest. *Character Person.*, **4,** 147–169.

Cattell, R. B. (1940). Sentiment or attitude? The core of a terminology in personality research. *Character. Person.*, **9,** 6–17.

Cattell, R. B. (1943). Fluctuation of sentiments and attitudes as a measure of character integration and of temperament. *Am. J. Psychol.*, **56**, 195–216.

Cattell, R. B. (1946). *The Description and Measurement of Personality*. World Book Co: New York.

Cattell, R. B. (1947). The ergic theory of attitude and sentiment measurement. *Educ. psychol. Measure.*, **7**, 221–246.

Cattell, R. B. (1948). Primary personality factors in the realm of objective tests. *J. Person.*, **16**, 459–487.

Cattell, R. B. (1948a). Concepts and methods in the measurement of group syntality. *Psychol. Rev.*, **55**, 48–63.

Cattell, R. B. (1949). The dimensions of culture patterns by factorization of national characters. *J. abnorm. soc. Psychol.*, **44**, 443–469.

Cattell, R. B. (1950). *Personality: A Systematical Theoretical and Factual Study*. McGraw-Hill: New York.

Cattell, R. B. (1950a). The principal culture patterns discoverable in the syntal dimensions of existing nations. *J. soc. Psychol.*, **32**, 215–253.

Cattell, R. B. (1950b). The discovery of ergic structure in man in terms of common attitudes. *J. abnorm. soc. Psychol.*, **45**, 598–618.

Cattell, R. B. (1951). New concepts for measuring leadership in terms of group syntality. *Hum. Relat.*, **4**, 161–184.

Cattell, R. B. (1952). *Factor Analysis*. Harper: New York.

Cattell, R. B. (1952a). The investigation of cultural dynamics: concepts and methods. In J. E. Hulett and R. Stagner (Eds), *Problems in Social Psychology*. University of Illinois Press: Urbana, Illinois.

Cattell, R. B. (1952b). P-technique factorization and the determination of individual dynamic structure. *J. clin. Psychol.*, **8**, 5–10.

Cattell, R. B. (1953). On the theory of group learning. *J. soc. Psychol.*, **37**, 27–52.

Cattell, R. B. (1955). The principal replicated factors discovered in objective personality tests. *J. abnorm. soc. Psychol.*, **50**, 291–314.

Cattell, R. B. (1956). Second order personality factors in the questionnaire realm. *J. consult. Psychol.*, **20**, 411–418.

Cattell, R. B. (1957). *Personality and Motivation Structure and Measurement*. World Book Co.: New York.

Cattell, R. B. (1958). The dynamic calculus: a system of concepts derived from objective motivation measurement. In G. Lindzey (Ed.), *The Assessment of Human Motives*. Rinehart: New York.

Cattell, R. B. (1959). The Dynamic Calculus: Concepts and crucial experiments. In M. R. Jones (Ed.), *The Nebraska Symposium on Motivation*. University of Nebraska: Lincoln.

Cattell, R. B. (1961). Group theory, personality and role: a model for experimental researches. In F. A. Geldard (Ed.), *Defense Psychology*. Pergamon: New York.

Cattell, R. B. (1963). Theory of fluid and crystallized intelligence: A critical experiment. *J. educ. Psychol.*, **54**, 1–22.

Cattell, R. B. (1965). *The Scientific Analysis of Personality*. Penguin: Harmondsworth.

Cattell, R. B. (1966). Multivariate behavioral research and the integrative challenge. *Mult. Behav. Res.*, **1**, 4–23.

Cattell, R. B. (1966a). Anxiety and motivation: theory and crucial experiments. In C. D. Spielberger (Ed.), *Anxiety and Behavior*. Academic Press: New York.

Cattell, R. B. (1966b). In K. S. Miller and C. M. Gregg (Eds.), *Mental Health in the Lower Social Classes*. Florida State University Press: Tallahassee.

Cattell, R. B. (Ed.) (1966c). *Handbook of Multivariate Experimental Psychology*. Rand McNally: Chicago.

Cattell, R. B. (1971). *Abilities: their Structure, Growth and Action*. Houghton Mifflin: Boston.

Cattell, R. B. (1972). The nature and genesis of mood states: theoretical model with experimental measurements concerning anxiety, depression, arousal and other mood states. In C. D. Spielberger (Ed.), *Anxiety: Current Trends in Theory and Research*, Vol. 1. Academic Press: New York.

Cattell, R. B. (1972a). *Real Base Factor Analysis*. Monograph of Multivariate Behavioral Research, Texas Christian University: Fort Worth, Texas.

Cattell, R. B. (1972b). *A New Morality from Science: Beyondism*. Pergamon: New York.

Cattell, R. B. (1973). *Personality and Mood by Questionnaire*. Jossey-Buss: San Francisco.

Cattell, R. B. and Baggaley, A. R. (1956). The objective measurement of attitude motivation development and evaluation of principles and devices. *J. Person.*, **24**, 401–423.

Cattell, R. B. and Baggaley, A. R. (1958). A confirmation of ergic and engram structures in attitudes objectively measured. *Aust. J. Psychol.*, **10**, 287–318.

Cattell, R. B. and Bartlett, H. W. (1971). An R–dR-technique operational distinction of the states of anxiety, stress, fear, etc. *Aust. J. Psychol.*, **23**, 105–123.

Cattell, R. B., Barton, K., and Dielman, T. E. (1972). Prediction of school achievement from ability, personality, and motivation measures (sixth and seventh grade). *Psychol. Rep.*, **30**, 35–43.

Cattell, R. B., Blewett, D. B., and Beloff, J. R. (1955). The inheritance of personality: a multiple variance analysis determination of approximate nature–nurture ratios for primary personality factors in Q-data. *Am. J. hum. Genet.*, **7**, 122–146.

Cattell, R. B., Breul, H., and Hartman, H. P. (1952). An attempt at more refined definitions of the cultural dimensions of syntality in modern nations. *Am. soc. Rev.*, **17**, 408–421.

Cattell, R. B. and Butcher, H. J. (1968). *The Prediction of Achievement and Creativity*. Bobbs-Merrill: Indianapolis.

Cattell, R. B. and Cross, K. P. (1952). Comparison of the ergic and self-sentiment structures found in dynamic traits by R- and P-techniques. *J. Person.*, **21**, 250–271.

Cattell, R. B., DeYoung, G. E., and Horn, J. L. (1974). Human motives as dynamic states: A dR analysis of objective motivation measures. (In press).

Cattell, R. B. and Dielman, T. E. (1973). The structure of motivational manifestations as measured in the laboratory rat: a test of motivational component theory. Submitted to *Personality: An International Journal.* (In press).

Cattell, R. B. and Dreger, R. N. (Eds) (1975). *Handbook of Modern Personality Theory*. Appleton-Century-Crofts: New York.

Cattell, R. B., Eber, H. W., and Tatsuoka, M. M. (1970). *Handbook for the Sixteen Personality Factor Questionnaire*. Institute for Personality and Ability Testing: Champaign, Illinois.

Cattell, R. B. and Gorsuch, R. (1965). The definition and measurement of national morale and morality. *J. soc. Psychol.*, **67**, 77–96.

Cattell, R. B. and Gruen, W. (1955). The primary personality factors on eleven year old children, by objective tests. *J. Person.*, **23**, 460–478.

Cattell, R. B., Heist, A. B., Heist, P. A., and Stewart, R. G. (1950). The objective measurement of dynamic traits. *Educ. psychol. Measur.*, **10**, 224–248.

Cattell, R. B. and Horn, J. (1963). An integrated study of the factor structure of adult attitude-interests. *Genet. psychol. Monogr.*, **16**, 89–149.

Cattell, R. B., Horn, J., and Butcher, H. J. (1962). The dynamic structure of attitudes in adults: a description of some established factors and of their measurement by the Motivation Analysis Test. *Br. J. Psychol.*, **53**, 57–69.

Cattell, R. B., Horn, J. L., Sweney, A. B., and Radcliffe, J. A. (1964). *Motivation Analysis Test (MAT)*. Institute for Personality and Ability Testing: Champaign, Illinois.

Cattell, R. B., Kawash, G. F., and DeYoung, G. E. (1972). Validation of objective measures of ergic tension: Response of the sex erg to visual stimulation. *J. exp. Res. Person.*, **6**, 76–83.

Cattell, R. B. and Klein, T. (1974). Inheritance of personality factors in the HSPQ. *Behav. Genet.*, **3**, 12–20.

Cattell, R. B. and Luborsky, L. B. (1950). P-technique demonstrated as a new clinical method for determining personality and symptom structure. *J. genet. Psychol.*, **42**, 3–24.

Cattell, R. B., Maxwell, E. F., Light, B. H., and Unger, M. P. (1949). The objective measurement of attitudes. *Br. J. Psychol.*, **40**, 81–90.

Cattell, R. B. and Miller, A. (1952). A confirmation of the ergic and self-sentiment patterns among dynamic traits (attitude variables) by R-technique. *Br. J. Psychol.*, **43**, 280–294.

Cattell, R. B. and Radcliffe, J. A. (1961). Factors in objective motivation measures with children: a preliminary study. *Aust. J. Psychol.*, **13**, 65–76.

Cattell, R. B., Radcliffe, J. A., and Sweney, A. B. (1963). The nature and measurement of components of motivation. *Genet. psychol. Monogr.*, **68**, 49–211.

Cattell, R. B. and Rickels, K. (1968). The relationship of clinical symptoms and IPAT-factored tests of anxiety, regression and asthenia: A factor analytic study. *J. nerv. ment. Dis.*, **146**, 147–160.

Cattell, R. B., Rickels, K., Weise, C., Gray, B., and Yee, R. (1966). The effects of psychotherapy upon measured anxiety and regression. *Am. J. Psychother.*, **20**, 261–269.

Cattell, R. B., Saunders, D. R., and Stice, G. F. (1953). The dimensions of syntality in small groups. *Hum. Relat.*, **6**, 331–356.

Cattell, R. B. and Scheier, I. H. (1961). *The Meaning and Measurement of Neuroticism and Anxiety*. Ronald: New York.

Cattell, R. B., Sealy, A. P., and Sweney, A. B. (1966). What can personality and motivation source trait measurement add to the prediction of school achievement? *Br. J. educ. Psychol.*, **36**, 280–295.

Cattell, R. B. and Stice, G. F. (1954). Four formulae for selecting leaders on the basis of personality. *Hum. Relat.*, **7**, 493–507.

Cattell, R. B. and Stice, G. F. (1960). *The Dimensions of Groups and Their Relations to the Behavior of Members*. Institute for Personality and Ability Testing: Champaign, Illinois.

Cattell, R. B. and Sweney, A. B. (1964). Components measurable in manifestations of mental conflicts. *J. abnorm. soc. Psychol.*, **68**, 479–490.

Cattell, R. B., Sweney, A. B., and Radcliffe, J. A. (1960). The objective measurement of motivation structure in children. *J. clin. Psychol.*, **16**, 227–232.

Cattell, R. B. and Tatro, D. F. (1966). The personality factors, objectively measured, which distinguish psychotics from normals. *Behav. Res. Ther.*, **4**, 39–51.

Cattell, R. B., Tatro, D. F., and Komlos, E. (1965). The diagnosis and inferred structure of paranoid and nonparanoid schizophrenia from the 16PF profile. *Ind. Psychol. Rev.*, **1**, 108–115.

Cattell, R. B., Wagner, A., and Cattell, M. D. (1970). Adolescent personality structure in Q-data, checked in the high school personality questionnaire. *Br. J. Psychol.*, **61**, 39–54.

Cattell, R. B. and Warburton, F. W. (1967). *Objective Personality and Motivation Tests*. University of Illinois Press: Urbana, Illinois.

Cattell, R. B. and Wispe, L. G. (1948). The dimensions of syntality in small groups. *J. soc. Psychol.*, **28**, 57–78.

Child, D. (1970). *The Essentials of Factor Analysis*. Holt, Rinehart and Winston: London.

Cofer, C. N. and Appley, M. H. (1964). *Motivation: Theory and Research*. Wiley: New York.

Comrey, A. L. and Duffy, K. E. (1968). Cattell and Eysenck factor scores related to Comrey personality factors. *Mult. Behavl. Res.*, **3**, 379–392.

Cordiner, C. M. and Hall, D. J. (1971). The use of the Motivational Analysis Test in the selection of Scottish nursing students. *Nursing Res.*, **20**, 356–361.

Cottle, W. C. (1950). A factor study of the multiphasic, Strong, Kuder and Bell inventories using a population of adult males. *Psychometrika*, **15**, 25–47.

Crissy, W. J. and Daniel, W. J. (1939). Vocational interest factors in women. *J. appl. Psychol.*, **23**, 488–494.

Cross, K. P. (1951). Determination of the ergic structure of common attitudes by P-technique. Unpublished *M.A. Thesis*: University of Illinois.

Curran, J. P. (1968). The dimensions of state change, in Q-data and chain P-technique, on twenty women. Unpublished *M.A. Thesis*: University of Illinois.

Curran, J. P. (1970). Analysis of factors effecting interpersonal attraction in the dating situation. Unpublished *Ph.D. Thesis*: University of Illinois.

Curran, J. P. and Cattell, R. B. (1974). *Eight State Questionnaire*. Institute for Personality and Ability Testing: Champaign, Illinois.

Darwin, C. 1859 (1917). *Origin of Species*. Murray: London.

Das, R. S. (1955). An investigation of attitude structure and some hypothesized personality correlates. Unpublished *Ph.D. Thesis*: University of Illinois.

Davies, E. and Binks, N. (1969). Some motivational characteristics of senior managers. *Aust. Psychologist*, **4**, 167–170.

Davis, C. (1966). (personal communication). See Sweney, A., *A Preliminary Descriptive Manual for Individual Assessment of the MAT*. Institute for Personality and Ability Testing: Champaign, Illinois, 1969.

Delgado, J. M. R., Roberts, W. W., and Miller, N. E. (1954). Learning motivated by electrical stimulation of the brain. *Am. J. Physiol.*, **179**, 587–593.

Delgado, J. M. R., Rosvold, H. E., and Looney, E. (1956). Evoking conditioned fear by electrical stimulation of subcortical structures in the monkey brain. *J. comp. physiol. Psychol.*, **49**, 373–380.

Delhees, K. H. (1968). Conflict measurement by the dynamic calculus model, and its applicability in clinical practice. *Mult. Behavl. Res.*, Special Issue, 73–96.

Delhees, K. H., Cattell, R. B., and Sweney, A. B. (1970). The structure of parents' intra-familial attitudes and sentiments measured by objective tests and a vector model. *J. soc. Psychol.*, **82**, 231–252.

Delhees, K. H., Cattell, R. B., and Sweney, A. B. (1971). The objective measurement of children's intra-familial attitude and sentiment structure and the investment subsidiation model. *J. genet. Psychol.*, **188**, 87–113.

Dielman, T. E. (1974). *The Child Rearing Practices Questionnaire*. Institute for Personality and Ability Testing: Champaign, Illinois.

Dielman, T. E., Barton, K., and Cattell, R. B. (1971). The prediction of junior high school achievement from objective motivation tests. *Personality*, **4**, 279–287.

Dielman, T. E., Barton, K., and Cattell, R. B. (1973). The prediction of junior high school grades from the culture fair intelligence test and objective measures of motivation. Institute for Personality and Ability Testing: Champaign, Illinois.

Dielman, T. E. and Cattell, R. B. (1972). The prediction of behavior problems in 6–8 year old children from mothers' report of child rearing practices. *J. clin. Psychol.*, **28,** 13–17.

Dielman, T. E., Cattell, R. B., and Kawash, G. F. (1971). *Three studies of the manipulation of the fear erg.* Advanced Publication No. 14, Laboratory of Personality and Group Analysis, Champaign.

Dollard, J. *et al.* (1939). *Frustration and Aggression.* University of Yale: Yale.

Dreier, T. A. (1969). A factor analytic study of personality, motivation, and risk-taking behavior. Unpublished *M.A. Thesis*: University of Wichita State.

Duffy, E. (1934). Emotion: an example of the need for reorientation in psychology. *Psychol. Rev.*, **41,** 184–188.

Duffy, E. (1962). *Activation and Behavior.* Wiley: New York.

Dunn, J. P. *et al.* (1963). Social class gradient of serum uric acid levels in males. *J. Am. Med. Assoc.*, **185,** 431–436.

Edwards, A. C. (1954). *The Edwards Personal Preference Schedule.* Psychological Corporation: New York.

Emmett, D. (1966). *Rules, Roles and Relations.* Macmillan: London.

Everett, J. W. (1964). The central nervous system and control of reproductive function. In C. W. Lloyd (Ed.), *Human Reproduction and Sexual Behavior.* Len and Febiger: Philadelphia.

Eysenck, H. J. (1953). *Uses and Abuses of Psychology.* Pelican: Harmondsworth.

Eysenck, H. J. (1967). *The Biological Basis of Personality.* Thomas: Illinois.

Eysenck, H. J. and Eysenck, S. B. G. (1964). *Manual of the Eysenck Personality Inventory.* University of London Press: London.

Ferguson, L. W., Humphreys, L. G., and Strong, F. W. (1941). A factorial analysis of interests and values. *J. educ. Psychol.*, **32,** 197–204.

Festinger, L. (1950). Laboratory experiments: the role of group belongingness. In J. G. Miller (Ed.), *Experiments in Social Process.* McGraw-Hill: New York.

Fiks, A. I. (1969). Student motivational patterns and second language learning. Unpublished Thesis: American Institute of Research.

Fleishman, E. A. and Hempel, W. E. (1954). Changes of factor structure of a complex psychomotor task as a function of practice. *Psychometrika*, **19,** 239–252.

Fleishman, E. A. and Hempel, W. E. (1956). Factorial analysis of complex psychomotor performance and related skill. *J. appl. Psychol.*, **40,** 96–104.

Freud, S. (1930). *Civilization and its Discontents.* Trans. from the German by J. Riviere. Hogarth: International Psycho-analytical Library, London.

Freud, S. (1949). Instincts and their vicissitudes (1915). In *A Collection of*

Papers of Sigmund Freud, Vol. I (translated by J. Riviere). Hogarth: London.

Freud, S. (1949). *Outline of Psychoanalysis*. Norton: New York.

Fuster, J. M. (1958). Effects of stimulation of brain stem on tachistoscopic perception. *Science*, **127**, 150.

Gibb, C. A. (1949). The emergence of leadership in small temporary groups of men. Unpublished *Ph.D. Thesis*: University of Illinois.

Gorsuch, R. (1962). National morale, morality and cultural integration. Unpublished *M.A. Thesis*: University of Illinois.

Gorsuch, R. (1965). The clarification of some superego factors. Unpublished *Ph.D. Thesis*: University of Illinois.

Gorsuch, R. (1973). *Factor Analysis*. Saunders: Philadelphia.

Gorsuch, R. L. and Cattell, R. B. (1967). Second stratum personality factors defined in the questionnaire realm by the 16PF. *Mult. Behavl. Res.*, **2**, 211–224.

Gottesman, I. (1963). Heritability of personality: a demonstration. *Psychol. Monogr.*, No. 9 (whole No. 572).

Graffam, D. T. (1967). Dickinson College changes personality. *The Dickinson Alumnus*, **44**, 2–7.

Grossman, S. P. (1973). *Essentials of Physiological Psychology*. Wiley: New York.

Guetzkow, H. (1958). Building models about small groups. In R. Young (Ed.), *Approaches to the Study of Political Science*. Northwestern University Press: Evanston.

Guilford, J. P., Christensen, P. R., Bond, N. A., and Sutton, M. A. (1953). A factor analysis study of human interests. A.R.D.C. Hum. Res. Centre. *Res. Bull.*, May issue, 53–111.

Guilford, J. P., Christensen, P. R., Bond, N. A., and Sutton, M. A. (1954). A factor analysis study of human interests. *Psychol. Monogr.*, **68**, No. 4.

Gundlach, R. H. and Gerum, E. (1931). Vocational interests and types of abilities. *J. educ. Psychol.*, **22**, 505.

Haber, R. N. (1966). *Current Research in Motivation*. Holt, Rinehart and Winston: New York.

Hammond, W. H. (1945). An analysis of youth center interests. *Br. J. educ. Psychol.*, **15**, 122–126.

Handbook for the Sixteen Personality Factor Questionnaire. Cattell, R. B., Eber, H. W., and Tatsuoka, M. M. (1970). Institute for Personality and Ability Testing: Champaign, Illinois.

Hare, A. P. (1963). *Handbook of Small Group Research*. Free Press: Glencoe.

Harlow, H. F. (1959). Love in infant monkeys. *Scient. Am.*, **200**, 68–74.

Harlow, H. F. and Harlow, M. K. (1962). Social deprivation in monkeys. *Scient. Am.*, **207**, 137–146.

Harlow, H. F. and Zimmerman, R. R. (1959). Affectional responses in the infant monkey. *Science*, **130**, 421.

Haverland, E. M. (1954). The application of an analytical solution for proportional profiles rotation to a box problem and to the drive structure in rats. Unpublished *Ph.D. Thesis*: University of Illinois.

Haythorne, W. (1953). The influence of individual members on the characteristics of small groups. *J. abnorm. soc. Psychol.*, **48**, 276–284.

Hemphill, J. D. and Weste, C. M. (1950). The measurement of group dimensions. *J. Psychol.*, **29**, 352–362.

Hendricks, B. C. (1971). The sensitivity of the dynamic calculus to short term change in interest structure. Unpublished *M.A. Thesis*: University of Illinois.

Herrington, L. P. (1942). The relation of physiological and social indices of activity level. In McNemar, Q. and Merrill, M. A. (Eds), *Studies in Personality*. McGraw-Hill: New York.

Herzberg, F., Mausner, B., Peterson, R. O., and Capwell, D. F. (1957). *Job attitudes: Review of Research and Opinion*. Psychological Service of Pittsburgh: Pittsburgh.

Herzberg, F., Mausner, B., and Snyderman, B. (1959). *The Motivation to Work* (2nd ed.). Wiley: New York.

Hess, E. H. (1964). *Imprinting in Animals*. Scientific American Reprint.

Hess, W. R. (1931). Le Sommeil. *C.R. Soc. Biol. Paris*, **107**, 1333.

Hess, W. R. (1936). Hypothalamus und die Zentren des autonomen Nervensystems: Physiologie. *Arch. Psychiat.*, **104**, 548.

Hess, W. R. and Akert, K. (1955). Experimental data on role of hypothalamus in mechanism of emotional behavior. *Archs. Neurol. Psychiat.*, **73**, 127–129.

Hetherington, A. W. and Ranson, S. W. (1940). Hypothalamic lesions and adiposity in the rat. *Anat. Rec.*, **78**, 149–172.

Hetherington, A. W. and Ranson, S. W. (1942). The spontaneous activity and food intake of rats with hypothalamic lesions. *Am. J. Physiol.*, **136**, 609–617.

Hokanson, J. E. (1969). *The Physiological Basis of Motivation*. Wiley: New York.

Holland, I. J. and Beazley, R. I. (1971). Personality, motivation and education needed in professional forestry. *J. Forestry*, **69**, 418–423.

Horn, J. L. (1961). Structures in measures of self-sentiment, ego and superego concepts. Unpublished *M.A. Thesis*: University of Illinois.

Horn, J. L. (1966). Motivation and dynamic calculus concepts from multivariate experiment. In the *Handbook of Multivariate Experimental Psychology*. Rand McNally: Chicago.

Horn, J. L. and Cattell, R. B. (1965). Vehicles, ipsatization, and the multiple method measurement of motivation. *Can. J. Psychol.*, **19**, 265–279.

Horn, J. L. and Sweney, A. B. (1970). The dynamic calculus model for motivation and its use in understanding the individual case. In A. R. Mahrer (Ed.), *New Approaches to Personality Classification*. Columbia University Press: New York.

Howarth, E. and Browne, J. A. (1971). An item-factor-analysis of the 16PF. *Personality*, **2**, 117–139.

Hull, C. L. (1943). *Principles of Behavior*. Appleton-Century-Crofts: New York.

Hundleby, J., Pawlik, K., and Cattell, R. B. (1965). *Personality Factors in Objective Test Devices*. Knapp: San Diego.

Hunt, J. McV. (1944). *Personality and the Behavior Disorders*. Ronald: New York.

Hurley, J. R. (1960). An attempt to reveal the dynamics of a maladjusted mental defective by objective analysis: A P-technique factor analysis. Unpublished *M.A. Thesis*: University of Illinois.

Jackson, D. N. (1965). *Personality Research Form*. Research Psychologists Press Inc.: New York.

Janowitz, H. D. and Grossman, M. I. (1949). Some factors affecting the food intake of normal dogs and dogs with esophagostomy and gastric fistula. *Am. J. Physiol.*, **159**, 143–148.

Jasper, H. (1941). In W. Penfield and T. C. Erickson (Eds), *Epilepsy and Cerebral Localization*. Thomas: Springfield, Illinois.

Katz, D. (1949). Morale and motivation in industry. In W. Dennis (Ed.), *Current Trends in Industrial Psychology*. University of Pittsburgh Press: Pittsburgh.

Katz, J. L., Weiner, H., Gurman, A., and Ts'ai-Fan Yu. (1973). Hyperuricemia, gout and the executive suite, *J. Am. Med. Assoc.*, **224**, 1251–1257.

Kawash, G. F., Dielman, T. E., and Cattell, R. B. (1972). Changes in objective measures of fear motivation as a function of laboratory-controlled manipulation. *Psychol. Rep.*, **30**, 59–63.

Kelly, E. L. (1944). *Activity-Preference Test for the Classification of Service Personnel*. Washington D.C.: Office of the Publication Board, U.S. Dept. of Commerce.

Kelly, E. L. and Fiske, D. W. (1951). *The Prediction of Performance in Clinical Psychology*. University of Michigan: Ann Arbor.

Keys, A. (1952). Experimental induction of psychoneuroses by starvation. In *The Biology of Mental Health and Disease*, 27th Animal Conference: Milbank Memorial Fund. Harper and Row: New York.

Kline, P. and Grindley, J. (1974). A 28 day case-study with the MAT. *J. Mult. exp. Person. clin. Psychol.*, **1**, 13–22.

Kohlberg, L. (1964). Development of moral character and moral ideology. In M. L. Hoffman and L. W. Hoffman (Ed), *Review of Child Development Research*, Vol. 1. Russell Sage Foundation: New York.

Kong, S. (1971). *The 16PF in Latin America*. Institute for Personality and Ability Testing: Champaign, Illinois.

Korth, B. (1970). Attitude change in relation to reward and initial dynamic structure. Unpublished *M.A. Thesis*: University of Illinois.

Kretschmer, E. (1931). *The Psychology of Men of Genius*. Kegan Paul: London.

Krug, S. (1971). An examination of experimentally induced changes in ergic tension levels. Unpublished *Ph. D. Thesis*: University of Illinois.

Lange, C. and James, W. (1922). *The Emotions*. Williams and Wilkins: Baltimore.

Laughlin, J. (1974). Prediction of action decisions by the dynamic calculus. Unpublished *M.A. Thesis*: University of Illinois.

Lavin, D. E. (1967). *The Prediction of Academic Performance*. Wiley: New York.

Lawlis, G. F. (1968). Motivational aspects of the chronically unemployed. Unpublished *Ph.D. Thesis*: Texas Technological College.

Lawlis, G. F. (1971). Motivational factors reflecting employment stability. *J. soc. Psychol.*, **84**, 215–225.

Levin, E. D. (1949). Some comparisons of the group performances of men and women in groups of ten. Unpublished *M.A. Thesis*: University of Illinois.

Levonian, E. (1968). Self-esteem and opinion change. *J. person. soc. Psychol.*, **9**, 257–259.

Lindsley, D. B. (1951). Emotion. In S. S. Stevens (Ed.), *Handbook of Experimental Psychology*, Wiley: New York.

Lindsley, D. B. (1957). Psychophysiology and motivation. In M. R. Jones (Ed.), *Nebraska Symposium on Motivation*. University of Nebraska: Lincoln.

Loehlin, J. C. (1965). Some methodological problems in Cattell's Multiple Abstract Variance Analysis. *Psychol. Rev.*, **72**, 156–161.

Loevinger, J. (1969). Theories of ego development. In L. Breger (Ed.), *Clinical-Cognitive Psychology: Models and Integrations*. Prentice-Hall: New York.

Lorenz, K. (1952). *King Solomon's Ring*. Pan: London.

Lorenz, K. (1967). *On Aggression*. Methuen: London.

Lunzer, E. A. (1968). *The Regulation of Behavior*, Vol. I. Staples: London.

Lurie, W. A. (1937). A study of Spranger's value types by the method of factor analysis. *J. soc. Psychol.*, **8**, 17–37.

Lynn, R. (1971). *Personality and National Character*. Pergamon: Oxford.

McClelland, D. C. (1955). *Studies in Motivation*. Appleton-Century-Crofts: New York.

McClelland, D. C., Atkinson, J. W., Clark, R. A., and Lowell, E. L. (1953). *The Achievement Motive*. Appleton-Century-Crofts: New York.

McDougall, W. (1908). *An Introduction to Social Psychology*. Methuen: London.

McDougall, W. (1900). *An Introduction to Social Psychology*. Scribner: New York.

Maier, N. R. F. (1949). *Frustration*. McGraw-Hill: New York.

Mann, R. D. (1959). A review of the relationships between personality and performance in small groups. *Psychol. Rev.*, **56**, 241–270.

Maslow, A. H. (1943). A theory of human motivation. *Psychol. Rev.*, **50**, 370–396.

Maslow, A. H. (1970). *Motivation and Personality*. Harper and Row: New York.

Masserman, J. H. (1950). Experimental neuroses. *Scient. Am.*, **182**, 38–43.

May, J. M. and Sweney, A. B. (1965). Personality and motivational changes observed in the treatment of psychotic patients. Paper presented at *Southwestern Psychological Association*: Oklahoma City.

May, R. (1950). *The Meaning of Anxiety*. Ronald: New York.

Mayer, J. (1953). Glucostatic mechanisms of regulation of food intake. *New England J. Med.*, **249**, 13–16.

Mayo, E. (1945). *The Social Problems of an Industrial Civilization*. Harvard University Press: Boston.

Merton, R. K. (1957). *Social Theory and Social Structure*. Free Press: Glencoe, Illinois.

Miller, K. M. (1968). *Manual for the Rothwell–Miller Interest Blank*. N.F.E.R.: Slough, England.

Milner, P. M. (1970). *Physiological Psychology*. Holt, Rinehart and Winston: New York.

Motivation Analysis Test (MAT). Cattell, R. B., Horn, J. L., Sweney, A. B., and Radcliffe, J. A. (1964). Institute for Personality and Ability Testing: Champaign, Illinois.

Murphy, G. (1949). *Historical Introduction to Modern Psychology (5th ed.)*. Routledge: London.

Murray, E. J. (1964). *Motivation and Emotion*. Prentice-Hall: New Jersey.

Murray, H. A. *et al.* (1938). *Explorations in Personality*. Oxford University Press: Oxford and New York.

Nauss, A. H. (1968). The ministerial personality: on avoiding a stereotype trap. *J. counsel. Psychol.*, **15**, 581–582.

Nesselroade, J. R. (1966). The separation of state and trait factors by dR-technique with special reference to anxiety, effort stress and cortertia. Unpublished *Ph.D. Thesis*: University of Illinois.

Nichols, K. E. (1974). Changes in structures and level of sentiments through character education. Unpublished *Ph.D. Thesis*: University of Illinois.

Noty, C. (1973). Personality, motivational and attitudinal correlates of persistence in religious vocations. Unpublished *Ph.D. Thesis*: Loyola University, Chicago.

Olds, J. and Milner, P. (1954). Positive reinforcement produced by electrical stimulation of septal area and other regions of rat brain. *J. comp. physiol. Psychol.*, **47**, 419–427.

Peters, R. S. (1958). *The Concept of Motivation*. Routledge and Kegan Paul: London.

Prescott, R. G. W. (1966). Estrous cycle in the rat: effects on self-stimulation behavior. *Science*, **152**, 796–797.

Prosser, C. L. (1959). Comparative neurophysiology. In A.D. Bass (Ed.), *Evolution of Nervous Control*. Publication No. 52. Am. Assoc. Adv. Sci.: Washington, D.C.

Purkey, W. W. (1970). *Self Concept and School Achievement*. Prentice-Hall: New York.

Putnam, M. L. (1930). Improving employee relations. *Personnel J.*, **8**, 314–325.

Ranson, S. W. (1939). Somnolence caused by hypothalamic lesion in the monkey. *Archs. Neurol. Psychol.*, **41**, 1–23.

Rickels, K., Cattell, R. B., Weise, C., Gray, B., Yee, R., Mallin, A., and Aaronson, H. G. (1966). Controlled psychopharmacological research in private psychiatric practice. *Psychopharmacologia*, **9**, 288–306.

Roby, T. B. (1957). On the measurement and description of groups. *Behavl Sci.*, **2**, 119–127.

Rosenberg, M. (1957). *Occupations and Values*. Free Press: Glencoe, Illinois.

Rummel, R. J. (1972). *The Dimensions of Nations*. Sage Publications: New York.

Sarason, S. B. *et al.* (1960). *Anxiety in Elementary School Children: A Report of Research*. Wiley: New York.

Sawyer, J. and LeVine, R. A. (1967). Cultural dimensions: a factor analysis of the world ethnographic sample. *Am. Anthrop.*, **68**, 708–731.

Scheier, I. H. (1965). *Eight Parallel Form Anxiety Battery*. Institute for Personality and Ability Testing: Champaign, Illinois.

School Motivation Analysis Test (SMAT). Sweney, A. B., Cattell, R. B., and Krug, S. E. (1970). Institute for Personality and Ability Testing: Champaign, Illinois.

Sheffield, F. D., Wulff, J. J., and Backer, R. (1951). Reward value of copulation without sex drive reduction. *J. comp. physiol. Psychol.*, **44**, 3–8.

Shotwell, A. M., Hurley, J. R., and Cattell, R. B. (1961). Motivational structure of a hospitalized mental defective. *J. abnorm. soc. Psychol.*, **62**, 422–426.

Singer, J. D. (Ed.) (1965). *Human Behavior and International Politics*. Rand McNally: Chicago.

Skelton, J. J. (1968). *The Vocational Application of an Objective Test of Motivation*. Report 4/68, Psychological Research Unit. Australian Military Forces.

Sorokin, P. A. (1937). *Social and Cultural Dynamics*, Vol. 3. American Book Co.: New York.

Spence, M. T. and Sweney, A. B. (1966). A factorial resolution of psychometric measures of anxiety. *Psychol. Rep.*, **19**, 2.

Spielberger, C. D. (Ed.) (1972). *Anxiety: Current Trends in Theory and Research*. Academic Press: New York.

Stice, G. F. (1951). The relation of attitude and interest changes to personality and syntality in small groups. Unpublished *Ph.D. Thesis*: University of Illinois.

Stogdill, R. M. (1952). Leadership and morale in organized groups. In J. E. Hulett and R. Stagner (Eds), *Problems in Social Psychology*. University of Illinois Press: Urbana.

Stone, C. P. and Ferguson, L. (1938). Preferential responses of male albino rats to food and to receptive females. *J. comp. Psychol.*, **26**, 237–253.

Strong, E. K. (1949). *Vocational Interests of Men and Women*. Stanford University Press: Stanford.

Sumner, R. and Warburton, F. W. (1972). *Achievement in Secondary School*, N.F.E.R.: Slough, England.

Sweney, A. B. (1967). *The Prediction of Adjustment from Dynamic Source Trait Measurement*. Contribution to the Symposium: New Evidence on Source Trait Measurement in Clinical Prediction. Midwestern Psychological Association Annual Meeting: Chicago.

Sweney, A. B. (1969). *A Preliminary Descriptive Manual for Individual Assessment of the Motivation Analysis Test*, Institute for Personality and Ability Testing: Champaign, Illinois.

Sweney, A. B. and Cattell, R. B. (1961). Dynamic factors in twelve year old children as revealed in measures of integrated motivation. *J. clin. Psychol.*, **17**, 360–369.

Sweney, A. B. and Cattell, R. B. (1962). Relationships between integrated and unintegrated motivation structure examined by objective tests. *J. soc. Psychol.*, **57**, 217–226.

Sweney, A. B., Cattell, R. B., and Krug, S. E. (1970). *School Motivation Analysis Test (SMAT)*. Institute for Personality and Ability Testing: Champaign, Illinois.

Sweney, A. B. and Rich, C. (1966). A response style interpretation for inventory anxiety measures. Paper presented to *Southwestern Psychological Association* Annual Meeting, Arlington, Texas.

Tapp, J. (1958). An examination of hypotheses governing the motivational components of attitude strength. Unpublished *M.A. Thesis*: University of Illinois.

Tatsuoka, M. M. and Cattell, R. B. (1970). Linear equations for estimating a person's occupational adjustment, based on information on occupational profiles. *Br. J. educ. Psychol.*, **40**, 324–334.

Thorndike, E. L. (1935). The interests of adults: 2. The inter-relations of adult interest. *J. educ. Psychol.*, **26**, 497–507.

Thurstone, L. L. (1935). A multiple factor study of vocational interests. *J. Person.*, **10**, 198–205.

Tinbergen, N. (1951). *A Study of Instinct*. Oxford University Press: Oxford.

Torr, D. V. (1953). A factor analysis of 49 variables. *Res. Bull.*, 53–67. Human Research Center A.R.D.C. Lackland A.F.B. Texas.

Tsujioka, B. and Cattell, R. B. (1965). Constancy and difference in personality structure from applying the 161 F in America and Japan. *Br. J. Soc. clin. Psychol.*, **4**, 287–297.

Tsushima, T. (1960). Notes on trends and problems of psychotherapy in Japan. *Psychologia*, **1**, 231–236.

Tucker, L. R. (1958). Determination of parameters of a functional relation by factor analysis. *Psychometrika*, **23**, 19–23.

Tucker, L. R. (1966). Learning theory and multivariate experiment: Illustration by determination of generalized learning curves. In Cattell, R. B. (Ed.), *Handbook of Multivariate Experimental Psychology*. Rand McNally: Chicago.

Vaughan, D. S. (1973). A test of Cattell's structured learning theory. Unpublished *M.A. Thesis*: University of Illinois.

Vernon, M. D. (1969). *Human Motivation*. Cambridge University Press: London.

Vernon, P. E. (1949). Classifying high grade occupational interests. *J. abnorm. soc. Psychol.*, **44**, 85–96.

Vernon, P. E. (1950). *The Structure of Human Abilities*. Methuen: London.

Vroom, V. H. (1964). *Work and Motivation*. Wiley: New York.

Walker, C. R. and Guest, R. H. (1952). *The Man on the Assembly Line*. Harvard University Press: Cambridge, Mass.

Warden, C. J. (1931). *Animal Motivation: Experimental Studies on the Albino Rat*. Columbia University Press: New York.

Wessman, A. E. and Ricks, D. F. (1966). *Mood and Personality*. Holt, Rinehart and Winston: New York.

Whisler, L. D. (1934). A multiple factor analysis of general attitudes. *J. soc. Psychol.*, **5**, 283–297.

Williams, H. V. (1954). A determination of psychosomatic functional unities in personality by means of P-technique. *J. soc. Psychol.*, **39**, 25–45.

Williams, J. R. (1958). The definition and measurement of conflict in terms of P-technique: a test of validity. Unpublished *Ph.D. Thesis*: University of Illinois.

Williams, J. R. (1959). A test of the validity of the P-technique in the measurement of internal conflict. *J. Person.*, **27**, 418–437.

Wilson, R. C., High, W. S., Beem, H. P., and Comrey, A. L. (1954). A factor-analytic study of supervisory and group behavior. *J. appl. Psychol.*, **38**, 89–92.

Wispe, L. G. (1947). The syntality of small groups. Unpublished *M.A. Thesis*: University of Illinois.

Wylie, R. C. (1961). *The Self-Concept: A Critical Survey of the Pertinent Research Literature*. University of Nebraska Press: Nebraska.

Yerkes, R. M. and Dodson, J. D. (1908). The relation of strength of stimulus to rapidity of habit-formation. *J. comp. neurol. Psychol.*, **18**, 459–482.

Young, P. T. (1961). *Motivation and Emotion*. Wiley: New York.

Young, P. T. and Greene, J. T. (1953). Quantity of food ingested as a measure of relative acceptability. *J. comp. physiol. Psychol.*, **46**, 288–294.

Subject Index

Achievement motivation (N'ach of McClelland), 105, 185, 191, 193, *see also* School achievement

Achiever (high and low), 191–193

Action potential (*Z*), 73

Activation theory, 147–151

Adaptation, *see* Dynamic learning

Adjustment, confluent, 91

Adjustment Process Analysis (APA), 59–64, 132, 168, 171, 193, 195; chart 60

Adrenergic response (Cannon), 151

Aggression, 36, 139

Ambient stimulus (*k*), 68–70, 195

Anxiety, 109, 116–117, 150, 170, 171–175; amongst nations, 254, components in level of, 173–174

Appetitive state strength, 73, 132–133, 142

Arousal States, 143–147; and personality, 145–147, 173

Assertiveness, *see* self-assertiveness erg

Attitude, 3; defined, 4, 21; elements, 5; intrafamilial, 249–250; measurement, 5–7; paradigm, 6, 25; strength, 5; vector summation, 48–49, 100–102, 248

Autism (alpha and U component test) 19, 20

Autonomic-endocrine activity, 152–154, 155, 173

Behavioral equation, 53, 104, 166; for achievement, 185; for group performance, 235

Behavioral index, 65–67, 91; negative on sentiments, 94; standard, 72

Bivariate experimentation, 2–3, 114

Cafeteria experiments, 119

Career sentiment, 33, 35, 39, 205–206

Cathexis, 103

Chiasms (dynamic crossroads), 59–61

Child Rearing Practices Questionnaire (CRPQ), 247

Children's Motivation Analysis test (CMAT), 18–19

Clinical psychology, 158

Coefficient of stability for dynamic factors, 51

Complexes, 45–50

Conflict, 50; action, 89–90; in animals, 120–121, 130–132, 155; confluence (stabilized, indurated), 89, 91–94, 180; at foci, 167–168; at loci, 167–168, 169–170; of two ergs, 88–89, 95–96; U-I as a measure of, 161, 228–229

Conflict index (*C*), 93

Confluent learning, 107

Conscious Id, *see* Motivational Components—alpha

Constructiveness (mechanical, material interest) erg, 36, 42

Consummatory behavior, 75, 133–134

Contact comfort, 125, 126

Critical period, 130

Cultural pressure factor, 251

Curiosity erg, *see* exploration erg

Deflection strain, 43, 96–97, 118
Devices: strength of attitude, 6, 7–10; validity of, 10
Dispositions, 50–51
Drive level or strength, 118–120; genetic elements, 44, 125; reduction theory (Hull), 133; Yerkes-Dodson law, 115–117
dR-technique, 30, 172
Dynamic calculus, 100–104
Dynamic Lattice, 22–23, 24, 25–26, 92, 100
Dynamic Laws: Modulation law (the first), 69, 72; Deflection strain law (the tenth), 118
Dynamic learning (adaptation), 59
Dynamic state equation, 69, 198
Dynamic structure, 22–26, 37–44; in animals, 121–127; and personality, 50–56; stability coefficients, 51
Dynamic structure profiles: chronically unemployed, 212–213; college students, 222; criminals, 160–161; disabled workers, 222; doctors, 213–219; engineers, 222; executives, 207–210; man and wife, 247; ministers 162–163; promoted v not promoted 226–227; schizophrenics, 165; servicemen, 210–211; teachers, 222
Dynamics of groups, 204–205, 232–233

Ego defense mechanisms, *see* Motivational Components—beta
Ego strength, 62, 106–107; and development, 108; experimental evidence, 107–110, 178–182; genetic component, 107; L- and Q-data, 106
Electroencephalograph (EEG), 143, 144
Engrams: nature of, 45–50, 85, 86, 95, 200–201
Ergic drive structures and goals, 24, 26, 27–31; in animals 114–116
Ergic investment in a sentiment, 48–50, 84–85, 86, 95, 98, 102–104, 176
Ergic tension, 37–44, 159; change in learning, 200; equation, 73–76, 78–79, 142, 149–150; modification, 72–76, 76–82, 83; tests of, 72, 76–77
Ergs, 26, 27–31, 37–44; appetitive and nonappetitive, 119, 132; defined, 117–118; hypothesized human, 40; modulation, 72–78

Ethology, 127–130; aggressive behavior, 131–132; appeasement, 130; displacement, 131; imprinting, 130; innate release mechanisms (IRMs), 127–128, 129; releasers, 128; sign stimuli, 127; territorial rituals, 128–129; threat displays, 130
Exploration (curiosity) erg, 29–30, 192–193

Factor analysis, 256–258; real base, 93
Factor C, *see* Ego strength
Factor G, *see* superego strength
Factor Q_3, *see* self-sentiment
Factor Q_4, *see* Ergic tension
Family as a group, 245–250
Family Attitude Measurement (FAM), 250
Fear Erg, 38, 76–77; and anxiety, 172
Focal stimulus (h), 68–70
Frustration-aggression theory (Dollard), 40; in animals, 132

General inhibition, 108
General states (contrast ergic tension states), 172
Glucostatic theory (Mayer), 138
Gregarious erg, 29–30, 192–193
Group morale and neuroticism, 245

Habits, 6
Homeostasis, 61, 118
Home-parental sentiment, 29–30, 39
Hull's theory of learning, 149
Hypothalamus, 136–140

Information (beta and I component test), 19–20
Instincts (McDougall), 1, 42–43, 113, 117–119
Integrated component, 15–18, 50, 79, 85, 94–95, 161, 162, 167, 191, 207–208; in animal research, 125
Integration: capacity for, 91; degree of, 91; index I, 94, 109
Integrative upbringing, 108, 177
Interest strength, *see* Devices

Job satisfaction, 219–224

Leadership, 237–239, 240
Learning change, 64–68
Learning Law matrix (multi-dimensional learning matrix calculation), 61–64, 199–202
Learning theory, *see* Structured learning theory
Liability: values, 72; term (*L*), 73
Loser's syndrome, 213, 225, 228–229

Marital compatibility, 245–247, 248
Mating (Sex) erg, 28, 38, 41, 76–77, 192–193
Matrix algebra, 62, 259–261
Modulation index (*s*), 68–70
Modulation theory, 68–72
Morale I (Leadership synergy), 238–240, 244
Morale II (immediate synergy or congeniality), 220, 238–240, 244
Morale III (Reward morale), 238–240
Morale IV (effective role morale), 238–240
Motivation: animal, 1, 113–135; and the brain, 137; definition of, 1–3; and emotion, 137, 151–155
Motivation Analysis Test (MAT), 18–20, 50, 51, 54, 56, 76–79, 159, 160, 166, 186, 198, 207, 208–212, 245, 275
Motivation profiles for various groups— *see* Dynamic structure profiles
Motivational Components (Primary), 10–15; alpha, 11–12, 13; beta, 12, 13–14; gamma, 12, 14; delta, 13, 14; epsilon, 13, 14–15; others, 13; in animals, 121–127; second-order in animals, 126; second-order factors, *see* Integrated and Unintegrated components
Multiple Abstract Variance Analysis (MAVA), 74
Multivariate experimentation, 2, 114

Narcism (or narcissism) erg, 38, 41, 176, 192–193
Need strength, 73, 74, 75; gratification (*G*), 75, 150; neural need (*N*), 75, 150;

physiological condition (*P*), 74; trait strength, 74
Needs (Murray), 1, 2
Nonviscerogenic appetite, 75–76, 122, 132

Occupational adjustment, 206–207, 219–224; of chronically unemployed, 224
Occupational efficiency, 206–207, 221
Occupational groups (*see* also career sentiment) 206–213, 221

Paired words (gamma and I component test), 20
Parental protectiveness, *see* Home-parental sentiment
Personality factors, 52, 54, 61, 108–110, 147, 158, 159, 172, 186–188, 189–191, 207, 215, 221, 225, 241–243, 246, 252–253, 271
Personality learning, 59
Personality and motivation, *see* Superego or Self-sentiment
Professional habits and MAT, 217–219
Propensities, 1, 113, 117
P-technique, 27, 70, 247
P-technique applied to: dynamic structure, 30–31; dynamic structure validation, 80–82; ergic investment in sentiment, 83–84; index of integration, 109; indurated conflict, 93–94; quantitative psychoanalysis, 164–167
Pugnacity erg, 37, 38, 40–41, 192–193

Quantitative psychoanalysis, 164–167

Reflexology, 3
Religious sentiment, 32, 35
Reticular formation, 145–146
R-technique, 30

Satisfaction, (*see* also Ergic tension and Need Strength—gratification): aversive behavior, 141; drive tension and reduction, 140; hedonic continuum, 141; pleasure-pain centers, 141
School achievement, 184–189, 189–194, 201

School Motivation Analysis Test (SMAT), 18, 20, 149, 160, 186–188, 190–191, 192, 207

Security seeking erg (fear, escape), 28

Self-assertiveness erg, 29–30, 36, 38, 41–42, 176, 191, 192–193

Self-sentiment, 35, 36, 38, 97–100, 209, 229, 233, 242; and achievement, 191, 192–193; and conflict, 90–91; and development, 108; and integrative behavior, 104–106, 175–178; L- and Q-data, 99–100; relationship to personality, 54–56, 175–178; and self-concept, 97–98

Sentiments, 24, 32–37, 47–49; in animals, 96; defined, 32; excitation equation, 86; hypothesized human, 46; modulation of 82–86; relationship to personality, 54; reward associated with, 86; stabilizing action, 95–97

Sex erg, *see* mating erg

Specification equation, 53, 65, 69, 88–89, 164, 166, 181, 195, 235

Sport and games sentiment, 34

State measures, 79–80, 164

Stimulus: level $(S_k + Z)$ 73, 76, 86; response theory, 3; term (S), 73

Structured learning theory, 64, 67; tri-vector model, 71, 194–196

Subsidiation, 22; chain, 23–24; and the dynamic lattice, 23; negative, 92; tract, 43–44

Superego, 35, 36–37, 97–100, 209, 229, 242; and achievement, 191, 192–193; conflict, 90–91; and development, 108; genetic component of, 98; and integrative behavior, 104–106, 175–178; L- and Q-data, 99–100; relationship to personality, 54–56

Sweetheart/spouse sentiment, 35, 39

Synergy, 234–235; efficiency, 236–237; maintenance, 236–237; structure, 236–239

Syntality, 233, 234–235, 237–239, 250–251

Taxonomic stage of science, 4

Territorial imperative, 41

Trait strength $(C + H + I)$, 73–74; Constitutional (C), 74; Investment (I), 74; Personal history (H), 74

Tri-vector theory, *see* Structured Learning theory

Unintegrated component, 15–18, 50, 79, 85, 94–95, 151, 161, 162, 167, 191, 207–208, 223; in animal research, 125

Utilities (epsilon and U component test), 19

Vectors: bearing or potency (**B**), 66–68, 71, 72, 195, 196–197; research on bearing change 67–68, 196–199; situation or modulator (**S**), 68–71, 72, 195, 197–198; summation, 48–49, 100–102, 248; trait (**T**), 64–65, 71, 195

Viscerogenic appetite, 75–76, 122, 132

Author Index

Aaronson, H. G., 276
Adelson, M., 76, 262
Akert, K., 143, 272
Alker, H. R., 204, 251, 262
Anand, B. K., 138, 262
Anderson, E. E., 96, 121, 262
Andersson, B., 138, 262
Anumonye, A., 185, 262
Appley, M. H., preface, 118, 119, 132, 268
Ardrey, R., 41
Atkinson, J. W., 37, 105, 262, 274

Backer, R., 276
Baggaley, A. R., 10, 40–41, 266
Baldwin, A. L., 247, 262
Bartlett, H. W., 172, 224, 266
Barton, K., 67, 146, 173, 185, 187–188, 189, 190–192, 194, 196, 198, 199, 225–227, 246, 247, 248, 250, 262–263, 266, 269
Bartsch, T. W., 51, 67, 173, 199, 227, 263
Bass, A. D., 275
Beazley, R. I., 272
Beem, H. P., 239, 278
Bellows, R. T., 133, 263
Beloff, J. R., 98, 266
Bendix, R., 240, 263
Benzinger, T. H., 138, 263
Berlyne, D. E., 1, 263
Bexton, W. H., 150, 263
Binks, N., 269
Birch, D., 262

Bishop, M. P., 141, 263
Blewitt, D. B., 98, 266
Bolz, C., 247, 263
Bond, N. A., 46, 271
Borgatta, E F., 204, 232, 237, 263
Boulding, K. E., 204, 263
Bowlby, J., 130, 263
Brady, J. V., 131, 142, 263
Breese, F. H., 247, 262
Breger, L., 274
Bretnall, E. P., 46, 264
Breul, H., 251, 266
Bridges, K. M. B., 152, 154, 263
Broadhurst, P. L., 115–116, 263
Brobeck, J. R., 138, 262, 263
Brogden, H. E., 264
Bronfenbrenner, U., 204, 264
Brookover, W. B., 98, 264
Brooks, G. W., 185, 264
Browne, J. A., 179, 273
Bullock, T. H., 150, 264
Burdsal, C., 164, 250, 264
Burt, C., 1, 44, 45, 101, 108, 117, 264
Butcher, H. J., 38–39, 173, 185, 186–187, 190. 194, 267

Caffelt, D., 160, 161–162, 264
Calder, N., 138, 264
Cannon, W. B., 61, 118, 148, 151, 152, 154, 264
Capwell, D. F., 220, 272
Carter, G. C., 242, 264
Carter, H. D., 46, 264
Cartwright, C. F., 61, 132, 147, 254, 264

Cartwright, D. S., 61, 132, 147, 238, 254, 264
Cattell, M. D., 268
Cattell, R. B., 6, 10, 16, 18, 24, 27, 30, 31, 34, 38–39, 40, 42, 46, 52, 54, 61, 65, 69, 72, 73, 76, 78, 83, 93, 96, 98, 106, 107, 108, 109, 113, 114, 116, 117, 120, 121, 122, 123–126, 131, 132, 140, 143, 145, 146, 147, 150, 151, 157, 166, 168, 172, 173, 175, 176, 177, 178, 179, 180, 181, 185, 186–188, 189, 190–192, 194, 196, 198, 201–202, 204, 206, 209, 210, 221, 224, 225–227, 232, 233, 237, 238, 240, 243, 245, 246, 247, 248, 250, 251, 253, 254, 256, 262, 263, 264–268, 269, 270, 271, 272, 273, 275, 276, 277, 278
Child, D., 256, 268
Christensen, P. R., 46, 271
Clark, R. A., 274
Cofer, C. N., preface, 118, 119, 132, 268
Comrey, A. L., 179, 239, 268, 278
Cordiner, C. M., 269
Cottle, W. C., 46, 269
Cottrell, L. S. (Jr.), 204, 232, 237, 263
Crissy, W. J., 46, 269
Cross, K. P., 30, 31, 83, 166, 247, 267, 269
Curran, J. P., 72, 146, 173, 269

Daniel, W. J., 46, 269
Darwin, C., 27, 113, 117, 269
Das, R. S., 109, 180, 269
Davies, E., 269
Davis, C., 160, 162, 163, 269
Delgado, J. M. R., 139, 141, 269
Delhees, K. H., 34, 50, 160, 228, 269
Dennis, W., 273
Devereux, E. C., 204, 264
DeYoung, G. E., 18, 30, 69, 78, 149, 198, 267
Dielman, T. E., 67, 76, 77, 96, 114, 120, 122, 123–126, 185, 187–188, 189, 190–192, 194, 198, 247, 263, 266, 267, 269–270, 273
Dodson, J. D., 115–117, 278
Dollard, J., 40, 132, 270
Dreger, R. N., 157, 267
Dreier, T. A., 270
Duffy, E., 143, 148, 270
Duffy, K. E., 179, 268
Dunn, J. P., 185, 270

Eber, H. W., 107, 108, 206, 221, 253, 254, 267
Edwards, A. C., 1, 270
Elder, S. T., 141, 263
Emmett, D., 204, 270
Erickson, T. C., 273
Everett, J. W., 139, 270
Eysenck, H. J., 15, 145, 146, 148, 150, 151, 172, 221, 245, 270
Eysenck, S. B. G., 221, 270

Ferguson, L. W., 46, 96, 270, 277
Festinger, L., 109, 239, 270
Fiks, A. I., 185, 270
Fiske, D. W., 245, 273
Fleishman, E. A., 65, 270
Freud, S., 1, 2, 30, 37, 41, 42, 43, 54, 113, 171, 172, 174, 176, 270–271
Fuster, J. M., 148, 271

Geldard, F. A., 266
Gerum, E., 46, 271
Gibb., C. A., 240, 271
Gorsuch, R., 37, 54, 108, 176–177, 180, 251, 267, 271
Gottesman, I., 107, 271
Gottlieb, D., 98, 264
Graffam, D. T., 196, 271
Gray, B., 180, 268, 276
Greene, J. T., 114, 119–120, 278
Gregg, C. M., 266
Grindley, J., 51, 80–82, 83, 198, 273
Grossman, M. I., 133, 273
Grossman, S. P., 137, 271
Gruen, W., 109, 267
Guest, R. H., 220, 278
Guetzkow, H., 232, 237, 271
Guilford, J. P., 46, 271
Gundlach, R. H., 46, 271
Gurman, A., 185, 273

Haber, R. N., preface, 271
Hall, D. J., 269
Hammer, A. G., 259
Hammond, W. H., 46, 271
Hare, A. P., 242, 271
Harlow, H. F., 74, 119, 125, 130, 271
Harlow, M. K., 119, 271
Hartman, H. P., 251, 266

Haverland, E. M., 120, 121, 272
Haythorne, W., 242, 272
Heath, R. G., 141, 263
Heist, A. B., 267
Heist, P. A., 267
Hempel, W. E., 65, 270
Hemphill, J. D., 232, 272
Hendricks, B. C., 67–68, 197, 198, 272
Heron, W., 150, 263
Herrington, L. P., 151, 272
Herzberg, F., 220, 272
Hess, E. H., 74, 130, 272
Hess, W. R., 136, 137, 139, 143, 272
Hetherington, A. W., 137, 272
High, W. S., 239, 278
Hoffman, L. W., 273
Hoffman, M. L., 273
Hokanson, J. E., preface, 272
Holland, I. J., 272
Horn, J. L., 7, 10, 30, 37, 38–39, 41, 50, 120, 140, 160, 176–177, 178, 180, 228, 267, 272, 275
Howarth, E., 179, 273
Hulett, J. E., 265, 277
Hull, C. L., 1, 85, 101, 133, 149, 273
Humphreys, L. G., 46, 270
Hundleby, J., 106, 109, 147, 172, 273
Hunt, J. McV., 61, 196, 273
Hurley, J. R., 83, 273, 276

Jackson, D. N., 1, 273
James, W., 97, 151, 152, 274
Janowitz, H. D., 133, 27?
Jasper, H., 144, 273
Jones, M. R., 265, 274

Kallborn, J., 247, 262
Katz, D., 239, 245, 273
Katz, J. L., 185, 273
Kawash, G. F., 76, 78, 123–126, 149, 198, 247, 248, 263, 267, 270, 273
Kelly, E. L., 245, 273
Keys, A., 60, 273
Klein, T. W., 98, 107, 267
Kline, P., 51, 80–82, 83, 198, 247, 273
Kohlberg, L., 177, 273
Komlos, E., 110, 268
Kong, S., 252–253, 273
Korth, B., 273
Kretschmer, E., 222, 273

Krug, S., 67, 149, 160, 175, 274, 276, 277

Lange, C., 152, 274
Laughlin, J., 197, 219, 274
Lavin, D. E., 185, 274
Lawlis, G. F., 160, 212–213, 223, 224, 274
Levin, E. D., 274
LeVine, R. A., 251, 276
Levonian, E., 274
Light, B. H., 267
Lindsley, D. B., 145, 148, 274
Lindzey, G., 265
Lloyd, C. W., 270
Lochlin, J. C., 107, 274
Loevinger, J., 177, 274
Looney, E., 269
Lorenz, K., 1, 27, 41, 42, 127–129, 130, 274
Lowell, E. L., 274
Luborsky, L. B., 173, 267
Lunzer, E. A., 129–130, 274
Lurie, W. A., 46, 274
Lynn, R., 254, 274

McClelland, D. C., 37, 105, 185, 191, 251, 274
McDougall, W., 1, 2, 23, 27, 32, 37, 42, 44, 46, 97, 101, 113, 117, 132, 140, 176, 274
McNemar, Q., 272
Mahrer, A. R., 272
Maier, N. R. F., 131, 274
Mallin, A., 276
Mann, R. D., 242, 274
Maslow, A. H., 1, 2, 274
Masserman, J. H., 131, 275
Mausner, B., 220, 272
Maxwell, E. F., 267
May, J. M., 160, 164, 275
May, R., 196, 275
Mayer, J., 138, 275
Mayo, E., 220, 275
Merrill, M. A., 272
Merton, R. K., 204, 275
Meyer, H. J., 204, 263
Miller, A., 140, 267
Miller, J. G., 270
Miller, K. M., 46, 275
Miller, K. S., 266

Miller, N. E., 269
Milner, P. M., 137, 275
Mueller, E., 185, 264
Murphy, G., 46, 275
Murray, E. J., 119, 137, 275
Murray, H. A., 1, 2, 37, 75, 118, 132, 275

Nauss, A. H., 221, 275
Nesselroade, J. R., 146, 173, 199, 263, 275
Nichols, K. E., 108, 219, 275
Noty, C., 207, 208, 209, 275

Olds, J., 136, 140, 141, 275

Packard, V., 41
Pawlik, K., 106, 109, 147, 172, 273
Penfield, W., 273
Peters, R. S., 275
Peterson, R. O., 220, 272
Prescott, R. G. W., 142, 275
Prosser, C. L., 73, 275
Purkey, W. W., 98, 276
Putnam, M. L., 220, 276
Pyles, M. K., 46, 264

Radcliffe, J. A., 10, 18, 34, 120, 140, 176, 178, 267, 268, 275
Ranson, S. W., 137, 143, 272, 276
Rich, C., 224, 277
Rickels, K., 62, 172, 179, 180, 268, 276
Ricks, D. F., 109, 278
Roberts, W. W., 269
Roby, T. B., 232, 237, 276
Rosenberg, M., 209, 239, 276
Rosvold, H. E., 269
Rummel, R. J., 204, 251, 276

Sarason, S. B., 172, 276
Saunders, D. R., 238, 268
Sawyer, J., 251, 276
Scheier, I. H., 61, 72, 109, 132, 147, 168, 172, 276
Scott, J. H., 150, 263
Sealy, A. P., 186, 188, 189, 268
Sheffield, F. D., 133, 140, 142, 276
Shotwell, A. M., 83, 276

Singer, J. D., 204, 276
Skelton, J. J., 210–211, 223, 276
Snyderman, B., 220, 272
Sorokin, P. A., 204, 276
Spence, M. T., 224, 276
Spielberger, C. D., 72, 116, 151, 173, 174, 224, 266, 276
Stagner, R., 265, 277
Stevens, S. S., 274
Stewart, R. G., 267
Stice, G. F., 209, 232, 237, 238, 240, 241, 243, 245, 268, 276
Stoghill, R. M., 232, 237, 276–277
Stone, C. P., 96, 277
Strong, E. K., 46, 277
Strong, F. W., 46, 270
Sumner, R., 185, 277
Sutton, M. A., 46, 271
Sweney, A. B., 10, 18, 34, 50, 120, 140, 160, 161–162, 164, 168, 174, 176, 178, 186, 188, 189, 199, 207, 209, 211, 213, 215, 223, 224, 225, 228, 229, 250, 267, 268, 269, 272, 275, 276, 277

Tapp, J., 277
Tatro, D. F., 110, 180, 268
Tatsuoka, M. M., 107, 108, 206, 210, 221, 253, 254, 259, 267, 277
Thorndike, E. L., 46, 140, 277
Thurstone, L. L., 46, 277
Tinbergen, N., 1, 27, 41, 42, 127–129, 277
Torr, D. V., 46, 277
Ts'ai-Fan Yu., 185, 273
Tsujioka, B., 65, 277
Tsushima, T., 189, 277
Tucker, L. R., 65, 278

Unger, M. P., 267

Vaughan, D. S., 197, 198, 278
Vernon, M. D., 278
Vernon, P. E., 46, 225, 278
Vroom, V. H., 225, 278

Wagner, A., 177, 268
Walker, C. R., 220, 278
Warburton, F. W., 10, 52, 109, 185, 268, 277

Warden, C. J., 88, 96, 120, 278
Weiner, H., 185, 273
Weise, C., 180, 268, 276
Wessman, A. E., 109, 278
Weste, C. M., 232, 272
Whisler, L. D., 278
Williams, H. V., 151, 278
Williams, J. R., 50, 109, 180, 228, 278
Wilson, R. C., 239, 278
Wispe, L. G., 237, 268, 278
Wulff, J. J., 276

Wylie, R. C., 98, 278

Yee, R., 180, 268, 276
Yerkes, R. M., 115–177, 278
Young, P. T., preface, 1, 114, 119–120, 140, 141, 142, 278
Young, R., 271

Zander, A., 238, 264
Zimmerman, R. R., 74, 130, 271